GREEK TRAGEDY
IN NEW TRANSLATIONS

GENERAL EDITORS
Peter Burian and Alan Shapiro

FOUNDING GENERAL EDITOR
William Arrowsmith

FORMER GENERAL EDITOR
Herbert Golder

THE COMPLETE AESCHYLUS, VOLUME II

D0954315

The Complete Aeschylus, Volume II

Persians and Other Plays

Edited by
PETER BURIAN
and
ALAN SHAPIRO

OXFORD
UNIVERSITY PRESS

2009

OXFORD
UNIVERSITY PRESS

Oxford University Press, Inc., publishes works that further
Oxford University's objective of excellence
in research, scholarship, and education.

Oxford New York
Auckland Cape Town Dar es Salaam Hong Kong Karachi
Kuala Lumpur Madrid Melbourne Mexico City Nairobi
New Delhi Shanghai Taipei Toronto

With offices in
Argentina Austria Brazil Chile Czech Republic France Greece
Guatemala Hungary Italy Japan Poland Portugal Singapore
South Korea Switzerland Thailand Turkey Ukraine Vietnam

Persians Copyright © 1981 by Janet Lembke and C. John Herington

Prometheus Bound Copyright © 1975 by James Scully

Seven against Thebes Copyright © 1973 by Anthony Hecht and Helen Bacon

Suppliants Copyright © 1975 by Janet Lembke

Compilation Copyright © 2009 by Oxford University Press, Inc.

Published by Oxford University Press, Inc.
198 Madison Avenue, New York, NY 10016

www.oup.com

Oxford is a registered trademark of Oxford University Press

Library of Congress Cataloging-in-Publication Data
Aeschylus.
[Selections. English. 2009]
Persians and other plays / edited by Peter Burian and Alan Shapiro.
    p.   cm. — (The complete Aeschylus ; v. 2)
(The Greek tragedy in new translations)
Includes bibliographical references.
ISBN 978-0-19-537337-0; 978-0-19-537328-8 (pbk.)
1. Aeschylus—Translations into English. I. Burian, Peter, 1943–
II. Shapiro, Alan, 1952– III. Title.
PA3827.A2B87 2009
882'.01—dc22   2008039935

9 8 7 6 5 4 3 2 1

Printed in the United States of America

EDITORS' FOREWORD

"*The Greek Tragedy in New Translations* is based on the conviction that poets like Aeschylus, Sophocles, and Euripides can only be properly rendered by translators who are themselves poets. Scholars may, it is true, produce useful and perceptive versions. But our most urgent present need is for a *re-creation* of these plays—as though they had been written, freshly and greatly, by masters fully at home in the English of our own times."

With these words, the late William Arrowsmith announced the purpose of this series, and we intend to honor that purpose. As was true of most of the volumes that began to appear in the 1970s—first under Arrowsmith's editorship, later in association with Herbert Golder—those for which we bear editorial responsibility are products of close collaborations between poets and scholars. We believe (as Arrowsmith did) that the skills of both are required for the difficult and delicate task of transplanting these magnificent specimens of another culture into the soil of our own place and time, to do justice both to their deep differences from our patterns of thought and expression and to their palpable closeness to our most intimate concerns. Above all, we are eager to offer contemporary readers dramatic poems that convey as vividly and directly as possible the splendor of language, the complexity of image and idea, and the intensity of emotion and originals. This entails, among much else, the recognition that the tragedies were meant for performance—as scripts for actors—to be sung and danced as well as spoken. It demands writing of inventiveness, clarity, musicality, and dramatic power. By such standards, we ask that these translations be judged.

This series is also distinguished by its recognition of the need of nonspecialist readers for a critical introduction informed by the best recent scholarship, but written clearly and without condescension. Each play is followed by notes designed not only to elucidate obscure references but also to mediate the conventions of the Athenian stage as well as those features of the Greek text that might otherwise go unnoticed. The notes are supplemented by a glossary of mythical and geographical terms that should make it possible to read the plays without turning elsewhere for basic information. Stage directions are sufficiently ample to aid readers in imagining the action as they read. Our fondest hope, of course, is that these versions will be staged not only in the minds of their readers but also in the theaters to which, after so many centuries, they still belong.

A NOTE ON THE SERIES FORMAT
A series such as this requires a consistent format. Different translators, with individual voices and approaches to the material at hand, cannot be expected to develop a single coherent style for each of the three tragedians, much less make clear to modern readers that, despite the differences among the tragedians themselves, the plays share many conventions and a generic, or period, style. But they can at least share a common format and provide similar forms of guidance to the reader.

1. *Spelling of Greek names*
Orthography is one area of difference among the translations that requires a brief explanation. Historically, it has been common practice to use Latinized forms of Greek names when bringing them into English. Thus, for example, Oedipus (not Oidipous) and Clytemnestra (not Klutaimestra) are customary in English. Recently, however, many translators have moved toward more precise transliteration, which has the advantage of presenting the names as both Greek and new, instead of Roman and neoclassical importations into English. In the case of so familiar a name as Oedipus, however, transliteration risks the appearance of pedantry or affectation. And in any case, perfect consistency cannot be expected in such matters. Readers will feel the same discomfort with "Athenai" as the

chief city of Greece as they would with "Platon" as the author of *The Republic*.

The earlier volumes in this series adopted as a rule a "mixed" orthography in accordance with the considerations outlined above. The most familiar names retain their Latinate forms, while the rest are transliterated; *-os* rather than Latin *-us* is adopted for the termination of masculine names, and Greek diphthongs (as in Iphigene*ia* for Latin Iphigenia) are retained. Some of the later volumes continue this practice, but where translators have preferred to use a more consistent practice of transliteration of Latinization, we have honored their wishes.

2. Stage directions

The ancient manuscripts of the Greek plays do not supply stage directions (though the ancient commentators often provide information relevant to staging, delivery, "blocking," etc.). Hence stage directions must be inferred from words and situations and our knowledge of Greek theatrical conventions. At best this is a ticklish and uncertain procedure. But it is surely preferable that good stage directions should be provided by the translator than that readers should be left to their own devices in visualizing action, gesture, and spectacle. Ancient tragedy was austere and "distanced" by means of masks, which means that the reader must not expect the detailed intimacy ("He shrugs and turns wearily away," "She speaks with deliberate slowness, as though to emphasize the point," etc.) that characterizes stage directions in modern naturalistic drama.

3. Numbering of lines

For the convenience of the reader who may wish to check the translation against the original, or vice versa, the lines have been numbered according to both the Greek and English texts. The lines of the translation have been numbered in multiples of ten, and these numbers have been set in the right-hand margin. The (inclusive) Greek numeration will be found bracketed at the top of the page. The Notes that follow the text have been keyed to both numerations, the line numbers of the translation in **bold**, followed by the Greek lines in regular type, and the same convention is used for all references to specific passages (of the translated plays only) in both the Notes and the Introduction.

Readers will doubtless note that in many plays the English lines outnumber the Greek, but they should not therefore conclude that the translator has been unduly prolix. In most cases the reason is simply that the translator has adopted the free-flowing norms of modern Anglo-American prosody, with its brief-breath-and-emphasis-determined lines, and its habit of indicating cadence and caesuras by line length and setting rather than by conventional punctuation. Even where translators have preferred to cast dialogue in more regular five-beat or six-beat lines, the greater compactness of Greek diction is likely to result in a substantial disparity in Greek and English numerations.

ABOUT THE TRANSLATIONS

The translations in this series were written over a period of roughly forty years. No attempt has been made to update references to the scholarly literature in the Introductions and Notes, but each volume offers a brief For Further Reading list that will provide some initial orientation to contemporary critical thinking about the tragedies it contains.

THIS VOLUME

The seven surviving plays of Aeschylus amount to less than one-tenth of what he wrote, at least to judge by the titles and fragments that have come down to us—and one of the survivors may not be his. Nevertheless, we can consider ourselves lucky to have one complete trilogy, the *Oresteia*, and the group of four very fine dramas that make up this volume.

The earliest is also the most unusual, in that it has a subject based on contemporary history rather than the distant, legendary past. Aeschylus was almost certainly at the battle of Salamis he describes so vividly in *Persians*, which was performed only eight years after the event, when Athenians' memories were still fresh. The most interesting thing about the play, however, is not its documentation of real events, but its transformation of those events into a true Greek tragedy, of history into myth. Thus, for example, the ghost of the previous Persian king, Darius, whom the chorus invokes as a king "who brought no evil" (1064 / 1071) despite the Persian disaster at Marathon, appears as a kind of idealized god-king, the legendary hero of an earlier and better time. Aeschylus is creating not merely an account of how but also an explanation of why Xerxes' attempt to subjugate the Greeks came to grief.

The explanation involves the same sequence of human over-reaching and divine chastisement that appears again and again in tragic myth. Scholars have debated whether Aeschylus' choice of telling this tale entirely from the point of view of the defeated Persians creates sympathy for the enemy's suffering, or whether it is designed to honor the Greeks' defeat of a supposedly invincible enemy. The two need not, of course, be entirely exclusive. In any case, we should note that the play defines the Greeks as everything the Persians are not, while at the same time it sounds a warning about the fate that could be theirs should they succumb, as the Persians did, to overweening ambition.

Seven against Thebes, produced five years after *Persians*, is also a war play—"full of Ares," says the character Aeschylus proudly in Aristophanes' comic *Frogs*. Yet, like *Persians*, it focuses on the fear and suffering war brings rather than on glory and victory. This is the third play of a trilogy that traced the fate of the royal house of Thebes through three generations, from Laios to Oedipus to Oedipus' children. In *Seven*, Oedipus' curse of his sons is fulfilled when they die at each other's hands, but the city of Thebes is saved from destruction.

At the heart of this drama is the "shield scene," a set of seven pairs of speeches in which a scout tells Eteokles which Argive commander has been stationed at each of Thebes' seven gates, describing the blazons on each of their shields. Eteokles responds by appointing a Theban captain to defend each gate. Only at the end of this process, when Eteokles hears that his brother Polyneices will attack the seventh gate, does he decide that he himself will oppose him; and only when he has made that decision does he recognize that his father's curses are being accomplished. Eteokles is at once the self-sacrificing defender of his city and the son whose choice fulfills the fate to which Oedipus consigned him along with his brother. The closing scene of the play, in which Thebes' magistrates refuse Polyneices' burial, is considered by most scholars to be a later addition to the play designed to harmonize it with Sophocles' *Antigone*, perhaps on an occasion when the two plays were being performed together. As Hecht and Bacon point out in their Introduction, however, the scene is well integrated into what precedes it and reinforces what every spectator knew: that the misfortunes of the House of Laios and the city of Thebes were not yet at an end.

Suppliants was long thought to be the earliest surviving tragedy, primarily because of the size and importance of the role played by its chorus, a supposedly archaic feature. Following the publication in 1952 of a scrap of papyrus that preserves a fragmentary performance record, it has become more or less universally accepted that *Suppliants* was written late in Aeschylus' career, most likely in the mid-460s. It formed part of the Danaid trilogy (so named for the daughters of Danaos, who form the chorus of this play); most scholars consider it the opening play, some think it came second. At any rate, its plot is incomplete, in that it leaves us in suspense about the daughters' final destiny. *Suppliants* shows only the arrival of Danaos and his daughters in Argos. They have chosen to flee rather than endure unwanted marriage with their Egyptian cousins, who are in hot pursuit. The Danaids' flight is turned into a dramatic action by their supplication, which forces the Argive king to choose between divine wrath if he rejects the suppliants, who are under the protection of Zeus, and an unwanted war with the Egyptians if he grants them refuge. The king and his people accept the suppliants, the Egyptians arrive to claim them as their "property," and the maidens take refuge within the city walls.

What will happen next? Although the trilogy cannot be reconstructed in detail, we know from other sources that the Egyptians were eventually victorious and married the Danaids, but that on the wedding night the maidens killed their husbands—all but one, Hypermnestra, who spared her bridegroom, bore him a child, and founded a new royal line in Argos. This outcome helps explain the significance of the Danaids' repeated and emphatic retelling of the story of their Argive forebear, Io. She fled the unwelcome advances of Zeus, who turned her into a cow and pursued from Greece to Egypt, where, rather than take her by force, he caressed her with a gentle, life-giving touch and made her pregnant. The maidens see themselves in Io's fearful flight but do not recognize the meaning of her story's outcome; they see only violence in sexuality and do not recognize the possibility it offers of fulfillment.

Prometheus Bound is believed by many recent scholars not to be by Aeschylus at all, but rather to be the work of a follower (perhaps even a descendant) who wrote two or three decades after his death

under the influence of dramaturgical, metrical, and stylistic practices of Sophocles and Euripides and the intellectual atmosphere of
Athens in the 450s and 440s. John Herington rejected this view and
considered *Prometheus Bound* to be a late work of Aeschylus,
written in the last two years of his life during his final visit to Sicily.
In the absence of documentary evidence, there can be no certainty
in the matter. In some respects, this play is *sui generis*; much in its
staging has no real parallel in extant fifth-century works earlier
or later. It is worth noting, however, that the argument for non-
Aeschylean authorship on grounds of the non-Aeschylean treatment
of Zeus as a ruthless tyrant falls away if, as Herington and others
argue, *Prometheus Unbound* (whose fragments are translated in the
Appendix to his translation and appear fully Aeschylean) was intended to follow *Prometheus Bound*. That play will have shown a
very different picture of Zeus, with whom Prometheus finally
reaches an understanding beneficial to all—including humankind.

Whatever the solution to the riddle of its authorship, whatever the
original solutions to the problems of its staging, *Prometheus Bound*
is a bold drama, animated by titanic passions and ideas. Its center-
piece is the Io scene, and although her sufferings continue the story
of Zeus the tormentor, they will end, according to Prometheus'
prophecy, in deliverance and fulfillment for Io through the touch
of a far different, gentler Zeus (1280–94 / 846–52)—a story central
also to *Suppliants*, as we have seen, and given a similar import in
that play. Even without adducing a sequel, *Prometheus Bound*,
whose rebellious hero is so fully tied by his benefactions to humanity to a world amenable to civilized life, offers prophetic evidence of
a resolution by which Zeus will come to preside over a world in
which human progress is enabled by divine good will.

The plays in this volume were originally published between 1973
and 1981. The poets and scholars who collaborated on them are a
distinguished crew. The late ANTHONY HECHT was one of America's
best-known poets, the author of five volumes of poetry and three of
criticism. Among many other distinctions, Hecht served as Poet
Laureate and was awarded both the Pulitzer Prize and the Bollingen
Prize. JANET LEMBKE has written poetry and numerous books of
essays on the natural world and the place of humans and other
animals in it. She also translated two plays of Euripides for this series,
a splendid volume of fragments from early Latin poetry, and, most

recently, Virgil's *Georgics*. JAMES SCULLY has achieved widespread recognition as an engaged poet who practices an impassioned and radical poetics. He is the author of a dozen books of poetry and two of criticism.

The late HELEN H. BACON was Professor of Greek and Latin at Barnard and author of *Barbarians in Greek Tragedy*, as well as of articles on Plato, Virgil, and Petronius, as well as Aeschylus. The late C. JOHN HERINGTON had a distinguished teaching career at a number of universities in England, Canada, and the United States, including serving as Talcott Professor of Greek and Chair of Classics at Yale. He was one of the most distinguished Aeschyleans of his generation. Among his books are *The Author of the Prometheus Bound*, *Aeschylus*, and the magisterial Sather Lectures *Poetry into Drama: Early Tragedy and the Greek Poetic Tradition*.

CONTENTS

CONTENTS

PROMETHEUS BOUND   Translated by James Scully and
                    C. John Herington

PERSIANS

Translated by

JANET LEMBKE

and

C. JOHN HERINGTON

INTRODUCTION

I BACKGROUND: HISTORY AND POETRY

Aeschylus was there, at the desperate struggle between Greeks and Persians in the Strait of Salamis. That is one of the few certainly attested facts in our poet's personal life.[1] Thus it comes about that the *Persians* is not merely a play but also a precious historical document: the description of the battle contained in its long scene (417–867 / 249–531) is in fact the only account of any event in the Great Persian Wars that has been composed by an eyewitness.

Yet it seems important, at the outset of any approach to the *Persians* as a whole, to draw a firm line between a historical document in the sense just described, and a conscious, deliberate attempt to record an event with the system and accuracy expected of a modern historian. Too often that distinction has been overlooked by critics of the *Persians*, with the result that they tend to concentrate disproportionately on the question of the poet's historical veracity or otherwise; sometimes with expressions of near-outrage at his apparent distortions of the history of the Persian Wars and of the Persian court, so far as they are known from other sources. Yet even those parts of the play—a relatively small proportion of the whole—that concern events that Aeschylus could have witnessed personally, should be enough to warn us against expecting from him a cool, objective historical account. He was indeed at the battle of Salamis in the fall of 480 B.C., and yet, for a start, his play imagines that battle from an angle of vision that he could not have literally shared. It is—it has to

---

It should be noted that at some points in the Introduction, for purposes of close exposition, a literal, word-for-word version of Aeschylus' Greek is given.

1. It was recorded in a now lost book, *Visits*, by the tragedian Ion of Chios, who was a younger contemporary of Aeschylus and knew him personally; the statement is quoted in the ancient Greek commentary (the "Medicean scholia") on the *Persians*.

be—a *Persian* who recalls, for instance, how swiftly the Greek fleet came into sight at the beginning of the battle (650 / 398). Further, no Greek personal names are mentioned either in this passage or, for that matter, anywhere in the entire play; and even the names of Persians, although very numerous, seem to be largely invented or misapplied, there for the sake of majesty and pathos.[2] Particulars about the battle, of the kind that we would rightly expect from a historian or even a memoirist, are remarkably few. The only exception is the exact detail of the numbers of ships engaged (555–64 / 337–43), and even that is probably included to emphasize the miraculousness of the Greek victory, and the error of the Persians in trusting to mere numbers. Otherwise, the account of the battle is so generalized that historians argue to this day even about its precise location in Salamis waters; perhaps only the wrecks of the Greek and Persian galleys, if they still survive where they sank under the now-polluted silt of the strait, can ever provide the answer.

Aeschylus' painting of the event is mostly a matter of selected tones and colors rather than of sharp-edged lines. We are left with a vivid *impression* of what it was like to be at Salamis on that day. We re-experience the determination, almost elation, of the Greeks as the moment of crisis arrived, the shouting, the rhythmic crash of oars, the masses of warships locked together in the narrows, and perhaps above all the frightfulness of the contrast between the human work of butchery and the serene, sunlit natural background.[3] The brilliance and beauty of that dawn are specially emphasized (627–28 / 386–87); Salamis itself is a "dove-broody island" (507 / 309); the islet on which so many noble Persians were battered and chopped to pieces is the dancing-place of the god Pan (727–28 / 448–49, a miniature pastoral poem obtruded into the scene of blood); the distorted Persian corpses are nibbled by what the Chorus calls, with an irony almost as painful in our time as in theirs, "the silent Children of the Unpollutable" (936 / 577–78, literally translated). Which, being decoded, means the fishes of the sea.

Thus Aeschylus' vision even of the shattering event in which he actually took part is to a great extent a poet's vision, not an objective historian's. But the greater part of the *Persians* concerns episodes and places that Aeschylus could not possibly have seen, and about which he could hardly have had much precise information. For affairs and personalities in the Persian capital at Susa, where his scene is set, and for the narrative of Xerxes' retreat through northern Greece, there was no way for a poet composing

2. On these see the preliminary note to the Glossary.
3. Those who lived through August 1914 in France, and September 1940 in southern England, have recorded rather similar impressions of the contrast between nature and the activities of man.

at Athens within eight years of the event to arrive at the objective historical particulars, even if it had occurred to him for one moment that such research was any part of a poet's trade. For we are, after all, dealing not merely with a poet, but with a classical Greek poet. And perhaps the most important single characteristic of the Greek poetic tradition within which Aeschylus worked, as opposed to poetry as it is usually understood in modern times, is this: the Greek poet consistently strove to set the transient doings of mortals against a permanent universe, a universe of ever-present death and ever-living gods. Unless so measured, the particular human act (whether a legendary event, or a contemporary victory at the Olympic Games, for instance) will scarcely be worth narrating, or even intelligible. Only the permanent will make sense of the ephemeral. So worked the mind of the Greek poet, whether epic, lyric, or tragic, from the earliest times into the late fifth century. (Somewhat so, indeed, worked the mind of classical Greek poetry's ultimate heir and enemy, Plato, with incalculable consequences for all our later thinking; but that is another story.)

It is with this tradition firmly in mind, rather than in the expectation of a historical narrative, that we should probably do best to approach the *Persians*. On one side of us we shall see, as the poet had seen, an awe-inspiring series of purely human events; but on the other side, a no less awe-inspiring universe against whose laws those events can alone be fully understood. To relate those two is the poet's task, not factfinding.

The great empire of the Persians was new, as empires go. It had sprung into being within the lifetime of Aeschylus' parents, in the middle of the sixth century B.C., and a thousand miles away, in the arid uplands eastward of the Tigris. Then it was that Cyrus the Great merged the realms of Media and Persia under Persian overlordship. The ancient kingdoms of the East fell to that combined power in swift succession: Lydia in Asia Minor, and with Lydia the rest of the peninsula, including the noble Greek cities along its western coast; Babylon; then, under Cyrus' son Cambyses (reigned 530–522 B.C.), the realm of the Pharaohs itself. By the end of the reign of the great Darius (who succeeded to the empire, after a confused interregnum, in 521 B.C. and died in 486), the eastward limit of the Persian rule lay on the banks of the Indus. Southwestward that rule reached out into the Cyrenaica, and northwestward through Thrace to the border of Macedon, so that Greece was already poised between its jaws. In recorded history there had never been such power and wealth under a single ruler, nor so quickly won, anywhere in the world west of China. What it felt like to be a Greek, faced with a threat of such a scale, can partly be imagined from the opening chant and song of the Chorus in the *Persians* itself (1–136 / 1–106), with their roll call of nations and captains in irresistible onward movement. For a modern, however, so much further removed from the terror of that time, and thus more in need of concrete detail, the most vivid sense of the vastness and diversity of the attacking empire can perhaps be gained from Herodotus' account of Xerxes' review of his forces at Doriskos in Thrace.[4] Here the massed nations of the empire are paraded before us, their equipment being described with all the precision of the historian-anthropologist that Herodotus was. First march the Persians and the Medes, wearing the turbanlike national headdress, clad in iron-scaled tunics and in trousers, and carrying wicker shields, short spears, great bows, and daggers; then Kissians, Hyrkanians, Assyrians (these wear outlandish helmets of plaited bronze, and carry knobbed cudgels), Bactrians, Scythians, Indians (these wear cotton tunics, and their bows and arrows are made of cane), Arians, Parthians, Chorasmians, Sog-dians . . . and so the catalogue of exotic names and outfits runs on for page after page of Herodotus. It embraces both the famous civilizations of the ancient East, and also many tribes scarcely known otherwise to history. Of the latter class, to take only one example, are the Aithiopians, who as described by Herodotus must have looked like the jokers of that monstrous pack. These are wrapped in the skins of lions or leopards; they shoot stone-tipped arrows; they carry spears tipped with antelope horn, and knobbed cudgels; "and when they went into battle," adds the historian, "they would smear half of their body with chalk and the other half with vermilion." It was as if all the known and half-known world, in all its phases of civilization from the Stone Age to the Iron Age, was converging against Greece.

Herodotus demands a brief introduction for himself, since it is he who provides us with the only extant full-length and near-contemporary account of the expansion of Persia and its clash with the Greeks, and he will therefore often have to be referred to in the course of this introduction. His *Histories* (as the title is conventionally translated; "*Enquiries*" would be a more accurate rendering), composed probably between ca. 460 and 430 B.C., are based on wide travels in the Near and Middle East, as well as in the Greek world. The information that he thus assembled about peoples, places, and customs is enormous and peren-nially fascinating. He is less strong on the political and military history of the Persians, partly because he was working two decades or more after the events, and to a great extent (it would seem) from oral communica-tions; partly because his informants were persons of very uneven reli-ability, and few if any of them are likely to have had direct access to the inner counsels of the Persian court and high command. The result is a

4. Herodotus, *Histories* VII.59–100.

6

narrative that will respond, to put it mildly, better to the historical standards of a Tolstoy than to those of Clausewitz or Mahan: Herodotus tends to represent a battle or a political development essentially as a series of personal anecdotes. His account of the battle of Salamis[5] is in fact a very good example of his method. It is almost the antithesis of Aeschylus' account, in that it presents a mass of discrete episodes, mostly linked to personalities, yet leaves us with scarcely any impression of the battle as a whole. But Herodotus remains by far the best source we have for the story of the great Persian invasion, and all too often the only source whatever.

As Herodotus tells that story in his Books VII–IX, King Darius had been actively preparing a massive amphibious expedition against Greece since 490 B.C., when he heard the news of the Athenian defeat of a Persian seaborne invasion at Marathon. On Darius' death in 486 B.C., Xerxes, his son by Queen Atossa, succeeded to the empire; and, after various delays and doubts, finally launched the expedition early in 480. The enormous land force crossed the Hellespont by a marvelously contrived bridge of boats,[6] and proceeded round the northern coast of the Aegean Sea. Offshore, in parallel, sailed a great fleet. To avoid the dangerous rounding of stormswept Mount Athos, says Herodotus, it passed through a great canal cut by Xerxes' orders across the base of the Athos peninsula.[7] Moving down the east coast of the Greek mainland, the expedition was only temporarily checked by the heroic action in the pass of Thermopylae, and the accompanying naval engagements off Cape Artemision. It flooded on, through Boiotia and into Attica, where the troops sacked and burned Athens, almost all the inhabitants having already fled. Thus by the fall of 480 the Persians had overrun about half of Greece, and their superiority by land and sea was still immense.

5. *Histories* VIII.83–96.

6. *Histories* VII.33–37 (the construction of the bridge) and VII.55–57 (its passage by the army); IX.121 (how the cables of the bridge were finally brought back to Greece, to be set up as trophies in the Greek temples). The bridge is also mentioned, with awe, in the *Persians* (96–99 / 65–72, 1177–79 / 721–23, 1192 / 736; also 1213–28 / 746–50, where it is criticized as an act of impiety against the Sea).

7. *Histories* VII.22–25 (construction), VII.122 (passage of the fleet through it). One of the most surprising omissions from the account of the expedition presented in the *Persians* is that of any mention of this great engineering work. It certainly existed (traces still survive on the peninsula), and—as almost every other Greek or Roman writer who refers to the expedition has not failed to see—it provided a neat rhetorical counterpart to the bridge: the impious Persian not only bridged the sea but also cut open the land! This omission may perhaps illustrate once again the fact that Aeschylus does not write in the first instance as a historian, but as a dramatist seeking to capture his Athenian audience. Few of that audience at that date could have seen, or perhaps even heard much of, the canal in the remote and dangerous corner of the Aegean; on the other hand, *Histories* IX.121 (cited in Note 7) makes it very likely that all of them would have seen relics of the bridge in one of the Athenian temples.

With the crushing defeat of Salamis, the apparently irresistible advance was suddenly stopped in its tracks; it is one of the neatest and most decisive peripeties in history. After a short period of indecision, the battered Persian fleet made off in its entirety for the Hellespont, and Xerxes pulled back his army to northern Greece. From there he himself left for Asia, guarded by a detachment from the main army: suffering many privations, it escorted him to the Hellespont and thence to the Lydian capital of Sardis, where he remained for about a year. Before leaving Attica, however, Xerxes had sent off a messenger carrying news of the defeat to Susa. On its arrival there, the people "were so shattered that all of them tore their robes, and cried and wailed without measure, blaming Mardonios (one of the chief Persian generals). And this the Persians did not so much because they were distressed about their ships as because they feared for Xerxes."[8]

But the danger to Greece was not over. A very large Persian army still wintered in northern Greece under Mardonios, and in the summer of 479 it advanced southwards as far as Attica, where it sacked what was left of Athens yet again. A few weeks later it met the Greek army near Plataia, just beyond the northwestern border of Attica, and was defeated with great slaughter. On that same day, Herodotus says, a Greek naval force destroyed much of the remainder of the Persian fleet at Mykale on the Asia Minor coast. The great expedition of Xerxes was thus, at last, conclusively defeated, just about a year after the battle of Salamis.[9]

That swift expansion and abrupt disgrace of the Persian Empire, even when told as sober history, have already the quality of drama; it is not often that the raw material of historical events arrives in such aesthetically satisfying shape. This fact in itself might to some extent account for the appeal of the Persian Wars to the Greek artists of the fifth century. Far more important, however, must have been its moral-religious aspect. For the events of the Persian Wars conformed almost miraculously to a law of our mortal existence that the Greeks had understood since time immemorial: a law that had been respected implicitly by the unknown Bronze-Age creators of many a Greek myth and that had been formulated explicitly by the archaic poets and thinkers. In its least refined form the law simply entails the visitation of God's ferocious punishment on anything that is unduly great, whether physical or mental. Its starkest

8. The direct quotation is from Herodotus, *Histories* VIII.99. For the story of the Persian retreat in general, see VIII.113–20; and for Xerxes' one-year stay in Sardis, IX.107 (here, of course, is a major discrepancy with the *Persians*, which has Xerxes back in Susa apparently within days after the defeat at Salamis, and certainly long before the battle of Plataia).

9. Herodotus describes the Plataia campaign in *Histories* IX.1–89, and the battle of Mykale in IX.90–107.

extant formulation is put, interestingly enough, into the mouth of a Persian by Herodotus. As Xerxes is debating with his Council whether or not to launch the expedition, his uncle Artabanos argues as follows:

> Thou seest how God strikes over-large animals with His lightning, and does not allow them to show off, whereas little creatures do not even irritate Him. Thou seest how He always shoots His missiles down upon the highest buildings and the highest trees. It is God's habit to chop back all things that are over-large. By the same rule, a great army is ruined by a little one, and this is the way of it: God in His jealousy hurls panic on them, or thunder, and so—behold! They are ruined in ways unworthy of themselves. For God allows no one to think thoughts of greatness, except Himself.

As stated by Artabanos, the law is automatic, and moral considerations scarcely enter into it: it applies to inanimate as well as animate objects with the chill impartiality of a law in physics. Even in this form, however, it might be invoked by the Greeks, and no doubt was, to explain the astonishing overthrow of the Persian hordes by a single small nation.[10]

For a subtler version, applying more specifically to humanity, we may turn to many of the Greek lyric and elegiac poets from the seventh century B.C. down to the lifetime of Aeschylus. The poetry of the Athenian statesman Solon, who composed ca. 600 B.C., provides some of the best examples. According to this formulation, individual or communal disaster is not simply due to greatness *per se*, but to a concatenation of circumstances, partly external, partly psychological. Overgreat prosperity (*olbos*) or satiety (*koros*), connected with infatuation or failure of judgment (*ātē*), will issue in an act of insolence or outrageousness (*hybris*), which brings destruction (also termed *ātē*: the ambivalent word can cover, in Greek, both the mental fault and its physical consequence).[11] As will be seen in more detail in the final section of this introduction, the same law, and even to a great extent the same terminology, is to be found in the *Persians*, above all in the pivotal scene where Darius' ghost explains the failure of the expedition.

The Persian Wars must have seemed to fifth-century Greeks a perfect exemplification of the ancient law of *hybris-ātē*; almost, one might dare to say, the incarnation of it, on the grandest conceivable scale. It is

10. The very words attributed to Artabanos in this passage (Herodotus, VII.10.5) may perhaps be an example of such interpretation. The likelihood that Herodotus or any of his informants could have known the actual words spoken at an imperial council held deep in Persia is minimal; Artabanos' speech must therefore be suspected of being a Greek invention, put together after the failure of the expedition.
11. See Solon, Fragments 6 and 13.9.26 (Greek texts in M. L. West, *Iambi et Elegi Graeci*, 2 vols. [Oxford, 1972], vol. II; text with English translation in J. M. Edmonds, *Elegy and Iambus*, 2 vols. [London and Cambridge, Mass., 1931], vol. I).

almost certainly for this reason that the Persian Wars, alone among the events of classical Greek history, were admitted into the repertoire of all the major arts. It is a well-known—a crucial—feature of Greek art in all media, visual and verbal, that its regular subject matter was divine myth and heroic legend, not contemporary events or personalities. But the Persian Wars broke that taboo. The great contemporary choral poets had several poems on, or alluding to, the wars, and toward the end of the century the famous musician Timotheos wrote a long lyric on the subject, which is still partly extant; its title, like that of Aeschylus' play, is the *Persians*.[12] Scenes of battle between Greeks and Persians are fairly common on Attic red-figure vase paintings, and occasionally even found their way into monumental paintings and sculptures.[13] Of the three fifth-century Attic tragedies certainly known to have had "historical" themes, two referred to the battle of Salamis, i.e., Aeschylus' *Persians* and Phryni-chos' *Phoinissai* (which will be described in the following section): the third, a tragedy by Phrynichos on the capture of Miletos, referred to an earlier incident in the struggle between the Greeks and Persians.[14] It might even be argued that the overwhelming shock of the Persian Wars widened the very boundaries of Greek literature (and of our own) by creating historiography, in the unprecedented life-work of Herodotus. But however that may be, it must be clear from the evidence of lyric poetry, painting, sculpture, and the tragedies of Phrynichos that Aeschylus' choice of theme in the *Persians* is not an isolated phenomenon, nor a surprising one, for its time.

Our play has all too often been labeled a "historical tragedy," as if it really belonged to a separate Greek genre comparable to the Roman genre of historical tragedies, the *fabulae* praetextae, or to the Shake-spearian Histories. But the superficial analogy seems to lead to a critical, and religious, and, indeed, historical dead end. It will be far more

12. The Greek texts of the fragments of the lyric poets are best consulted in D. L. Page, *Poetae Melici Graeci* (Oxford, 1962); for translation, see J. M. Edmonds, *Lyra Graeca*, 2nd ed. (Cambridge, Mass., and London, 1928). The great Simonides, who died in 468 B.C., left lyrics on those who were slain at Thermopylae (Fr. 532, Page, 21 Edmonds), on the *Sea Battle off Artemision* (Frr.522–25 Page), and on the *Sea Battle off Salamis* (Fr.536 Page). A lyric poem concerning Marathon, by a now unidentifiable composer, survives on papyrus (Fr.932 Page). For the *Persians* by Timotheos, see Frr.788–91 Page. Pindar twice refers explicitly to the Persian Wars in his surviving works: in the fifth and eighth Isthmian Odes.

13. We hear of a painting of the battle of Marathon in the Stoa Poikile at Athens, by the great painters Panainos and Mikon. Still extant is the sculptured frieze showing Greeks fighting Persians (supposed by some to represent the battle of Plataia) from the little temple of Athena Nike on the Acropolis.

14. Herodotus, *Histories* VI.21, preserves all we know of the play on the capture of Miletos. The sacking of that great city by the Persians in 494 B.C. was the greatest disaster suffered by the Ionian Greeks in their revolt against Persia. For other Greek tragedies on "historical" themes—none, it seems, earlier than the fourth century B.C.—see H. D. Broadhead's edition of the *Persians* (Cambridge, 1960), p. xvii, n. 2.

profitable to approach the *Persians* simply as a member of the genre "Attic tragedy," but one which also happens to belong to a class of fifth-century Greek works—in *all* media—which accepted the Persian Wars as worthy to be received without delay into the ancient repertoire of the national myths.

II FOREGROUND: THE TRAGEDIAN AND HIS WORK

"Aeschylus used to say that once, as a youth, he was guarding the grapes in the countryside and went to sleep. Dionysos appeared over him and told him to compose tragedy. When daylight came, since he wanted to obey the god, he tried it, and found it easy from that time on."[15] With such charming stories as this the later Greeks sought to repair their ignorance about the poet's career, and to account for a miracle of a quite different order: the genesis in his hands of tragedy as a great art-form. But the really certain facts in Aeschylus' biography are few; they are confined almost entirely to information about certain of his dramatic performances, which seems to derive ultimately from the official Athenian archives. We know that he first produced a tragedy at the Great Dionysia in about 500 / 499 B.C. This fits well enough with the traditional date given by the later Greeks for his birth, namely 525 / 24 B.C., which may therefore be tentatively accepted. In that case Aeschylus will have been about thirty-five years old at the time of the battle of Marathon, in which he fought;[16] forty-one when he at last gained first prize in the tragic contests (spring, 484 B.C.); forty-five when he fought at Salamis; and fifty-three when he produced our play, the *Persians* (spring, 472 B.C.), which is both his first extant tragedy and, of course, the earliest surviving drama in the entire Western tradition.

At the time of the *Persians*, nearly two-thirds of Aeschylus' career as a playwright already lay behind him (it was only about sixteen years later, in 456 / 55 B.C., that he was to die in Sicily). Very little is known for certain about the character of his work, or indeed about the tragic art in general, during that long period. The majority of Aeschylus' total output of dramas (at least eighty, and very probably eighty-nine) will presumably have been composed then, although none of the last works is individually datable. Scanning their titles, which have mostly been preserved, and the all too

---

15. Pausanias (second century A.D.), *Description of Greece* I.21.2.
16. The evidence for this is strong, although perhaps not quite as certain as the evidence for his presence at Salamis (for which see Note 1). It includes the famous epitaph, which according to some ancient sources was to be seen on Aeschylus' tomb in Sicily, and was thought to be by the poet himself; this said nothing whatever about his poetry, but ended: "The glorious, sacred field of Marathon could tell of his valor, and so also could the longhaired Mede, who had good cause to know." A few late and not especially trustworthy sources add that Aeschylus also took part in the actions at Artemision and Plataia.

scanty fragments, one carries away the general impression of an enormous range of subject matter and treatment, and an imaginative and poetic power that scarcely ever seems to falter, however short or mutilated the fragment; we shall see some typical examples shortly, in examining the last plays of the *Persians* tetralogy. But their character as *plays* is impossible to make out. All that can be said with reasonable certainty is that at some time before 472 Aeschylus must have taken the important step of adding a second actor to the single actor with whom the earliest tragedians had been content; for a second actor is already required in parts of the *Persians*.[17]

The only other substantial information that we have about the nature of any tragedy produced before 472 is derived from accounts of the work of Phrynichos, who first appeared in the tragic contests at least ten years before Aeschylus did. The ancient reports about his tragedies agree in stating that they were remarkable for the high proportion and fine quality of song that they contained. One source, a little poem ascribed to Phrynichos himself, adds the element of *dance*: "my dancing art found me (dance-) figures as many as the waves which the cruel night raises in a storm." At least in its high proportion of sung-and-danced lyric poetry, Aeschylus' *Persians* is evidently still close to the tragic art of Phrynichos. But the resemblances may not have gone much deeper than that. The ancient Greek *Argument* to the *Persians*, which is prefixed to our manuscripts of the play, begins: "Glaukos in his work *On the Plots of Aeschylus* says that the *Persians* was adapted from Phrynichos' *Phoinissai*, of which he quotes the beginning: 'These, of the Persians who long ago have marched . . .' The difference is that there a eunuch appears in the beginning, announcing the defeat of Xerxes and laying certain thrones for the counsellors of the realm, but here [i.e., in the *Persians*] a chorus of elders deliver the prologue."[18] Some difference! In the *Phoinissai* the grand catastrophe was evidently announced in the first moments of the play, whereas in the *Persians* Aeschylus can already be seen employing one of his most characteristic and effective techniques: the building up of suspense and doubt before the catastrophe finally explodes over the actors. Further, the very title of Phrynichos' play (literally "The Phoenician Women"), as well as two of its fragments,

---

17. *Persians*, 417–833 / 249–514 (Queen and Messenger), 1090–1383 / 681–842 (Queen and Ghost). The chief ancient authority for Aeschylus' introduction of the second actor is Aristotle, *Poetics*, chapter IV.

18. The Glaukos quoted in the *Argument* may perhaps be one Glaukos of Rhegion, who wrote about 400 B.C., but nothing else is known about his book (if it was indeed his) on Aeschylus' plots. Nor can we judge just what this Glaukos meant by saying that the *Persians* was "adapted from" the *Phoinissai*. The sole resemblance that he cites is a superficial verbal one, between the opening lines of the two plays (line 1 / 1 of the *Persians* runs, literally translated: "These, of the Persians who have gone . . ."); but the differences, as we shall see, appear to be far more striking.

indicates that his Chorus was feminine, and non-Persian. Hence, presumably, the character of its singing, and the entire atmosphere of the tragedy, would have been totally different.

Phrynichos' latest recorded victory in the tragic contests was in spring, 476 B.C., and there are some grounds for thinking that this may have been the occasion on which he produced the *Phoinissai*. However that may be, there is no doubt as to the plays produced by the victor in spring, 472 B.C.; the record, preserved in the ancient *Argument* to our play, runs: "Aeschylus won, with the *Phineus*, the *Persians*, the *Glaukos of Potniai*, and the *Prometheus*." An Athenian inscription adds to this the name of Aeschylus' *Choregos* (the term for the citizen who financed the production); it is none other than Perikles, who here appears in a public capacity for the first time in history.

The record shows Aeschylus already following the practice that was standard in the tragic contests for the rest of the fifth century. He competes with a tetralogy: three tragedies, followed by a satyr-play. Not a great deal has survived of any of them, except of course the second on the list, but it is worthwhile putting together what we know of the dramatic frame within which the original spectators experienced the *Persians*.[19] The *Phineus* concerned the blind seer of that name, who lived at Salmydessos (on the Black Sea coast, northward of the Bosporos) and was harassed by onsets of the Harpies on his food. He was relieved by the twin sons of Boreas, the North Wind, who arrived in the company of the Argonauts; they pursued and eventually killed the Harpies. Next in order of performance came the *Persians*; and then, last of the three tragedies, the *Glaukos of Potniai*.[20] Its title-character was a king of Corinth, whose obscure legend is told in many versions. Most agreed, however, that he died being devoured by his own team of horses during the funeral games held for Pelias. The exact version followed in Aeschylus' play is uncertain, but the fragments allow us glimpses of two scenes. In one, the Chorus is wishing a prosperous journey to a departing traveler, who could well be Glaukos on his way to the games. In the second, preserved in a badly tattered papyrus, a woman who may well be Glaukos' queen seems to be relating a dream that involves *horses*,

19. The only near-complete collection of the evidence for the tetralogy of 472 B.C. is to be found in H. J. Mette, *Die Fragmente der Tragödien des Aischylos* (Berlin, 1959), pp. 158–66. The reconstruction of the tetralogy is discussed at some length by Broadhead in his edition of the *Persians*, pp. lv–lx. There exists no complete English translation of Aeschylus' fragments, but H. Weir Smyth, *Aeschylus*, 2 vols. vol. II (second ed., with appendix by Hugh Lloyd-Jones [London and Cambridge, Mass., 1957] provides translations of most of the fragments of any length, with good discussions, in brief, of what is known of the lost plays.

20. The manuscript evidence for the *Argument* of the *Persians* shows almost conclusively that this, at least, was what the Alexandrian scholars believed to be the title of the third tragedy. Modern attempts to substitute *Glaukos Pontios* ("Glaukos of the Sea") for it rest on no evidence at all.

the *nave of a chariot-wheel*, *biting*, and *dragging*. A Messenger then tells her about Glaukos at the games; in his fragmentary speech there is mention of a *race*, a *charioteer*, and again of *biting*. If the papyrus is correctly interpreted, there were close parallels here to the first episode of the *Persians* (lines 183–867 / 140–531), where also a Queen narrates an ominous dream concerning an absent male relative, the true meaning of which is subsequently revealed by a Messenger. Aeschylus may thus have displayed his characteristic suspense-building technique in the *Glaukos* also. But it is difficult to make out any further connection among the three tragedies produced on this occasion.[21]

The title of the fourth and last play is recorded (as we saw) simply as *Prometheus*. Since the fourth play was normally a satyr-play, it is natural to identify it with the only Promethean satyr-play now identifiable among the fragments of Aeschylus: the work known to the Alexandrian scholars as *Prometheus Pyrkaeus*, "the Firelighter." The fragments of this show that it concerned Prometheus' carrying of fire to earth. In one of them we glimpse a member of the satyr-chorus so enchanted by his first sight of a flame that he tries to kiss it. In another, preserved on papyrus, there are parts of a marvelously lively song performed by the satyrs as they reel around this world's very first bonfire.[22]

So far as we can reconstruct it as a whole, the tetralogy of 472 B.C. presented the original audience with an amazing range both of theme and of tone; the primeval winged monsters on the far-off Thracian coast, and the all too familiar galleys grappling in Salamis waters; the terror of an empire's pride (of *all* human pride?) brought to nothing, and the comic fantasy, light-as-fire, of the *Prometheus Pyrkaeus*. Yet almost from the first, the *Persians* seems to have been singled out in popular favor. Even in Aeschylus' lifetime it received the distinction (unparalleled, so far as is known) of a command re-performance at the court of the tyrant Hieron of Syracuse, which brought the poet, we are told, "great fame."[23]

---

21. Broadhead, in the discussion referred to in Note 20, discusses attempts, mostly by certain nineteenth-century students of Aeschylus, to show that all three tragedies may have been connected by a single overriding theme, namely the Persian Wars. It seems now to be generally agreed that this theory must be abandoned, or at least shelved; not because it is impossible *per se*, but because the evidence so far available is simply inadequate to justify it.

22. This fragment is edited, with English translation, by Lloyd-Jones in his Appendix to Smyth's *Aeschylus* (see Note 20), pp. 562–66. The attribution of the fragment to the satyr-play *Prometheus Pyrkaeus* is not quite certain, but seems extremely likely. The main objection that has been raised to it is that the singers in the papyrus refer to a *chiton*, a kind of tunic not associated by most people with the uncivilized satyrs; but this objection seems to be disposed of by an unnoticed remark in the lexicographer Pollux, who, describing various kinds of satyr-play dress, includes "the shaggy *chiton*, which is worn by the Silens" (Pollux, *Onomastikon* IV.118).

23. The evidence is given in Broadhead's edition of the *Persians*, pp. xlviii–xlix. This re-performance must have taken place within five years of the original production at Athens, since Hieron died in 467 / 66 B.C.

Long after, in the declining years of the Roman Empire, it was included in the selection of seven plays of Aeschylus for school reading, which has been preserved in one or two of our medieval manuscripts. Even a thousand years after that, when the schools of a shrunken and threatened Byzantine Empire cut down the reading selection yet again to three plays, only, of Aeschylus, the *Persians*—this memorial of a Greek triumph over the powers of the East, this solemn warning about the way life is—remained on the syllabus. So it has come to us, in our turn.

III STAGING AND DELIVERY

The guise in which the *Persians* (like the other six plays of Aeschylus) has come to us from antiquity through medieval Byzantium is essentially that of a bare verbal text. Most of the manuscripts on which we depend offer an *Argument* at the beginning of the text, and some also offer a marginal commentary. In part, at least, the *Argument* and commentary can be traced back to some of the best ancient Greek scholars, working, many of them in the Alexandrian Library, with materials and information that would otherwise be quite lost to us. Every student of Aeschylus owes a great debt to these men for their preservation and explication of the texts. Unfortunately, however, even the earliest of them worked at least two centuries after Aeschylus' death, and in any case their interests were almost exclusively verbal. Either they could not, or they would not, comment to any significant extent on the manner of staging, the masks and costumes, the properties, the delivery, the melodies, the rhythms of speech, song, and dance—in fact, on any of those elements that were combined with the verbal poetry to make up the totality of an Aeschylean drama.

There are two resources available for the modern student of Aeschylus, or indeed of any Greek tragedy, who is seeking, as he or she should, to re-experience that totality—to conjure it up in all its dimensions from these written symbols that lie silent and flat on this paper. The first resource is the general information that has been built up from miscellaneous ancient sources, literary and archaeological, about the Attic theater, its physical layout, its costumes, its music, and so on.[24] Unfortunately, this is less helpful than usual when we are dealing with a play produced as early as 472 B.C. We simply do not know what the Theater of Dionysos looked like only seven years after the second Persian sack of Athens, although it is a reasonable guess, which will be adopted in this book, that its main elements were much the same as they

---

24. T. B. L. Webster's *Greek Theatre Production*, second ed. (London, 1970), is one of the many convenient general surveys of these questions. An invaluable detailed sourcebook for most of them is Arthur Pickard-Cambridge, *The Dramatic Festivals of Athens*, second ed. by J. Gould and D. M. Lewis (Oxford, 1968).

are known to have been later. There will have been a circular dancing floor, the *orchēstra*, and a few yards south of it the façade of a stage building, the *skēnē*; entrance passages, *parodoi*, will have led from either side into the area between those two. The Chorus' usual territory will have been the *orchēstra*, while the actors will most often have been stationed in the area between it and the *skēnē*; but very free interplay was possible in the earliest extant dramas. Finally, sloping down toward the *orchēstra* and embracing it on the north, east, and west, was the *theatron* proper, the audience area, shaped out of a natural hollow in the southern slope of the Acropolis. The few visual representations of tragic actors and choruses that date from as early as Aeschylus' lifetime suggest in general that the costumes will have been gorgeous, and that the features of the masks (worn by actors and choruses alike) will have shared the simplicity and elegance of other early classical art. The masks were not yet the caricatures of the human face that grimace from above the portals of our Schools of Drama.

But here, so far as the *Persians* goes, the external evidence for the production gives out, and we must turn to our other major resource, the indications obtainable from the verbal text in itself. As in most ancient Greek dramatic texts, such indications are surprisingly numerous and enlightening. It seems that in the absence of the convention of regular stage directions (which are extremely rare in Greek manuscripts of any date, and in no case can be proved to go back to the original authors), the Greek dramatists took considerable care to embody hints on the play's production in the actual words that they composed for their choruses and actors.

It is clear from allusions in our text (e.g., 1259 / 760–61) that the imagined scene is somewhere in Susa, capital of the Empire. The earlier part of the play is enacted before "this ancient roofed-building" on which the Chorus "sit down" (183–84 / 140–41, literally translated). That is all the poet has told us, and it seems rather pointless to speculate on what, exactly, the ancient building is.[25] We may fairly deduce, however, that in the original production the façade of the *skēnē* played the part of the "ancient roofed-building," presumably being fitted with a bench or step on which the Chorus could seat themselves. A second structure whose presence is required by the text is the tomb of Darius, which is in the form of an earth-mound (1037 / 647, note). Just where this would have been placed is uncertain; we ourselves would prefer to imagine it in the center of the *orchēstra*, to allow ample room all around

---

25. Speculations are enumerated in Broadhead's edition of the *Persians*, pp. xliii–xlvi: Council-Chamber? Darius' tomb? (But would this Chorus actually *sit* on the tomb of the divine ruler, whose eventual appearance strikes them dumb with terror?) The city gates of Susa . . . ?

it for the spectacle of the ghost-raising. It any case, it will be noticed that the stage-set of the *Persians* as a whole clearly resembles the set required for Aeschylus' *Libation-Bearers*. In both these plays, there are two structures, a building and a tomb; and the focus of the action may shift from the one to the other according to the requirements of the drama. In the *Persians*, the passage 961–1397 / 598–851 (perhaps even as far as 1469 / 906) will be centered around Darius' tomb; the opening scenes of the play (certainly the first entrance of the Queen, and perhaps the entire passage 1–960 / 1–597) will probably be concentrated in front of the *skēnē*; there is no clear indication in the text as to the acting locale of the finale, 1470 / 907 onward, but one might imagine the Chorus advancing from the tomb of Darius to meet Xerxes as he enters through one of the *parodoi*, and remaining thenceforth in the area between *orchēstra* and *skēnē*.

The text also offers several indications as to the personal appearance of the Chorus and actors of the *Persians*. The Chorus were white-bearded (1690 / 1056), and voluminously robed (1694 / 1060). Darius' ghost was certainly represented in Persian costume (1060–61 / 660–61, where he is conjured to appear in saffron-colored sandals, and in the national headdress with its peak upright, as only the King of Kings might wear it). It may fairly be assumed from this that the other characters in the play were likewise costumed as Persians, probably with some attempt at accuracy; after all, it was only a few years since Aeschylus and many of his audience had looked at close quarters on Persians, living and dead. Without being unduly fanciful, we might envisage the characters in our play as resembling the figures who can still be seen on the marvelous reliefs of the palaces built by Darius and Xerxes at Persepolis: handsome but austere-featured men, with a superb majesty in their expression and bearing—of a kind which Greek sculptors tended never to assign to human beings, only to Gods.[26]

On close inspection, the Greek text also provides quite detailed information about entrances, exits, and stage-properties. For the modern reader's convenience, we have incorporated that information in marginal stage directions. Where necessary, our textual justification for such directions is given in the notes. Also in the margins of the translation we have noted the manner in which each part of the play was delivered when it was performed in Greek. For a classical Greek drama might vary between three modes of delivery in any given passage, with profound consequences for that passage's tone and tempo. They were

---

26. A fairly recent short account of the Persepolis palaces, with illustrations and bibliography: Donald L. Wilber, *Persepolis: The Archaeology of Parsa, Seat of the Persian Kings* (New York, 1969).

unaccompanied verse (normally a six-foot iambic line in the Greek, but sometimes also, in this play, a seven-and-a-half-foot trochaic line); *chant*[27] *with instrumental accompaniment* (in an anapestic metre rather like the anapestic drum-roll that accompanies modern marching); and *fully melodic song* accompanied by instrumental music and, usually, by the dance (in a very wide variety of lyric metres). The metres found in the Greek text allow scarcely any doubt about the moments where Aeschylus shifts from one of the three modes to the other. What cannot, of course, be reproduced in a modern English version, are the precise metres that he used in Greek, in all their subtlety, and variety of emotional effect. Yet to this writer, at least, it seems that the composer of the version offered here has succeeded as well as any translator could hope to succeed in allowing the reader to feel the varying texture of Aeschylean dramatic poetry. Not for the first time she has shown that she knows how

To get the final lilt of songs,
to penetrate the inmost lore of poets ....
to diagnose the shifting-delicate tints of love and pride and doubt
                    —to truly understand.

IV GODS

It is recorded that as Xerxes was journeying through Asia Minor to take command of his expedition, "he came upon a plane-tree, which for its beauty's sake he presented with ornaments of gold; and he assigned one of his Immortals to be its attendant."[28] This incident in the Great Persian Wars, trivial though it must seem at first sight, serves well to introduce an aspect of archaic Greek and Near Eastern religious thinking that has been almost beyond Western comprehension until quite recently (the ecological movements, and the growing realization of the limitations of technology for the ordering of human fate, may have begun to alter things). Rightly or wrongly, the ancient peoples recognized the existence of a divine power and beauty not merely in their heavenly and infernal Gods, but also in the nonhuman phenomena of the visible world. The art of living was to walk cautiously and reverently among all the forces of this divine landscape, knowing one's place; if not, the law of *hybris* and *ātē* would be enforced. Seen in that light, Xerxes'

---

27. "Chant" or "recitative" seem to be the nearest modern equivalents to this kind of delivery, which the ancient Greeks called *parakatalogē*; it is clear that it lay somewhere between spoken verse and melodic song.

28. Herodotus, *Histories* VII.31. The "Immortals" were the elite division of the Persian army, as Herodotus explains in VII.83.

gesture to the plane-tree might be counted as his last sane act in the course of the expedition.

Aeschylus' *Persians* happens to be the most spectacular example in Greek literature of this ancient attitude to our world. For the attitude was already an integral element in the ancient and complex system of Greek mythology, which other early Greek poems and dramas naturally draw on quite freely; in a play whose setting and characters are entirely Persian, however, recourse to that system was obviously out of place.[29] Hence it is, perhaps, that the ancient world-vision is here most apparent to a modern observer. The nonhuman world is alive, and all its members are akin. Most explicitly, and most beautifully, this sense is expressed in the Queen's loving description of the offerings that she brings to Earth (lines 979–87 / 611–18), a little lyric poem in itself. They consist of flowers, "children of Allbearing Earth," and also of liquids for Earth to drink (994 / 621–22); in return she will release Darius from the company of the dead, themselves mighty powers (1106–9 / 689–92). But Earth is not always kindly. When the Persians break the law of moderation, of respect for the way things are, she will ally herself with the Greeks to punish them (1301–3 / 792–94). At the terrible crossing of the river Strymon, the Persians grovel in vain both to her and to Sky (809 / 499); here Sun joins in the destruction (815–17 / 504–5). Sea, also, is a powerful force in this play. We have already seen her children at their quiet work on the Persian dead (935–36 / 577–78); that might not have happened had they and Xerxes respected the "shrine" of her windswept waves (133 / 100–101), or the "holy" Hellespont and the Bosporos which "streams from god" (1214–16 / 746–47).

Yet those elemental powers at least the Persians could see and consequently respect (as, indeed, can we) if they were not blinded by *ātē*. Trickier to deal with, and no less powerful, were the *invisible* powers of the universe, whom Aeschylus normally refers to in this play by the vague names of *theos* or *daimōn*. *Theos* may be, and here usually is,

---

29. Aeschylus does introduce a few Greek divine names into the *Persians*. For reasons of clarity and emphasis, some of them have been replaced by paraphrases in this translation, but the fact is in each case recorded in the notes. The full list of occurrences may be given here (line numbers in parentheses indicate where a paraphrase has been used): Phoibos, **323** / 203 and note; Hades, (**1039–42** / 649–50, **1493** / 923); Hermes, (**1004** / 629); Pan, **728** / 448–49; Poseidon, **1228** / 750; Zeus, (**868** / 532), **1198** / 740, **1260** / 762, **1357** / 762, (**1481** / 915). But such names occur infinitely less often than in any other Greek play, and in most cases Aeschylus seems to introduce them simply because a Greek audience will recognize them with greater ease (better, for instance, to speak of Apollo than of Ahuramazda!). Nondivine names from Greek mythology are even rarer in this play, and each single one of the instances occurs simply as an alternative way of naming a geographical site; see the Glossary under AJAX and HELLĒ, and the notes on **922** / 570 and **1432–55** / 880–96 for Kychreus and Ikaros, respectively. There may be a covert allusion to the legend of Zeus and Danae in **106** / 79–80 (see the note there).

translated "god," and this word will not be too misleading—provided we understand in it the nature of the gods as Homer has depicted them, rather than of the God whom we know in the Judeo-Christian tradition. *Daimōn* is very much more difficult to translate. In Greek it can mean anything from a rather passive and impersonal concept, "fortune," at one end of the spectrum, to a personal being who is not merely active but also spiteful, at the other. In its sense "fortune," and also in the middle bands of the spectrum, *daimōn* roughly overlaps with the possible senses of *theos* (the dead Darius, for instance, is *daimōn* in the Greek text of 1030 / 641–42, but *theos* in 1031 / 643): at the opposite end from "fortune," however, it may almost approach the sense of its modern derivative, "demon." There is no word of comparable range in English, and various paraphrases have therefore been used in the translation. Notable passages in which Aeschylus' word is *daimōn* will be found in the translation at 567 / 345 ("some Power"), 581 / 345, 764 / 472, 834–37 / 515–16 (here the *daimōn* jumps down on the Persians with both feet!), 1180 / 724 ("Something divine"), 1181 / 725, 1474 / 909–10 ("undying Lust for human flesh"), 1489 / 921.

And yet, vague and variable as the nomenclature of divinity here is, in any of its visible or invisible manifestations, there seems to be one function that is shared by everything that is divine: it will enforce the ancient law of *hybris* and *ātē*.

V THE TRAGEDY OF THE PERSIANS

It seems that the *Persians* is best understood, both in its structural and in its religious aspects, if it is viewed primarily as *a progressive revelation of divinity* (in the sense explained in section IV) *and of its law*. As the means toward this revelation, Aeschylus orchestrated all the resources at the disposal of an early Attic tragedian: the entire heritage of pre-tragic Greek poetry, song, and dance; and also the new, visual element, which was the crucial innovation of the tragedians. The visual resource, however, he husbanded, just as he does in all his extant plays. He reserves it mostly for the middle and the finale of his *Persians*, with shattering effect.

The audience, no doubt, was (and is) impressed at the outset by the magnificent appearance of the Chorus of Persian Counsellors, and by the pomp of the entrance of the Persian Queen. In that sense, the visual resource of tragedy is drawn on from the beginning. And yet, in the actual development of the drama from its first line through more than half its course, it is *words* that count. The spectator of Aeschylus—more than the spectator of any later classical tragedy, and infinitely more than the spectator of most modern drama—must learn in the first place to listen to the verbal poetry, almost with the same attention that he would give to polyphonic music. For it is in the words that the dramatic themes are usually first developed and interlaced. The eye will have its turn later.

The play's sole great reversal—its peripety, if you will—occurs in the first speech of the Messenger at 417–25 / 249–55, the (in Greek) seven monumental lines that announce the defeat at Salamis. It is an excellent lesson in Aeschylean verbal dramaturgy to follow out the means whereby both the message and the appalling shock that it contains have been quietly prepared for from the first words of the play. Here is a translation of the first four lines of that Messenger-speech (literally translated, for the sake of exact verbal exposition; the same will be true of most of the other phrases quoted in the following paragraphs):

O cities of *all the Asian* land!
O *Persian soil*, and abounding harbor of *wealth*!
How in one stroke has been destroyed the abounding
prosperity, and the *flower of the Persians has gone*, fallen!

Now the phrases italicized are not here for the first time in the play. They, and related phrases, have been uttered before both by the Chorus and by the Queen—not, however, with this horrifying finality, but in shifting tones of love, and pride, and doubt. In the Messenger's speech the phrase "has gone" is the decisive one, which clinches the awful truth (if any doubt were left, it would be removed by the added "fallen"). Commentators have long noticed that the verb used in Greek, *oichomai*, has an inherent double sense; either neutral, "has departed," or abominable "is dead-and-gone, is done for." That same verb is heard in the first line of the play, "These, of the Persians who have gone"; and again in 15–16 / 12–13, "for all the Asian-born might has gone"; and in 81–83 / 59–60, "such is the flower of the men of the Persian soil that has gone"; and in 271–73 / 176–78 (the Queen is speaking), "since my son...has gone." In two of these passages the verb *oichomai* is coupled with other phrases that are echoed in the Messenger's first lines: "all the Asian-born might," "flower...of the Persian soil." Further, the Persian "wealth," *ploutos*, and prosperity, *olbos*, in the Messenger's speech echo an ominous meditation on these themes that is put into the Queen's mouth at 228–47 / 163–68 ("lest great *ploutos*...kick over the *olbos* which Darius won...our *ploutos* is beyond blame").

Thus the Messenger's first speech gathers up all the aspects of the Persian Empire that have emerged ambiguously so far in the play— wealth, majesty, command over all Asia, towering pride, and persistent doubts about the doom inherent in all these things—and in one final phrase, "has gone, fallen," determines the true meaning of them all.

This is but one example of Aeschylus' thematic use of words in the *Persians*. Once alerted, the modern reader (who must also, with this poet, learn to be hearer and visualizer too) will find many more, which so far as conditions allow have been brought out in the translation. Some of the phrases we have already observed will re-echo later in the play, if with less shocking effect: the "Persians' flower," at the eventual appear-ance of Xerxes himself (1496 / 925), and perhaps also in Darius' great metaphorical formulation of the *hybris-ātē* law (1347–49 / 821–22); the "abounding harbor of wealth," in Darius' fear for his "abounding toil of wealth" (1232–33 / 751). Other verbal themes that are worth listening for are the pervasive gleam of *gold* in the Chorus' opening chant (here the resonant Homeric word *polychrysos*, "much-golden," occurs four times within fifty lines, but is never found again in the *Persians* or in the rest of Aeschylus); the sinister word-game, throughout the tragedy, with the antithesis *fullness-emptiness*; the *yoke*; and *clothing*. To this last we shall have to return at a later stage in our account of the tragedy, for it is an example of the technique—brought to perfection long after, in the *Oresteia*—whereby Aeschylus may develop an ambiguous verbal theme, ultimately, into an all too clear visual epiphany.

The Messenger's appearance brings to an end the first of the play's four major movements,[30] which has built up a picture of the great wealth and power of the Persian Empire, and of its vulnerability to the laws of the universe (for this last, see above all 137–48 / 107–14; also 225–45 / 162–67, and the dream and omen narrated in 270–338 / 176–210). The second movement (417–960 / 249–597), like the first, is essentially verbal and descriptive. It begins from the Messenger's definitive announcement of disaster; and thereafter is occupied with presenting the full dimensions of that disaster, both objectively, in the words of the Messenger, and emo-tionally, in the reactions of the Queen and Chorus.

When the Messenger leaves the scene toward the end of that second movement, the tragedy has run for almost half its total length. During that time the Persian Empire has been both built up and torn down, through poetry of tremendous power. But two points should be noticed: the effects so far have been overwhelmingly verbal (reinforced, it is true,

---

30. By "movement" we refer to the principal divisions of the play's *content*. These divisions do not closely coincide with the traditional divisions of a Greek tragedy by *meter—parodos, episode, kommos,* and so on—which will be pointed out in our notes to the translation.

to an unreconstructible degree, by melody and dancing in the choral passages); and the story has been presented entirely at the human level, and through human eyes. Humanly speaking, the tragedy of Salamis is all over, bar the wailing, by 833 / 514; and that without a single dramatic spectacle, or even dramatic episode, in the sense that "dramatic" is nowadays understood. But to a composer and an audience still living within the ancient poetic tradition, the human action is only one half of the tally. There can be no completeness until that action has been seen and interpreted against the background of divinity.

That is the function of the third movement, from the re-entry of the Queen at 961 / 598, through the conjuring and the epiphany of Darius' Ghost, to the point where he sinks back into the tomb-mound at 1383 / 842. With this movement, the entire texture and technique of the *Persians* changes. The focus of the actors' and audience's attention shifts from the ancient building (i.e. the *skēnē?*) to the tomb (in the center of the *orchēstra?*); the divine world is opened wide, in terrifying majesty; and the visual element in Aeschylus' dramaturgy at long last is brought into full play and will remain so until the end of the drama. It is no great exaggeration (and if there is exaggeration at all, it may be pardoned as an attempt to emphasize a crucial aspect of Aeschylus' art) to suggest that an Athenian spectator who had the misfortune to be stone deaf would have made out, at best, only the general drift of the first two movements; but that from 961 / 598 onward he would have been able to follow the *Persians* with increasing assurance, until at the finale he would scarcely be at a disadvantage compared with the rest of the audience.

Central to this third movement is of course the noble figure of the Ghost of Darius, clothed in the full regalia of a Persian monarch. In three aspects Darius makes his impact on the drama: as successful father of the incompetent son Xerxes; as symbol of the splendor of that great empire that Xerxes has shattered; and above all, as one who in death has joined the Gods, and thus can expound the significance of what has happened with divine knowledge and authority. In passing, he also adds yet more to the unhappiness of his hearers (and to the historical coverage of the *Persians*), for he prophesies the great defeat by land which is still to come at Plataia. But the central message of this scene seems to be of universal import. In part it is a magnificent restatement of the old law of *hybris* and *ātē*. The bones of the dead piled high on the field of Plataia, the Ghost says, "will be a wordless signal to the eyes of mankind that, if you are human, your thoughts must not be over-high; *hybris*, flowering out, bears the wheat-ear of *ātē*, and from there reaps a harvest, all of tears" (1344–49 / 819–22, literally translated). The great expedition, in the end, ran up against the way things are. To those who would probe further, and would ask about the personal responsibility of Xerxes for the breaking of the law, the scene responds with a riddle. "Some one of the *daimones*, I dare say, joined with his will," says the Queen, speaking of Xerxes' bridging the Bosporos; to which the Ghost responds, paradoxically, "Ah, yes: it was a great *daimon* that came upon him, so that he should not have right thoughts" (1180–81 / 724–25, literally translated). At 1204–6 / 742 the Ghost puts it yet another way: "but when a man himself is eager, the *theos* too joins in."

Spirit or man? Circumstance or individual will? Whether or not Aeschylus knew of the philosophy of his older contemporary Herakleitos of Ephesos (*floruit* ca. 500 B.C.), there can be no proving; but there is a remarkable similarity here to Herakleitos' three-word enigma:

$$\text{\textit{Ēthos} \qquad \textit{anthropōi} \qquad \textit{daimōn}}$$
$$\text{"Character \qquad for-man \qquad Destiny"}$$

There is no verb here. Man sits in the middle, in the Greek dative case, the case of the recipient. On either side of him, each in the nominative case, loom Character and Destiny. Question: which of those two is subject, which is predicate? "Character for Man is Destiny?" or "Destiny for Man is Character?" Greek idiom will admit of either translation, equally. No more than Herakleitos, will Aeschylus provide the solution. At the core of his tragedy is the riddle of human responsibility, as it continues to be at the core of our life.

The fourth and final movement (1398–1714 / 852–1077) reverts to the human level. Its central theme is the contrast between the splendor of Darius' Empire, and the squalor to which Xerxes has reduced it. The splendor is first recapitulated by means of verbal poetry, in the sonorous choral ode 1398–1469 / 852–906. Immediately on this follows the entrance of a tattered figure, Xerxes himself. In characteristically Aeschylean fashion, the *name* that has echoed through the whole course of the play at last, and at the most effective moment possible, becomes a visible, tangible *person*. Xerxes is set in deliberate visual, and moral, contrast to his father's ghost. From his entry until the end of the play the greatness of the Persian disaster, so far described only in words, is finally brought before the eye.

It is perhaps only at this moment that most spectators will fully realize the extent to which *clothing*, from early in the play, has gradually been manipulated into position as the predominant image of Persian luxury and glory, and of Persian failure. As one thinks back, one remembers the soft, almost subliminal first entry of the theme: the Chorus' fear that they may come to hear the mourning of the women, as "ripping falls on the fine-linen robes" (163 / 125). It becomes increasingly insistent and closer to realization, as first the Queen narrates her dream-vision of Xerxes tearing his clothes (315–16 / 199), and then the Messenger reports how he actually did tear them when he saw the depth of the disaster at Salamis (756 / 468). From the beginning of the third movement, however, clothing moves to the forefront of the action, visually and thematically. The Queen, on returning with the libations for Earth, has changed her adornment from its former splendor (975–76 / 607–8); the Chorus, as we have already seen, conjure the Ghost to appear in the full imperial regalia; the parting words of the Ghost to the Queen, and again of the Queen to the Chorus, heavily emphasize the concern of both for the torn regalia of Xerxes, as if it were the most important thing on earth (1364–97 / 831–51). In the solemn context of national disaster, that emphasis, especially in the words of the Queen (1388–92 / 845–48), has struck many students of the *Persians* as a lapse of taste, and the criticism may well be justified: Aeschylus seems to come perilously close to the borderline between tragedy and black comedy. Even so, his ultimate dramatic purpose in the passage seems beyond doubt. He is preparing us for the ultimate realization of the clothing image, in this fourth and final movement. Here, it is not merely the splendid robes of the Chorus that are rhythmically torn apart to the accompaniment of an antiphonal of terrible lament; it is the imperial majesty of Persia that is destroyed before our eyes.

Looking down the years after the production of this first surviving tragedy in 472 B.C., we see Athens in its turn acquire an empire, and lose it disastrously, before the century is out. During those same years we see a vast upheaval in art, literature, and political and philosophical thinking—a revolution in the mode of human consciousness, the effects of which are with us yet. To the course of that revolution, the successive Attic tragedies, including the later tragedies by Aeschylus himself, are a major witness. As the century advanced, Aeschylus' successors concentrated with increasing psychological subtlety on *individuals*, on their interactions with one another, on their struggles with themselves and with the divine forces that shape (or seem to shape) their personal destinies; and in so concentrating they created an art that is recognizably drama as the world has since understood the term. The gain so achieved is there for all to see and wonder at. Sometimes overlooked is the inevitable corresponding loss. It is the loss of an archaic wholeness of vision, a perception of humanity's place in the great nonhuman world. Never again after the *Persians* would a tragedy display the fate of an entire nation that clashed with the law of that world. Never again would the law itself be so clearly expounded.

It has quite disappeared from the Attic tragedies that were enacted in the last quarter of the century, under the shadow of the calamitous Peloponnesian War.

C. JOHN HERINGTON

ON THE TRANSLATION

The story of this translation is partly and appropriately a ghost story. The ghost is not, however, that of King Darius, whose oracular presence commands the third movement of *Persians*. Instead, a more solid hand delivered a message from the fifteenth century A.D., which gave the work of translation a mysterious and urgent push. It happened this way:

On a warm summer evening in 1975, C. J. Herington exhibited a photostat of the last page of the tragedy's medieval N manuscript (Madrid 4677). That page contains emendations and a subscription in writing other than that of the original copyist. The subscription is signed "Konstantine Laskaris the Byzantine." Some facts about Laskaris' life are known. Born in Constantinople to a princely family, he lived there and pursued the scholarly study of Greek. But when the Turks took the city in 1453, he went into exile, first on Corfu, then in various Italian cities, where he continued to study and teach. It was perhaps not an unusual life, given the times, for a well-born man dedicated to learning. His prime claim to an entry in today's encyclopedias is authorship of a text on grammar, the first book in Greek ever to be set in type and printed. By an odd coincidence, Laskaris' death at the end of the fifteenth century took place in Sicily where Aeschylus himself had died, though in another town, nearly two thousand years earlier.

The N manuscript of *Persians* is not an authoritative version lying in the mainstream of the tradition from which our current texts derive, but it does have a small, sweet history of its own. Laskaris' subscription is a personal note that tells an astonishing tale:

> One must expect anything. For, before the fall of the city, the present very old book—also comprising others of the poets—was, as it were, mine. And, after the capture, finding it in Pherrai, I bought it for a pittance and entrusted it to a certain very good friend along with many other books which—I don't know how—he lost. Then, eighteen years

later while living in Messina in Sicily, I obtained it again. I restored it and wrote in the missing parts for the use of those who have nothing better.

Remarkable! Not all the details are clear. Did Laskaris regain the entire book in Sicily or only a part of it? Is the Pherrai mentioned to be equated with Pera, a suburb of Laskaris' Constantinople, or with the location of the modern village of Pherrai in Thrace? It doesn't matter. The basic story is cause enough for wonder, that a manuscript then over a century old, containing *Persians* and work by poets other than Aeschylus, was lost—twice?—in the aftermath of Constantinople's fall and serendipitously recovered, though in damaged condition, nearly two decades later.

Laskaris' restoration seems to have been a labor of love. And the footnote written in his swift hand became a voice reaching, that summer night, across centuries to issue working orders: Go to it and do your best for the use of those who have nothing better.

The next two years were spent in the fifth century B.C., inside *Persians*. The text confronts the translator like a rusted tangle of barbed wire, somehow to be straightened out and given a shiny new coat of language. The job cannot be done. For the text of a piece meant for performance is a tiny fraction of the whole; the words are only clues to a host of actions, vocalizations, tempi, pacing, conventions, memories, and emotions that elude print. Where are the actors, the audience, and the currents that once bound them? The absence of all these poses the eternal question of lamentation: *Ubi sunt?* And because *Persians* is a work dependent for many of its dramatic effects, especially in the last movement, not merely on verbal meanings but on sounds—sheer, swelling, inarticulate, overwhelming sounds of heartbreak at its most extreme, the play cries out for its lost breath, its forever lost music. How can such a play be reimagined?

Its message is clear. Pride goeth before a fall; the fall can be bitter indeed. Humankind must check its mortally presumptuous urge to alter and control lest sure retaliation be provoked from Earth and Heaven. These, the statements of *Persians*, are as suited to a technological society as to one of farmers, seafarers, and fighters. And Aeschylus makes them by closing a moment in history within a poetry that is enduring strange and heartrending. The poetry is worth trying to rediscover.

The world of *Persians* is a world that gives no room to metaphor. It is totally alive. Everything human and natural is inseparably linked, and all feelings, all things are potentially sentient and powerful. The fertile Nile flows seaward, literally giving birth to Xerxes' Egyptian contingents.

Sardis the city actually stands beside the commanders Mitrogathes and Arkteus to subjugate and mount Ionian Greeks in the service of Persia. The plain of Marathon itself is murderous, killing Darius' splendid troops. Care scratches hearts with real claws, and runaway wealth kicks up real dust. The Sea is outraged at being bridged in chains like a slave. Asia falls to her knees. Men flower and are cut down, but in death they may still hear, see, and speak. And the invisible energies of Heaven do indeed have feet and use them to trample the immoderate flesh.

But such marvels and the old acceptance of pervasive vitality are shared by much Greek poetry, especially that on the edge of the archaic. *Persians* is extraordinary for the ways in which Aeschylus combines elements that may now seem to be oil and water, not to be mixed. He mingles the account of a timebound event, the defeat of the Persian forces at Salamis, with magic and the supernatural—a dream, waking omens, soul-raising, prophecy, and the unseen, constant presence of the *daimōn*. Today the play is beyond price as a document of history witnessed. The fact that it is also history dramatized is sometimes viewed as a frustrating blind pulled down on what really happened at Salamis. What, for example, is the identity of the small, nameless island off the coast of Salamis? All the poet tells us is that there, on its harborless rock, Pan dances and many Persians die. The essential drama of the play, however, lies in just such combinations of poetic and historical truths. In the combining the temporal world is surrounded—permeated—by all that is timeless and divine. The tragedy occurs not only on the battlefield and in the wildly lamenting court at Susa; it plays out through eternity. The result is a document of human feeling, a stunning piece of *emotional* realism. The defeat at Salamis becomes all defeat; the grief spawned there in blood is all grief anywhere at any time.

If the translation succeeds in bringing some of this time-freed drama into the present moment and into playable English, there are living people to be thanked. Not all the impetus behind the work was ghostly. I am grateful to my firm and gentle ally, C. J. Herington, with whom it has been a joy to collaborate. He knows Greek with head and heart. Without his guidance my version of the Persian defeat and withdrawal would have poeticized historical facts past recognition, and ships, not temples, would have crowned the hills. Nor, without him, would the directive from Konstantine Laskaris have reached me.

There are others whose help and participation deserve happy acknowledgment. In the beginning the task of translation was to have been a three-way effort, with the poet James Scully, translator of this volume's *Prometheus Bound*, tackling all but the odes, introduction, and notes. The pages he provided gave me a starting point—finding English for the lyrical choral responses to the Messenger's announcement of disaster. Thanks are also due D. S. Carne-Ross, who read an early version of the translation and rescued it from several kinds of unspeakability. Deepest appreciation goes to William Arrowsmith, the first to believe that we might make a *Persians* for our day.

The translation is based primarily on the text edited by H. D. Broadhead, *The Persae of Aeschylus* (Cambridge University Press, 1960). Broadhead's critical notes and commentary furnished many useful explanations of historical, if not dramatic, facts. A second text was also consulted, that of H. Weir Smyth, *Aeschylus*, volume I, Loeb Classical Library (Harvard University Press, 1922). In supplement, two scholarly studies helped me to come to contemporary terms with the ancient art of lamentation. They are Margaret Alexiou's *The Ritual Dirge in Greek Tradition* (Cambridge University Press, 1974) and Gareth Morgan's "The Laments of Mani" (*Folklore*, Volume 84, winter 1973). Professor Morgan was brave enough, too, to give a telephoned rendition of a dirge-tune used today in the southern Peloponnese. And there is one translation of *Persians* that must be credited simply for the pleasure it has given me: the version robustiously made in the late eighteenth century by the Rev. R. Potter, Prebendary of Norwich, and the first to find English verse for the Aeschylean corpus. It is luckily accessible in the Random House collection of Greek tragedies, which may be found in many public libraries.

Throughout its years the work of translation was enhanced by thoughts of two special people. Without any textual justification, I have imagined the Chorus of the Faithful, Persia's elderly regents, as veterans of Darius' wars and fathers of sons gone, and gone forever, with Xerxes' host. To my own two sons, Peter and Charles, young men both at the time of this writing, my translation is dedicated in hope that they will all their lives see days of safe return.

Janet Lembke

PERSIANS

Translated by

JANET LEMBKE

and

C. JOHN HERINGTON

CHARACTERS

CHORUS   of old men, regents of Persia

ATOSSA   the Queen, mother of Xerxes and Darius' widow

MESSENGER   a Persian runner

GHOST OF DARIUS

XERXES   King of Persia, son of Darius

Ladies in waiting

Persian soldiers, survivors of the defeat at
Salamis and the subsequent retreat

Line numbers in the right-hand margin of the text refer to
the English translation only, and the Notes beginning at
p. 187 are keyed to these lines. The bracketed line numbers
in the running headlines refer to the Greek text.

An open square in Susa, capital of Persia. In the background, a building reached by steps. Nearer to the spectator, and probably in the center of the dancing-floor, a mound representing the tomb of Darius.

> *Enter the* CHORUS *right, marching slowly and delivering anapestic chant.*

CHORUS We the old men

     while Persia's young strength has gone
onto Greek soil   stay at home
     appointed their Faithful,
the lavish and goldwinning throne's
loyal regents
     whose age and experience he
Lord Xerxes   King   son of Darius
chose himself
     to safeguard his country.   10

King   royal army   blazoned in gold
WILL THEY COME HOME?
               My heart's ragged beat
prophesies doom:
     all Asia's strong sons
are gone   gone
     and now rumors bruit
the young King's name
but not one runner and not one rider
     bring word to Persia's capital.   20

They rallied, they marched   leaving Susa's defenses
     and Ekbatana's
          and safe ancient stones that barricade Kissa
some mounted on horses, others on ships
footsoldiers, too, stepping it steady
     eager for combat

          man packed on man.
You, Amistres
and you, Artaphrenes
you, Megabates   30
and you, Astaspes
Persian commanders
kings in your own right under the Great King
leaders who hurl on the battling horde
you bowtamers, horsebreakers
          chilling to watch
               deadly in war
                    because endurance gleams hard in your souls.

You, Artembares, war-joyful horseman
you, Masistres   40
you, the bowtamer shining Imaios
you, Pharandakes
you, too, stallion-driver Sosthanes.

And you
          whose command fertile Nile outpoured
Sousiskanes born in Persia
Pegastagon sundark Egyptian
and godbelov'd Memphis' lord, towering Arsames
and satrap at Old Thebes, Ariomardos
          with swampskippers, rowers   50
               oars dipping silent
                    dangerous men, too many to number.

And following close throng
the Lydian thousands
          who relish the rich life
and lord it over every last man
               of the Asia-born race whom
Mitrogathes
and valiant Arkteus
          kingsent commanders   60
and goldladen Sardis
          made to wheel out, chariots clanging

three horses, four, each
a fear-breeding sight.

And pressing on them
Lydia's neighbors
who live in eyes' reach of her godswept peak
Mardon, Tharybis, lance-breaking anvils
Mysians, too, masters of javelins–
all, all have vowed   70
to throw slavery's yoke
firm on the Greeks.

And Babylon the gold-proud
fields motley troops in long horizon-crowding lines
some for a ship's bench
others who trust bowtugging rage
and scimitars from every fort in Asia
surge behind
obeying the King's
deadly orders to march.   80

The CHORUS *come to a halt.*

This
is the flower of Persian earth
the men now gone
and Asia's land that held their roots
groans out loud,
aflame with yearning.
Parents, wives in cold beds
count the days.
Time stretches thin.
They wait and shiver.   90

The CHORUS *begin to sing and dance the invasion of*
Greece.

The army HAS won through! Persians,
Breakers-of-cities, the King's men
sweep countries lying on the far shore

They've crossed the strait
    that honors Hellē
      by binding their ships
and clamping a bolt-studded road—
a yoke
   hard on the Sea's neck!

And teeming Asia's headstrong   100
    lord has shepherded his flocks
        godsped against the world on two fronts
land and sea
    and trusts his leaders
        stern rocks among men
As heir to a gold-showered line
he gleams
        casting a god's light

But the heart of his eye darkens,
    the death-dealing stare of a snake   110
        Countless its hands!
        Countless the ships!
And he while his chariot sings
    has targeted War's taut bow
        on spearmen trained for close combat

And not one has proved he can stand up
    to men in a ceaseless stream
      nor ever build
      a sure seawall
to stay the unstoppable waves   120
    Resistless, Persia's armed flood
        and the war-joy that crests in her sons

For gods decree
Fate's age-old power here and she
has long charged Persians
with a holy task:
    Wage tower-splitting war
    Hurl forward horse-drawn battle glee
    Lay cities waste

And they have learnt   130
when galewinds lash the saltroad white
to look unshaken
at the Sea's deep shrine:
    entrusting life to slender
    ropes and man-supporting tricks
    they stride the waves

But how crafty
    the scheme of God!
What mere man outleaps it?
What human foot jumps fast enough   140
to tear loose
        from its sudden grip?

For with gestures
    of kindness as bait
Blind Folly fawns a man
into her net, nor can he hope
to work loose
        and escape unhurt

   The CHORUS *begin a lament, ominous in its prematurity.*

My thoughts
    scratched raw by fear   150
        wear black
Shall we wail   WAAAAW!
    for the wide-ranging Persians?
What word for our people?
    That Susa's great heart is
        bled empty of men?

And will
    Kissa's old walls
        din back
that death caw   WAAAAW!   160
    and the thump of the womanhorde
howling and croaking

ripping fine linen and
        pummeling breasts?

For horseback troops
and troops on foot
        all, all of them
have left home
        in a stinging swarm behind their chief
and all have crossed   170
        the Sea-dividing span
                that juts from two shores
yoking two lands

Here double beds
bereft of men
        are filled with tears
and each wife
        who has rushed to war a headstrong spear
is left to spend
        her gentle elegance   180
                bereft of love, one
yoked but alone

> *At ode's end the* CHORUS *are scattered, each member
> standing alone to give visual emphasis to the last line.*

CHORUSLEADER *(chanting)* Persians! Assemble.
Gather on the steps below this ancient roof.
We should discuss
our carefullest, most deep-debated thoughts,
        for need presses close.

How does he fare
Xerxes   our King   son of Darius?
Where lies the victory?   190
                        Taut bow
or lance's spearing force—
        which one has conquered?

> *With her retinue* ATOSSA *enters right in a chariot.*

Look up!
        Dazzling as gods' eyes,
a light moves toward us.
Mother of the Great King.
My Queen.

        Prostrate yourselves!
Salute her as adorns her dignity.   200

The CHORUS *prostrate themselves.* (ATOSSA *and the*
CHORUS *speak in unaccompanied trochaic verse
from here through line 269.*)

CHORUSLEADER My lady, all honor.
        My lady most blest
           among sonbearing women,
grey mother of Xerxes,
        Darius' wife
           born to share
our god's bed
        and born also
           to mother a god unless—
unless the age-old   210
        Lust for Winning has
           taken itself from our men.

ATOSSA *descends from her chariot. The* CHORUS *rise.*

ATOSSA Yes, there's
        the reason urging me
           to leave the gold-wrapt
shadow of my house
        and room where once
           Darius slept beside me.
Sharpest care is
        clawing at my heart.   220
           It's you,
good friends,

      to whom I'd speak out
         unvoiced thoughts.
Nothing
      guards my inmost self
         against the fear
that vast Wealth,
      kicking up dust
         as it pelts headlong,   230
may overturn
      continued joy
         in the prosperity
Darius
      by some god's grace
         lifted high.
There's the reason
      an unspeakable, two-pronged
         anxiety sits at my core:
not to bow low   240
      honoring
         a manless treasure-hoard
nor does a light shine
      on the treasureless,
         no matter what their bodies' strength.
Surely our wealth
      is beyond reproach!
         My fear
centers on the Eye,
      for in my mind   250
         the house's Eye
is its master's presence.
      There
         my thoughts rest.
Persians,
      old faithful confidants,
         advise me.
All,
      all my hopes lie in you.
         Guide me.   260

CHORUS Our country's Queen,
                no need
                        to ask twice.
        A word, an act—
                we'll help if we can
                        when you
        command our counsel.
                We do intend
                        to serve you well.

ATOSSA (*in unaccompanied iambic verse*) Night after night   270
                since my son left with the army he mustered
        I am joined with many dreams.

                                        He's gone,
        gone to Greece,
                bent on making it Persian and *his*.
        But never has a vision showed more clear
        than what I saw last night
                in the kind-hearted dark.
        I'll tell you:
                        It seemed to me   280
        two well-dressed women—
        one robed with Persian luxury,
        the other in a plain Greek tunic—
        came into view, both
        taller far than any woman now living,
        and flawless in beauty,
        and sisters from the one same
        parentage.
                And for a fatherland, a home,
        one was allotted Greek soil,   290
        the other, the great world beyond.

                        Then I saw
        the two of them build bitter quarrels,
                one against the other,
        and when my son learned this,
        he tried to curb and gentle them:
                under his chariot

he yokes the two, and on their necks
he straps broad leather collars.
And the one towered herself   300
    proud in this harness
and she kept her mouth
    well-governed by the reins.
But the other bucked stubborn
    and with both hands
she wrenches harness from the chariot fittings
and drags it by sheer force,
    bridle flung off, and she
shatters the yoke mid-span
and he falls,   310
        my son falls,
and his father is standing beside him—
Darius, pitying him,
    and when Xerxes sees *that*,
he shreds around his body
the clothes that a king wears.

                I tell you
I did see these things last night.

Today, when I'd risen
and dipped both hands in a clear-rippling spring   320
    to cleanse me of bad dreams,
hands busy with offerings,
I stood by Phoibos' altar
wanting to give mixed honey and wine,
    their expected due,
to the undying Powers that turn away evil.
And I see
        an eagle
fleeing toward the altar's godbright flame.
Frightened, mute, my friends, I   330
    just stood there,
and soon I see a hawk in downstoop
raising wings to break the fall and working
talons in the eagle's head, and the eagle did
nothing,

only cringed and offered up
its flesh.

Terrors! I saw them!
Now you've heard them.
And you surely know   340
that if my son succeeds, he'll be marveled at,
but if he fails,
his people cannot call him to account.
When he is safely home,
he'll rule the country as he always has.

(*From here through line 416* ATOSSA *and the* CHORUS
speak in trochaic verse.)

CHORUS Mother,
here's advice
meant neither to alarm
nor overgladden you.
Gods abide: 350
turn toward them suppliant,
if anything you saw stirs faintest doubt,
praying them
to turn it away and bring
goodness to its peak
for you and
children in your line,
for Persia, too,
and those you love.
Afterward, pour out   360
the drink due Earth
and give the thirsty dead their sip
and pray, appeasing him,
your husband Darius—
you say you saw him
in the kind-hearted night—
asking him to send up
from his depth into our light
blessings for you and your son
and hold the reverse back   370

earth-coffined
till it molders in that dark.

For this advice
I have consulted
my prophetic heart.
Be appeased,
for as we
read the signs,
everything
shall   380
turn out well.

ATOSSA Yes, you
the first
to read my dream,
with goodwill toward my son and house,
have found
its true interpretation.
Would that the omens
turn out well!
I'll do all you say   390
for gods and old friends under earth
when I go home.
But first
I'd like to know, dear friends,
where
Athens is.

CHORUSLEADER Far west where the Lord Sun fades out.

ATOSSA My son really wanted to hunt down this city?

CHORUSLEADER Yes, so all Greece would bend beneath a Shah.

ATOSSA Does it field a manhorde of an army?   400

CHORUSLEADER Such that it has worked evils on the Medes.

ATOSSA Then bowtugging arrows glint in their hands?

CHORUSLEADER No. Spears held steady, and heavy shields.

ATOSSA What else? Wealth in their houses?

CHORUSLEADER Treasure, a fountain of silver, lies in their soil.

ATOSSA But who herds the manflock? Who lords the army?

CHORUSLEADER They're not anyone's slaves or subjects.

ATOSSA Then how can they resist invaders?

CHORUSLEADER So well that they crushed Darius' huge and shining army.

ATOSSA Terrible words! You make the parents of those gone shudder.   410

CHORUS (*severally*)
     But I think you will soon hear the whole story.
     Someone's coming!

                              He's ours—
     a Persian clearly by the way he runs.

     Something's happened. Good or bad,
     he brings the plain truth.

                         The MESSENGER *enters left.*

MESSENGER (*in unaccompanied iambic verse throughout this episode*)
     Listen! cities that people vast Asia.
     Listen! Persian earth, great harbor of wealth.
     One stroke, one single stroke has smashed
     great prosperity,   420
          and Persia's flower is gone, cut down.
     Bitter, being first to tell you bitter news,
     but need presses me to unroll the full disaster.

Persians,
> our whole expedition is lost.

CHORUS (*singing from here through line 469*)
> Cruel cruelest evil
>> newmade, consuming Oh
>>> weep, Persians, who hear
> this pain

MESSENGER Everything over there has ended. And I—   430
> against all hope, I'm here, seeing this light.

CHORUS Life stretches long
>> too long for grey old men
>>> who hear of all hope
> undone

MESSENGER I was *there*. I can tell you, no hearsay,
> the evils that sprang up hurtling against us.

CHORUS No nonono
>> That bright storm
> of arrows showing Asia's massed colors   440
> advanced
>> all for NOTHING
>>> into hostile Greece?

MESSENGER They met hard deaths. The corpses
> pile on Salamis and every nearby shore.

CHORUS No nonono
>> You're saying
> those we love are floating, foundering
> awash
>> DEAD MEN shrouded   450
>>> in sea-drowned cloaks?

MESSENGER Our arrows didn't help. The whole force

went down, broken, when ship rammed ship.

CHORUS Rage
for the Persians killed
Wail the death howl
All that began well
comes to the worst end   CRY!
CRY OUT
for the army slaughtered!   460

MESSENGER Salamis, I hate that hissing name.
And Athens, remembering makes me groan.

CHORUS Athens
bears Persia's hate
We will recall
wives she has widowed
mothers with no sons   NO!
and all
ALL FOR NOTHING!

(ALL *speak in iambic verse from here through*
line 867.)

ATOSSA Silence has held me till now   470
heartsore,
struck by the blows of loss,
for this disaster so exceeds all bounds
that one can neither tell,
nor ask,
about the suffering.
Yet there is terrible need
for people to bear pain
when gods send it down.
You must   480
compose yourself: speak out,
unrolling *all* the suffering,
though you groan at our losses.
Who is not dead?

47

And whom shall we mourn?
Of all the leaders
 whose hands grip authority
which one
 left his post unmanned, deserted
when he died?   490

MESSENGER Xerxes—he lives and sees light—

ATOSSA You speak: light blazes in my house,
and white day after a black-storming night!

MESSENGER —but Artembares,
  commander of ten thousand horse,
is hammered along Sileniai's raw coast
and thousand-leader Dadakes,
  spearstuck,
danced back without any effort I could see
   overboard   500
and Tenagon,
  pureblooded Bactrian and chief,
scrapes against Ajax' sea-pelted island.

Lilaios,
Arsames,
and a third, Argestes,
  wave-tumbled around that dove-broody island,
kept butting resistant stones
and so did Pharnoukhos
  whose home was Egypt, by Nile's fresh flow, 510
and so did they
  who plunged from one same ship,
Arkteus,
Adeues,
and a third, Pheresseues.
And Matallos from a golden city,
  leader of ten thousand,
dying, stained his full beard's tawny brush
  changing its color with sea-purple dye.

And the Arab, Magos,   520
with Artabes the Bactrian,
      who led thirty thousand black horse,
took up land as an immigrant
by dying there
      on that harsh ground.

Amistris
and Amphistreus,
      whose spear delighted in trouble,
and bright-souled Ariomardos,
      whose loss brings Sardis down grieving,   530
and Seisames the Mysian,
Tharybis, too,
      sealord of five times fifty ships,
      Lyrnaian by descent, a hard-bodied man,
lies dead,
      a wretch whose luck went soft,
and Syennesis,
      first in courage, the Cilicians' chief,
      one man who made most trouble for the enemy,
died with glory.   540

                        These are the leaders
of whom I bring my memories.
But we suffered many losses there.
I report a mere few.

                        The CHORUS *cry out sharply.*

ATOSSA Noooo!
                  These words I hear
lift evil to its height.
O the shame cast on Persians,
and the piercing laments!

But tell me,   550
            turn back again,
was the count of Greek ships so great

49

they dared launch their rams
    against Persia's fleet?

MESSENGER If numbers were all, believe me,
Asia's navy would have won,
for Greek ships counted out
at only ten times thirty
    and ten selected to lead out that line.
But Xerxes, this I know,   560
commanded a full thousand,
    two hundred and seven
    the fastest ever built.
That is our count. Perhaps you thought
we were outnumbered?
                No.
It was some Power—
    Something not human—
whose weight tipped the scales of luck
and cut our forces down.   570
Gods keep Athens safe for her goddess.

ATOSSA You're saying that Athens is not yet sacked?

MESSENGER Long as her men live, her stronghold can't be shaken.

ATOSSA But at the beginning, when ship met ship,
tell me, who started the clash?
                Greeks?
Or my son
    who exulted in his thousand ships?

MESSENGER My lady,
    the first sign of the whole disaster came   580
when Something vengeful—
    or evil and not human—
appeared from somewhere out there.

For a Greek,
    who came in stealth from the Athenian fleet,

whispered this to your son Xerxes:
As soon as black night brought its darkness on,
Greeks would not maintain their stations, no,
but springing on the rowing benches,
    scattering here, there in secret flight,   590
would try to save their own skins.
And at once,
    for he had listened not understanding
      the man's treachery nor the gods' high jealousy,
he gave all his captains this command:
As soon as Sun's hot eye let go of Earth
and darkness seized the holy vault of Sky, then
they should deploy ships
    in three tight-packed ranks
to bar outsailings and the salt-hammered path,   600
while others circled Ajax' island.
And if the Greeks should somehow slip the trap
    by setting sail, finding a hidden route,
Xerxes stated flatly
    that every last captain would lose his head.
So he commanded in great good spirits.
He could not know the outcome set by gods.

There was no disorder. Obediently
the crews prepared their suppers,
and each sailor, taking a thong,   610
    made his oar snug to the tholepin.
And when Sun's glow faded and Night
was coming on,
        each oarlord,
each expert man-at-arms
    boarded his ship.
Squadron on squadron, cheers for the warships
roared from the decks,
        and they sailed,
each captain maintaining his position.   620
And all night long the lords of the fleet
kept fully manned vessels plying the channel.
And night was wearing on.
        The Greek forces never

tried sailing out secretly.
Not once.

But when Day rode her white colt
dazzling the whole world,
                the first thing we heard
was a roar, a windhowl, Greeks   630
singing together, shouting for joy,
and Echo at once hurled back
that warcry
      loud and clear from island rocks.
Fear churned in every Persian.
We'd been led off the mark:
                the Greeks
weren't running, no,
but sang that eerie triumph-chant
as men   640
          racing toward a fight
              and sure of winning.

Then the trumpet-shriek blazed
      through everything over there.
A signal:
          instantly
their oars struck salt.
                We heard
that rhythmic rattle-slap.
It seemed no time till they   650
all stood in sight.
              We saw them sharp.
First the right wing,
      close-drawn, strictly ordered,
led out, and next we saw
the whole fleet bearing down, we heard
a huge voice
          Sons of Greece, go!
          Free fatherland,
          free children, wives,   660
          shrines of our fathers' gods,
          tombs where our forefathers lie.

> *Fight for all we have!*
> *Now!*
Then on our side shouts in Persian
rose to a crest.
                    We didn't hold back.
That instant, ship rammed
bronzeclad beak on ship.
                              It was   670
a Greek ship started the attack
shearing off a whole Phoenician
stern. Each captain steered his craft
        straight on one other.
At first the wave of Persia's fleet
rolled firm, but next, as our ships
        jammed into the narrows and
              no one could help any other and
                    our own bronze teeth bit into
our own strakes,   680
                        whole oarbanks shattered.
Then the Greek ships, seizing their chance,
swept in circling and struck and overturned
our hulls,
                and saltwater vanished before our eyes—
shipwrecks filled it, and drifting corpses.
Shores and reefs filled up with our dead
and every able ship under Persia's command
broke order,
        scrambling to escape.   690
We might have been tuna or netted fish,
for they kept on, spearing and gutting us
        with splintered oars and bits of wreckage,
while moaning and screams drowned out
the sea noise till
        Night's black face closed it all in.

Losses by thousands!
                    Even if I told
the catalogue for ten full days I
could not complete it for you.   700

But this is sure:
                        never before in one day
have so many thousands died.

ATOSSA It's true, then, true.
        Wild seas of loss have come crashing down,
        down over Persians and all Asia's tribes.

MESSENGER You must understand:
           disaster—
                    I've told you less than half.
           The next load of suffering   710
           outweighed the first twice over.

ATOSSA What more hateful Luck
        could still beset our men?
                                  Answer me!
        What fresh disaster, what
        new losses weighted them down?

MESSENGER Persians at the peak of life,
               best in soul, brightest in lineage,
               first always to give the King loyalty—
           they're dead without glory,   720
               and shamed by that fate.

ATOSSA (to the CHORUS)   Cruel chance!
        O my friends, it hurts me.

                                           (to the MESSENGER)

        How did *they* die? Can you say?

MESSENGER An island fronts the coast of Salamis—
           tiny, harborless,
                             where dance-wild
           Pan likes stepping it light through the breakers.
           There

Xerxes posted these chosen men,   730
planning that when the shipwrecked enemy
swam ashore desperate for safety,
they'd kill that Greek force easily
and rescue friends caught in the narrows.
How badly he misread the future,
        for after some god had
handed Greeks the glory in the seafight,
that same day
        they fenced their bodies in bronze armor
and leapt from their ships   740
                        and cordoned off
the island so completely that our men milled
helpless,
                not knowing where to turn
while stones battered at them
and arrows twanging from the bowstrings
hit home killing them.
                        It ended
when the Greeks gave one great howl
and charged, chopping meat   750
        till every living man was butchered.
Then Xerxes moaned out loud
to see how deep disaster cut.
        Throned on a headland above the sea, he'd
        kept his whole army clear in sight.
And he ripped his clothes
and screamed
and gave shrill hasty shouts to his whole land force
dismissing them.
                        They fled in disorder.   760

Here is disaster greater than the first
to make you groan.

ATOSSA *(looking up into the sky)*   You!
        Hateful, nameless, not human Power,
how You cheated Persians of their senses!
How bitter the vengeance
        meant for this talked-of Athens

that found its way home to my son!
Marathon killed men. Weren't they
enough?   770
            It was for them
my son cast retribution
and hauled in countless cruelties
            upon himself and us.

But the ships that outran doom—
            where did you leave them?
Do you know what happened?

MESSENGER   The captains of the ships left
            ran in no order before the wind.
And the army left   780
            kept dropping off, first on Boiotian ground,
some of thirst,
            though water flowed beside them
                  out of exhaustion's reach,
while some of us,
            empty from panting,
drove through to the Phōkians' land
            and Dōris' fields
                  and the Mēlian Gulf where
Sperkheios quenches the plain with earthkindly drink,   790
and after that Akhaian soil
and the cities of Thessaly took us in
            when we were starving.
There the most died.
                        Thirst and hunger,
both of them stalked us.
And slogging north
            on to Magnesia and on to Macedon,
we reached the Axios' ford
            and Bolbē's reed-choked marsh   800
                  and Mt. Pangaios where Ēdōnians live.
It was that night
                  some god
blew down winter out of season and froze
holy Strymōn bank to bank.

Then any man
who'd once thought gods were nothing
sought them out, praying, begging
as he lay face down before Earth and Sky.
When the army finished its godcalls,   810
it started to cross the icelocked water,
and those of us who step out quick
before the god can shed his rays
find ourselves safe,
but when the fireball of Sun came up,
blazing light and heat,
its flame melted the iceroad midstream
and men kept falling,
falling one on another, and he is lucky, yes,
whose life breath was quickest cut.   820

And those of us left to gain safety,
working through Thrace against hard odds,
have slipped away,
not many,
and come back to our homefires,
to this earth of home.

Reason enough, chief city of Persians,
to cry out
longing for your best belovèd youth.
True reasons, though there's much   830
I've left untold of horrors
that a god hurled
crackling down on Persians.

The MESSENGER *exits right.*

CHORUS (*looking skyward*)   You!   Troublebringer!
nameless and not human,
how hard
You've jumped both feet into Persia's people!

ATOSSA I am heartsick. The army slaughtered!

O vision in the night
    that roiled through dreams,   840
the cruelties you clearly promised me
came true.

(*to the* CHORUS)   And you,
you read them much too lightly.
Even so, there's only your advice
to seize and act on.
                I will
first of all pray to the gods,
then bring gifts from my royal house—
    wine poured out with honey—   850
to soothe the appetites of Earth and ghosts.
When these are done, I shall
return to you.
            There's no regaining
what is gone, I understand that,
but I act so that something better
    may happen in days to come.

And you,
    with due regard for what has happened,
must, as my Faithful,   860
give advice worthy of my faith.

My son—
    if he comes back before I can return,
comfort him,
           escort him home
so that he heaps on existing evils
    no self-inflicted evil.

        ATOSSA *remounts her chariot and exits right with her*
                              attendants.

CHORUS (*chanting*)   God, greatest King!
    The Persians' proud and manswollen army, now
You've destroyed it,   870
You've hidden

Susa and Ekbatana in lowering grief

and mothers
whose gentle hands savage their veils
whose eyes rain tears on breasts already drenched
give tongue to sorrow

and wives, Persian brides
wailing softly
longing to see the men who were yokemates
stripping the soft beds where bursting youth reveled   880
wail, wail out the hungriest grief

And I, too,
raise a griefswollen voice
at the fate of men gone
dead and gone

(*singing and dancing*)

Listen   To the outmost ends
Asia's earth groans now
emptied of sons
Xerxes   convoyed them
He CONVOYED THEM   890
Xerxes   destroyed them
He DESTROYED THEM
Xerxes   the hothead brought on the whole rout
he and his riverdhows rigged for the sea

Once
we knew Darius' rule
a bowchief who
never volleyed such hurt
and Susa's men loved him
WHY HAVE TIMES CHANGED?   900

Soldiers and seamen lost!
Sailwings unfurled, bluedark
eyes on the sea

warships   convoyed them
                 Ships   CONVOYED THEM
warships   destroyed them
                 Ships   DESTROYED THEM
warships
        brought every one of them down
     rammed them and left them to Greeks' hacking   910
     hands

     Now
         we learn the King himself
         by slender chance
         runs for life down snowblocked
         roads in sweeping Thrace
     HOW CAN THIS BE?

Those doomed to die first
              DOOMED
are left
        there was no choice   920
               LEFT
to wash on Salamis' wavebroken rocks
               THEY ARE GONE
Groan
        Bite lips till the blood shows
         Howl, griefweighted voices, howl
          anguish at heaven
               DEAD AND GONE
Hold sorrow's burden
        till breath sobs and breaks   930

Flesh torn in the surge
              TORN
is stripped
        clean off the bone
               STRIPPED
by voiceless young of the unsoilable Sea
               THEY ARE GONE
Grieve

you houses robbed of your men
        Wail, childless parents, wail   940
            inhuman anguish
                                DEAD AND GONE
and learn in your grey years
        the whole reach of pain

And those who live on Asia's broad earth
will not long be ruled
                        by Persian law
nor longer pay tribute
under empire's commanding grip
nor fling themselves earthward   950
        in awe of kingship
            whose strength now lies dead

No longer will tongues in vassal mouths
be kept under guard
                        for people are freed,
set loose to bark freedom
now that dominion's yoke is snapped
The bloodsodden beaches
        of Ajax' sea-bruised island
            now hold Persia's heart   960

            ATOSSA, *on foot and dressed in mourning, enters right*
                with her ladies, who carry the jars and garlands
                        needed for making libations.

ATOSSA (*speaking in iambic verse*) Good friends,
        whoever lives learns by experience
that when a wave of evils crests
and breaks, it's natural for humankind
        to be afraid of everything,
but when the deathless Power flows calm,
        to trust
that Fortune's wind will always blow fair.
But now, for me,
        everything is packed with fear,   970

61

before my eyes the gods' hostility shows plain,
and the roar in my ears is battle din,
    not a healing song:
Evils attack so fiercely panic storms my heart.

That's the reason I've returned
    without a chariot or queenly luxury
to bring my son's father the appeasing drinks
    that serve as sweeteners to dead men:

        (*pointing to the jars her ladies carry*)

an unblemished Cow's white freshtasting milk
and the Flowerworker's droplets, lightsteeped honey,   980
with moisture poured sparkling from a virgin Spring
and unwatered drink from a wild country mother—
    this, the ancient Vine's new brightness,
and the fresh-scented harvest of one who blooms life
always in her leaves, the sundrenched Olive Tree—
    here it is,
and woven flowers, children of Allbearing Earth.

But, O my friends,
    these libations to the ones below
need solemn hymns.   990
            Chant them
and call his spirit, call up Darius
    while I send down
these Earthdrunk honors to the gods below.

CHORUSLEADER (*chanting*) Our Queen, our lady,
    whom Persians revere,
yes,
    send your libations to Earth's hidden rooms
while we, chanting, calling, pour out our breath
to beg kindness from those who marshal   1000
    men's shadows through Earth.

ATOSSA *and her ladies make their ceremonies of libation,*
while the CHORUS *look on with increasing anxiety. When*
she has finished, they begin the ghostraising. ATOSSA,
weeping, muffled, sits at the tomb's base.

CHORUS *(chanting)* Help us, You Powers undying and holy
                    that thrive beneath graves.
            You, Earth and the Soul-Guide
            and You who are King of the dead below us,
            send him out of his utter darkness,
                    send his spirit up into light.
            Disasters keep stalking us,
                                    and if
            he knows of any cure   1010
                    more powerful than offerings and prayer,
            only risen near us into light
                    can he reveal it.

                                    (singing and dancing)

            Can he hear me?
                    Blest in death
                            and potent as a deathless Force
            can my King hear these broken words
                    earthmuffled
                            tumbling from my lips and touching
                                    every note of pain in   1020
            ceaseless sorrow-roughened breath?
            Or must I shout
                    so that my anguish reaches him?
            Can he heed me in his buried dark?

            Wake and hear me
                    Earth and You
                            Who rule that world where dead men go
            Give complete consent to prayer:
                    set free
                            his proud and deathless glory   1030

Let Persia's god, born a man in Susa
rise now from his funeral house
Now, speed him up
         whose peer does not nor ever shall
rest hidden in this Persian earth

Man I loved, yes
         tomb I love, for
everything I love lies covered there
Hand of Death
         Yours alone the power to open graves   1040
and lead him lightward
                              Hand of Death
         free our hallowed lord Darius
Free him

Never once
         did he kill men with
Folly's blind and life-devouring haste
He was
         called the Persians' godbright counselor
and godbright counselor   1050
                    he was
         who steered the army on a true course.
Free him

The CHORUS *fall to their knees and begin to hammer and*
claw at the earth as if to help free the GHOST OF DARIUS.
                    In their next words they invoke him directly.

Shah once and Shah forever
         come close
                    break through
Go to the high prow of your tomb
Make yourself known
         showing signs of your kingship
                    crocus-dyed shoe   1060
                    turban's upright crest
Make yourself seen

Break free
Father who brought us no evil
Darius
          break free

Wake and hear loud suffering
          Hear strange
                    new pain
Lord of our lord, find daylight form   1070
The deathmist
          that grows on the eyes of the dying
                    opens dark wings:
                    the young men, our sons
are all of them gone
                    Wake now
Father who brought us no evil
Darius
          awake

                    The CHORUS, *moaning, slowly stand.*

CHORUSLEADER Why, why   1080
          must friends who deeply mourned your death
     [now mourn again —
          sorrows twice borne, new grief exciting old?]
Where have we erred?
The fleet all Asia built
is smashed and sunk,
                              the three-tiered
ships
          ghostships ghostships.

     The GHOST OF DARIUS *rises, spectral, from his tomb.*

DARIUS (*speaking in iambic verse*)
          Most Faithful of the faithful,   1090
               comrades of my youth,
                    Persians grown honorably grey,
what trouble oppresses my people?
The earth ceiling groans —

    hammered, scratched open.

                                              (*to* ATOSSA)

And seeing you, who shared my bed, here
        huddled now beside my tomb,
I sense fear.
                Yes,
I drank the sweetenings that you poured down.   1100

                                        (*to the* CHORUS)

        And you who stand before my tomb
                wail dirges
and dolefully chant out soulraising spells
to summon me.
                    There is no easy exit:
Gods in the underrealms have always been
better at taking than letting go.
Yet, now that I am one of them and powerful,
I come.
                Be quick, for I would have   1110
no blame for moments spent beneath the sun.
What new strange evils
        weigh down my Persians?

            ATOSSA *sobs. The* CHORUS *prostrate themselves.*

CHORUS (*singing*) I praise you
            and awe blinds my eyes
    I praise you
            but awe binds my tongue
    Your nearness fills me
            with death's age-old chill

DARIUS (*speaking in trochaic verse*)
    Because you chanted spells   1120
            persuading me to leave the buried world,
                I come.
    Tell everything, not rambling on,

              but make the story brief.
                   Speak and be done.
         I frighten you?
              Then reverence exceeds its bounds.
                   Let reverence go.

CHORUS (*singing*) I dread you
              and would not displease   1130
         I dread you
              but cannot find speech
         to tell those I love
              news better left untold

         ATOSSA *laments.* (DARIUS *and* ATOSSA *speak in trochaic
                        verse from here through line 1254.*)

DARIUS Because you feel the old dread
              pounding in your hearts,
                   restraining you,
         then let the one
              who shared my bed,
                   my aged lady wife,   1140
         cease her lamenting
              to give me
                   plain account.
         Mankind is
              bound to suffer
                   the hurts of being human.
         Many the evils spawned in the sea
              and many on land
                   for you who must die.
         And the longer you live,   1150
              the greater
                   your pain.

ATOSSA My husband, you
              above all other men were destined
                   to a wealth of happiness.
         How fortunate you were!
              While your living eyes

beheld the sun,
Persians,
    filled with praise and envy,   1160
        called you a god.
Now do I envy you
    because you died
        before you looked in the depths of loss.
Listen, Darius,
    I need few words
        to tell you everything:
Persia's power,
    her prosperity
        are completely crushed.   1170

DARIUS How? Thunderbolts of plague? Civil war?

ATOSSA Neither. Near Athens the whole expedition was lost.

DARIUS Which of my sons invaded Greece?

ATOSSA Headstrong Xerxes. He emptied Asia.

DARIUS Stubborn child! Did he go by land or sea?

ATOSSA Both. With a double front of two contingents.

DARIUS But how could footsoldiers cross the sea?

ATOSSA He made a path by yoking the Hellespont.

DARIUS What? He closed mighty Bosporos?

ATOSSA Yes. I think Something divine gave him help.   1180

DARIUS Something so monstrous it twisted his good sense!

ATOSSA And we see his achievement—disaster.

DARIUS What happened? Why do you groan?

ATOSSA Because the ships sank, the army was lost.

DARIUS You mean the whole army fell to the spear?

ATOSSA And Susa's man-empty streets are groaning.

DARIUS Lost, a great army! Our defense, lost!

ATOSSA And Bactria's men, even the old ones, are all dead.

DARIUS Wretched man! He killed his allies' young sons.

ATOSSA But Xerxes—it's said that he and a few others—   1190

DARIUS Is he safe?

ATOSSA —happily did reach the bridge yoking two shores.

DARIUS And arrived safe in Asia? You're sure?

ATOSSA Yes, it's been clearly reported. There is no doubt.

DARIUS Too swiftly then
                the Oracles came true,
                    and on my son
            Zeus hurled down
                prophecy completed,
                    and I had somehow   1200
            hoped that gods
                would take a longer time
                    to work their plan.
            But when a man
                speeds toward his own ruin,
                    a god gives him help.
            Now a fountain of defeats
                has been struck
                    for everyone I love.
            And my son in his ignorance,   1210
                his reckless youth,

69

brought on its spurt:
he hoped to dam
the flow of holy Hellespont—
the Bosporos
that streams from god—
by locking it
in shackles like a slave
and he altered the strait
and, casting over it   1220
hammered chains,
made a footpath
broad enough
for his broad array of troops.
Mere man that he is,
he thought, but not on good advice,
he'd overrule all gods,
Poseidon most of all.
How can *this* not be
a sickness of mind   1230
that held my son?
The wealth
I earned by my own hard work
may be overturned,
becoming nothing more than
spoils to the first looting hand.

ATOSSA Consort with evil-minded men
taught headstrong Xerxes
what to think: 1240
they told him
that the vast wealth
you handed on
was won at spearpoint
while he,
not half the man,
secretly played toy spears at home
and added nothing
to inherited prosperity.
Hearing such taunts
over and again   1250

from evil-minded men,
he planned
    his expedition
        and the invasion of Greece.

(ALL *speak in iambic verse from here till the end of the*
episode.)

DARIUS And so did his work,
    the greatest ever,
        to be remembered always,
such work as never before fell
    and emptied out Susa
since the Lord Zeus granted this honor: 1260
that *one* man
    should rule vast sheepbreeding Asia,
his sceptre held
    as a steersman holds the rudder.
The Mede himself was the army's first leader,
and another, his son, gained the succession
because reason stood at his passions' helm,
and third after him Cyrus ruled,
    Heaven's favorite,
who gave peace to everyone he loved   1270
and made subject Lydia's people and Phrygia's
and rounded up all Asian Greeks by force
nor did the god despise him,
    for his heart was righteous,
and Cyrus' son, fourth, piloted the army,
and fifth Mardos led, a disgrace to fatherland
    and long-established throne,
but there was plotting
and Artaphrenes, potent in virtue,
    helped by friends whose duty it was,   1280
cut him down inside the palace.
Then I ruled.
    Chosen by lot, I gained what I wished for
and fought a thousand times with my fighting thousands
but never
    threw evil like this on the nation.

But Xerxes my son, green in years,
    thinks green
and forgets what I taught him.

                              (*to the* CHORUS)

But you, men of my own generation,   1290
    plainly understand
that everyone of us who has held power
cannot be shown
        to have worked such devastation.

CHORUS What next, lord Darius?
            Where will your prophecy attain
        its end? How, after the worst,
        may we, Persia's people, win through to the best?

DARIUS Beware: mount no soldiers against Greek holdings.
        Beware: not even if Medes count more soldiers.   1300
        Know: Earth Herself is their ally.

CHORUS What do you mean? How, their ally?

DARIUS She starves a manglutted enemy.

CHORUS But you must know
            we shall select choice, action-ready troops.

DARIUS But *you* must learn
            the army still remaining on Greek soil
        shall not see a day of safe return.

CHORUS What are you saying?
            That not all the forces left   1310
        will cross the Hellespont from Europe?

DARIUS Few out of thousands,
            if one can trust godspoken oracles.
        But when you look at those that have come true,
        you know they are fulfilled—

complete, not just in part.
And if this be so, then
          empty hopes have persuaded him
to leave behind a force selected from the army,
and there they linger   1320
          where Asōpos pours kind floods on Boiotia's soil:
for them the height of evil waits implacable
to pay them back in suffering
          for pride and godlessness
who came to Greek earth lacking the reverence
          to stay their hands
from desecrating gods' images
          and putting temples to the torch,
and altars are vanished
          and shrines dedicated to the undying   1330
Dead are torn, root and branch, from their bases
          and shattered.
It is sure
          that having done evil, no less
do they suffer and more in the future
and not yet has evil's wellspring run dry
          but still spurts unchecked:
so great shall be new
          sacrifices of clotting blood
poured out   1340
          on Plataia's battleground by Dorian spears,
so great the piles of bones,
even to the third generation they shall be
seen by human eyes as speechless warnings
that those who must die
          not overreach themselves::
when stubborn pride has flowered, it
ripens to self-deception
          and the only harvest is a glut of tears.

                              (*directly to the* CHORUS)

These are the punishments   1350
          and as you behold them,

remember Athens and remember Greece
    lest someone
scorning the immediate blessings Heaven grants,
lusting for others,
      pour away his worldly goods and happiness.
Zeus the Pruning Shear of arrogance run wild
is set over you, a grim accountant.
Because events have prophesied
      that my son learn to know himself,   1360
teach him in gentle admonitions
to stop
      wounding gods with young reckless pride.

                          (*to* ATOSSA)

And you,
    agèd mother whom Xerxes loves,
after you have gone to your house
    and found him splendor that suits a king,
go out to face your son
whose anguish at the fullness of disaster
has torn his bright embroideries   1370
    to shredded rags around his body.
But speak kind words in a calming voice.
He will listen only to you
    and only you can comfort him.

  DARIUS *begins to descend into the tomb, his voice fading.*

I go, I must,
down below earth to the shadowworld.
Goodbye, wise old friends.
Though evil surrounds you,
give joy to your souls
all the days that you live   1380
for wealth is
      useless to
        the dead

                DARIUS *vanishes.*

CHORUSLEADER Disasters present and disasters coming on—
                I listened with anguish
                    to the Asians' fate.

ATOSSA (*looking skyward*) You! Nameless, inhuman!
                How cruel the anguish
            invading me! And one disaster
                most of all bites deep—   1390
            to hear that shame's clothing
                hangs in ragged shreds around my son's body.

                                          (*to the* CHORUS)

            But I'm going home, and when I've taken
                kingly splendor from my house,
            I'll try to face him.
            Though evil surrounds us,
                I shall not forsake my best belovèd son.

                          With her ladies ATOSSA *exits right.*

CHORUS (*singing and dancing*)   GOD, PITY US
                for once we knew
            the life of grandeur and virtue   1400
                    under stable rule
            when he whose years and dignity we honored—
            the All-Enabler, the Evil-Shunner,
            the Battle-Winner—
                    when King
            Darius cast a god's light
                and governed us wholly

            AND PITY US
                for once we showed
            an armed force whose praises rang sharp   1410
                    through the chastened world
            The laws that steered us stood bold on towers
            and days of return led men safely home
            Unwearied, unwounded,
                          the men

of Persia came back from war
    to houses that prospered

How many cities he captured
    without once crossing the Halys river
      nor leaving his hearth: 1420
city on city—
    the Rivergod's cities
        piled on the floodplain near Strymōn's gulf
and hillguarded cattletowns in Thrace

and cities east of the coastal marshes—
    tower-enclosed mainland cities
    bowed to him as lord,
and boastful cities
    by Hellē's broad current
        and strung on the shores of the Inland Sea   1430
and cities clustered at the Black Sea's mouth

And wave-caressed islands
    held in the Sea's arm
        close off our homeshores:
Lesbos
and olive-silvery Samos
Khios
and Paros
Naxos
Mykonos   1440
Tenos, too
    that rises out of the deep near
Andros
and salt-embraced islands
    set in the Sea's midst—
        he mastered them, too:
Lemnos
and Ikaros' settling place
Rhodes, Knidos
and Cypriote cities—   1450

Paphos
and Soloi
Salamis, too
        whose mother-city now causes
our groans

And more,
that rich estate Ionia
        teeming with Greeks—
he bent it to his will
and drew on strength that never failed: 1460
            fighters under heavy arms
            allies from a thousand tribes

But now
        beyond a doubt
we must endure
being god-overturned in war,
for we are tamed
        greatly tamed
            by seastruck blows

        XERXES *enters left hidden from view in a curtained car-*
        riage drawn by ragged men. A few other survivors straggle
                        in, pulling worn equipment carts.

XERXES (*chanting*)   No!   1470
                    Nonono!
Heartsick have I confronted hateful doom.
No warning signs, not one, foretold me
some undying Lust for human flesh
would stamp savagely on Persia's clans.
What now?
            I am helpless,
my body's last current of strength runs out
and I must
            face townfathers, fathers of sons.   1480

Dear God!

Would that I were with the men
now gone. I wish
the doom of death had curtained me.

CHORUSLEADER (*chanting*)   My King,
devote your sorrow to the skillful thousands,
the sweeping primacy of Persia's rule,
and the straight rows of men
some deathless Power cut flat.

CHORUS (*rising from chant into full song*)
And Earth herself   1490
mourns. Listen! She cries out
wailing her own young   slaughtered by Xerxes
who crammed them into the huge maw of Death,
for those now dead
were thousands of men
the country's flower
tamers of great bows   thickets of men
all wasted and withered
by tens of thousands.
Cry! Can you cry?   1500
Their courage kept us safe.
And Asia
whose mountains and plains you rule
is forced   forced in blood
down on her knees.

XERXES, *dressed in rags, climbs from the carriage. Both
he and the* CHORUS *sing from this point until the end.*

XERXES Look at me
and weep
I am
your sorrow, a sad hollow
son to Earth and my fathers   1510
born to bring home woe

CHORUS There are greetings for your safe return:
bleak howls of woe

       bleak melodies of woe
          torn from the throats of
             dirge-keening men
     I promise you
        promise you
           tear-darkened notes

XERXES Let every breath   1520
        you draw
          sound out
     a din of endless lamenting
     Divine wind has shifted   Heaven
         blows against me now

CHORUS Every breath drawn shall din a lament
     sounding your pain
     and sea-battered sorrows
        But listen! a nation
           howls for her children   1530
     And I ring
        I ring out
          a tear-spilling change

XERXES It was Greeks
        who stole our victory!
     Yes, Greeks
        for whom ship-armored War
          decided
     to harvest
        the black as night plain   1540
        and that Luck-hated shore

CHORUS Thousands
        the thousands!
           Anguish puts questions:
     Where are the friends
        who marched legion behind you?
     Where, the men
        who stood proud beside you?

Where, Pharandakes?
Where are Sousas, Pelagon, Dotamas?   1550
Where, Agdabatas, Psammis, too
and where Sousiskanes
             who left Ekbatana?

WHERE ARE THEY NOW?

XERXES Past all help
        I *had* to leave them
They fell
      from a Tyrian ship
          and washed on
Salamis'   1560
      rocks and there they died
      on that wave-broken shore

CHORUS Thousands
      the thousands!
         Where are the others?
Where, your Pharnoukhos
      and Ariomardos?
Where is his brave heart?
      And where, lord Seualkes
or highborn Lilaios?   1570
Where are Memphis, Tharybis, Masistras?
Where, Artembares, Hystaikhmas, too?
We ask you, keep asking you
        over and over

WHERE ARE THEY NOW?

XERXES Sorrow
     sorrow
         is mine, mine
Looking with one same look at
    Athens   old as time, anciently hated   1580
all of them now   at one same sweeping stroke
are cast on the dry land
to lie there

               lie there
          gasping for breath

CHORUS Then it's true?
                       Your most faithful Persian
your very own Eye
         whose rollcall counted those thousands
TEN thousands —   1590
Batanokhos' son Alpistos
           [you left HIM there]
with the son of Sesames, Megabates' son?
Parthos, too, and brawny Oibares?
You left them all
               left them
slaughtered or drowned?
          To Persia's old men you
call out a roll
         of grief, unbounded grief   1600

XERXES Sorrow
          sorrow
              If only I
could charm back the souls of
         brave men   comrades you make me remember
as you call   the roll of boundless grief
hateful, unforgettable grief
My heart howls
             howls
      from its bony cage   1610

CHORUS And I ache
           with longing for others:
Xanthes who led out
        ten thousand nomads
and war-hungry Ankhares, too
Diaixis with another, Arsakes
          horselords both of them
and Ēgdadatas and more, Lythimnas
Tolmos, too, whose spear always thirsted
I am stunned   1620

                                     stunned
                    They'll not march again
                                   beside these men, these few
                    who came home
                              following your carriage wheels

XERXES Gone, the leaders who set my army's pace

CHORUS   Gone, gone, their names become dust

XERXES Ache   aching sorrow

CHORUS   Sorrow sorrow
                              Undying Powers   1630
                    You willed this hopeless loss
                    wide and chilling as Blind Folly's gaze

XERXES Struck, we are struck lifelong by Luck's blows

CHORUS   Struck, struck down, I know it to the bone

XERXES By new   strange new anguish

CHORUS From the moment
                              Greek sailors
                    loomed on fortune's horizon
                    War-broken   no, not Persia's sons!

XERXES How not?   1640
                    Thousands lost—
                    struck through my army I suffer

CHORUS Great fool!
                        What is NOT
                    ruined   that made Persia proud?

XERXES (*fingering his rags*)   Do you see the remnant left as my
              cover?

CHORUS   I see, I do see!

XERXES (*holding up his quiver*) And see this arrow-concealing—

CHORUS   You're telling us something is saved!

XERXES —this storehouse where shafts were crowded?   1650

CHORUS   Few left of many, too few

XERXES Defenders are few, we are helpless

CHORUS   Greeks never ran from the spear

XERXES War-mad,
                    they made me
         see shame   I never expected—

CHORUS   You speak
                    of DEFEAT!
         Ship-armored thousands   went down

XERXES —and I tore my clothes when I saw them drowning   1660

CHORUS   Despair despair

XERXES Far more than despair

CHORUS   Disasters by twos, disasters by threes

XERXES In my shame I give joy to our enemies

CHORUS   And strength is wholly destroyed

XERXES My bodyguard's gone, I am naked

CHORUS   Stripped of friends, tricked at sea

XERXES Wail tearsongs, wail pain, wail me home

CHORUS   Gone, gone, they are gone, dead and gone

XERXES Din back my howling, my thumping   1670

CHORUS   Sad voices sadly moan sadness

XERXES Cry doomsongs, tune them to mine

CHORUS   Gone   gone
&   dead and gone

XERXES   gone

CHORUS How brutal the losses on land and sea
             How helpless my grief

XERXES Strike deathnotes, drum breasts, drum me home

CHORUS   Dead, dead, they are dead and I weep

XERXES Din back my howling, my thumping   1680

CHORUS   Lead and I follow, my lord

XERXES Lift voices, beat out the dirge

CHORUS   Gone   gone
&   dead and gone

XERXES   gone

CHORUS And black-bruising hands and voice bruised black now mingle
             in grief

XERXES And keep striking breasts and keep crooning wails

CHORUS   Wail thousands the thousands

XERXES And tug, pull out white hair from your beards   1690

CHORUS   With tearing, tearing nails and a dirge

XERXES And rake air with cries

CHORUS   Hear my cries

XERXES And rip heavy robes with fingers hooked

CHORUS   Mourn thousands the thousands

XERXES And strip out your hair, lament an army lost

CHORUS   With tearing, tearing nails and a dirge

XERXES And eyes rain down tears

CHORUS   See my tears

XERXES Din back my howling, my thumping   1700

CHORUS   Thousands the thousands

XERXES Lament as you go to your houses

CHORUS   Sorrow the sorrow
                     Hard now to tread Persia's downtrodden Earth

XERXES Wail as you step through the city

CHORUS   Wailing wails, weeping

XERXES Tread soft as you sob out your dirges

CHORUS   Sorrow our sorrow
                     Hard now to tread Persia's downtrodden Earth

XERXES Mourn mourn   1710
                     the men in the ships   three-tiered ships
             Mourn mourn
                     your sons dead and gone   dead and gone

CHORUS To slowdinning dirges we shall lead you home

The CHORUS *surround* XERXES. *Together, lamenting and making all the gestures of mourning, they circle the stage as if walking through the city.*

Exeunt ALL *right.*

NOTES

1–182 / 1–139 During this long passage, which occupies more than one-eighth of the total running time, the Chorus alone carry the play—are the play. Although the effects produced are both varied and, in a certain sense, highly dramatic, they are brought about by costume, movement, and rhythm, not by any interplay between separate characters on the stage. This is Aeschylean poetic drama at its most remote from our modern theatrical experience; here, therefore, the visual and aural imagination, whether of the reader or of the director, must work at its hardest.

In Greek theatrical terminology (see on **183–867 / 140–531**) the whole passage is called the *parodos*, the "side entrance" of the Chorus. In the Greek, **1–90 / 1–64** are in the anapestic marching rhythm; here we are to imagine the Chorus as entering from one of the side passages (also called *parodos*), and chanting as they move around the orchestra, their movement perhaps reinforcing the onward-marching effect produced by the great roll call of the imperial forces, which is the predominant content of the chant. In **91–182 / 65–139** the metre shows that they are no longer chanting but singing; dance and mime will now replace the marching. The singing in turn falls into three parts: **91–136 / 65–106, 137–48 / 107–14** (see also the separate note on those lines), and **149–82 / 115–39**. The first two parts are composed in the same song-metre, the Ionic (basically), a rhythm that heaves like the sea's swell. In **91–136 / 65–106** we hear of the still unclouded majesty of the expedition, and of its invincible progress, but at **137–48 / 107–14** those thoughts are suddenly interrupted—still in the same metre!—by a meditation on the deceptiveness of God, and on the man-trap set by *átē*. This leads, at **149 / 115**, to a violent change in the metre and presumably also in the character of the dance. From here until the song's end at **182 / 139**, the Chorus mourn for a land imagined as empty of its menfolk. The iambo-trochaic rhythm that predominates here has been thought by some students to derive originally from Greek funeral laments; however that may be, it will certainly recur, loud and clear, in the Greek of the play's finale, from **1626 / 1002** until the end. Thus, it will be seen, almost all the varied emotions of this play, and its arc of triumph and disaster, have been foreshadowed by the Chorus before a single actor has set foot in the theater.

17–18 / 13 *and now...King's name* We offer a guess at the meaning underlying the Greek here, which seems almost certainly corrupt; as it stands, it seems to say "and yaps young man!"

28–44 / 21–32 *You, Amistres...and you* The Greek is in the third person throughout this passage. The word "you" is used in our version to capture the effect of the repetitive *kai* and *te...te* ("and," "both...and"), which link the names in the Greek.

91–92 / 65 *Persians, Breakers-of-cities* By a strange fatality of language, the word *persai* means in Greek both "Persians" and "to destroy," and more than once Aeschylus seems to play on this ambiguity. Our words attempt to translate the heavy compound adjective, *perse-ptolis*, which he applies to the invasion-force here; the second part of it, *ptolis*, means "city."

106 / 79–80 *gold-showered line* The Greek text, on the most commonly accepted reading, says, literally, "born-of-gold line." Aeschylus probably alludes here to a Greek belief that is recorded by Herodotus (VII.61 and 150) and by some later writers: that the Persians are so named because they trace their descent from one Perses, a son of that great Greek hero Perseus who was begotten by Zeus upon Danae in a shower of gold.

137–48 / 107–14 *But how crafty...escape unhurt* The metre and reading of this passage, as it appears in the manuscripts, present many difficulties in detail, but there is no doubt as to the general sense. It is a sudden and frightful intuition of the fragility of human greatness in face of the Divine, and of the vast power of "Blind Folly" (for which the Greek is *ātē*). For the present, this remains mere intuition; only much later in the play, with the epiphany of Darius' Ghost, will its true application to the Persian expedition be made clear. A very difficult question, which has been debated for a century and a half with plausible arguments on either side and yet still without a generally agreed solution, is, where should this passage stand? In all the manuscripts it appears *before* the lines that we number **123–36 / 94–106** ("For gods decree...they stride the waves"). It was a nineteenth-century German scholar, Karl Otfried Müller, who first argued that its original position must have been after those lines, so that it would provide at once a sinister coda to the climactic passage on the Persians' achievements, and a natural transition to the wild lamentation that sets in at **149** / 115. After much pondering of the arguments, we have come down on the side of Müller, but we do not pretend to certainty here.

183–867 / 140–531   This is the first *episode*, according to the terminology that has been used to describe the formal, metrical-musical articulation of a Greek tragedy since at least the time of Aristotle (*Poetics*, chapter XII, where an *episode* is defined as that part of a tragedy that "lies between complete choral songs"). As has been seen in the Introduction, p. 25, n. 31, these formal divisions do not necessarily coincide with the main phases in the dramatic development of our play. This particular *episode* is, in fact, unusually rich and complex both in its content and in its metrical effects. So far as content goes, a decisive break occurs at the first speech of the Messenger in 417–25 / 249–55 (on which see the Introduction, pp. 21–23). Before that, we have felt only vague apprehensions about the vulnerability of the Persian host to the operation of divine law; after it, the truth of the calamity is certain, and its details are spelled out in the long narrative speeches of the Messenger. Metrically, Aeschylus' Greek moves through all three of the levels of utterance available to a Greek tragedian: unaccompanied speech, chant, and full song (see the Introduction, p. 18). He further uses the metre called the trochaic tetrameter (on which see **201** / 155, note). These shifts in metre are indicated, as usual, in our marginal notes, and it will be observed how closely they follow, as it were, the contours of the *episode*'s content: chant to accompany the physical movements at the opening, trochaics for the flustered dialogues between Chorus and Queen, steady iambic speech for prolonged exposition, and bursts of full song to bring out the Chorus' horror as the news strikes home.

184 / 141   *this ancient roof*   See the Introduction, pp. 16–17.

189 / 145   *son of Darius*   After these words the Greek manuscripts offer a mysterious phrase, apparently to be translated "related to us in virtue of his father's name." Following most modern editors, we have omitted it; it looks like a fragment of some ancient Greek reader's marginal comment, mistakenly copied into the poetic text.

194 / 150   *Look up*   The stage direction before this line is based on **975–76** / 607–8, where the Queen, on re-entering, says that she comes this time *"without* a chariot or queenly luxury." Following an editorial tradition that goes back through the medieval manuscripts of Aeschylus to the Alexandrian scholars, we have named the queen ATOSSA in our *Dramatis Personae*, our stage directions, and often elsewhere. Modern scholars have pointed out that that name never, in fact, occurs in the verse-text of the *Persians*, and have deduced that Aeschylus (either for dramatic reasons or because he actually did not know much about the historical Atossa) did not care to particularize; all he intended his audience to see here was a nameless Oriental Queen-Mother. This deduction is almost certainly correct and is worth bearing in mind when one comes finally to assess the play in its aspect as a historical document. On the other hand, the point did not seem important enough to justify the inconvenience that would result if we broke with the age-old convention still retained in most of the major editions. See further in the Glossary, under ATOSSA.

201 / 155 *My lady* From here to 269 / 175 the Chorus and the Queen converse in the metre called the trochaic tetrameter. The *Persians* contains two other dialogue-passages composed in this metre: 346–415 / 215–48 in the present episode, and 1120–1254 / (with the exception of the lyric passage at 1129–34 / 700–702) in the Darius episode. In Greek it is a long and agitated verse-line—a fairly close English analogue to it is Browning's line in *Home-Thoughts from the Sea*, "Nobly, nobly Cape Saint Vincent to the North-West died away"—and not too easy, one would imagine, for an actor to sustain at any length. In this translation it has been handled for the most part by short triplets, each beginning and ending with an accented syllable.

According to chapter IV of Aristotle's *Poetics*, the trochaic tetrameter was the prime dialogue-metre of the very earliest Attic tragedy, being replaced only after some time by the more natural and more easily speakable iambic trimeter. The presence of so many trochaic tetrameters in this, the earliest tragedy to survive, may perhaps be a vestige of that earliest phase of the art. Aeschylus never uses them on anything like this scale again in his extant plays; nor does Sophocles; only Euripides, in the plays composed at the very end of his career, reintroduces them for long dialogue scenes, apparently as a deliberate archaism and to enhance the operatic quality that he aimed at in his latest work. Opinions vary as to whether they were delivered as recitative with instrumental accompaniment (like the anapests), or unaccompanied (like the iambic trimeters). For practical production purposes, we have assumed the latter in our stage directions.

203 / 155 *sonbearing* The Greek word is *bathyzōnōn*, deep-girdled or -belted. The word has been re-imagined here as referring to more than a woman's mode of dress. It seems to suggest the set of a belt on hips and the deep roundness of a pelvis that gives easy passage to children: Persia's mothering-lifegiving-sonbearing women. And Atossa, for mothering a king, is most honored among them. Pindar uses the same word to describe the Graces, goddesses of fertility and increase, in his ninth Pythian ode, lines 2–3.

211 / 158 *Lust for Winning* The Greek has *daimōn*.

221–45 / 161–67 *It's you...bodies' strength* The text and meaning of these lines are much debated; particularly problematic are the details of the tremendous image of personified Wealth (*ploutos*) in **228–33 / 163–64**, and the syntax of **238–45 / 165–67**, both of which are confused in the Greek text presented by the manuscripts. To us, it does not seem beyond the bounds of possibility that that text is actually what Aeschylus composed, the hectic quality of the trochaic metre being quite deliberately matched by a certain stylistic confusion in order to bring out the tumult of the Queen's emotions as the scene opens. But in any case, the general drift of her words is certain: like the Chorus in their preceding song, she is assailed by thoughts of the fragility of success.

275 / 178 *bent on making it Persian and his* The Greek says, literally, "wishing to *persai* it"; for the pun, see **91–92 / 65**, note.

278 / 180 *kind-hearted dark* This translates a single word, *euphronē*, which the tragedians sometimes use for "night"; literally "kind-heart" or "glad-heart," it seems to derive from some primeval desire to propitiate the dark time, the time of dreams, by speaking well of it. The same word is used below, **366 / 221**.

291 / 187 *the great world beyond* The Greek has "the *barbaros* earth." This is the first of ten occurrences of the word *barbaros* in this play, mostly with reference to the Persians. We have paraphrased it on each occasion, because the English derivative words "barbarian," "barbaric," with their evil nuances, are clearly ruled out. *Barbaros* originally had a neutral meaning: "non-Greek" in speech, race, or location; and although the fatal dichotomy between Greek (or Western) "civilization" and non-Greek "barbarism" was beginning to open up in the course of the fifth century, it is scarcely perceptible in this play. Those critics who, at least in the past, have represented the *Persians* (especially its finale) as a kind of mocking triumph over a silly and alien race, might have given more thought to this very passage: in the dream, Persia and Greece are seen as *sisters*, both of marvelous majesty and beauty (**284–88** / 183–86; and compare **106** / 79–80, note).

321 / 201–2 *to cleanse me of bad dreams* Not in the Greek; we have included the words because to a modern reader the reason for the Queen's recourse to spring water will probably not be so self-evident as it would have been to the first audience.

323 / 203 *Phoibos' altar* This is perhaps the most striking of the occasional appearances of Greek gods in this Persian setting (on which see the Introduction, p. 19, note 30). It has been argued, unprovably but plausibly, that Aeschylus may have had some knowledge of the religious practices of the Persians; and that what we have in this passage is a perfectly realistic fire-altar of Ahuramazda, with merely a change in the God's name as a concession to the Athenian audience. *Phoibos*, "Shining One," is of course an often-used epithet of Apollo.

324 / 203–4 *mixed honey and wine* The Greek for this is *pelanos*; see **1339** / 816, note.

343 / 213 *his people cannot call him to account* The Greek says, literally, "he is not accountable, *hypeuthynos*, to the city." Here Aeschylus uses terms that are really applicable only to a Greek democratic city-state, not to the Persian monarchy. There can be no doubt that he is stressing what to a Greek (and most notably to Herodotus, a generation later) was one of the most important issues in the struggle between Greek and Persian: it was not merely a clash between nations, but also a clash between political systems; and it was the democratic system that won, against all odds. *Hypeuthynos*, in particular, stands out as an Athenian democratic technical term, referring to the *euthynē*, the public accounting, which every elected magistrate was bound to undergo at the end of his annual term of office. It is surely no accident that much later in the play a similar term will occur in the Greek: Darius' ghost, in **1358** / 826, will explain that over the proud thoughts which resulted in the disaster of Plataia there stands as corrector "Zeus, a grim accountant, *euthynos*." In the end, it will prove, even a Shah must undergo his *euthynē* . . . but before God.

401–5 / 236–40 *Such that . . . in their soil* There is much debate as to the reading, meaning, and even the order of these lines. Doubtfully, we have accepted the line order and interpretations offered in Broadhead's edition. In spite of these uncertainties, the historical allusions in the lines are clear enough. 401 / 236 will refer to the Athenian repulse of the Persians at Marathon (see the Glossary under that name), and perhaps also to the Athenian part in a raid on the Persian provincial capital at Sardis in ca. 498 B.C. (described in Herodotus, V.99–102 and 105); **405 / 238**, the "fountain of silver," must refer to the recent opening up of exceptionally large veins of silver ore in the Attic mines at Laureion (Herodotus, VII.144).

409 / 244 *So well...army* Another reference to the battle of Marathon (see the Glossary, and the preceding note).

462 / 285 *Athens, remembering* Here, and again at **1352 / 824**, Aeschylus seems ironically to put into a Persian mouth an allusion to the story that after the Athenian attack on Sardis (**401–5 / 236–40**, note) King Darius was so incensed that he ordered a servant to repeat three times, every time he dined: "My Lord, remember Athens!" The first extant version of the anecdote may be read in Herodotus, V.105.

508–23 / 310–19 *kept butting...immigrant* Again, as in **401–5 / 236–40**, there is doubt as to the correct order of the lines; and here a case can also be made for the theory that one or two lines have been entirely lost. Certainty does not seem possible, but we have adopted what seems to us the likeliest order of the many possible orders that have been suggested.

516 / 314 *from a golden city* The Greek here has the adjective *Chryseus*, which strictly should mean "belonging to the (town of) Chrysa." The only Chrysa generally known to antiquity was an insignificant town in the neighborhood of Troy (cf. *Iliad* I.37), but this seems an improbable residence for a Persian divisional general; we therefore prefer, with several commentators, to believe that Aeschylus has here simply invented an exotic-sounding Persian place-name. The glint of gold (Greek *chrysos*) in it may not be in any way accidental; J. L. comments: "This is the last reference to gold in the play. Here its light winks out."

571–73 / 347–49 *Gods keep...can't be shaken* The city of Athens, of course, *had* been sacked in the campaign preceding the naval battle, and indeed was to be sacked again in the following year (see the Introduction, pp. 6–7), but it would scarcely have been in human nature for an Athenian dramatist to have labored this point before an Athenian audience. Aeschylus neatly has the Messenger avoid this admission by citing a thought that had long been current among Greek writers, in various forms: *not walls, but people, make a city*. He may have in mind the rather similar retort made by the great Athenian leader Themistokles, just before the battle, to one who taunted him with having lost his city (Herodotus, VIII.61).

579–94 / 353–62 *My lady . . . high jealousy* Perhaps more clearly than any other single passage in the play, this illustrates the difference between our poet's vision of the events, and the vision of a historian. Underlying it, evidently, is the same incident that Herodotus recorded a generation or so later (VIII.75–6): Themistokles, seeing that the Greek fleet as a whole was bent on retreating from the anchorage at Salamis to cover the Peloponnese, sent a household slave of his, Sikinnos, to the Persian fleet. As instructed, Sikinnos persuaded the Persian admirals that Themistokles secretly wished them to succeed, and was therefore letting them know that the Greek fleet was panicking and preparing to sail away out of their grasp. The Persians therefore disposed their ships to block the exits from the straits during that same night. By this trickery Themistokles made up the minds of the non-Athenian Greek admirals for them: like it or not, the fleet must stay where it was, and give battle in the straits. So he ensured not only that the battle would be joined in a place where the Persian numerical superiority would count for least, but also that Attica would not be irrevocably abandoned by the Greek forces.

By contrast, it will be seen that Aeschylus lets the responsibility for starting the battle float mysteriously in the interspace between Man and God; this is brought out with heavy emphasis both at the beginning and the end of the passage. To translate literally: at **581–83 / 353–54** the anonymous individual who begins it all is "a vengeance-spirit (*alastor*) or an evil *daimon* who appeared from somewhere; for a Greek man, who came from the Athenian fleet . . . " (that "for," when one reflects on it, is seen to be one of the most enigmatic occurrences of the little word in literature). Then, at the close (**592–94 / 361–62**), Xerxes "as soon as he heard, not understanding the deceit of the Greek man nor yet the jealousy of the Gods," issues the orders that will bring on the battle.

What Aeschylus has done is to suppress the Greek individuals' names and personalities (just as he does throughout this play); on the Persian side, to concentrate attention on the grandiose and tragic figure of Xerxes, ignoring the anonymous Persian officers who bear the responsibility in the version known to Herodotus; and above all, to distribute the action between God and Man at the opening, and Man and God at the close.

691–93 / 424–26 *We might have been tuna ... bits of wreckage* The appalling character of this image does not seem to have been fully grasped by Aeschylus' commentators. We are made to be present at a tuna round-up of the kind still to be witnessed until recently in Southern European waters. Alan Villiers, *Give Me a Ship To Sail* (New York, 1958), pp. 59–67, gives a general account, and also an eyewitness report of a round-up off Cape Santa Maria; here are some extracts, which may throw light on the Aeschylean lines. The tuna were funneled by a great barrier of nets into a kind of corral of nets and boats, within which the tuna

> swims and swims, looking for a shadowless passage. There is none. He is trapped–doomed .... Near-naked men ... thrust deftly with their hooks and long gaffs among the tuna, cutting at them with swift blows, the red blood spurting thick .... Great shapely blue bodies are everywhere, with wild staring eyes, and the water is soon tinged and then stained red with the tuna's blood.

707–51 / 435–64 *You must understand ... butchered* In the Messenger's account, the climax of the battle is this massacre of the Persian nobles trapped on the islet. Again, Herodotus' version is worth comparing. In VIII.76 he briefly mentions that the Persian commanders, on the evening before the battle, disembarked "many of the Persians" on an islet to which he gives the name Psyttaleia, in order to intercept any shipwrecked Greeks. In VIII.95 he records with almost equal brevity how in the midst of the battle the great Athenian statesman Aristeides "took along with him many of the heavy infantry who had been stationed along the shore of Salamis, being Athenians, and conveyed them to the island of Psyttaleia, and there landed them; and they slaughtered the Persians on the islet to a man." Here is the now familiar contrast between poet and historian: Herodotus gives names and particulars, but does not render the atmosphere or the pathos as Aeschylus does. And the two authors differ profoundly in the importance that they attach to this engagement: what to Herodotus is a passing incident is the ultimate disaster in Aeschylus' account. On the evidence that we have, it is probably idle to speculate on the reasons for this; just as it seems impossible now to be sure whether Psyttaleia is to be identified with the islet known as Lipsokoutali on modern maps, lying across the mouth of the strait, or that known as St. George, within the sound. A good account of the debate on these questions is given in Broadhead's Appendix VI to his edition of our play.

752–833 / 465–514 *Then Xerxes ... on Persians* This account of the aftermath of the battle differs greatly from that given by Herodotus (VIII.97–120), which is summarized in the Introduction, pp. 6–7. In part, the reason may well be that neither author possessed reliable information about the details of Xerxes' calamitous retreat to Asia; the historian, indeed, actually admits that he had heard two quite different versions of its final stage, from the River Strymōn onward (VIII.118–20). It further seems very likely, however, that Aeschylus has deliberately omitted some events and foreshortened the course of others. He has made Xerxes retreat immediately after the battle (just as does Timotheos in his lyric poem on the battle three-quarters of a century later, and no doubt for the same artistic reasons); Herodotus, however—who should have been able to find witnesses enough to this point—makes Xerxes delay for some days in Attica. While Aeschylus brings Xerxes directly home to Susa (apparently—such is our poet's lordly attitude to mere time—still wearing the clothes that he had rent at Salamis), Herodotus has him repair to Sardis and remain there for nearly a year. Aeschylus also says nothing, in this passage, of the Persian army that was left behind to winter in northern Greece (see **1306–13** / 796–801, with the note there). Everything, in fact, is so arranged as to heighten the impression of immediate and total humiliation both for Xerxes and for his forces. Finally, the climax to Aeschylus' version of the retreat, the freezing and melting of the River Strymōn, is not even hinted at in Herodotus, and has seemed incredible to many commentators on meteorological grounds, if on no others.

At this distance in space and time, it is hard to decide where the factual truth of Aeschylus' story of the retreat ends, and where the poet-moralist's shaping imagination begins. But we can still admire the grim, majestic poem that he has made out of it, from 780 / 482 onward. In the Greek, these lines seem to trudge and struggle almost like the battered army itself, through a malevolent landscape that rings with names rich in the association to an ancient Greek audience; for in the evocative use of place-names Aeschylus perhaps has no equal among the European poets until Milton.

780–805 / 482–97 *And the army... bank to bank* The modern reader will not be so familiar with the geographical names in this passage as the original audience was, and we therefore give some account of them here. For a production or reading aloud of the *Persians*, some might prefer a version that cuts out the names, giving instead the associations that they might be thought to have evoked for a Greek hearer; such a version, composed by J. L., is added at the end of this note.

The army more or less retraces the route that it had taken in the spring of 480: northward through the provinces of central Greece—Boiotia, Phokis, and Doris—until they hit the sea at the Mēlian Gulf (here is

Thermopylae, site of the battle, and here the River Spercheios enters the sea); then into the northern section of the Greek peninsula, passing through Phthiotic Achaia (Achilles' country, this), Thessaly, and the mountainous coastal region of Magnesia. Entering half-Greek Macedonia, they cross the River Axios at the northwest corner of the Aegean Sea, and wheel eastward into eastern Macedonia and then into Thrace—a wild, magical landscape, best known to a Greek for its association with the legends of Dionysos and Orpheus, which Aeschylus himself treated in his now lost cycle of Dionysiac plays. The great river Strymōn enters the north Aegean at a point between Lake Bolbē and Mount Pangaios (here live the Ēdonoi, a tribe once ruled by King Lykourgos, the early persecutor and victim of Dionysos); it is at this river, as we have seen, that Aeschylus sets the most terrible incident of the retreat. *Alternative version of 780–805 / 482–97:*

> And the army left
>   kept dropping off,
>   first on ground a short march from Athens,
> some of thirst
>   taunted by bright springs
>   out of exhaustion's reach,
> while some of us,
>   empty from panting,
> drove on through plundered orchards
> and fields that once held bounty, and on
>   along that sea-grazed coast where
> the Rapid River spills earthkindly drink.
> After that hardscrabble farms
> and towns in the lean north took us in
>   when we were starving.
> There the most died.
>   Thirst and hunger,
>   both of them stalked us.
> And slogging on
>   through high white passes
>   and a wilderness of trees
> we came to the Worthy's ford
> and a bubbling swamp choked with reeds
> and the mountain called All-Earth—
>   a fox-haunted place
>   that tears men apart.
> It was that night
>   some god
> blew down winter out of season and froze
> the holy Harsh River bank to bank.

850 / 524 *wine poured out with honey* The Greek has *pelanos*; see 1339, note.

868–960 / 532–97 In Greek theatrical terminology, this is the first *stasimon*, i.e. the first complete choral song after the *parodos* (1–182 / 1–139, and note). The song proper actually begins at 886 / 548; it is prefaced by a passage of anapestic chant, during which the Chorus may perhaps be envisaged as moving forward in a body from the *skēnē* to take up position for dancing in the orchestra. If we have guessed correctly at the setting of the play (cf. the Introduction, p. 17), this move will almost be the equivalent of a scene change in the modern theater, since it will bring the Chorus close to the tomb-mound of Darius—that is, to the focal point of the ensuing action.

    The song is full of the clearly articulated wailing-words in which ancient Greek is so rich, and which are almost entirely lacking in modern English. Against English "alas!" (and even this is now an archaism), the Greek of this song alone can set *popoi, totoi, pheu, ē-ē,* and *o-ā,* balancing each other with antiphonal effect. Direct translation of them being impossible, this version seeks to render them by repetitions of phrases and by concentration on long vowel-sounds.

868 / 532 *God* The Greek has "Zeus."

873 / 536–37 *mothers* This is not in the Greek text, but was conjecturally supplied by the nineteenth-century scholar W. Dindorf.

894 / 553 *riverdhows rigged for the sea* The Greek has "ocean-*barides,*" *baris* being a rather vague term for any non-Greek, non-seagoing vessel, especially those which plied on the Nile. The phrase, therefore, is paradoxical, and probably scornful too.

902–3 / 557 *Sailwings unfurled, bluedark eyes on the sea* The Greek reading in the first phrase here is uncertain; following many others, we have adopted a conjecture by the eighteenth-century scholar C. G. Schütz, which literally will mean "linen-winged." The second phrase is also, in the Greek, a single, magnificent compound word, which could be interpreted either as "dark-blue-faced" or as "dark-blue-eyed." We prefer the latter, recalling the eyes commonly shown painted on ships' prows in Greek vase-paintings (and still to be seen on some southern European fishing boats), as well as Aeschylus' words in *Suppliant Maidens* 716, where an Egyptian warship has a "prow scanning with its eyes the course ahead."

922 / 570 *Salamis* Here the Greek has "the Kychreian shore." Kychreus was an ancient hero-king of Salamis, of whose legend not much is now known. According to a relatively late source, Pausanias (*Description of Greece*, I.36.1), he manifested himself during the battle of Salamis, in the guise of a snake; it is not impossible that this story was already current in Aeschylus' time, and that this phrase is therefore a muted allusion to it.

961–1001 / 598–627 By the received terminology (cf. **183–867 / 140–531**, note), this is the second *episode* of the play, although in fact the action develops without a real break from **961 / 598** to **1397 / 851**. Throughout, the center of attention is the tomb-mound of Darius. The Queen's change of dress and equippage (see our stage direction before **961 / 598**, which is based on the Queen's own words at **975–76 / 607–9**) similarly emphasizes the somber and unearthly atmosphere into which the play now enters.

This is, of course, not the only occasion in Greek tragedy on which offerings and invocations are made at a tomb; compare, in particular, Aeschylus' *Libation-Bearers* 1–509 (and, for such practices in actual Greek life from the earliest times until today, Margaret Alexiou's *The Ritual Lament in Greek Tradition* (Cambridge, 1974). What makes our scene unique among the extant instances is that here, finally, the *dead man actually rises up out of his grave*, to the consternation of the mourners. This need by no means have been a foregone conclusion—in the *Libation-Bearers* the pleas to the dead man to return are scarcely less passionate than they are here, and yet Agamemnon does not manifest himself visibly—and the first audience of this play may well have been as shocked by the ghost's eventual appearance as are the Chorus on the dancing-floor.

995–1089 / 623–80 The second *stasimon*: after a few introductory lines of anapestic chanting (**995–1013 / 623–32**), the Chorus break into full song and dance. It is likely that this ghost-raising ode was accompanied by unusually violent movement; compare out tentative stage direction at **1053 / 656**, and our note at **1094–95 / 683**.

1004 / 629 *Soul-Guide* Hermes (one of whose many aspects is that of *Psychopompos*, Escort of Souls) is named in the Greek.

1037 / 647 *tomb* Here and at **1057 / 659** the word used for this in the Greek is *ochthos*, literally "tomb-mound."

1039 / 642, 1042 / 650 *Hand of Death* In both places the Greek text has *Aidoneus*, an old poetic name for the god Hades.

1054 / 657 *Shah* Here Aeschylus uses a rare and strange word, *Balēn*; the ancient Greek writers themselves, while agreeing that it meant "King," were uncertain about its origin, but the balance of the evidence seems to favor the theory that it belongs to an Oriental language. On some views, it is to be connected with *Baal* and *Beelzebub*. This stanza is, indeed, heavily Oriental; Darius' clothing also, as specified in the ensuing lines, is the characteristic clothing of a King of Kings.

1082–83 / 676 *now mourn...exciting old?* The Greek words here are hopelessly corrupt; we can offer no more than a guess at the original meaning.

1088–89 / 680 *ships...ghostships* Greek has a negativing prefix a-, roughly equivalent to English un-. Aeschylus here writes *naes* "ships," and follows it with a unique adjective, apparently invented for the occasion, *a-naes*. On this fearful note he ends his ode.

1090–1397 / 681–851 The third *episode* (cf. 183–867 / 140–531, note).

1094–95 / 683 *The earth...scratched open* All the Greek manuscripts give a text that will translate, word for word: "moans, has been struck, and is being scratched the earth." Students of Aeschylus have long debated whether this text can be correct, what is the subject of the first two verbs (all seem to agree that the subject of the third one is "the earth"), and what is the meaning of the statement as a whole. Without claiming certainty, we believe that the best solution is to take "the earth" as the subject of all three verbs—the flow of the line in Greek seems very much in favor of this—and to take those verbs in their literal senses. We assume that they describe the activities of the Chorus during, and perhaps just after, the preceding ode (cf. our stage direction before 1054 / 657). For the ghastly detail of the scratching at the earth, one might possibly compare the Roman poet Horace's parody of a ghost-raising ritual (*Satires* I.8.26–27), where the necromancers "score the earth with their nails"; although there the object seems to be to open up a pit for blood-offerings.

1171–94 / 715–38 *How? Thunderbolts...There is no doubt* The dead Darius is by now so far detached from life on earth, and so near divinity, that he knows nothing of the recent actions of Xerxes and of the Persian forces. Only after Atossa has informed him of the expedition and its defeat at Salamis is he able to connect the news with his supernatural knowledge of the doom stored up in Heaven (1195–1203 / 739–41, 1312–16 / 800–802): the folly of taming the Hellespont and crossing the water to invade Greece, whenever it takes place, must entail a Salamis and, beyond that, a Plataia.

Aeschylus is not the only great poet who has attributed this *selective* vision to the dead. As the great Dutch commentator, Groeneboom, notes on this scene, the inhabitants of the Inferno are somewhat similarly described: we can dimly see events that are to come on earth, says the shade of Farinata degli Uberti, "but when they are near, or are, our intelligence is vain" (compare the whole passage, *Inf.*X.94–108).

1188 / 732 *even the old ones* So says the Greek text; it is almost certainly corrupt—would *aged* Bactrians have been drafted into the expedition?—but no convincing emendation has been put forward.

1256 / 759–60 *the greatest* We translate literally here; but the reader should bear in mind that in the Greek poets, conscious as they were of the law of *hybris* and *átē*, "greatness" in human beings and their works is usually a sinister attribute.

1265–94 / 765–86 *The Mede...devastation* To emphasize by contrast the folly of Xerxes and the heights from which the Persian realm has so suddenly fallen, Aeschylus puts into the ghost's mouth a review of the line of earlier kings. There are some doubts in this passage about the readings, the order of the lines, and the identification of one or two of the monarchs. These doubts—most of which are not finally resolvable on present evidence, and none of which affect the general effect of the speech—are well discussed by Broadhead in his commentary, especially in his Supplementary Note on pp. 278–79. Here we need only remark that, following most editors, we have omitted a line that occurs in the manuscripts after **1281 / 778**, "and sixth was Maraphis, seventh Artaphrenes," since 1. no such Persian kings are mentioned in any other source and, perhaps more decisively, 2. it seems next to impossible to squeeze two monarchs in between the assassination of Mardos and the accession of Darius. The line may be a fragment of an ancient comment, mutilated and mistakenly worked into the poetic text. (The names mentioned in the speech are explained in the Glossary.)

1306–11 / 796–99 *But you must...from Europe?* The important fact that a Persian army had remained in Greece after Xerxes' flight was omitted from the Messenger's narrative, no doubt on account of dramatic considerations (cf. **752–833 / 465–514**, note). Only here does the ghost—relying, as he says in the following lines, on the information provided by the divine oracles—reveal it to the Chorus.

1330–31 / 811–12 *shrines...the undying Dead* The Greek has "shrines of the *daimones*"; the translator has accepted the theory favored by some commentators that this is Aeschylus' way of saying "tombs," since in a few specialized contexts the dead may be called *daimones*.

1336–37 / 814–15 *wellspring...unchecked* The reading of the Greek here is evidently corrupt. We have tentatively accepted the emendation made by the scholar-poet A. E. Housman. Its merits are that it introduces not merely an image that is fine in itself, but an image that seems to have been near the surface of Aeschylus' consciousness anyway, during the composition of this play; compare the "fountain of silver" at 405 / 238, and the "fountain of defeats" at 1207 / 743.

1339 / 816 *sacrifices of clotting blood* The Greek has "bloodslaughtered *pelanos*," which may provide yet another instance of Aeschylus' manipulation of words and their meanings through the course of a play. *Pelanos* is used in Greek to refer to certain substances that are viscous, on the borderline between liquid and solid. Most often it is found in ritual and sacrificial contexts, to mean offerings of meal and honey, or of blended liquids. At 324 / 204, and again at 850 / 524, Atossa has spoken of offering a *pelanos*, in this ritual sense, to the supernatural powers, to avert disaster. Here the word occurs for the last time in the play, but in another well-established sense: of a sticky clot of blood.

1341 / 817 *Dorian spears* Although the Athenians were present in force at the battle of Plataia, it was the Dorian Greeks of the Peloponnese, and above all the Spartans, who played the greatest part in the victory. This line seems to pay tribute to that fact.

1359–60 / 829–30 *Because...himself* The reading is uncertain. We have doubtfully followed Broadhead's text (which adopts a reading found in a minority of the manuscript witnesses) and interpretation.

1379–83 / 841–42 *give joy to your souls...the dead* Darius' parting words have worried many readers and commentators: why this apparently hedonistic advice to his old counsellors, to conclude a series of speeches so dignified, so rich in insight into the ways of the universe? In seeking to interpret them, one should probably begin from the fact that *Darius here speaks in the authentic language of the dead*—that is, of the pagan dead. He expresses an understanding of death and life—the finality of the one, the limitations imposed on the other—which not only permeates Greek poetry from Homer onward, but is also formulated with an especial poignancy in many a pagan epitaph, both Greek and Roman. Broadhead's commentary cites a number of examples. One could add more, like this (from a Roman tombstone): "See, I lie in my tomb and I have no feeling; I warn you, *enjoy*, while life is given you!" Or this (from a Greek tombstone of Roman imperial date): "I, Euodos, give this advice to all mortals: let your soul have a share of pleasure [cf. **1379** / 841 here], knowing that if once you go down to the stream of Lethe you will never see, there below, anything of what is above." Darius, like the plebeian dead who speak to the passers-by in such epitaphs, has a double message; of which the one component, the advice to enjoy what life we have, seems but a foil to the other, which is the utter hopelessness and finality of death. It is that cloud, we are reminded as the royal ghost sinks back into the tomb, that hangs over all human endeavor: over the Persian expedition, and over the Persian accumulation of wealth, *ploutos*, which word occurs here for the last time in the play.

1398–1469 / 852–906 The third *stasimon*; in the Greek, this song stands out among all the other songs in the *Persians* because it is composed almost entirely in the magnificent dactylic rhythm, which may have had heroic connotations for a Greek hearer (the dactylic hexameter is, of course, the metre of the Homeric epics). Certainly the content is heroic, or heroizing. It is an evocation of the effortless power of the dead Darius, bitterly contrasted in the final lines (**1463–69** / 905–6) with the calamity that Xerxes' efforts have brought upon the Persian empire. The core of the ode is the great roll call of cities and islands (**1418–62** / 864–902) which, say the Chorus, Darius caused to be conquered without ever stirring from his own fireside, and without ever a reverse to the Persian army. (All these places, as a matter of history, were lost to the empire after the failure of the expedition, and in the very period of this play the Athenians were recruiting them into a naval league which in time was to become an empire itself.)

Comparison with the historical evidence about Darius' reign suggests that Aeschylus has either knowingly suppressed certain particulars of it, or (as is quite possible in some cases, given the date and place at which he composed) knew little or nothing about them. For instance, one of the most extensive episodes in Herodotus' account of the reign is the Scythian Expedition (IV. 1–144), in which, so far from sitting on the far side of the Halys River, Darius marched from Susa to the Thracian Bosporos, *threw a bridge across it*, threw a second bridge across the

Danube, and penetrated far into southern Russia, from which he was obliged to retreat with considerable danger and humiliation. As so often in the study of this play, we have to remind ourselves that Aeschylus does not set out to compose history, but poetry. As so often also, we may find in the last analysis that his poetic intuition, his sense of the underlying realities, is not so wide of the historical truth after all. The *general* contrast drawn in this ode between the reigns and personalities of Darius and Xerxes is in accord with the general tenor of Herodotus' accounts of them, and of the other evidence.

1398 / 852 *GOD, PITY US* The Greek has an exclamation of anguish, not directly translatable.

1412 / 859–60 *The laws . . . on towers* The correct reading and interpretation of this line are hotly, and quite inconclusively, debated. Our translation renders the apparent meaning of the Greek words offered in nearly all the manuscripts, but we are not confident they are anything like the words that Aeschylus originally wrote here.

1419 / 864 *the Halys river* The Halys runs into the Black Sea midway along the northern coast of Asia Minor, and was the ancient boundary between western Asia Minor and the kingdoms further east (Herodotus, I.6 and 72; compare also the story of the sixth-century Lydian king Croesus' fatal crossing of it from west to east, *ibid.* 75–91).

1422–31 / 867–77 *the Rivergod's cities . . . Black Sea's mouth* This first section of the survey of Darius' conquests in the Aegean area covers the coastal region of the province called Thrace in ancient times. It begins from the neighborhood of the River Strymōn at Thrace's western border, and then ranges eastward to the Hellespont, the Propontis (Sea of Marmara), and the Thracian Bosporos (the strait between the Propontis and the Black Sea). So much is clear, but there are the gravest doubts about the details of all but the last three lines. The text offered by most of the manuscripts in **1422–27 / 867–73**, literally translated, runs approximately: "(cities) such as those of Acheloos [a river-god] belonging to the Strymōnian water-expanse, neighboring the Thracian settlements; and those outside the lake, along the dry land, with fortifications running around them; these listened to him as lord." Some think that the "cities of Acheloos" can be identified with the lake-dweller settlements on the lower Strymōn, described by Herodotus (V.16).

It will be noted that the Chorus' survey begins from the very region at which the Messenger's detailed narrative broke off (820 / 507). This is surely deliberate: by the play's end the hearer will have traversed a poetic map of the entire theater of the Greco-Persian wars.

1432–55 / 880–96 *And wave-caressed . . . our groans* Now comes a long list of islands — their names, perhaps, being more evocative to Aeschylus' first audience than to a modern reader, for during the years since Xerxes' defeat Athenian squadrons had been constantly cruising these very waters. The exposition is not so orderly as in the previous section of the survey, as a glance at a map of the Aegean will show, but there are fewer obscurities in detail. First come three important islands close to the Asian mainland, Lesbos, Chios, and Samos; then the isles of the Cyclades, Paros . . . Andros; then an oddly assorted group, Lemnos sitting solitary in the middle of the North Aegean, Icaria (presumably meant by "Ikaros' settling place," 1448 / 890) well to the south, Rhodes off southwest Asia Minor, and Knidos (an interesting error, for Knidos is no island, but sits on the end of a slender tongue of land projecting from the continent; had Aeschylus only seen it from the sea?). Then comes Cyprus, with three of its major cities mentioned by name; appropriately, the last is Cyprian Salamis, which legend held to be a daughter-city of Athenian Salamis (see the Glossary, under AJAX).

1456–62 / 899–903 *And more . . . a thousand tribes* The survey ends with the mainland province of Ionia, stretching along the central portion of the western coast of Asia Minor, and perhaps the bitterest loss of all for the Persians to bear. Since Cyrus' time, with a brief interlude of revolt in the opening years of the fifth century, this land, with its many rich and populous Greek cities, had been a Persian fief. In Xerxes' expedition many Ionian Greeks, whether they liked it or not, had served on the Persian side; now they too, like the Greeks of the islands, were free.

1470–1714 / 908–1077 The concluding section of the tragedy, following the last complete *stasimon:* the *exodos,* in the terminology that we have received from Aristotle. In the *Persians* the *exodos* contains not a single line in unaccompanied speech. The opening passage, at Xerxes' entry (1470–89 / 908–21), is in chanted anapests. At 1490 / 922 the character both of the metre and of the dialect used in the Greek suggest that the style of delivery changes, almost certainly to the level of full song. From 1506 / 931 until the end of the play there is no question that everyone is *singing,* and presumably dancing as well. The reader of the play in English will be able to observe for himself how the tempo quickens: at first Xerxes and the Chorus exchange fairly lengthy passages, but they end by exchanging single lines (and indeed, in two passages, probably half-lines only). In all Greek tragedy there is only one other such totally operatic, antiphonal *exodos*, and that is in Aeschylus' next surviving dated play, the *Seven against Thebes* of 467 B.C. (if we assume, as many students do, that the passage there from 1005 to the end is probably by a later hand).

For the translator, the problem becomes similar to that already presented by the choral ode 868–960 / 532–97 (compare the end of the note on that passage). As J. L. writes: in the Greek

> verbally meaningful lines yield to lines in which rhythm and sheer sound carry the messages. There is a heavy emphasis in the translation on these sounds: long o, long a, oo, ow, and long e. Certain words, such as sorrow and gone, are repeated often in an attempt to capture the repeated howls and cries in the text.

But even when the translator's task has been carried out as sensitively as it has been here, the reader who would do proper honor to the poet's conception must also labor for his part to hear and see this climax to the play, where all the performing arts finally merged: verbal, musical, choreographic, and scenic.

1470 / 908 The stage direction before this line is based on what seems to us the most probable interpretation of lines 1620–25 / 1000–1001, which read literally: "I marvel, I marvel at them [the lost Persian soldiers] not following behind you, around the tent drawn on wheels." There is little doubt that this passage describes the vehicle called the *harmamaxa*, a kind of caravan *de luxe*, in which Xerxes did in fact occasionally ride during his expedition (Herodotus, VII.41). Commentators debate whether the vehicle would actually have appeared on the scene at this point. In concluding that it did, we have borne in mind the Queen's original entry in a chariot (194 / 150, note); the contrast and parallel to it, which would be produced by the appearance of Xerxes in a *harmamaxa* here; the importance of the yoke-image in this play; and Aeschylus' standing tendency to create symbolic visual effects. The other points in the stage direction, however, should be taken as guesses only. Another guess relates to the exact point at which Xerxes will descend from the vehicle (see the stage direction before 1506 / 930). That, whenever he first comes into the audience's view, he will be pitifully dressed in torn clothes, is made certain by 1370–71 / 834–36, 1391–92 / 847–48, 1646 / 1018, 1660 / 1030.

1474–75 / 911–12 *some undying Lust . . . Persia's clans* The Greek reads, literally: "how rawheartedly a *daimon* stamped on the race of the Persians!"

1481 / 915 *Dear God* The Greek has "Zeus!"

1489 / 921 *deathless Power* The Greek has, again, *daimōn*.

1493 / 923–24 *maw of Death* The Greek has *Hades*, the God.

1513–18 / 936–40 *bleak howls . . . promise you* The Greek has, literally: " . . . I will send, I will send you the cry ominously uttered, the howl well versed in evil, of a Mariandynan keener." The Mariandynoi, a tribe of Asia Minor, were known for the passionate and unrestrained kind of mourning that they practiced in their tribal cult. Aeschylus' allusion to them may well be taken as a hint to future directors about the style of song and dance that he intended for this last section of the play. A similar hint may be incorporated at **1688 / 1054** (see the note there).

1524 / 942 *Heaven* The Greek has *daimon*.

1540 / 953 *black as night plain* This seems to be a riddle, very much in Aeschylus' manner, for the expanse of sea off Salamis.

1542–1625 / 955–1001 *Thousands . . . carriage wheels* This passage is the third and last of the three long roll calls of Persian commanders that span our play. In the first (**28–68 / 21–51**) we hear of them in all their pride and pomp, marching against Greece; in the second (**494–540 / 302–28**) their varied deaths are narrated by the Messenger; in the third the names are heard through a storm of wailing. In translating the long stanzas of the Greek (each stanza divided between Xerxes and the Chorus, the Chorus taking the larger share), the translator has rendered the Greek fairly freely, for here above all it is a matter of responding *sounds*. Thus the long drawn out "Thousands the thousands!" and the refrain "WHERE ARE THEY NOW?" for instance, are her additions—but additions made for rhythmic ends not unlike those at which Aeschylus seems to have aimed. As a model, she has had in mind the *ubi sunt*, an ancient device used in the lamentations of many times and countries; for example, in the Anglo-Saxon *Erdstoppa* (Where is the horse? Where is the man? Where is the giver of treasure?); or in the twelfth-century passion play, the *Planctus Mariae* (*Ubi sunt discipuli? Ubi sunt apostoli?*).

1587–88 / 978–79 *Your most faithful... Eye* This is very probably a reference to an official Persian title, "Eye of the King," of which we know otherwise from a hilarious episode in Aristophanes' comedy, the *Acharnians* (91–125), and from a sober mention in Xenophon's *Cyropaedia* (VIII.2.10). Holders of the office were apparently confidential agents who reported directly to the King.

1592 / 982 *you left HIM there* This line is conjectural; the Greek metres show that a line has been lost from the text here.

1614 / 993 *nomads* The Greek has *Mardoi*; Herodotus mentions them (I.125) as being a nomadic clan of the Persians.

1622–25 / 1000–1001 *They'll not... carriage wheels* See **1470 / 908**, note, for a discussion of this passage.

1626 / 1002 *Gone, the leaders* At this point there is a sudden change in the character of the singing. From now until the end of the play Xerxes and the Chorus for the most part exchange line for line, instead of partstanza for partstanza; the metre becomes overwhelmingly iambotrochaic (this is that same lament-rhythm that was heard in the final section of the *parodos*, **150–82 / 115–39**); and, perhaps most interestingly, Xerxes gradually assumes more and more initiative in the singing. Instead of being the mere target for near-insults and pointed questions directed at him by the Chorus, he becomes first a partner in the lament and then, from **1668 / 1054** onward, its conductor, issuing instructions that the Chorus dutifully obey. There does not seem to be enough evidence to allow one to do more than speculate on Aeschylus' dramatic motive in causing this near-reversal of roles. Possibly the intention might be to remind us that under the Persian system, as Atossa remarked long ago, *Xerxes still reigns*, however much he has abused his charge; in the last resort he is not accountable to any earthly auditor (**343 / 213**, note). And indeed, it is almost never without a shock that one recalls, on emerging from the dramatic illusion created in the *Persians*, that when it was first performed Xerxes was still alive and holding court in one of his great throne-halls, whether in Susa or in that whose ruins still survive at Persepolis.

With the change in the singing comes increased stage-business, culminating in the wild breast-beating, hair-tearing, and robe-rending of **1678–97 / 1046–63**.

1630 / 1005 *Undying Powers* The Greek is *daimones*.

1632 / 1007 *Blind Folly* The Greek is *ātē*. We are reminded here, and again at 1643 / 1016 (where "Great Fool" represents a word meaning approximately "greatly beset by *ātē*"), of the interlude in the *parodos*, 137–48 / 107–14.

1688 / 1054 *crooning wails* The Greek has, literally, "and cry in accompaniment, in the Mysian style." The Mysians, a people of Asia Minor, were known, like the Mariandynoi (1513–18 / 936–40, note), for their passionate manner of mourning. Again, this may be an indication of the way in which the poet wished this last scene to be delivered and acted.

SEVEN AGAINST THEBES

Translated by

ANTHONY HECHT

and

HELEN H. BACON

To Frank E. Brown

INTRODUCTION

I

With some important exceptions, scholars and translators, from the nineteenth century onward, have been virtually at one in their indifference to *Seven against Thebes*: an indifference that has been deflected from time to time only into overt hostility and contempt. The play has been accused of being static, undramatic, ritualistic, guilty of an interpolated and debased text, archaic, and, in a word, boring. The present translators find themselves in profound disagreement with such assessments, and cherish a slight hope that the translation offered here—which is also an interpretation, as any translation must be—will help restore to the play some of the dramatic and literary interest it deserves to have even for those with no knowledge of Greek.

This translation has aimed at literal accuracy insofar as that was possible within the limitations of our own imaginations and understanding; our English text departs from the original mainly through that sort of extrapolation we have thought useful to a modern audience not likely to be acquainted with all the minor Greek deities, for example, or with their ritual attributes. Thus, where Phobos alone will do in the original, here he is identified as the god of fear. This kind of expansion, as well as complete independence from the Greek of the English lineation, has made our text some three hundred lines longer than the original. But we are confident—as confident as our scruples and a certain fitting modesty will allow us to be—that in this we have not violated the tone or dramatic intention of the play. A scholarly defense of such liberties as we may be thought to have taken will appear, as it ought to, elsewhere.

Still, it must be admitted that even to the most sympathetic of readers *Seven against Thebes* suffers under a special handicap. It is the last play of a trilogy of which the first two plays have been lost. It is, of course, impossible accurately to reconstruct the enormous dramatic and linguistic forces that must have been contrived and set in motion to culminate in this play; but one may perhaps guess at the magnitude of the loss if one were to think of the Oresteia as surviving only in the text of the *Eumenides*. We do know the names of the first two plays of this trilogy: *Laios* and *Oedipus*. And what we know of the ancient legends and sagas of the Curse of the house of Laios, of the traditional lore concerning the founding of Thebes by Kadmos, and of the subsequent history of the city, may provide us with some of the background with which Aeschylus approached this final drama in the series.

II

Like the "history" of the Trojan War, Theban "history" was preserved in epic poems, now lost, but almost as familiar to fifth-century Athenians as the *Iliad* and *Odyssey*. Aeschylus could count on his audience knowing not only his specific shaping of the stories of Laios and Oedipus in the two earlier plays, but also the broad outlines of the whole story of Thebes as preserved in the poetic tradition. It is a story of violence and wrath from beginning to end.

Kadmos, the founder of the city and the royal house, came from Tyre seeking his sister Europa. He killed a dragon that guarded a spring at what would become the site of Thebes and, at Athena's direction, sowed the dragon's teeth in earth. The teeth sprouted as a crop of armed men who, when Kadmos pelted them with stones, began to murder each other. The five survivors of this fratricidal battle, the "sown men" (Spartoi), were the ancestors of the people of Thebes. The lost epics went on to tell the stories of Laios and his descendants, but did not end, as the trilogy does, with the defeat of the Argive army, the death in battle of the army's leaders, and the fratricide of the sons of Oedipus. They pursued a narrative that took up the story again ten years later when, just before the Trojan War, the sons of the leaders of the Argives returned for their revenge at the head of another Argive army and completely destroyed Thebes. This sack of Thebes by the Epigonoi, as the sons of the seven Argive captains were called, was one of the most firmly fixed elements of the tradition: among the famous cities of Greece, only Thebes is missing from the catalogue of the ships in the *Iliad*. Aeschylus' audience could not fail to associate the many hints of future disaster for Thebes appearing throughout this play with the total destruction of that city by the sons of the "Seven."

The principal mythological figures of *Seven against Thebes*, Ares, the Fury, the Curse (also referred to in the plural as Curses, perhaps suggesting the separate words of the imprecation), Dike, and Apollo, interact in a context taken for granted by Aeschylus' audience, but which for us perhaps requires some explanation. Ares, the Fury, and the personified Curse of the house of Laios (the Curse of which Laios and Oedipus were the victims and which in turn Oedipus laid upon his two sons) represent the forces that are let loose when Dike, the personification of the fundamental principle of right and order, is violated. The trilogy dramatized a chain of outrages (outlined in this play in the third choral song, 908–1009 / 720–91,[1] the Fury chorus) starting with Laios' defiance of Apollo's word—which said that if Laios refrained from begetting offspring the city would be safe. The traditional reason for this prohibition was that Laios had kidnapped, violated, and murdered the little son of his host and friend, Pelops. For this violation of the sacred tie of hospitality, childlessness was a fitting punishment. Like the banquet of Thyestes in *Agamemnon*, this, or a similar outrage, was probably the crime behind the crimes in *Laios*. To these acts of violence, Laios added the attempt to destroy his own son, Oedipus, the child of forbidden intercourse. And violence begets violence. Oedipus killed his father and married his mother; his sons, by an act of outrage against him (we do not know which of several versions of their crime Aeschylus used in *Oedipus*), provoked their father's Curse, and they then attempted to take possession of their mother city by violence (Aeschylus in the lament [1118–29 / 875–85] makes plain that Eteokles too has used force on Thebes) and ended by murdering each other. Dike represents the sanctity of the basic relationships between god and man, host and guest, parent and child, brother and brother, relationships that Laios and his descendants defied. When these are violated Dike is violated.

The Fury, wrath (her Greek name Erinys is derived from *eris*, wrath or strife), and Ares, violence and hostility, are the instruments with which Zeus comes to the defense of Dike, but they are in turn the cause of new outrages in an apparently endless sequence. The Curse is another expression of the same psychological fact. It is the prayer of a victim, which is implemented by Ares and the Fury in their capacity as enforcers of Dike. Where this complex of forces occurs, Delphic Apollo will always be found as well, in his role as restorer of harmony and health, the purifier from all kinds of contagion. Only when the miasma of violated Dike has been cleansed away does the Fury cease raging and become the gentle cherisher that she is at the end of the *Oresteia*. Though in *Seven against Thebes* she appears only as a destroyer, it should not be forgotten that she destroys in defense of the helpless and in order that life and the social order that sustains life shall be cherished.

---

1.   Unless otherwise indicated, line references throughout are to our English version.

Her contradictoriness is the contradictoriness of woman—the tender mother ready to kill in defense of those she cherishes. Several images and figures in this play express this enigmatic quality of the female—the moon, Hekate, Artemis, the land of Thebes, the Sphinx (notes to 473 / 389–90 and 661 / 541–42).

An Athenian audience would also have recognized the parallels in *Seven against Thebes* with their own recent history, and responded to them with a special set of feelings and values. The return of an exiled ruler to claim his rights with the support of a foreign army, a not infrequent occurrence in Greece, was regarded with the same kind of religious horror as was felt toward attacks on parents. *Seven against Thebes* was produced in 467 B.C. Twenty-three years earlier, in 490 B.C., Hippias, the exiled son of the tyrant, Peisistratos, and himself a former tyrant, landed at Marathon with the Persian army, prepared to be reinstated as ruler of the Athenians. According to Herodotus (VI, 107), whose account is later than our play and could even have been influenced by it, the night before the landing Hippias dreamed that he slept with his mother. At first he interpreted this hopefully, as a sign that he would pass his old age peacefully in Athens. However, when he landed there was another portent. He was seized with a fit of sneezing and coughing, and, being an old man, coughed out one of his teeth, which fell upon his native soil and could not be found again. He then said, "This land is not ours and we will not be able to conquer it. My tooth has my whole share of it." Herodotus adds that this statement was Hippias' interpretation of the dream. In this story, as in *Seven against Thebes*, the attack on the parent land is equated with incest, and its consequence is that the attacker receives only a token share of his native soil. Hippias received as much Attic earth as his tooth possessed, Eteokles and Polyneices each as much Theban earth as it takes to bury a man. Whether this story of Hippias is older than Aeschylus' play, or came into being as a result of it, its existence suggests that the Athenians would have understood the play in the light of their own great national crisis. It also suggests that parallels between the crimes of Oedipus and those of his sons would have been more immediately obvious to the Athenians than they are to a modern audience.

III

The action of *Seven against Thebes* we conceive to be profoundly unified and profoundly dramatic. It unfolds in four stages, of which the Fury is the organizing principle. In the first stage the Fury is set in motion when Eteokles calls on her in conjunction with his father's Curse, to defend the city, which is being attacked by one of her own children (96–107 /

69–77). In his prayer Eteokles seems clearly to assume that if any violation against Dike has been or is being committed it is by his brother, Polyneices; he seems to have forgotten or blocked out of his mind the earlier crimes performed jointly with his brother that brought down on both their heads their father's Curse; and seems as well to have forgotten that his exiled brother has as much right as he to be king in Thebes. In the second stage the Fury comes to the defense of Dike by implementing the Curse. She rages unchecked as Eteokles decides to meet his brother in single combat (816–907 / 654–719). In the third stage, Dike is temporarily re-established and the Fury seems to subside. The inheritance is justly divided when the brothers, in death, are apportioned their equal shares of Theban earth. The play ends with a new outbreak of the Fury as the magistrates of Thebes reopen the conflict by refusing burial to Polyneices — refusing him, that is, his just share of the inheritance — and in so doing once more implicate the city in the fate of the house of Laios, edging Thebes and her entire population one step nearer to their ultimate destruction at the hands of the Epigonoi.

Modern scholars, with a few notable exceptions, regard this last scene, which dramatizes the final stage, as a fourth-century interpolation whose purpose is to bring the play into line with the popular Sophoclean version of the aftermath of the brothers' deaths. They see no justification for introducing a new speaking role in the person of Antigone, who raises what they consider to be a problem new to this play and wholly outside the dramatic unity of its action: the problem of the burial of Polyneices, after the conflict of the brothers has been resolved. Yet the scene is integrated with the entire design of the play; and to an audience familiar with the Theban epics, the second song of the Chorus (362–451 / 286–368), which visualizes the sack of the city, is not an unfulfilled fear but a prophecy of her ultimate fate. And that prophecy is brought nearer to its consummation in this final scene when the city brings upon herself the promise of total annihilation by repeating Eteokles' repudiation of Dike. The scale of the tragedy is enlarged, pity and fear intensified by this fresh outbreak of the Fury. It is not a new problem but a new stage and development of the old problem: how to allay the wrath let loose in Thebes by the chain of outrages stemming from Laios' original violation of Dike. It is a wrath that spreads from the individual members of the house of Laios until it includes, first, the magistrates of Thebes rising up to deny Polyneices his inheritance, and ultimately all the inhabitants of the city that is to be brought to destruction; a wrath that promises a countering wrath, a continued struggle to an exhausted and demolishing end.

IV

The language of *Seven against Thebes* is markedly concerned with noise, and with two kinds of noise in particular: the noise of battle and the noise of lamentation, that is, of strife and of weeping. At the start of the play, the noise of battle is outside the walls of Thebes, and the noise of lamentation (in the form of the first choral song, 108–212 / 78–180) within. By the time the drama is over, these two noises will come to be identified with the two contending brothers, Eteokles and Polyneices; and not merely because one has been inside and the other outside the walls, but because of their names and their fates, as will appear. Eteokles is more than merely "justifiably angered" by the fears and lamentations of the Chorus: he is enraged and unhinged by them, and proceeds to some quite extraordinary calumnies upon womankind in general. His nominal grounds for wrath are that the Chorus, by their womanly weakness, are undermining manly courage and endangering military morale inside the city. There is a certain plausibility to this, to which, after all, the Chorus acquiesce. But Eteokles' rage seems so extravagant that we might at first suppose that he is himself afraid of losing his nerve. Since, in the event, this does not prove to be the case, there must be some other reason for it. And, indeed, as the drama unfolds, we come to see that this play is not merely the culmination but the terrible re-enactment of the tragedies of Laios and Oedipus, of disobedience, parricide, and incest. And Eteokles' misogyny might be not only an unconscious sense of his inheritance, but a fear that he is doomed to repeat it. He is determined not to. Nevertheless, he does.

As in the case of his father, he is called upon to protect Thebes from what appears to be an outward danger. And, as in his father's case, he seems to undertake this in a manly way. The city of Thebes and its outlying pastures and folds are consistently spoken of in maternal terms, in metaphors of a mother who nurtured, cherished, and brought up her sons, and who must therefore not be violated. The violent desire for exclusive possession of the mother is a tragedy Oedipus unconsciously acted out, becoming blind that he might see what he could not see with his eyes. The violent desire for the exclusive possession of the mother land, the unwillingness of either to be content with a lesser or equal share, drives Oedipus' two sons, who are also his brothers, to murder each other, each one blindly believing justice to be on his side. And each, by murdering his brother, sheds his father's blood. As in the case of Oedipus, a problem is posed, a riddle must be untangled, in order that the city may be saved. For Eteokles this is, in fact, not one riddle but seven. These are the devices on the shields of the seven champions who attack the city.

It may be worth attending to this scene (457–907 / 375–719) in some detail, for it has often been singled out as one of the most tedious blemishes of the play, and it constitutes about a third of the whole. In hearing the report of the Scout and undertaking to construe in terms of magic and numinous power the nature of each of seven successive threats to Thebes, and in proposing a counter-magic for the defense of the city, Eteokles is taking upon himself the role of seer, as once his father did. Yet even before these seven opportunities for divination occur, Eteokles has several times been warned; what he is at pains to conceal from himself is precisely who he is, the nature of his inheritance, and the possibility that he cannot see everything clearly and for what it is. And while the Scout punctiliously addresses him as "most fittingly king of the Kadmeians," the Chorus, with more intimacy and greater point, address him as "son of Oedipus." Moreover, in their high-strung emotional debate with him, they defend their devotion to and utter reliance on the gods by observing that not only are the gods more powerful than men, but that the gods alone can assist humankind when its vision and understanding are obscured. These are implicit warnings against blindness and impiety, and they are augmented by the off-stage but telling presences of two genuine seers and diviners, who are also priests: Teiresias and Amphiaraos. Nevertheless, as commander of the defending troops, Eteokles does not hesitate to assume the role of seer.

There are seven contending champions, and therefore, seven riddles (though there is in addition one great and central riddle, concerning Eteokles' name, which lies at the very heart of the play, and which we will come to later). In general, it may be said that Eteokles conceives these riddles as applying purely to the fate of the contending champions and, by extension, to the fate of Thebes; never does he seem to suppose that the riddles might have any bearing upon his own fate. It may be added that with most of the defending champions he nominates, Eteokles takes pains to advertise the distinction of their genealogies as well as their military prowess and excellence of character. This is, of course, quite in accordance with heroic tradition. But in emphasizing the nativity—the legitimacy, as it were—of these local sons of the mother land, their title by birthright to be her defenders, he appears never to consider that this is a right he must, by the same token, share equally with his own brother. And the fact that two of the defending champions, Hyperbios and Aktor, are themselves brothers, does nothing to remind him of this.

1. The first of the attacking champions is Tydeus. We learn that he abuses and insults a priest of Apollo, Amphiaraos. Yet, while Eteokles does not hesitate to accuse Tydeus of impiety (as indeed he does in the

case of every attacker but one—and that one worth noting), neither does he scruple himself to abuse and insult Amphiaraos when later the priest, the true seer, presents himself as the sixth of the champions outside the walls. It is true that Eteokles cannot quite bring himself to accuse so unblemished a man as Amphiaraos of impiety; but the priest is charged with blindness and bad judgment, which Eteokles might do well to consider with respect to himself. And in abusing Amphiaraos, he is imitating the impious enemy, Tydeus. In addition to the dark night (ignorance, inability to see), which is Tydeus' device, the moon, associated with Hekate, goddess of the three ways, might serve to remind Eteokles of the beginning of his father's catastrophe, the curse of the house of Laios, the penalty for blindness. Tydeus' helmet is triple-crested, a part of the riddle to which we will return in due course. Most important, Eteokles proclaims that his defending champion, Melanippos, is a blood-relative of Dike, "goddess of all orders, of justice human and divine," and that she will favor him. If Dike is to side with the defending forces, she cannot at the same time side with the attackers, as from the claims of Polyneices it appears she does, unless she is to play some impartial role, and deal with the claims of both sides as being equal.

2. The second of the attackers, Kapaneus, the giant, is an enlargement, a grotesque exaggeration, of the impiety of Tydeus; he defies all the gods, and Zeus in particular. As opposed to Tydeus, whose emblem was darkness, Kapaneus' device is a naked man armed with a flaming torch (which is light and knowledge, the ability to see, to construe the truth), but this light has been perverted into a destructive weapon, intended to reduce the city to ashes (just as the Chorus has feared and prophesied). It might therefore be a warning to Eteokles in his self-assumed office of seer.

3. The third is Eteoklos, whose name is so close to the protagonist's as surely to invite a moment's thought. He is clearly "Eteokles Beyond the Walls," the attacking double of the defender; Eteokles, by this extension, is both outside and inside the city, and therefore it is folly to fear, to observe, to take precautions chiefly against the danger of what is outside. Here is a representation of Eteokles as his own worst enemy and, pointedly, he has nothing whatever to say about the character of this attacker. Whereas in every other case he is quick to bring accusations of blasphemy, impiety, and folly, here he moves swiftly to name his chosen defender, and makes unusually brisk work of the matter, turning instantly to the next contender.

4. This is Hippomedon, who bears Typhon, the earth god, on his shield. Now, from the very first speech of Eteokles, the earth has been seen as a nourishing parent, child-bearer, kindly provider. But just as the

Fury has what seems to be a double nature, or at least two aspects of a single nature, so here is the earth transformed, represented by a monstrous offspring, "breathing fire, black smoke, sister of glittering fire, pouring from his mouth," the universal tomb. This is not unlike the earlier vision of the Chorus.

5. Parthenopaios, "savage-minded" but with a boyish beauty, himself suggests the two aspects of the Fury. And his device, the Sphinx, not only recalls the whole Theban and family saga, but specifically points it toward the problem of knowing who you are. It is declared of Parthenopaios that he reverses his blade "above god and his own eyes," which is to say that he puts violence, military glory, and ambition above piety and knowledge; and it recalls the theme of blindness.

6. The case of Amphiaraos is rich and complicated. He is, first, a priest of Apollo, the god who is foreteller, knower of what awaits, who long ago warned Laios of what would happen if he begot a child, and who warned the youthful Oedipus of his parricidal and incestuous fate. These facts are all clearly known to the Chorus, and therefore may be supposed to be known to Eteokles as well. As the god's priest, Amphiaraos is not merely a holy man, one who wishes not to seem but in fact to be the best, undeceived by appearances and undeceiving; he also has special access to the wisdom of the god. He clearly denounces the impiety, violence, and violation that Tydeus and Polyneices are about to offer the city, and in the most condemnatory terms; he speaks of this in the highly charged language and metaphor of rape and incest. Eteokles' answer to this riddle is noticeably weak and evasive. Perhaps that is because there is no device for him to perform magic with. But possibly the true piety and self-knowledge of this man has come home to him. In any case, he makes Amphiaraos guilty by association, and, while not doubting the priest's piety—which, incidentally, consists in part in his refusal to attack the city—all but calls him foolish and blind for getting mixed up with wicked men against his better judgment, that is to say, ignorantly. Yet if, as Eteokles himself says, Apollo does not lie, then all the prophecies of disaster which have been accumulating throughout the drama, and which Eteokles has now been given six chances to fathom and to attempt to avert, are obviously pointing to something he does not see, yet knows to be inexorable.

7. At last, the brother, mighty Polyneices (784–815 / 631–52). His claim is plain, violent and sexual.

> He declares he will scale and bestride the walls,
> proclaimed lord and subjugator of the land.

He makes explicit his equality with Eteokles (which Eteokles has never acknowledged):

> he will fight you hand to hand;
> and either, in killing you, lie dead beside you,
> or else drive you into dishonored exile
> just as you forced such banishment on him.

The insistence on "equality" in Polyneices' boast should be noticed. He does not propose, as he might, to kill his brother and take upon himself the kingship; rather he says that either they shall both die, or they shall change places with each other. And just as Eteokles has done, he calls upon the gods of the race of his own land, entreating their support. This exclusive claim to the motherland as a sexual possession is stated at its clearest in Polyneices' device.

> A stately woman guides forward a warrior
> in full armor who is hammered out in gold.
> She says she is Dike—goddess of all orders,
> human and divine—
> and inscribed there are these words:
> "I shall bring this man to his harbor,
> and he shall enjoy his father's city,
> shall tumble and make free with his house."

The great blow, and the final irony, for Eteokles, is not that his brother should be revealed as a champion, for it was generally known that his brother was among the attacking troops, and no doubt the entire siege has been undertaken at his behest and with an eye to his restoration to the kingship. Clearly, then, he could have been expected to play a major role in the attack. What unhinges Eteokles is in part the claim that Dike is aligned with the forces outside the walls, and with his brother in particular, since he has already assumed that she has allied herself with the defenders. Her impartiality in this, as well perhaps as the discovery that Eteokles is not only inside but outside the walls in the person of Eteoklos, reveal to us at last the true equality of the two brothers in their inheritance, their fate, their shared guilt of origin and of ambition.

But this sense of equality Eteokles is determined to resist to the end, and while he feels he has been mocked and manipulated by fate, he goes to meet his brother in a frenzy of blindness, a man fully armed, turned into iron, himself a weapon. And the Chorus, perhaps recalling the warning that appeared with the very first of the attackers, the triple-crested helmet of

Tydeus, proceeds, in the next ode (908–1009 / 720–91), to recall the first of
all the warnings to this blind family:

> Three times the Lord Apollo
> in the midmost Pythian navel,
> the prophetic center, spoke:
> if Laios were to live
> childless, without issue,
> then the city would be safe.

And they echo the present storm outside the walls:

> Like a plunging and storm-agitated sea,
>   disaster drives the wave;
> first one wave falls, a second rises up,
> a third three-crested, crashes at the stern
>   of the city in angry foam.
>   Between our perilous home
>   and total jeopardy,
> our hull is the mere width of the city walls.

While it is clear enough that, in the first instance, these waves represent
the hordes of attacking troops, they have also by this time come to refer
to the three destructive and self-destructive generations of the house of
Laios, each of which in turn put Thebes in peril, and were themselves
the whole cause of her troubles, and, in effect, her attackers.

V

Like Oedipus, whose name means both "knowing foot" and "swollen
foot," the sons of Oedipus have names that express their fates. The
applicability of Polyneices' name, "full of strife," to his actions as the
leader of a foreign army attacking his native city is reasonably clear.
Amphiaraos, Eteokles, and finally the Chorus, all brood over it in the
section of the play (701–907 / 568–719) that leads up to Eteokles' climactic decision to meet his brother in single combat. The etymologically
correct meaning of Eteokles is "justly famed" (from *eteos*, just, true, and
kleos, fame), and in the argument with the Chorus about whether or not
he will go to the seventh gate, Eteokles dwells and honor as though, in
deciding to confront his brother, he hoped to implement this meaning of
his name. However, another possible meaning of Eteokles, "truly
bewept" or "true cause of weeping" (combining *eteos* with *klaio*, weep),
is fearfully suggested in Eteokles' opening speech, and alluded to with
increasing dread throughout the play. It suggests to him a fate that he tries
with all his powers to evade; hence his prohibition of weeping to the

Chorus, and his own refusal to weep when he feels that fate has pointed him toward fratricide at the seventh gate. And just as the measures Oedipus took to avoid the fate spelled out for him at Delphi nevertheless brought about its complete fulfillment, so Eteokles' attempt to avoid the fulfillment of this second, more ominous meaning of his name results in its implementation; as even he himself perhaps begins to recognize when he says,

> let the generations of Laios go down to the last man,
> blown wind-wracked along the weeping river of Hades.

In the act of killing his brother he finds the answer to the riddle of his own identity and fate, a riddle posed by the double meaning of his name. The second, or buried meaning, "true cause of weeping," "truly bewept," is literally acted out as the Chorus of Theban women, joined by Antigone and Ismene, perform their lament (1044–1280 / 821–1010) over the bodies of the brothers who have murdered each other. At this point it is clear that the names and fates of the brothers are interchangeable. Reconciliation and total equality are achieved together. Polyneices is just as "truly bewept" in this scene as Eteokles. In the preceding scene the Chorus warns Eteokles,

> do not take on the violence of your brother
> of evil name and fame . . .

But by the end of the scene Eteokles has done just that. In deciding to meet his brother at the seventh gate he becomes the counterpart of Ares, the emblem of strife in the house of Laios.

Both in imagery and action the play is an elucidation and dramatic unfolding of these two names. The storm of strife, presided over by Ares and the Fury, is realized in the Argive army outside the walls, and in the Chorus' fearful visualization of the final destruction of Thebes in their second song. The storm of weeping is realized in the Chorus' entrance song as well as in the final lament.

VI

There are many texts, both ancient and modern, that maintain, with elegiac eloquence, that it is the lot of mankind to be born, to suffer, and to die. However sagely we may assent to this universal condition of existence, no particular man likes to think that this is the governing limit of his own life; and when he speaks of his lot, though he may acknowledge it as a limited one, he is inclined at the same time to feel that it entails certain rights and prerogatives, that it is truly and only his, and not to be shared by anyone else. It is therefore associated most easily with what he comes to regard as his just due, his personal fortune, a wealth, either earned or inherited, though that wealth may be expressed in any number of ways, such as strength or courage or a gift for music or telling jokes.

Aeschylus takes the richest possible advantage of these ambiguities in *Seven against Thebes*; and behind the ambiguities, of course, lie the unresolved problems of free will and justice. That is to say, does a man choose his lot, or is it chosen for him? Does he get what he deserves, and by what or whose standards? While these problems are woven into the background of almost every tragedy, in this drama we are made to take particular notice of them. The first speech of the Scout recounts the drawing of lots. It appears that both Eteokles and Polyneices, while realizing that a part of their inheritance must include their father's Curse, seem also to feel that it includes title to the kingship of Thebes. As for the Curse itself, Eteokles at least seems to feel, when at last he is brought to acknowledge that it cannot be evaded, that it is confined purely to the prophecy that the sons of Oedipus shall divide his wealth with a sword; that is to say, he thinks of the Curse as something laid upon his brother and himself by his father, not as something laid upon his grandfather, his father, and the two brothers in their turn, for the original and continuing violations and crimes of the house. The father's wealth, for which the brothers are prepared to fight to the death, is the city of Thebes, its land, its fecund, life-giving sustenance. What they actually win in their duel is just enough of that land to be buried in. Yet the land is truly a part of their wealth, and indeed of the wealth of all the inhabitants of Thebes; it is life itself. To the Chorus, who are women, this appears to be much clearer than it is to the two ambitious brothers. The Chorus sing movingly about the richness and fertility of the land, and the horror of its despoilation; and their sympathy with the land might perhaps derive from their sharing with it a common gender. At the same time, and perhaps for the same reason, they conceive human life itself as being a form of wealth (372–73 / 295–98):

> Our city's wealth of men
> climbs to the battlements.

And, again, later (977–79 / 769–71)

> The city's wealth,
> this heavy freight of men, this swollen horde
> must, from the stern, now be cast overboard.

That, as in the Book of Jonah, a forfeit must be paid, some wealth rendered up to protect and preserve the remainder, the mariners on the ship to Tarshish or the inhabitants of Thebes, appears to these women a natural if terrible part of the economy of justice; life must be paid out that life may be sustained. For the two brothers it means, with a disastrous, ultimate irony, that the wealth for which they fight is precisely what they must forfeit: their lives.

Our translation is based on the text of Gilbert Murray, *Septem Quae Supersunt Tragoediae*, Oxford Classical Texts, 2nd ed., 1955. To have acknowledged individually the work of every scholar who has contributed to our understanding of the play would have made the Notes unduly cumbersome. Students of Aeschylus will recognize how great our debt is.

This translation was undertaken in Rome at the American Academy, where we were both the happy beneficiaries of the hospitality of Frank E. Brown, to whom, in gratitude, this work is dedicated.

It was also undertaken at a time when citizens of Aeschylus' native land were suffering (as they continue to, even now) oppression, imprisonment, and torture, for speaking out against the regime that today controls Greece and its culture.

It was undertaken, finally, at a time that can be regarded as possibly the most shameful in our nation's history; in which we have prosecuted a war for which there can be no moral, political, or military justification. A nation can rarely redeem itself from its follies and errors, the cost of which in human misery is incalculable. It is our forlorn but continuing hope that our government may look with some charity upon the young men who thought it from the first a foolish, brutal, and dishonorable undertaking. Our commitment to the work involved in this translation has, in some measure, been colored by these feelings.

HELEN H. BACON
ANTHONY HECHT

SEVEN AGAINST THEBES

Translated by

ANTHONY HECHT

and

HELEN H. BACON

CHARACTERS

ETEOKLES son of Oedipus, ruler of Thebes

ANTIGONE
} sisters of Eteokles
ISMENE

SCOUT a soldier

MESSENGER of magistrates of Thebes, a civilian

KORYPHAIOS Chorus leader

CHORUS of Theban women

Male citizens of Thebes

Magistrates of Thebes

Champions assigned to defend the gates of Thebes:
MELANIPPOS, POLYPHONTES, MEGAREUS, HYPERBIOS, AKTOR, LASTHENES

Theban soldiers

Six slave girls, attendants of Eteokles

Mourning women, attendants of Antigone and Ismenc

Line numbers in the right-hand margin of the text refer to the English translation only, and the Notes beginning at p. 177 are keyed to these lines. The bracketed line numbers in the running headlines refer to the Greek text.

An open square on the citadel of Thebes. Three doors with porticos reached by
steps—council chamber right, temple center, palace left. In front of the temple a
round altar with steps. Grouped around the altar from left to right, statues of Ares
in full armor, Athena with aegis, spear, and helmet, Poseidon with trident, Zeus
with thunderbolt, Artemis in hunting dress with bow and quiver, Apollo with lyre,
Aphrodite with doves.

Enter severally, a crowd of male citizens between the ages of sixteen and sixty—i.e.,
capable of some kind of military service. Some are armed, some not. Those with
weapons stack them, then gather in front of the council chamber.

Enter ETEOKLES *from the council chamber attended by magistrates (men over sixty)*
of the city of Thebes, in civilian dress. He stands in the portico of the council
chamber and addresses the citizens.

ETEOKLES   Citizens, children of Kadmos,
             whoever has charge of affairs in the stern of the ship,
             holding the rudder, sleepless, unblinking,
             must say what has got to be said.
             If things go well for us, it's because of the god.
             If, on the other hand,
             a disaster should strike (which heaven forbid),
             the moiling, the tidal groans, the sea-lamentation
             would sound the name "Eteokles"
             as wail and dirge all through the city.   10
             And I, Eteokles, alone the cause of weeping,
             Eteokles bewept,
             would be multiplied in the surge
             and raving of all your voices,
             and so prove fitly named
             for the city of the Kadmeians.
             May Zeus, Averter, forbid it.
             But all of you now must come to assist the city

129

and the altars of her gods.
The young boy, not yet a man,   20
the one who, past his prime, has already planted
many a sapling child,
and you in the fullness of manhood,
shall each have his function.
So the honor of this mothering land may not be
    extinguished,
either for her children whom she brought forth and
    cherished,
or for herself, their parent and devoted nurse.
For when you were infants on all fours,
dandled upon her nourishing hills and valleys,
she welcomed the familiar burdens of child-rearing,   30
tended you, brought you up, so that
you would be filial keepers of her house,
bearers of shields, and fit
for such need and moment as this is.
Up to this point
the god has inclined the scales in our favor;
so far during this siege the war goes well
in the main, thanks to the gods.
As of this moment our priest, shepherd of birds,
Teiresias, without benefit of light,   40
by ear and by thought alone, sorts out
the omen-giving birds with his trustworthy science;
this lord of divinations keeps saying
that the chiefs of the Achaians, in council all this night,
have planned an attack on our city.
Then, run, all of you,

The citizens rush to pick up their weapons and adjust them.

rush to the battlements and gates of our walls.
Fall out in full armor, crowd to the gunwales,
position yourselves at bow and stern of the towers,
stand firm at the gates, and be of good heart.   50

Do not give in to panic before this mob of outsiders.
It is the god who brings about good conclusions.

> A *few citizens take command and lead the rest off in*
> *various directions.*

SCOUT, *in light armor, runs in from left as the citizens run*
out. ETEOKLES *comes down from the steps of the council*
chamber to meet him. Magistrates follow at a distance.

But I myself have sent out scouts, sure-footed, clear of eye,
to spy on the camp. Their reports will save me
from all traps and deception.

SCOUT   Eteokles, most fittingly king of the Kadmeians,
I come with clear news from beyond the walls,
for I have seen myself all I can tell you.
This night there were seven men, violent, terrible, captains,
they slit the throat of a bull, catching the blood   60
in an inverted shield, bound with black iron.
They splashed their hands in bull blood, they swore
by the trinity of battle, Ares, god of strife,
Enyo, goddess of frenzy, and Phobos, god of fear,
either to sack and gut this city,
or by dying to smear and defile
this life-giving land with their blood.
Tearfully they brought keepsakes to send home to their
    parents
in the event of their deaths
and hung these on the chariot of their general, Adrastos;   70
and though they wept, no one uttered a word of grief,
because courage, an iron passion, gripped them
so that their eyes glared like the eyes of lions,
blazing with Ares.
Scared as I was I kept my head,
watched, made note of these things, and brought you the
    news
as fast as possible. As I was leaving

they were casting lots, each to divine by fortune
against which of our gates he would lead his battalions.
To answer this, therefore, instantly tell off as captains   80
the fittest, the chosen, the most select of the city
for each gate.
Already the Argive hosts in full battle array
are advancing in their own storm of dust.
The mouths of their stallions drip thick foam;
they defile our plowlands.
But like a steady helmsman, you must secure your ship
before Ares strikes in wind and lightning.
The sea-surge of that army shrieks a blood cry.
You must deal with them now and in the readiest way.   90
And I will continue to serve as your distant, enlightening eye
by day, as I have by night,
and informed by the clearness of my reports,
at least when it comes to what is outside our walls,
you will be free from danger and harm.   *Exit left.*

ETEOKLES *and the magistrates approach the altar and
statues of the gods.*

ETEOKLES Zeus, Earth, Olympian gods, this city's defenders,
my father's Curse, and you who will bring it to pass,
Fury, whose power is great,
let not this war capsize us
or overturn our city to ravaged desolation—   100
our city where the mother tongue of Hellas
rings in the sanctuary of our homes.
Do not bind the free city of Kadmos
in a slave's manacles, but become our defense.
I should think that I speak in our common cause,
for only a free and prosperous city
can make proper gifts to the gods.   *Exeunt into the council
chamber.*

Enter CHORUS *from left in disorder.
They carry seven garlands and seven robes as offerings
to the gods.*

CHORUS   I shriek fear, a frighted cry of pain.
         The attackers have flooded out of their camp,
         a rushing host, turbulent, thronged with horsemen   110
              foremost.
         A stormcloud of dust in heaven, a voiceless messenger,
         truth-telling but without sound, speaks and convinces.

         Slamming, clashing of steel, hoof-stomp and clubbing
         increase, possess and deafen our land.
         They rumble and thunder
         like a swollen, rock-dashed, hillside torrent.
         Ai, Ai, gods, goddesses,
         avert the swelling storm.

         *They run around wildly, alternately addressing each other
                               and the statues of the gods.*

         Beyond the walls
         that host with shields like staring eyes   120
         rears, tense and lithe, to spring
         against our city.

         Who will turn them aside? Who will come to our rescue?
         What god? What goddess?
         Shall I fall down before the images of the gods?
         O tranquil, thronèd gods,
         now is the time to clasp your images.
         Why do we stand lamenting when we should be at prayer?

SEMI-CHORUS   Can you hear,
         can you not hear the clanging of shields?   130
         When if not now shall we have recourse to
         supplication with gifts?

SEMI-CHORUS   I can see the sound: the hailstone clatter of spears.

What will you do, Ares?
Ancestral god of this homeland,
will you betray it?

God of the Golden Helmet,
look, look to the city
you once chose for your own.

They form a religious procession, approaching the statue
of each god as he or she is addressed and laying a robe and
                                    a garland at his or her feet.

CHORUS   Now all gods of this land, city's defense,   140
                    look down on us, take care
         of this pathetic legion of suppliants,
         mothers, young brides, virgins who make this prayer,
         and stand in danger of slavery, rape, and death.
         The helmet crests, blown in the brilliant air,
         are foam-froth flung by Ares' lustful breath.
         Around this rock, this city, a wind-whipped sea
         crashes and roars. O great divinity,
                    Zeus, God, Accomplisher, keep out
         the enemy, who would bind us with straps and chains.   150
         Argives encircle our stronghold. Panic, fear,
         terrors of Ares put the soul to rout.
         The iron bits, the links of the horses' reins,
         ring hard with murder. Seven men, cold breastplates,
                    greaves, shields, swords, helmets, and spears,
                         each as his lot dictates,
                         stand at our seven gates.

                    Athena, Zeus' daughter,
         lover of battle, become our present balm.
         And Lord Poseidon, regent of the water,   160
         ruler of sunken hulls and sailors' graves,
         tamer of horses, bridler of the waves,
                    bring us to harbor's calm.

And thou, fierce god of strife,
    glad when the battle joins,
Ares, who lives upon the spilling of life,
guard and avow us descendants of your loins
        that fathered Harmonia, Kadmos' wife;
        and Aphrodite, ancestress,
who bore Harmonia in your celestial womb,   170
        give ear to our distress,
hear our petitions, guard us from iron doom.

And thou, Apollo, Lord of Accords, for whom
the wolf in annual sacrifice is slain,
        turn to a wolf against our foes,
with your clear fire drive back the encircling gloom,
        and with your fang disclose
their bitten fear, their boast and purpose vain;
and unwed Artemis, goddess, silver-chaired,
now let your cleansing arrows be prepared.   180

      They resume their wild running and exclaiming.

O Artemis, Artemis, the clear heavens are crazed
        with glint and flash of spear.
What will become of the city? Whip and goad
        hasten the clanking chariots.
        They circle us. I hear
shrill scream of ungreased axle under its soldier load.
        Artemis, mistress of untamed beasts,
release us, O relieve us from the cold iron that divides,
        we who observe your feasts.
To what conclusion shall we be   190
        brought by the god that guides?

        Apollo, son of Zeus,
who gives the cleansing ceremony of war,
the pass and purpose of battle, the struggle's use,
I hear at the gates a clanging of brazen shields.
        Huge stones batter our tower-tops,

a terrible shower falls.
Apollo, foreteller, knower of what awaits,
and blessed Athena, enshrined beyond the walls,
protect, defend this fortress of seven gates.   200

They return to formal supplication and end up clasping
                                        the images of the gods.

O governing gods, goddesses who fulfill,
            long honored and adored,
do not betray this city to the will
            of a strangely spoken horde.
Listen, O hear, hear justly these cries, these free
breast-beaten claims upon your sovereignty.

Healers, emancipators, gods who save,
            be partisan, incline
your hearts to remember the offerings we gave,
            harken to this your shrine.   210
Be mindful of future gifts, relieve our groan,
hear our petition, make our cause your own.

Enter ETEOKLES *and magistrates from the council chamber.*
He approaches the CHORUS, *followed by the magistrates,*
and addresses the CHORUS *while they continue to cling to*
                                        the images of the gods.

ETEOKLES You—animals, repulsive beasts—I ask you,
is this screaming and bawling,
this hysterical prostration before the shrines
any way to save our city
or to encourage defending troops?
To sane men in command of themselves
this is an outrage.   220
Neither in disaster
nor in the careless calm of life
may I ever get cornered and quartered with any female.
When a woman is confident, her insolence can't be endured;

When frightened she's even worse, a danger to house and
        to city.
At this moment, with your storming sea-noise
and your skittering about,
you have drained our souls and paralyzed our citizens,
assisting the tides that threaten our walls:
thus we are being sacked from within.
This is what comes from sharing life with women.   230
And if command is violated by anyone,
man, woman, any who joins with such a one,
the judges shall find against him,
the pebble shall drop its fatal weight on his name,
nor shall he escape his sentence:
to be stoned to death as a traitor at the people's decree.
Outside things are a man's concern.
Let no woman debate them.
You, who belong inside, must stop this havoc and damage.
Can you hear? Can you understand?   240
Or are you beyond comprehension?

CHORUS Beloved son of Oedipus, his dear child,
                I trembled and shook with fear
        at the chariots' shaking, the terrible shaking, the wild
                pipe scream, the piercing, clear
        panic scream of the axles, and the forged
        ringing bits of the horses as they charged.

ETEOKLES Stop. Does the helmsman
        who flees to the bow
        when the ship is tossed in the swell of the sea   250
        find a means of safety
        if he lets go of the tiller at the stern?

CHORUS No. But I am a woman, and threw myself
                upon the Blessed Ones,
        trusting in them, when a hailstorm seemed to engulf
                the gates with thundering stones.
        In terror I cried aloud to them who dwell
        above to gird and protect this citadel.

ETEOKLES Then pray that our towers
                    stand against the spears of the attack—   260
                    for this does come from the gods.
                    There is a saying that
                    when a city is captured
                    the gods desert her.

CHORUS O may I die, may I be safely dead
                            before the gods remove
                    from the city, before the sacred gods have fled;
                            and may I never live
                    to see the breaching of walls, the brutal shame
                    of penetration, the home and shrine aflame.   270

ETEOKLES It is folly to invoke the gods
                    with such unlucky words.
                    Submission-to-Proper-Authority
                    is the Mother-of-Well-Being
                    and, so men say,
                    the Wife-of-Him-Who-Saves.

CHORUS True, but the strength of gods is greater than man's,
                            and if disaster come
                    can often lift the weak with invisible hands
                            from depths no eye can plumb,   280
                    from pits of anguish, from the deeps of doubt,
                    when his own vision is darkened and put out.

ETEOKLES But at the moment of enemy attack
                    it is for men to slaughter
                    the sacrificial beast
                    and to perform divination.
                    It is for you to remain silent
                    and to stay indoors.

CHORUS Though the hordes of attacking men be held at bay
                            by strength and the city's towers,   290
                    it is the gods alone allot the day;

theirs are the holy powers
to secure our walls, and give us hope to live.
What cause for anger and hatred could this give?

ETEOKLES I feel no anger
that you honor the race of gods,
but you are making our citizens
faint-hearted with your lamentations.
Use words of more hopeful omen
and do not incite to panic.   300

CHORUS Hearing the clashing of armor, the metal ring
and cacophony of arms,
I, a mere woman, came to this place to sing
prayers against battle's harms,
came to the sacred acropolis, in fear
of strife and bloodshed, came to the citadel here.

ETEOKLES If you hear of men
dying or wounded,
do not besiege the city
with your wailing laments.   310
For Ares must pasture
on the murder of mortals.

CHORUS (1st voice) I hear the snorting of horses.

ETEOKLES If you do, act as though you didn't.

CHORUS (2nd voice) The surrounded city groans at its cornerstones.

ETEOKLES This is purely my concern—not yours.

CHORUS (3rd voice) I'm frightened: the clangor at the gates
swells and grows louder.

ETEOKLES But you must stop this dangerous noise inside the city.

CHORUS (*4th voice*) O company of gods, do not betray
the defenses.

ETEOKLES I don't give a damn what you feel. You must keep
quiet and endure.   320

CHORUS (*5th voice*) Native and citizen gods, don't let me
be taken in slavery.

ETEOKLES But you yourselves are enslaving me and the whole city.

KORYPHAIOS All-powerful Zeus, turn your bolt against the enemy.

ETEOKLES O Zeus, what a race of women you gave us.

KORYPHAIOS Miserable, just as men are, when their city is taken.

ETEOKLES How dare you speak of defeat while touching the images?

KORYPHAIOS Fear has charge of my tongue, and my heart is faint.

ETEOKLES Grant me, I beg, a small favor.

KORYPHAIOS The sooner you speak it, the sooner I can comply.

ETEOKLES Be silent, wretched women; don't panic your friends.   330

KORYPHAIOS I am silent. I will endure with the others what is to come.

ETEOKLES I like these last words better.
Now stand from the images,
and instead of raving,
offer this useful prayer: *The* CHORUS *move away*
from the statues.

"May the gods strengthen our men and direct our spears."
But first, hear my sacred vow;
then raise Apollo's chant, holy, propitious,
a victory cry and halleluiah,
the appropriate ceremonial of Hellas,   340

as at our sacrificial rites,
giving confidence to friends,
letting loose fear to the enemy.

He approaches the statues
of the gods.

I speak to the defending gods of the land
who oversee the plowland and marketplace,
to the springs of Dirke and the waters of Ismenos I speak;
and this I make my vow:
if things turn out well and the city survives,
the sons of Kadmos shall make the altars of the gods
run with blood and slaughter bulls upon them.   350
I will erect trophies, and with enemy spoils, taken by spear,
I will adorn the fronts of the temples, the gods' holy houses.
This is my prayer and vow.
(*To the* CHORUS) Imitate this prayer, without lamentation,
without keening and moaning like beasts.
Whatever is to come will come; your noise can't stop it.
I will go and assign six men, myself the seventh,
all fully armed oarsmen,
against the champions at the seven exit-points of the city
before swift sea-lashing words of a messenger   360
come and ignite new panic.

Exeunt the magistrates into the council chamber,
ETEOKLES *right to join the defenders. The* CHORUS *address*
each other.

CHORUS   I will try to do my part,
to shape my prayer as these formulas require,
but the pulse of fear will not be lullabyed;
and in the neighboring regions of my heart
anxieties ignite, terrors catch fire,

and agitations, fanned by the blown sound
           of the circling hosts outside,
           smolder and burn. I quake,
like the mild paralyzed dove who, from her perch,   370
huddled with unfledged nestlings all around,
           eyes the thick snake.

           Our city's wealth of men
           climbs to the battlements.
What shall become of us all, our prayers and hopes?
From the enemy skies a hail of jagged stones
whistles and plunges around our defending troops.

They turn and address the gods in a controlled and orderly
manner.

           O gods from Zeus descended,
may our embattled soldiery and the city
of the descendants of Kadmos enlist your favor   380
and by your invincible powers be defended.

If you abandoned this our deep-soiled ground
           into the enemy hand,
where could you find its equal, where would you go,
           to what dark alien land?

To leave the springs of Dirke, of all sweet waters
           most life-giving and clear
among the gifts of Poseidon and Ocean's daughters!
           O gods, let naked fear,
man-eating cowardice possess our foe   390
           outside the walls. Implant
panic that makes men drop their arms and run;
           and in our voices grant
a glory to yourselves. Hearing these drones
of lamentation and prayer, knowing the outward danger,

become the city's wardens; secure your thrones.

Their gestures became more excited.

Pitiful and terrible it would be
to deliver so august, so famous a city
        to the Dark House of Death;
brought down in flaking ashes, like a felled beast,
        rent without pity   400
        or honor by the enslaving rod,
        the wooden-shafted spear
hurled by a fellow Hellene, backed by a god;
        and terrible, a pity
for all these women assembled here today,
the withered and white-headed, the young and fair,
to be led off, like horses, by the hair,
        their clothing ripped, their breasts
        exposed to the conqueror's view.
Eviscerated, the stunned city screams.   410
        Ulooloo, Ulooloo
The booty hauled away. Shouts. Brutal jokes.
I quake. I dream the most terrible of dreams.

They leave the statues. For the rest of the ode the sack of
                                        the city is mimed.

O terrible, before a woman is ripe,
without accustomed procession, accustomed song,
to go the awful road from her own home
under the sword's compulsion. I say the man
who dies in battle is better off than this.
For when a city is doomed to armored rape,
blades flash in the firelight; murderers throng   420
the streets. Gigantic Ares, in his bliss,
dazed and insane with the towering flame and fume,
befouls the pieties, harvests his dead wealth,
and breathes from our black smoke his terrible health.

The city echoes with loud, bellowing howls;
it is a death-trap, fatally self-ensnared.
A thin blood-cry of infants, a shrill reed
      of nursling terror wails,
and lumbering spearmen pierce each other's bowels.
      Pillagers loot each other   430
in plundering brotherhood; greed joins with greed;
      the empty-handed hails
with rallying cry his empty-handed brother;
no one content with a lesser or equal share.
Who shall account for this portioning, by what law
comes this allotment of pain, grief, and despair?

It is a bitter sight for the housewife
to see, spilled piecemeal from her cherished store,
the foison and wealth of earth, the harvest riches,
grain, oil, and wine, dashed from their polished jars,   440
      sluicing the filthy ditches.
      And by the rule of strife,
the pale, unfamilied girl become the whore
and trophy of her captor, forced to spread
for the sweating soldier, triumphant, hate-inflamed.
Perhaps a dark deliverance may occur
      in that foul bridal, the untamed
violence of that battle-grounded bed.
      And there may come to her
      a species of relief,   450
an end of tidal groans, weeping, and grief.

CHORUS (*1st voice*) The spy, the army seer, is bringing us news.
He is coming in haste, quick-footed, and zealous.

               Enter the SCOUT *from left, running.*

CHORUS (*2nd voice*) And here is the lord himself, the child
      of Oedipus,
at the right moment to hear the messenger,
equally swift and full of zealous purpose.

Enter ETEOKLES *from right, also in haste, attended by a*
group of armed men—six captains, each with a small
company of foot-soldiers.

SCOUT I speak, with knowledge, of matters outside,
of what lot and what gate each champion drew.
Tydeus already thunders near the gate of Proitos,
but the priest Amphiaraos will not permit the enemy army   460
to cross the ford of Ismenos
because the omens are not propitious.
But Tydeus, raving and gluttonous for battle,
bellows like a chimera in noonday clangor.
He abuses and berates Apollo's priest, Amphiaraos,
alleging that he licks the hand of fate and avoids battle
out of cowardice. Shouting such things as this,
he shakes the three crests of his helmet,
and, behind the rim of his shield,
brass-forged bells clash fear.   470
On the shield itself he bears this top-lofty blazon:
heaven forged with flaming stars, and at the center
the triple goddess of the three ways,
a brilliant full moon, the most revered,
the queen of all the stars, the eye of night,
stands out, embossed.
And now, raving and brandishing
this boastful, haughty-blazoned shield,
he bellows at the banks of the stream,
lusting for battle,   480
like a horse that, hearing the brazen horn-blast,
snorts in rage at this bridle, rears and stamps.
Whom will you send against this man?
When the bars of the gate of Proitos are drawn,
who will stand firm in that place?

ETEOKLES I am not overcome by the trappings of any man.
Blazons don't wound.
Crests and bells lose their sting, without spears.
And this midnight, shining with heavenly stars

on the shield that you speak of,   490
perhaps this dark folly will be an oracle for someone.
For if it should fall upon his eyes in death,
then the boastful device would be named,
fittingly and with justice,
darkness for him who carries it.
And he himself
against himself
will become his own oracle of impious violence.
But I shall station against Tydeus,
to stand firm at the gate, this man,   500
the worthy son of Astakos,
named "the black horse," Melanippos,

MELANIPPOS *steps forward, followed by his men.*

a noble man who honors the throne of Reverence,
a hater of arrogant words.
He is slow in all shameful practices,
avoiding what is base and cowardly.
He is a thorough son of this land,
a shoot sent up from the seed of the dragon's teeth
sown by Kadmos, and by Ares spared,

MELANIPPOS *holds up his shield with the image of*
Ares on it.

therefore genuinely of our soil.   510
Of course, the chances of battle are as dice in the
        hands of Ares.
But Dike, goddess of all orders, of justice human and divine,
his blood-sister, shall send him forth
to fend off the enemy spear from the mother who bore him.

MELANIPPOS *and his men salute first* ETEOKLES, *their com-*
mander, then all the gods together, last of all the statue of
Ares, under whose sign they fight. They then exeunt right.

CHORUS   May the gods grant good fortune to this one
                        who rises in the name
               of justice at the city's need, a son
                        worthy of enduring fame.
               Yet I tremble lest I look upon the blood
               of those who perish for their kindred's good.   520

SCOUT   As you say, may the gods give him good fortune.
             Kapaneus drew the lot for the gate of Elektra.
             A new breed of giant, larger than Tydeus,
             he boasts of something beyond the power of man;
             he launches terrible threats at the towers;
             may fate not fulfill them.
             For he says he will sack the city
             whether the gods wish it or not.
             And not even Zeus,
             striking the earth with giant-slaying lightnings,   530
             shall get in his way.
             He likens those flashings and thunders
             to the quiet warmth of noon.
             He bears, as his sign, a naked man
             armed with a flaming torch
             who is crying out in golden letters,
             "I shall burn the city."
             Against such a man, who will join in battle?
             Who will hold his ground without trembling
             against this haughty man?   540

ETEOKLES   This boast of gain over us will breed our own gains.
                 The tongues of vain men turn out to be
                 their clearest accusers.
                 Kapaneus, fully prepared, threatens to act
                 in disregard of the gods;
                 and, running off at the mouth in the joy of vanity,
                 though a mortal, he directs at heaven
                 and against Zeus a scathing wave of words.
                 I firmly believe that the flaming thunder-torch
                 will come against him in justice—   550
                 and not as a mere likeness, but the god's torch itself.

147

Loud-mouthed though he is
a man is chosen to stand against him,
a torch of courage, a mighty man, Polyphontes,

> POLYPHONTES *steps forward, followed by his men.*

"killer of many." By the good will of Artemis,
whose shrine stands at that gate,
and of the other gods, he will be a firm defense.

> POLYPHONTES *holds up his shield with the*
> *image of Athena with helmet, spear, and aegis on it.*

Therefore, name an enemy at another gate.

> POLYPHONTES *and his men repeat the ritual performed by*
> MELANIPPOS, *except that their final salute is to the statue*
> *of Athena. They then exeunt right.*

CHORUS   May he who vaunts so hugely taste the dust;
       may lightning stop him dead   560
before he mounts my house in bestial lust
       to soil the marriage bed,
and with long lance gut and despoil my home,
my penetralia, my dark and sacred room.

SCOUT   I name the man at the next gate.
The third lot leaped from the upturned
brazen helmet in favor of Eteoklos,
who is to hurl his squadron against the gate of Neïs.
His raging horses wheel, snorting in their armored headgear,
avid to fall on the gate.   570
Iron whistles at their nostrils
pipe an inhuman noise, filled with animal breathing.
His shield is arrogantly devised.
A man, fully armed, mounts a ladder against the walls
of an enemy, preparing to sack;
and he bellows in lettered speech

that not even Ares could cast him down from the tower.
Against this man assign a firm defender
to fend off the yoke of slavery from this city.

ETEOKLES Here is the man I would send;   580

> MEGAREUS *steps forward, followed by his men.*

and a certain apt fortune goes with him.
Here he is, assigned; his boast is in the strength of his arm;
Megareus, of the seed of Kreon, of the race of sown men.
Unmoved by the thunder
of the snortings of maddened horses,
he will not budge from the gate;

> MEGAREUS *holds up his shield with the image of Poseidon
>   wielding his trident on it.*

but either by dying will repay his nurture to mother Earth,
or by capturing both a man
and a man and city upon a shield,
he will adorn the home of his father with spoils.   590
Tell me the boast of another—the full, clear facts.

> MEGAREUS *and his men perform the ritual of salutation,
>   ending with the statue of Poseidon, and exeunt right.*

CHORUS O champion of my house, may you fare well,
                and so, for them, fare ill;
just as they roar against us, rail and yell,
                vaunting their ravening will,
shouting the blood-theme of their brazen boasts,
May Zeus Avenger's wrath behold their hosts.

SCOUT Another, the fourth, stationed at the gate of Athena,
comes forward with a shout, the huge
aspect and frame of Hippomedon.   600
The enormous threshing-floor,

that is, the circle of his shield—
I shuddered when he twirled it, I must confess.
The maker of the blazon, whoever it was
embossed that work on his shield,
was no common artisan:
Typhon, breathing fire, black smoke,
sister of glittering fire, pouring from his mouth;
and the border of the hollowed shield
is encoiled with his tail.   610
The man himself yells out his war cry,
and filled with the god Ares, like a very Maenad,
revels in blood-glee, glaring forth fear.
Take thought of the test in meeting such a man,
for Panic is already boasting at that gate.

ETEOKLES First of all, Athena, close neighbor of the city gate,
hating irreverent violence,
will ward off the wintry snake from the nestlings.
Hyperbios, "queller of violence," noble son of Oinops,

> HYPERBIOS *steps forward, followed by his men.*

is chosen champion against this contender,   620
a man who wishes to search out his fate
in the extremity of the occasion.
Neither in form, in spirit, nor in the bearing of arms
can he be faulted.
Hermes, by divine reason, has matched this pair;
for this man is the other's natural enemy,
and the gods on their shields are at enmity.
One has fire-breathing Typhon,
but Hyperbios has immovable Zeus, the father,

> HYPERBIOS *holds up his shield with the image of Zeus*
>   *wielding his thunderbolt on it.*

and vanquisher of Typhon, planted on his shield,   630
and the god bears aloft his flaming lightning dart.

Such are the portents the gods have given each side.
We are clearly on the winning side,
they on the losing,
if Zeus is mightier than Typhon in battle.
Perhaps the two champions will fare accordingly.
To Hyperbios, by his own blazon,
Zeus would become a savior,
being, by good fortune, upon his shield.

HYPERBIOS *and his men perform the ritual of salutation,*
        ending with the statue of Zeus, and exeunt right.

CHORUS Certain I am that he who bears as crest   640
                the anti-type of Zeus,
        the hideous earth god, serpentine, unblessed,
                with whom there is no truce
        in lasting enmity of gods or men,
        shall fall before our gates, nor rise again.

SCOUT May it be so. And now I name the fifth,
        stationed at the fifth, the Northern gate,
        beside the tomb of Amphion, of the race of Zeus.
        He swears by the blade he carries—
        revering it above god and his own eyes—   650
        that he will gut the citadel of the Kadmeians
        in spite of Zeus.
        Thus speaks the fair-faced whelp of Atalanta,
        his mother, huntress in the wilderness;
        he is a man with the beauty of a boy,
        the down just visible on his cheeks, the soft beginnings
        of what will be a shaggy mane as his youth flourishes.
        He does not stand before the gates without a boast,
        for on his bronze-bound shield,
        his masking metal riddle and device,   660
        he wields the shame of this city, the Sphinx,
        eater of raw flesh, clamped to the shield with bosses,
        a shining, hammered body,
        pinning down a Kadmeian in her claws.

He means to make a target of himself,
attracting most of our weapons
to himself and the vanquished man upon his shield.
There he stands, with brilliant eye but savage mind
unsuited to his name, Parthenopaios,
"maiden-faced," the Arcadian, not Argive-born,   670
yet repaying his fair and recent nurture
to Argos as if she were his mother.
Having come this far, such a man is not likely to stint
in his carnage, nor let so long a journey
repay him less than it's worth.
May Zeus avert the horrors with which he threatens our
    walls.

ETEOKLES If only they could feel at the hands of the gods
the things that they dream against us
in their unholy boasts,
they would be flatly and totally destroyed.   680
Against this one also, the one you call the Arcadian,
a man is set who does not boast
but his hand sees what must be done,
Aktor, "the doer," brother of him who was named before.

                AKTOR *steps forward, followed by his men.*

He will not permit an unbridled tongue,
flowing within the gates, to breed evils,
nor will he permit
the bite of that most hateful beast
to get from outside in.
That beast will blame the man who carries her   690
when she feels the thick shower of weapons

          AKTOR *holds up his shield with the image of Artemis,*
                    huntress, drawing her bow on it.

under the city walls.
With the help of the gods,

I, too, may rightly answer her riddle.

AKTOR *and his men perform the ritual of salutation, ending*
with the statue of Artemis, and exeunt left.

CHORUS My hair rises. The impious message daunts
                my heart and mind again.
        May the undoubted gods, hearing these vaunts
                of loud, unholy men,
        wipe them from earth forever, stop the breath
        of blasphemous mouths in slack and silent death.   700

SCOUT I name the sixth.
        The most restrained in spirit and the best,
        the priest, strong Amphiaraos,
        stationed at the Homoloian gate.
        He rebukes Tydeus,
        who drew the first of the lots,
        calls him, "man-slayer, city's bane,
        a disastrous counselor to Adrastos
        king of the Argives,
        a mighty teacher of evil to Argos,   710
        conjuror of the Fury, a servant of murder."
        And then he calls on your brother,
        whose heritage and fate you share,
        strong Polyneices,
        and repeatedly sounds the ending of his name,
        which means "strife."
        And this is his pronouncement:
        "How can the gods delight in such a deed?
        How can posterity admire it,
        to sack your father's city and your native gods,   720
        launching a foreign force against them?
        What natural or divine law, what Dike,
        could sanction the quenching of the maternal spring
        and source of your life?
        How can your mother land, wife to your father,
        ravaged by your lust and looming spear,

accept and espouse you?
But this land that you would make your enemy
shall open and take me into her bosom,
take me, Apollo's priest—so I foresee   730
and hide me from this violence and desecration;
and I shall make her fertile.
Let the battle begin.
The fate I expect is not without honor."
So speaks the priest
as he deftly wields his shield of solid bronze;
its circle carries no device,
because he does not wish to seem best
but in fact to be the best,
harvesting the fruit of his great mind and heart   740
where good counsels take root and flourish.
Against this man I recommend you send
a wise and good oarsman.
The man who honors the gods is a dangerous adversary.

ETEOKLES Alas for the mortal fortune that links
one just man with an impious mob.
There is nothing worse
than wicked companions; no fruit is reaped therefrom.
The field of Ate, of self-will,
yields a harvest only of death.   750
A reverent man aboard a ship
of hot-headed sailors or pirates
perishes with that god-rejected race of men.
When men lose their humanity and forget the gods
they are obliged to suffer the Fury's lash.
A just man in their company
is caught in the same trap, though without deserving.
He is marked and damned.
So the priest Amphiaraos, a man
of self-control, a just man, good and reverent,   760
and a great prophet, is joined with unholy
bold-mouthed men against his better judgment,
men who have come too far to turn back now.

If the god so decrees, he shall be dragged down with them.
Perhaps he will not even attack the gates—
not because he lacks courage, or is base in spirit,
but he knows how he must end in battle,
if the prophetic saying of Apollo bear fruit.
Still, I shall station a man against him,
mighty Lasthenes, a gate-keeper who hates outsiders.   770

> LASTHENES *steps forward, followed by his men.*

In mind a man of many years, youthful in flesh and bodily
        form,
with a swift-footed eye, a quick-witted hand
to divine with keen spear-point

> LASTHENES *holds up his shield with the image of*
>   *Apollo on it.*

the unarmored, naked patch of flesh
under the masking shield.
But good fortune for mortals
is a gift of the god alone.

> LASTHENES *and his men perform the ritual of salutation,*
>   *ending with the statue of Apollo, and exeunt left.*

CHORUS O gods, hear our just entreaties, stem the attack,
                take part in this our strife.
        Turn the invader's spear-point evils back   780
                even against his life.
        May Zeus thunder against him, may he fall
        under the god's fierce bolts outside the wall.

SCOUT The seventh man at the seventh gate—I name him now:
        your own brother. And you shall know what Curses
        he calls down upon the city
        and what fate he vows for it.
        He declares he will scale and bestride the walls,

proclaimed lord and subjugator of the land.
Yelling his full-lunged victory song   790
over the trapped and the beaten,
he will fight you hand to hand;
and either, in killing you, lie dead beside you,
or else drive you into dishonored exile
just as you forced such banishment on him.
This is what he bellows,
and calls on the gods of our mother land,
wife to his father, begging them to
be wardens of his fortunes—
this mighty Polyneices.   800
He has a newly forged, perfect-circled shield,
and clamped on it a twofold device.
A stately woman guides forward a warrior
in full armor who is hammered out in gold.
She says she is Dike—goddess of all orders,
human and divine—
and inscribed there are these words:
"I shall bring this man to his harbor
and he shall enjoy his father's city,
shall tumble and make free with his house."   810
Such are the engines of the enemy.
Now you alone can decide whom it is best to send.
If there's a fault to be found
in the situation, it is not with my report.
Now you alone can decide how best to pilot this vessel.
                                                    Exit left.

ETEOKLES God-hated, hateful, beaten and trapped,
          O god-maddened, O race of Oedipus,
          ringed round with hate my patrimony, full of tears;
          the Curses of my father once again
          bring forth a sickening fruit.   820
          But no weeping now; no lamentation.
          They could engender a greater and wider grief.
          Polyneices, full of strife, much striven over,
          you are well named. Soon we will know

how his blazon and device will do its work—
whether in fact the gold-incised letters on the shield
will bring the babbling, aberrated brother to his harbor.
If Dike, maiden daughter of Zeus,
had been present in the deeds and heart of this man,
perhaps it might come about.   830
But neither when he fled from the darkness of his mother,
nor at the breast, not as a boy,
nor when his first beard began
did Dike ever look upon him, or find him
worthy of her company.
Then she is not likely to be at his side
or help him in this violence,
this crime against the parent land.
If she did she would be, quite justly,
falsely named Justice; linked with a man   840
who would dare anything.
Trusting in this, I shall go;

> *He steps forward alone into the place where the other*
> *champions stood.*

I shall stand against him myself.
Who has a juster claim than I?
Ruler against ruler, brother against brother,
hater against hater, I must take my rightful place.
Quickly, bring my armor,

> *One of the remaining soldiers steps up to the door of*
> *the palace, opens it, and makes a summoning gesture to*
> *those within.*

the masking metal riddle to ward off stones and spears.

CHORUS   Son of Oedipus, dear to this land,
do not take on the violence of your brother   850
of evil name and fame. Surely it is enough that the
        Kadmeians
fight at close quarters with the Argives;

there is a ritual of purification
for the spilling of such blood.
O but of this consanguinity,
of two men who share the same blood,

Enter from the palace six slave girls, each carrying a piece of
armor—greaves, breastplate, sword and sword belt, helmet,
shield (held so that the inner side faces the audience), spear.
They stand in the portico of the palace holding the arms in
front of them.

the death of one by the hand of the other
who is the image of himself—
such blood spills pollution which endures
and fouls beyond cleansing.   860

ETEOKLES If a man's lot be to suffer evil, let it be without shame.
That is our only gain when we are dead.
But take note that there is neither glory
nor gain when shame and misfortune go together.

Slave girl helps him buckle on greaves.

CHORUS Why this mad eagerness in you, my child?
Do not be borne away now by the flood
of blind, spear-maddened rage, heart-swollen and wild.
Cast out this corrupting lust now and for good.

ETEOKLES Since the Fury brutally forces on the event,
let the generations of Laios go down to the last man,   870
blown wind-wracked along the weeping river of Hades,
even as is their lot, right from the first,
being hated of Phoibos, branded and unclean.

Slave girl helps him buckle on breastplate.

CHORUS A stinging desire, like a poisoned fly,
bites at you even to the mind's dark root,

goads to a man-lopping harvest, a crimson dye
of unlawful blood, a vile and bitter fruit.

ETEOKLES It is true. The hateful Fury, the black Curse
of my beloved father has picked out its meat.
It settles down with dry and tearless eyes.   880
It speaks of a gain to be had from a doom that will follow.

Slave girl helps him buckle on sword.

CHORUS Resist this voice. A prosperous career
and prudent is thought cowardly by no man.
No black cyclonic Fury will appear
when the gods accept a sacrifice at your hands.

ETEOKLES Somehow, for a long time,
We have ceased to be a concern of the gods.
Our death is the only sacrifice they would value.
Why any longer lick
at the bone hand of man-harvesting Fate?   890

Slave girl helps him buckle on helmet.

CHORUS Now, while the storm towers about you, wait;
hold back, consider, before the day is lost.
In time the wind-swept goddess, the cold Fate,
might veer more gently. Now she is tempest-tossed.

Slave girl offers the shield to ETEOKLES, *still with inner side
facing the audience.* ETEOKLES *fits his arm through the grips
of the shield, then turns and holds it up so that the audience
can see the device—the Fury.*

ETEOKLES She is tempestuous because my father's Curse
opened again like a pustule. They were all too true,
those omens that came in dreams, those whisperings
of the wealth of Oedipus, split by an iron sword.

KORYPHAIOS Though it is hard for you, be persuaded by women.

ETEOKLES Then speak only of what can be done, and to the point.   900

KORYPHAIOS Do not go that road to the seventh gate.

> *Slave girl hands* ETEOKLES *the spear. Exeunt slave girls into palace.* ETEOKLES *holds up the spear.*

ETEOKLES Your words cannot blunt me, whetted as I am.

KORYPHAIOS And yet there are victories without glory,
and the gods have honored them.

ETEOKLES These are no words for a man in full armor.

> *Takes the same attitude as the statue of the god Ares, behind him.*

KORYPHAIOS Can you wish to harvest your very brother's blood?

ETEOKLES If the gods dispose evil, no man can evade it.

> ETEOKLES *salutes all the statues of the gods as a group and exists left, running. The remaining soldiers stand in confusion for a moment, then exeunt left more slowly. The* CHORUS *group themselves around the altar and deliver the following ode with relatively little movement.*

CHORUS I shudder at this goddess, home-wrecker,
true oracle of evils and of doom,
     foreteller of the worse,   910
     the ordained aftermath;
so unlike all the gods, this mighty Fury
     the father called upon.
I fear that she is working out the wrath
of unhinged Oedipus in his dark frenzy
     who spoke the awful Curse.

An ancient blood-strife, a child-murdering
inheritance, and terrible heirloom
of folly and disobedience drives these brothers on.

It is savage-minded iron, the Chalybian stranger,   920
Scythian immigrant Ares doles out their lot,
a bitter executor of the family wealth.
From his great shaken helmet he plucks out
the scrap that says they shall dwell in as much land
as the dead may need, and have no part or share
in the wide fields, sweet waters, the living air.

When these self-slaughterers lie
in mutual murder pierced,
and the dry dust of earth
with parched, inhuman thirst   930
drinks up the criminal blood
where it leaks, black and clotted,
who would perform the rites
that purify, would wash
the hacked and ruined limbs?
New miseries for this house
mixed now with furious evils
anciently allotted.

I speak of an old breach
of law, long since begotten,   940
but bitterly swift to bring
retributive disaster;
and yet it lingered on
to the third generation.
Three times the Lord Apollo
in the midmost Pythian navel,
the prophetic center, spoke:
if Laios were to live
childless, without issue,
then the city would be safe.   950
But madly overcome

by lust, the body's folly,
despite the speaking god
Laios begot his doom,
the father-slaying son,
King Oedipus, who sowed
his outrageous agony
in the inviolate field
of his mother, the same womb
that bore and cherished him;   960
and planted there in blood
the wrath-bearing root.
Madness, mind-shattering,
brought bride and groom to bed.

Like a plunging and storm-agitated sea,
          disaster drives the wave;
first one wave falls, a second rises up,
a third, three-crested, crashes at the stern
          of the city in angry foam.
          Between our perilous home   970
          and total jeopardy,
our hull is the mere width of the city walls.
I fear shipwreck, I fear unspeakable things,
the city's destruction, the foul death of two kings.

Busy destruction will not spare these two.
A heavy settlement of ancient curses comes
inexorably home. The city's wealth,
this heavy freight of men, this swollen horde
must, from the stern, now be cast overboard.

For who was so marveled at   980
by the very gods themselves,
by those who shared with him
the self-same city hearths,
by the generations of men
that populate the earth,
or by them so much honored

as Oedipus, the king,
destroyer of the Sphinx,
that man-destroying fate
crouching upon our land?   990
But when he realized,
poor man, the nature and truth
of his impossible marriage,
then, raving in agony,
he brought two crimes to pass.
With father-slaying hand
he tore out his own eyes,
more valuable to him
than the sight of his two sons,
who were hateful to his eyes.   1000
And then, against these sons,
in wrath at twisted lineage,
he launched these bitter-tongued
Curses: that in due time
they should be dealt their wealth
with a hand that wields cold iron.
I tremble, I fear, lest this
should now be brought to pass
by the fleet-footed Fury.

> *Enter* SCOUT, *running, from left.*
> CHORUS *cluster around him.*

SCOUT Take heart, you need not fear   1010
the horrors reserved for women in war.
The city has been delivered from the yoke of slavery.
The boastings of storming men have fallen to the ground.
The city rides at calm; we have shipped no water.
The walls were sea-worthy, and we shored up our gates
with firm combatants and defenders.
In the main, things go well at six of the gates.
But Apollo, the holy Lord of Sevens, Lord of Accords,
took as his own the seventh gate,
bringing to completion for the race of Oedipus   1020

the ancient follies of Laios.

KORYPHAIOS What further awful news have you got to tell us?

SCOUT The men are dead, slain by each other's hands.

KORYPHAIOS What men? What did you say?
You're driving me mad with fear.

SCOUT Take hold of yourself and listen. The race of Oedipus…

KORYPHAIOS Woe unto me, I foresaw this evil.

SCOUT Incontestably brought low…

KORYPHAIOS Did they come to that? Go on; speak your heavy things.

SCOUT The city is safe, but the two kings of one blood   1030
have spilled their shared stream out. Earth has drunk up
the blood of their mutual slaughter. So they were hewn,
felled at the same moment by brother-hands.

KORYPHAIOS So fatally equal was the spirit they shared.
So utterly has it consumed the ill-fated race.

SCOUT This is occasion both for rejoicing and weeping—
that the city fares well, but that those who stand
over the city, the two generals,
shared out by lot their full inheritance
with hammered Scythian iron. So they shall have   1040
what they won: to be buried in earth,
who were so ill-fatedly carried away
on the wind of their father's prayer.   *Exit right.*

The CHORUS *turn to the statues of the gods.*

CHORUS O city-defending gods who oversee
these towers of Kadmos,

shall I rejoice and raise a victory cry
to Zeus, the city's savior,

Enter from left a cortège of soldiers carrying the bodies of
ETEOKLES *and* POLYNEICES *on litters. The* CHORUS *face*
them as they advance.

or shall I instead bewail
the pitiful, unkindly-godded,
and hatefully misbegotten warriors;   1050
who, out of grave, unholy motives,
perished in clear accordance with their names:
Eteokles, true cause of weeping,

Soldiers set down body of ETEOKLES *on right of altar.*

and Polyneices, full of strife?

Soldiers set down body of POLYNEICES *on left of altar.*
The CHORUS *stand over the bodies, making ritual gestures*
of mourning.

O black, conclusive prayer of Laios' race,
        Oedipal Curse, O dark.
An evil coldness whelms round, laps at my heart.
When I heard of the leaking corpses, terribly fated
        to this polluted death,
like a Maenad, I contrived a melody   1060
        and chant of burial.
But what grim, ominous harmony was made
by these brothers in their concert of the spear!

The word invoked by the father, the potent word
        went its unwearied way
and was acted out, bloodily, to the last.
The defiant act conceived in Laios' day
        has pierced from the buried past
into their midst and bodies, has pierced through.
        Ulooloo, ulooloo.   1070

Therefore I fear for the city, soiled with this blood.
Nothing can blunt the prophecies of the god.

You two who now lie dumb and strengthless here
defied the pieties, and like bad seed begot
only this barren groan, this sterile tear,
and these distracted words to mourn your lot.
You were yourselves misfortune's instruments,
the silenced theme infecting these laments.

SEMI-CHORUS Articulate these slack and wordless mouths;
to the eye they are the speech of a messenger;   1080
here lie our double griefs, a deathly couple,
twin-fated ancient sorrows, ancestral errors
mutually murdering, brought to this dark conclusion.

What shall I say? What is there to be said
but that these are woes come home, to dwell at the hearth
and share a bed with the ancient woes of this house.

SEMI-CHORUS But, dear ones, sisters, row
an escorting funeral oarbeat
with our head-smiting hands
down the cold winds of wailing   1090
to bear away the dead
across dark Acheron
like a sacred, black-sailed ship
of grief, on expedition,
sailing the sunless way
untrodden by Apollo
to the all-welcoming,
the unseen, bitter shore.

Enter from the palace ANTIGONE *and* ISMENE *followed by
    a group of women making gestures of mourning. The*
CHORUS *make room for the procession to take a stand about
        halfway between the palace door and the biers.*

CHORUS For that ungrateful task,
           the lament of these two brothers,   1100
           here now come these two,
           Antigone and Ismene.
           They will surely utter
           loud, unstinted grief
           from lovely breast and throat.
           But it is right for us
           before we hear their voices
           to chant the grating hymn,
           the harsh hymn of the Fury,
           and over the dead to sing   1110
           the hate-filled paean of Hades.

           O in your brothers most unfortunate,
           of all women swayed to the menstrual pulse
                     most luckless and set apart,
                     I groan and weep for you;
           without riddle or mask, but openly
           I make these shrill sounds in the blood of my heart.

           The CHORUS *stand near the biers, alternately addressing*
           ETEOKLES *and* POLYNEICES, ANTIGONE *and* ISMENE, *and*
                                                   each other.

SEMI-CHORUS And you, defiant ones, foes to your kindred,
           enemies to yourselves, your family's blood,
           perverse and obstinate in evil paths   1120
           who seized at spear-point what had been your father's,
           O full of grief, unfortunates, who found
           in the deep violation of your home
           misfortune, and the angry, fatal wound;
           who pierced the very walls of your own house,
                     breached, hacked and defiled,
           to taste the sweet prerogative of rule
                     and solitary might,
           at last, by iron, you are reconciled.

167

The words of your father, of King Oedipus,   1130
were made true sayings by the listening Fury
who brought these things to pass.
Here two young men lie, pierced through the left side;
the lungs are pierced that once in darkened waters,
unbreathing, floated calm in the same womb.

SEMI-CHORUS Ai, Ai, alas for those Curses brought about
by divine intervention of the gods.
Yet you speak only of these two thrust down,
invaded, pierced in their bodies and their homes
because of an unholy, kindling wrath   1140
and even-handed fate, a father's gift.
But O our city also has been cleft,
cut through with groans. The very towers groan.
Earth groans, the mothering earth that fosters men.
To others there still remain holdings of land,
pasture and fold for those who are still to come,
their possession, the sweet earth. It was for this,
for this that there came to these ill-fated ones
the strife that linked them, the consummation of death.
With hearts like blades, these two young men shared out   1150
this inheritance in just and equal lots.

CHORUS To kindred, bonded in blood to these two men,
the justice of their reconciler, Ares,
is stern, forbidding, costly, without beauty.
Struck down by the god's iron and their own hands,
it is likely that in time someone will ask
what portion of a father's tomb they share
who spilled each other's blood, his blood, with iron.
A chill, echoing wail, "Eteokles,
Heart-Cleaver, Sea of Tears, Eteokles!"   1160
          A very groan of woe,
joyless and savage-minded, weeping salt
from the sickened spirit, rises from their house,
and makes me, in my wailing, waste away
          for the sake of these two lords.

SEMI-CHORUS Of these contentious young it can be said
                        they altered the fortunes of many in their city
                        and marshaled into the bloody ranks of death
                        many who lie full-length in the fields outside.

SEMI-CHORUS O most unfortunate in her hovering god   1170
                        was she who gave them birth; unfortunate
                        above all women brought to bed of a child.
                        Making a husband of her own first-born,
                        she brought forth these, his brothers, whose brothering
                                hands,
                        warmed in the same recess, dark womb and blood,
                        came to their limit and last in mutual slaughter.

SEMI-CHORUS Sperm-linked, twinned in the seed, united
                                in wrath and loveless strife,
                        these rivals went to school their killing hatred
                                in the first waters of life;   1180
                        in bowels and belly, in the narrow tubes
                                of birth they nursed their wrath,
                        madness of blade-wounds, hidden ravagement
                                brought to this aftermath;
                        unstrung their limbs in which all strife is spent.

CHORUS Their hatred now is ended, and their lives
                                spilled on their mother earth,
                        where pitifully their only blood lies pooled,
                                calm, and of nothing worth.
                        Truly, at last, they share one common blood.   1190
                        Ares, that bitter settler of strife,
                        is the guest foretold from across the hostile sea,
                        the fire-born, whetted iron of prophecy.
                        Bitter is Ares, Lord Apportioner,
                        who dealt such balanced bounty, equal lots,
                        making the father's furious wish come true.

SEMI-CHORUS They have won the lot they drew
                                at the hands of fate,

God-given lot of sorrow, 1200
      gift of hate.
Under the body lies
      the wealth it seized:
the plumbless deeps of earth,
      silent, appeased.

CHORUS O they have burst into bloom,
they blossom, unfold like petals,
these twin red flowers of a family grief!
Now that the seed of this line, the race of Laios,
      has turned on itself, and turned
everything into overturning flight, 1210
the sharp-turned cry of triumph, the victory earned,
      belongs by evident right
      but to the Curses.

Only the trophy of Ate, of blindness, stands
      firm at the fatal gate
where these two perished at each other's hands.
      The Fury's strength and hate,
having wrought the wills of men, the god's commands,
      begins now to abate.

The CHORUS *draw back as* ANTIGONE *and* ISMENE *and their*
      attendants come and stand over the bodies.

ANTIGONE Stricken, you struck back... 1220
  ISMENE But died as you cut him down.
ANTIGONE With a spear you slew...
  ISMENE But by a spear you died.
ANTIGONE Pitiful in your struggle.
  ISMENE Pitiful in your suffering.
ANTIGONE Give vent to the wail.
  ISMENE Open the sluice of the tear.
ANTIGONE You are stretched out for good...
  ISMENE Having done murder.

ANTIGONE E, e,   1230
   ISMENE E, e,
ANTIGONE My mind is unhinged with wailing.
   ISMENE My heart groans in my body.
ANTIGONE Io, Io, thou all-wept for.
   ISMENE Thou, also, all-striving.
ANTIGONE You perished by the hand of one who is dear...
   ISMENE And slew one who is kin.
ANTIGONE A double grief to croon.
   ISMENE A double grief to see.
ANTIGONE Here lies sorrow beside brother sorrow.   1240
   ISMENE Here stand sisters of those sorrows.

   CHORUS Terrible, ungenerous is Fate,
         and so are you, dark shade of Oedipus,
         lady, whose gifts are cruel pain and weight,
         black and abiding Fury, whose power is great.

ANTIGONE E, e,
   ISMENE E, e,
ANTIGONE (to POLYNEICES) Sorrows unbearable to the eye...
   ISMENE Were revealed to me in his return from exile.
ANTIGONE And though he killed, he didn't even get home...   1250
   ISMENE But as he got within reach of his goal, he perished.
ANTIGONE (to ETEOKLES) And this one also breathed his last...
   ISMENE And killed this one.
ANTIGONE Pitiful race...
   ISMENE Which pitifully suffered...
ANTIGONE Hard-groaning cares, mourners of like name...

   ISMENE Which drowned three generations in a flood of grief.

   CHORUS Terrible, ungenerous is Fate,
         and so are you, dark shade of Oedipus,
         lady, whose gifts are cruel pain and weight,   1260
         black and abiding Fury, whose power is great.

ANTIGONE You know her, having passed through her terrors.
   ISMENE You, also, learned her ways, no later than he...

ANTIGONE When you came home to the city . . .
  ISMENE As a rival oarsman to his spear.
ANTIGONE Hopeless to speak.
  ISMENE Helpless to see.
ANTIGONE Alas for suffering.
  ISMENE Alas for evil.
ANTIGONE For the house . . .   1270
  ISMENE For the land . . .
ANTIGONE Above all, for me . . .
  ISMENE And no less for me.
ANTIGONE Io, Io, of all men, most full of struggle, Polyneices,
               my lord . . .
  ISMENE Io, Io, lord of harsh, groaning evils, Eteokles, my ruler . . .
ANTIGONE Io, Io, possessed by spirits of blindness . . .
  ISMENE Io, Io, where shall we lay them in earth?

ANTIGONE Io, Io, where they have most right to be . . .
  ISMENE Io, Io, two griefs to sleep beside the father,
               and share the father's bed.   1280

          Enter MESSENGER *of the magistrates of Thebes, in civilian
                                   dress, from council chamber.*

MESSENGER I am commanded to announce
           the decreed resolution voted
           by the magistrates of this City of Kadmos,
           and their present pleasure, as well.
           They determined to bury this man, Eteokles,
           with honor and pomp, in recognition
           of his good will toward the land;
           for he contained the enemy,
           and, in choosing death at the gates of the city
           to protect the sanctities of his father,   1290
           he was brought to a blameless death.
           To die for such things is noble in the young.
           I have been told to speak accordingly of this man.
           His brother here, the corpse of Polyneices,
           I am commanded to say, is to be cast out,

unburied, a thing for dogs to tear at,
because, as they choose to put it, he would
have driven from their lawful homes
the people of Kadmos, if one of the gods
had not thwarted his spear.   1300
Even in death he shall suffer contamination
from the gods of his father, which he dishonored
in trying to bring an outside force within,
and to sack the city. It therefore seems to them right
that this man receive what he deserves:
to be buried only by the winged birds,
without honor.
And there shall not follow him any hands
pouring earth to make a tomb, nor shall he be
honored with shrill songs of mourning,   1310
or borne away by any cherishing kindred.
Such were the things decreed by those
in authority over the Kadmeians.

ANTIGONE I tell those who stand in authority
over the Kadmeians:
if no one else is willing to bury this man,
I shall bury him;
and shall take upon myself any danger
that may be incurred.
Nor am I ashamed to show this defiance   1320
against the city.
Dreadful and terrible, the common entrails
from which we both have come:
from an unfortunate mother and miserable father.
And so my willing soul
shares in my brother's unwilling evil,
and living,
shares his dead misery,
being like-hearted, born of the same bowels.
On this man's flesh no famished wolf shall feast;   1330
let no one decree it.

For I myself, though only a woman,
shall contrive the digging and the funeral rites,
drag him, if need be,
in the folds of my cloak, to the grave of his father and
        brother.
But I shall cover him. Let no man command otherwise.
This shall be done; a way shall be found to do it.

MESSENGER I enjoin you, do not show this defiance to the city.

ANTIGONE I enjoin you, do not come to me with extravagant
proclamations.

MESSENGER A people is harsh toward the contriver of misfortunes   1340
from which they have just escaped.

ANTIGONE Let them be harsh, but this man will not go unburied.

MESSENGER Will you honor in funeral one whom the city hates?

ANTIGONE Have not the gods already determined
that he should inherit his native earth?

MESSENGER So to decide before he cast this land in peril
could not have been just.

ANTIGONE Suffering, he answered with evil.

MESSENGER But he did this deed against all, instead of one.

ANTIGONE I shall bury this man. Don't lengthen the argument.   1350

MESSENGER Be self-willed, but I forbid the act.

Exit into council chamber.

ANTIGONE Last of the gods, the Fury, sower of discord,
has still the last word.

CHORUS O vaunting, blood-corrupting spirits of doom,

The soldiers form two groups, one with ISMENE *around the
bier of* ETEOKLES, *the other with* ANTIGONE *around the bier
of* POLYNEICES.

Furies, who shattered the line of Oedipus,
            once proud in the guiding stern,
what will become of me? Where now will I turn?
How could I summon the hardness, the brutal hate
not to lament you and bear you to the tomb?
            And yet I hesitate   1360
in fear and awe of the magistrates' command.
            It is the lot and right
of one of you to have many a mourning voice
            to sing you to your grave,
but the other is denied song, tomb and all
but one sole mourner to lament his fall.
O who would dare follow her path and choice?

Half the CHORUS *join* ANTIGONE. *The other half join*
ISMENE.

SEMI-CHORUS Whether or not the city rage and cry
            against the pitiful mourners of this man,
            we will bring Polyneices to his grave   1370
            and help you bury him. The grief for kindred
            is the bond and link of mankind, common to all,
            unchanging. Whereas the city declares
            now one thing, now another, to be just.

SEMI-CHORUS But we will go with this one, whom the city
            and Justice both join and delight in praising.
            For second only to the blessed gods,
            to mighty Zeus, this one man most of all
            defended the city of Kadmos, kept the ship
            steady against capsize, guiding it through   1380
            the breakers, the swamping waves of men from without.

Soldiers pick up biers. POLYNEICES *is carried out left, followed by* ANTIGONE *and* SEMI-CHORUS. ETEOKLES *is carried out right, followed by* ISMENE *and* SEMI-CHORUS.

NOTES

The play was produced at the festival of the Greater Dionysia (the principal occasion for the performance of tragedies in Athens) in 467 B.C. As was the custom, it was joined with two other tragedies to form a trilogy—*Laios, Oedipus, Seven against Thebes*—and followed by a satyr play—a burlesque of a tragedy with a chorus of satyrs—the *Sphinx*. As was also the custom, the author wrote the music to which the lyrics were sung, trained the chorus, directed the actors, and played one of the speaking parts. Under such conditions of production, stage directions and indications about properties and nonspeaking parts (what Aristotle in the *Poetics* called spectacle, *opsis*) were superfluous, and none have come down to us. Those supplied in this version represent what we consider the minimum of visual effects necessary to make the play intelligible in production. Some of these, such as the statues of the gods that Eteokles rebukes the Chorus for touching, are explicitly demanded by the text. Others, such as the shield devices of the defenders, are more controversial, but seem to us justified as a means of showing in action how the emblems of attackers and defenders prepare for the confrontation of Eteokles and Polyneices, with their riddling shield devices.

On the seven gods of Thebes and their attributes, and the meaning of seven in this play, see notes on the Chorus' entrance song (108–212 / 78–180) and on the central messenger scene (457–907 / 375–719).

The play has a Chorus of twelve (the traditional number for this period) and five speaking parts. There is some disagreement among manuscripts about the distribution of lines among Chorus and solo voices in the final lament. If the one we have followed is correct, the role of Ismene is limited to a few lines of lyric and can be assumed to have been played by an extra singer rather than by a full-fledged actor.

In that case, *Seven against Thebes* is a two-actor play—that is, all the speaking parts were distributed between two actors. On the other hand, if Ismene was played by an actor, it must be a three-actor play, since the text allows no time for an actor to leave the stage, change his mask and costume, and re-enter at 1281 / 961 as the Messenger of the magistrates of Thebes. This apparent economy in construction (two actors plus twelve members of the Chorus) is somewhat misleading. With the maximum of doubling (Theban citizens, at least twelve, become Theban soldiers; six Theban magistrates become six Theban champions; six armor-bearers become attendants of Antigone and Ismene) the play cannot be produced without twenty-four people on stage in addition to the actors and Chorus, and the smallest possible number of masks required (speaking and nonspeaking parts together) is sixty-five.

NOTES ON THE TEXT

1 / 1 *children of Kadmos* The original city on the site of Thebes was called after Kadmos, the first settler (see Introduction II and Glossary). Perhaps as a reminder that the action takes place in a distant past, the play never speaks of Thebes or Thebans, only of the city of Kadmos, children of Kadmos, Kadmeians, etc.

2–3 / 2–3 *whoever has charge of affairs . . . holding the rudder* The metaphor of the ship of state, struggling in a stormy sea, a commonplace from Homer on, is the controlling image of *Seven against Thebes*. Its treatment in this play is the most extended and developed in classical Greek literature. Nautical language is constantly used of the city and of the fighting men on both sides (e.g. 48–49 / 32–33, 87–89 / 62–64, 99 / 71–72, 248–52 / 208–10, 815 / 652, 965–79 / 758–71, 1014–16 / 795–98, 1265 / 992, 1379–81 / 1078–81). The ship metaphor, which seems at first to apply entirely to the city, gradually comes to be associated with the house of Laios. The focus shifts from the ship of state, threatened by the storm of war, to the bark of death in which Eteokles and Polyneices are swept away by winds of wrath and surges of weeping (particularly 869–71 / 689–90 and 1087–1196 / 855–946). The gods of this storm are Ares and the Fury, the personifications of the violence and wrath of the house of Laios (Introduction II).

11–16 / 5–9 *And I, Eteokles, . . . so prove fitly named / for the city of the Kadmeians* This passage has hitherto been understood to say, "And I, Eteokles, would be multiplied in songs of mourning throughout the city. May Zeus, Averter, forbid it and so prove fitly named for the city of Kadmeians." A minor change in the standard punctuation makes Eteokles rather than Zeus the one who is fitly named, and gives the first of many indications that his name may turn out to mean "truly bewept," rather than "justly famed" (Introduction v). The reference to weeping in Eteokles' name has gone undetected in modern times, hence the preference for the other punctuation.

97–98 / 70 On summoning the Curse and the Fury to defend the city, see Introduction III. The consequences of this act begin to appear in the central scene (819–20 / 655, 869 / 689, 878–79 / 695–96, 884–85 / 699–701, 895–96 / 709). The choral song that follows that scene (908–1009 / 720–91) gives the history of the joint operation of Curse and Fury in the house of Laios, and the final lament (1044–1280 / 821–1010) celebrates the power of the Fury as the implementer of the Curse, saluting her in the same words as those with which Eteokles originally summons her, "Fury, whose power is great" (1245 / 975 and 1261 / 988).

108–212 / 78–180 Chorus' entrance song: the Chorus alternate between excited exclamation (108–39 / 78–107, and 181–200 / 151–65) and a formal prayer in which the seven gods are invoked first jointly (140–48 / 109–15), then individually (148–80 / 116–49), and again jointly (201–12 / 166–80). At 188 / 152, the Greek text names an eighth deity, Hera. Unlike the other gods named, she is given no attributes in the ode and has no function elsewhere in the play. These facts, combined with the thematic importance of the number seven in this choral song and in the design of the play, seem to us to justify the assumption that Hera does not belong in this prayer, but is there as the result of a copyist's misreading of one of Artemis' attributes, possibly *potnia theron*, "mistress of wild beasts." The Greek letters of this epithet could easily be mistaken for the reading of our MSS., *potnia Hera*, "Mistress Hera."

118 / 87 *ai* Ai, E (1231 / 966), and Io (1234 / 969) are some of the many inarticulate cries of grief used in Greek tragedy.

120 / 90 *shields like staring eyes* The Greek says "round white shields," a reference to the distinctive shape and color of the Argive shield, invented by the hero Proitos (see 459 / 377 with note). In the central messenger scene, the association of this round white shield with an eye that can cast an evil spell is repeatedly suggested.

137 / 106 *God of the Golden Helmet* Perhaps Ares' helmet is connected with his role as apportioner of lots (see 920–25 / 727–33). For Ares as ancestral god see note on 164–72 / 135–44.

149–50 / 116–17 Zeus, king of the gods, is invoked first and alone as Accomplisher, and defender of Dike (Introduction 11). His thunderbolt, several times invoked in the central scene, symbolizes his power to uphold Dike, the principle of order. The remaining six gods are invoked in pairs.

154–57 / 124–26 *Seven men…seven gates* The number seven is stressed again in this song at **200 / 165**. It also structures the central scene. The seventh gate is the gate of destiny for Eteokles and Polyneices. The other gates have names, this one is simply called seventh, though in other versions of the story, it too had a name (note to **459 / 377**). Apollo, who presides at the seventh gate, has the title *Hebdomagetes*, Lord of Sevens (**1018–21 / 800–802**). The structuring of the action by this number contributes to the sense of a fateful symmetry that brings the sons of Oedipus together. But for this purpose, another number might have served. The special significance of seven in this play seems to be its connection with Apollo, who, as god of harmony, musical (the seven-stringed lyre) and cosmic (the seven planets), presides over the ceremony of reconciliation and purification performed at the seventh gate.

158–63 / 128–34 Athena, armed with helmet, spear, and aegis, is a defender of civilization and order, Zeus' ally against the giants. (The aegis, symbol of Zeus' authority, is a goatskin worn in battle, either on her left arm as a shield or poncho-style as body armor, usually decorated with a gorgon mask; when shaken by Zeus, it makes a thunderstorm that creates panic in men.) She and Poseidon, inventor of the bridle that tames horses, and the ship that masters the waves, are coupled here (as in their joint cult in Athens) as expressions of the controlled force that overcomes the kind of mindless violence (storm of Ares and the Fury, brute animal rage) that threatens to engulf the city (see notes on **530 / 428–29** and **557 / 449**).

164–72 / 135–44 Ares and Aphrodite are the ancestral gods of the city, parents of Harmonia, the wife of Kadmos. The ambiguity of the relationships among the members of the house of Laios, linked to each other by the unbreakable ties of blood, but also enemies to the death, is expressed in the treatment of Ares, who is not only invoked as an ancestor and protector (see also **134–39 / 101–7, 509 / 414**) but also imagined as inspiring the attackers (**63 / 45, 74 / 53, 88 / 64, 152 / 115, 612 / 497**). Like Oedipus and his sons, he is both outsider and insider, friend as an ancestral god; stranger because of his links with the alien world of Thrace. At **311–12 / 244**, and **421–24 / 341–44**, he seems to be neither friend nor stranger but simply the spirit of violence. Aphrodite is not named elsewhere in the play, but her force is felt in the perverted blood-lust of **866–68** / 686–88, **874–77** / 692–94, and in the many passages that more or less explicitly suggest incestuous desire as the cause of the hostility among the males in the house of Laios (see particularly **559–64** / 452–56, **719–32** / 580–89, **951–64** / 750–56, **1086** / 851, **1118–29** / 875–84, **1170–76** / 926–31, **1279–80** / 1004).

173–80 / 158–65 Apollo, wolf-slayer, and his sister Artemis with her arrows are both invoked as hunters, that is, curbers of the wild animal force that threatens the city; also as purifiers, since it is with their arrows that Artemis and Apollo both inflict sickness and restore health.

204 / 170 *strangely spoken* Aeschylus uses an adjective that means "speaking differently." The most natural explanation is that he is referring to the fact that the attackers, with the exception of Polyneices, are not Thebans, and therefore speak different dialects of Greek. Their alien speech makes them more menacing. Some think "strangely spoken" means that the attackers actually speak a foreign language. These are the critics who read the play as a commentary on the Persian Wars, in which the attackers represent impious barbarism, the defenders rational and restrained Hellenism. Such an interpretation restricts the reference of the play by ignoring many aspects of the imagery. It also has to explain away the fact that Aeschylus twice uses the adjective "Achaian" in connection with the attackers (**44** / 28, **403** / 324). At **403** / 324 we have translated "Achaian" with "Hellene."

232 / 197 *man, woman, any who joins with such a one* The Greek, which, as it stands, means, "man and woman and whatever is in between," is not intelligible. We have therefore assumed a corruption and substituted a plausible conjecture.

234–36 / 198–99 *the pebble...the people's decree* Judges, casting their votes for acquittal or conviction, sometimes used pebbles as ballots. The penalty for treason was to be stoned to death. The pebbles that convicted a man of treason are here assimilated to the stones with which the sentence was executed. Perhaps the storm of stones hurled at the towers of Thebes (**255–56** / 212–13 and **376–77** / 298–300) should be connected with this passage.

273–76 / 224–25 Eteokles offers the Chorus a bit of popular wisdom in the form of a riddle whose full implications he seems not to understand. Like Laios and Oedipus before him, he hopes to save the city and be the author of well-being for himself and others; but, also like Laios and Oedipus, he is a defier of authority (Introduction II, III, IV). Perhaps there is a play on the notion of mother/wife. Eteokles would, like to be at once the child (Well-Being) and the husband (Him-Who-Saves).

283–88 / 231–33 Eteokles is referring to the pre-battle ritual of taking the omens (see 460–62 / 378–79). However, the women are not usurping this masculine role. The supplication of the gods of the city in times of crisis is a traditional function of women. Compare the supplication of Athena by the women of Troy (*Iliad*, VI. 286–310).

338–39 / 267–68 Apollo's chant is the paean—a song of victory, but also of healing and purification. The Greek does not name Apollo but uses a verb that means "to sing a paean" (see 790 / 635, 1046 / 826, 1111 / 869–70, 1208–13 / 953–55).

346 / 273 *Dirke...Ismenos* In the dry climate of Greece, where water quite visibly brings life, to invoke the local springs and rivers is to draw attention to the life-giving, that is, parental aspect of the land.

388 / 311 *Ocean's daughters* In the Greek text, they are called Tethys' daughters. Springs and rivers are the daughters of Okeanos and his consort Tethys. We have substituted the parent more likely to be recognized by a modern audience.

414–17 / 333–35 Part of the marriage ceremony was the procession of singing boys and girls that escorted the bride from her father's house to her husband's house. The sack of the city is imagined as an inverted marriage ritual whose consummation is rape and death (446–51 / 363–68).

457–907 / 375–719 Central messenger scene: The scene has two sections. In the first, which ends at 848 / 676, the Scout describes the attacking champions, with their shields, and for each of these Eteokles selects and dispatches to the walls a suitable opponent. The climax of this section is Eteokles' decision to defend the seventh gate in person. The climax of the whole scene is the revelation of the device on Eteokles' shield. This is postponed until near the end of the second section. It is gradually built up to as Eteokles assumes his armor piece by piece and the Chorus tries to dissuade him from his decision to go to the seventh gate. Both the descriptions of the shields and the arming of the hero are conventions of the epic, which Aeschylus has converted to dramatic purposes. See the shields of Agamemnon and Achilles (*Iliad* XIX.32–40, XVIII.478–608) and the arming of Paris and Agamemnon (*Iliad* III.330–8, XIX.16–45). As in the epic, the emblems on the shields provide an opportunity for enlarging and deepening the meaning of the action. Shield devices were traditionally a kind of magic designed to terrify the enemy and make the bearer invincible—"engines" (*exeuremata*, **811** / 649) of war against which appropriate countermeasures must be taken. Compare the song that Eteokles orders the Chorus to sing, "giving confidence to friends, / letting loose fear to the enemy" (**342–43** / 270). Each of the first five emblems of the attackers is designed to unman the Thebans by an allusion to the potentially disastrous problems of the house of Laios. The first and last are the most overt—the moon, with her reminder of Oedipus' fatal meeting with his father (note to **473** / 389), and the Sphinx, symbol of Oedipus' and Thebes' failure to understand their true identity. The other three express, in ascending order of violence, the defiance of Dike which undid Laios and all who associated with him (Introduction II and IV). The language leaves it uncertain as to whether the defenders named by Eteokles are actually on stage, and, with one exception, we are not told what devices they have on their shields. But that exception is instructive. Hyperbios, confronting Hippomedon who has Typhon on his shield, has as his device the slayer of Typhon, thunder-wielding Zeus (**629–39** / 512–20), one of the seven gods whose images stand on the stage (**148–80** / 116–49). In this case, anyway, Eteokles pits device against device. Furthermore, we must imagine that when Eteokles takes shield in hand (**895** / 709) he displays a suitable device, even though the text does not allude to it directly. For not only is the blank shield reserved for Amphiaraos (**735–41** / 590–94); Polyneices' shield device is carefully described and strongly emphasized. Since the brothers are counterparts of each other in every way, Eteokles' shield must have an answering device. And the Fury is the proper counterpart of Dike (cf. note to **895–96** / 709–11). In two cases, then, the shield device is a significant part of the defender's equipment. It seems likely therefore that the devices of the other defenders were not overlooked. Since these devices are not mentioned they can only have been presented visually, by the defenders themselves present on the stage with their shields. Dramatically too it is more satisfying if, as in the case of Polyneices, the description of each attacker is answered not simply by another description but also by an actual champion with an answering shield device. Hyperbios' device provides the clue to what the devices of the remaining five might be. For each attacker one of the seven gods to whose statues the Chorus pray and make offerings in their opening song is as appropriate an opponent as Zeus is for Hippomedon. If each defender has on his shield one of these gods, Eteokles' prayer (336 / 266), "May the gods strengthen our men and direct our spears," is, in the most literal sense, enacted. As the time approaches for Eteokles to reveal his shield device, the presence of the image of Aphrodite, the only one of the seven gods not yet assigned to a shield, increases the irony and suspense. Symmetry would make her Eteokles' device, and the Chorus speak of lust (868 / 682) and desire (874 / 692–93). But Aphrodite remains unassigned. For the emblem of love and creation Eteokles substitutes the Fury (note to 895–96 / 709–11), the emblem of hatred and death—confirmation that, like Laios and Oedipus, he too can father only destruction. The Curse is still at work. The assignment of gods to shields, dictated by the attributes of the gods and the character of the warriors, as well as the device which each confronts, results in a meaningful symmetry: Ares, Athena, Poseidon, Zeus, Artemis, Apollo, Fury, with Zeus, the giver of Dike, in the center, Ares and the Fury, the implementers of the storm, framing the group, and the two pairs Athena/Poseidon and Artemis/Apollo in between.

459 / 377–78 *the gate of Proitos* On Proitos see note to 120 / 90. By naming the gate of Proitos first and repeating the name at the end of the speech (484 / 395–96) Aeschylus draws attention at the beginning of the scene to the roundness and whiteness, the resemblance to eyes that can cast evil spells, of the shields of the attackers. In addition, Tydeus' device, the moon, is actually referred to as "the eye of night" (475 / 390). The names and locations of the gates of Thebes were established by tradition, though there are minor variations from author to author. Aeschylus gives the seven gates with the captains attacking and defending them as follows:

1. *Proitides* (gate of Proitos)—Tydeus, Melanippos.
2. *Elektrai* (gate of Elektra)—Kapaneus, Polyphontes.
3. *Neïstai* (gate of Neïs)—Eteoklos, Megareus.
4. *Onkaiai* (gate of Athena Onka)—Hippomedon, Hyperbios.
5. *Borrhaiai* (Northern gate)—Parthenopaios, Aktor.
6. *Homoloides* (Homoloian gate)—Amphiaraos, Lasthenes.
7. Seventh gate, not given a name by Aeschylus, though elsewhere called *Hypsistai* or *Kreneiai*—Polyneices, Eteokles.
   The order is dramatic not geographical. The geographical order, proceeding clockwise from the northernmost point of the citadel, is *Borrhaiai* (5), *Proitides* (1), *Homoloides* (6), *Elektrai* (2), *Onkaiai* (4), the seventh gate (7), *Neïstai* (3).

461 / 378 *Ismenos* To cross the stream with an armed force would signal the opening of hostilities. The gods oppose this as sacrilege.

473 / 389 *the triple goddess of the three ways* This epithet is not in the Greek text. We have added it to make the allusion to Hekate more explicit. Hekate ("Diana of the Crossways") presides over the fork in the road, the place of fateful choice. For Aeschylus' audience the allusion to the moon would have been sufficient to suggest Hekate and the place "where three ways meet" (Introduction IV). Both Hekate and the moon express the enigmatic, changeable (threefold) nature of woman, and are closely associated in myth and cult with each other and with the Fury (Introduction II).

508 / 412 *seed of the dragon's teeth* Here and at 583 / 474, Aeschylus calls attention to the strife-torn origins of Thebans (Introduction II)—another hint that the springs of violence are inside as well as outside the city. To Tydeus, who expresses nothing but battle lust, the Ares on Melanippos' shield is a suitable answer, and his concentrated maleness is directed against the moon/Hekate, the embodiment of all female power, creative and destructive.

513 / 415 For Dike, see Introduction II and IV and Glossary.

530 / 429 *giant-slaying lightnings* This phrase renders the single Greek word *eris* (strife). According to a very probable suggestion, Aeschylus is here following Hesiod (*Theogony* 709–10), who used this word of the lightning which was Zeus' weapon in the war between the gods and giants. The Scout compares Kapaneus to one of these giants (523 / 424–25), and his emblem, a naked man with a flaming torch, recalls their primitive methods of warfare. In the battle with the gods, they relied on brute strength and such weapons as nature offered—enormous rocks, and torches made from trees.

557 / 449–50 The warrior Athena, who helped Zeus quell the giants, is frequently represented in the act of piercing a fallen giant with her spear (note on 158–63 / 128–34). She is the natural antagonist for giant-like Kapaneus and his shield device.

581 / 472 *and a certain apt fortune goes with him* Both Eteoklos, with his maddened horses, and the man on his shield hurl themselves against the walls of the city like a tidal wave. It is "apt fortune," therefore, that Poseidon, bridler of horses and tamer of the waves, is arrayed against them on the shield of Megareus. The description of Megareus standing firm in the storm of war (584–86 / 475–76) suggests Poseidon calming the storm.

598 / 486–87 The gate is named for the shrine of Athena Onka (a local cult name of unclear significance), which stood just outside the gate. Cf. the shrine of

Artemis outside the gate of Elektra (555–56 / 449–50) and the tomb of
Amphion outside the Northern gate (648 / 528).

601 / 489 *the enormous threshing-floor* This image alludes both to the roundness of the
shield, since the Greek threshing-floor is circular, and to the fecundity of
violence—a pervasive theme. See particularly 749–50 / 601.

625 / 508 Hermes is, among many other things, a god of luck or fortunate coincidence.

628 / 511 Typhon, earthborn like the giants, was more monstrous and more powerful
than they. (See Glossary.) Hippomedon seems to share some of the
monstrous quality of his shield device.

658–76 / 538–49 There is a fairly general feeling among editors that the line-order of this
passage as it appears in the MSS. is not correct. We have profited from their
arguments by producing a new line order, which seems to us to give the
speech a more coherent structure than do any of their suggestions.

661 / 539–40 The Sphinx (see Glossary) is another type of the mysterious threefold
female goddess (cf. note to 473 / 389). Like her, Parthenopaios is an
enigmatic combination of opposing qualities—resembling both a beautiful girl and a beast of prey. The threat of the Sphinx is answered
by Artemis who also expresses woman's multiple enigmatic nature.
As mistress of wild beasts and huntress, she is both the patron of
Parthenopaios, the wild animal of the Arcadian mountains, and the
one who will hunt him down (Introduction IV).

714–16 / 577–79 On the meaning of Polyneices' name see Introduction V.

734 / 589 "*The fate I expect is not without honor*" Amphiaraos knew the expedition
against Thebes was impious and doomed, but was tricked into joining it. As
a reward for his uprightness he was spared death in battle, the fate of the
other Argive leaders. During the fighting Zeus caused the earth to open
and swallow him up with his chariot and horses. (See Introduction IV.)

754 / 606 *When men lose their humanity* This expresses the pejorative meaning of the
adjective *echthroxenos* (literally, "hating strangers," i.e., violating the
laws of hospitality). At 770 / 621, Eteokles applies the same adjective as
a term of praise to Lasthenes, "who hates outsiders." This is one of the
many instances where Aeschylus exploits the ambiguities of language to
point up the fundamental similarity of attackers and defenders.

769–75 / 620–24 The blank shield of Amphiaraos expresses the refusal of all disguises, the commitment to truth of a seer and priest of Apollo, the god of truth and prophecy. In sending out Lasthenes, with Apollo on his shield, against him, Eteokles pits truth against truth, just as in confronting the Sphinx with Artemis he pits female enigma against female enigma.

805 / 646 Dike (see Introduction II and IV) now appears in visible form. Eteokles, in the first speech of this scene, has claimed her as an ally and blood-relative of the Thebans (**512–13 / 415–16**). Amphiaraos has denied that she can sanction violence against parents (**722–32 / 584–88**).

808 / 647 *"I shall bring this man to his harbor"* Aeschylus uses the same verb (*katagein*) here and at **827 / 660**. It means both "to lead down into Hades" and "to bring to shore." The shore that both brothers ultimately reach is in fact the shore of Hades (**1087–98 / 852–60**).

816–48 / 653–76 Eteokles confronts a triple enigma—his own name, his brother's name, and the name of Dike. He first links his name with weeping and then tries to deny the connection (Introduction V). He then reiterates Amphiaraos' interpretation of Polyneices' name (**714–16 / 557–79**), and finally decides to test in action whether Dike is fitly named.

847 / 675–76 *Quickly, bring my armor* In the Greek text, Eteokles calls not for his armor but for his greaves. In the arming scenes of Greek literature (note to **457–907 / 375–719**) the greaves are the first item that the hero puts on. To call for one's greaves is therefore the signal to begin arming. The order in which the other pieces of armor are assumed is also, with one minor variation, fixed—breastplate, sword, helmet, shield, spear. In contrast to the relatively small hoplite shield carried by Eteokles (he refers to himself as *hoplites*, "man in full armor," **905 / 717**), which was simply secured by two grips to the left arm and hand, the "man-covering shield" of Homeric epic was put on *before* the helmet, since it was anchored to the body by a strap that went over the head.

861–907 / 683–719 On Eteokles' preoccupation with fame in this passage, see Introduction V.

873 / 691 *Phoibos* The use of this epithet of Apollo, which means "the shining one," suggests that the race of Laios are not fit to see the light of day. Compare the description of their ultimate fate in **1087–98 / 852–60**.

885 / 700–701 *when the gods accept a sacrifice at your hands* The gods accept sacrifice only from ritually clean hands. The Chorus try to persuade Eteokles that purification is still possible since he has not yet shed kindred blood.

895–96 / 709 Eteokles' shield device must answer the shield device of Polyneices with a comparable and related force. The proper counterpart to Dike is her implementer the Fury, whose renewed onslaught Eteokles acknowledges as he takes his shield in hand. Since the Fury and Dike are two aspects of one cosmic order, their confrontation expresses a deadlock which only the death of both brothers can resolve.

897 / 710–11 *They were ... omens that came in dreams* This must refer to a prophetic dream in one of the earlier plays of the trilogy, whose real meaning only now becomes clear to Eteokles. Compare the dreams of Atossa in *Persians* and Clytemnestra in *Libation Bearers*.

898 / 711 *split by an iron sword* Iron, which was imported from the region north of the Black Sea (Scythia, Chalybia), and Ares, who is associated with the neighboring region of Thrace, become identified in the following song, and are used interchangeably throughout the rest of the play to represent the just divider and apportioner of the inheritance (920–26 / 727–33 and 1039–40 / 815–17, 1129 / 883–84, 1150–58 / 906–14, 1191–96 / 941–46). In this scene, Eteokles is turned into iron ("man in full armor"), the remorseless instrument of justice. He becomes the embodiment of Ares.

946 / 747 *the midmost Pythian navel* Apollo's shrine at Delphi, reputed to be the navel of earth. Woman is the ultimate source of this enigmatic pronouncement, as she is of the other enigmas that confront the race of Laios.

968–69 / 758–60 The threefold wave alludes, among other things, to the three generations of the house of Laios (Introduction IV).

1009 / 791 *the fleet-footed Fury* Like her inability to weep or sleep, the Fury's swiftness of foot is proverbial. The transgressor cannot move her to pity, or hide from her all-seeing eye, or run fast enough to escape her overtaking stride.

1018 / 800–801 *Apollo, the holy Lord of Sevens* See note on 154–57 / 124–26.

1022–43 / 803–21 That the line order of this passage is not correct in our MSS. is clear from the fact that line 1030 of our version occurs twice—as line 804 of the Greek text, the second line of the passage, and again as line 820, the next to the last line of the passage. In the MSS., the passage ends, "The city is safe, but the two kings of one blood / have spilled their shared stream out, earth has drunk up / the blood of their mutual slaughter" (820–21 of the Greek text). The repeated line is connected by sense and syntax with the line that follows it at the end of the passage, but not in any necessary way with the line that precedes it there. It makes nonsense of the sequence of thought at the beginning of the passage. Editors have called either for drastic rearrangement of the line order of the whole passage, combined with elimination of one occurrence of the repeated line, or for elimination of various blocks of lines, including one or both occurrences of the repeated line, on the assumption that the repetition is the result of the conflation of the original text with the work of a fourth-century interpolator. Our solution is simpler. It removes only one line, and transposes only two. If the repeated line is removed from the beginning where it clearly does not belong, the pattern of the exchange between Chorus and Scout becomes clear. By their questions and exclamations, the Chorus, who guess what has happened, finally induce the Scout to announce the news that both they and he find almost too horrible to put into words. This information, contained in the lines quoted above, belongs not at the end of the passage, after the news it conveys has already been commented on, but where we have put it, after the Chorus' last demand, "Go on; speak your heavy things."

1044–1280 / 822–1004 The lament: Some, but not all, of the editors who regard the final scene as an interpolation consider the participation of Antigone and Ismene in the lament and the lines that the Chorus address to them (**1099–1117** / 861–74) as part of the interpolation (see note on **1099–1117** / 861–74 and Introduction III).

1046–50 / 825–28 The Chorus build into the lament a victory song of Hades, Ate; and the Curses (**1111** / 868–69, **1208–16** / 953–60). Since the city has been, at least temporarily, delivered by the triumph of these forces, to lament the deaths of Eteokles and Polyneices is to celebrate the victory of the city.

1060 / 836 *like a Maenad* The followers of Dionysos improvise songs and dances in a state of ecstatic possession by the god of life and creativity. But the Chorus' ecstatic song celebrates death, not life (compare **612–13** / 497–98). The victory song, which is also a lament (see note to **1046–50** / 825–28), involves a similar inversion.

1087–98 / 854–60 Another ritual is alluded to here, and inverted. The language that describes the ship suggests the sacred ship of Apollo that the Athenians annually sent to the island of Delos on the anniversary of Theseus' victory over the Minotaur—a victory that saved seven youths and seven maidens from being sacrificed to the monster. The sacred ship went to Delos (the name means "clearly visible"), Apollo's shore, in commemoration of a rescue; the "black-sailed ship of grief" goes to the "unseen" shore, "untrodden by Apollo." For the transfer of ship imagery from the city to the house of Laios, see note to 2–3 / 2–3.

1099–1117 / 861–74 Editors who regard the participation of Antigone and Ismene in the lament as the work of an interpolator bracket these lines, and give the lines attributed to Antigone and Ismene to semi-choruses.

1113 / 872 *the menstrual pulse* The Greek text refers not to menstruation, but to a piece of female dress with which a modern audience is not familiar—the band that restrained the breasts. The purpose of the allusion is to emphasize the common femininity of the Chorus and Antigone and Ismene—their sisterhood in grief.

1332–33 / 1038–39 *drag him . . . folds of my cloak* We read this passage as a reference to the tradition that Antigone dragged the body of Polyneices in her robe to Eteokles' funeral pyre. Pausanias (IX.25,2) refers to a monument that marked the place of "Antigone's dragging." The Greek is ambiguous. According to some, what Antigone carries in the folds of her robe is earth to sprinkle on the corpse of Polyneices, so that he will have token burial. This is the version that Sophocles follows (or invented?) in *Antigone*.

1352–53 / 1051 *Last of the gods . . . the last word* In the MSS., where these words (one line in the Greek) follow 1349 / 1050, the sequence of thought from 1349 to the end of the passage is, as many editors have noted, somewhat jumbled. If they are moved to the end of the passage, where we have put them, they provide a fitting commentary on the whole episode, and the three preceding lines follow naturally one from the other.

SUPPLIANTS

Translated by

JANET LEMBKE

INTRODUCTION

I

Aeschylus' *Suppliants* is a stepchild in the house of surviving Greek tragedy: a beautiful but intractable bundle of contradictions that have prompted perplexity and argument. The play has therefore been tucked away and put to work in academic chimneycorners. It has admirers among scholars, yes, but few students of drama and fewer everyday readers encounter it. It deserves better.

Yet, it is not an easy play. The many lyrics have been acclaimed, justly, as the loveliest of all tragic lyrics, but an eighteenth-century translator described the play as "fraught with fine poetry and pious sentiment, but on the whole a drama devoid of nice art in its construction and a tragedy without a tragical conclusion." Then, the play's language is opulent, but the stage action implied by the words—no stage directions ever accompanied the play proper—seems so meager that some modern critics have thought of *Suppliants* as an oratorio rather than a theater piece. The feelings expressed by the lyrics are profoundly religious, but the myths informing them are fabulous, exotic, cruel, and repellent.

The play's construction also presents problems. It has been termed archaic and even primitive. Choral odes are uniquely predominant, commanding more than half the present text. The story seems to call not for the classic twelve-member chorus but for a stage-filling crowd of fifty suppliant women, each with an attendant maid. No one knows how many Suppliants actually appeared on stage, but however large the Chorus, its role is that of a single protagonist.

For these and other purely internal reasons of structure and style, *Suppliants* was long believed to be truly archaic, a not quite classical work that reached pastward to tragedy's lost antecedents for its form. And it was long thought to be the oldest tragedy extant, composed and presented perhaps as early as 490 B.C. It would thus have preceded *Persians* (472) by almost two decades and the *Oresteia* (458) by more than thirty years. The play seemed, therefore, the work of a young poet whose skills and dramatic imagination were still green. Recent evidence, however, supports a date in the last decade of Aeschylus' seventy years. *Persians* now lays fair claim to seniority.

That evidence merits a few words, for its discovery is an example of the kind of miracle scholars pray for but are seldom granted. In Egypt, appropriately, a papyrus fragment was found. Its publication in 1952 struck classicists with the force of Zeus' customary weapon, for it bears external information on *Suppliants'* date. It declares, in a widely accepted reconstruction of time-eroded words, that a tetralogy by Aeschylus—the tragic trilogy of which *Suppliants* is the first member and a concluding satyr-drama, *Amymone*—took first prize in a dramatic competition and defeated a group of plays by Sophocles. And the fragment mentions the name of the archon then presiding in Athens. The dates for these magistrates are established. *Suppliants'* production is thus placed no earlier than 466 and most likely in 463.*

This new information in no way explained the play's unusual features. It provoked instead a host of prickly questions. Was the play a bit of juvenilia pulled out of storage? If so, why was it produced decades after it was written? If not, its archaism must have been intentional. Why then did the mature poet reach deep into the past for his form? Barring future miracles, there may never be an end to argument.

Nor is the conflict between internal archaism and late date the only source of argument. Many of the play's tensions are obvious: male–female, barbarian–Hellene, private interest–public welfare, chastity–marriage, and fantasy–reality. But the play's fifth-century implications can only be guessed at. Did it celebrate the establishment of a women's festival or support women's rights? Did it comment obliquely on Athens' relations with Egypt and Argos? The play's theme is also elusive. Is it the inscrutability of Zeus' mind that in its perfect stillness moves to order the universe? Is it the clash between manmade law and the laws of heaven? Is it perhaps a cautionary defense of marriage? Opinions bristle; nothing is proved. The present text is corrupt, and attempts at interpretation are made triply difficult by the loss of the two plays, *Egyptians* and *Danaids*, that followed *Suppliants* and brought its story to a conclusion. It is as if *Agamemnon*—an

---

* *Oxyrhynchus Papyri*, xx (1952), 2256, fr. 3. For a thorough discussion of its possible reconstructions and interpretations, I am indebted to A. F. Garvie, *Aeschylus' "Supplices": Play and Trilogy* (Cambridge University Press, 1969), pp. 1–28.

Agamemnon robbed by time of its climactic murder—were all that survived of the *Oresteia*. Agreement exists only on these points: *Suppliants'* lyrics are numinous, and its substance almost as inscrutable as Zeus.

But the scholars' arguments do identify the questions that challenge any new translation. Is the play tragic? (Are there tints and shades of tragedy, fractions of tragedy?) Then, what is the play about? And are the play's peculiarities dictated by dramatic necessity? Ancient Greeks, like Delphic oracles, are not available for consultation. The answers found must be answers that work here and now without slighting the play's antique strangeness.

II

Suppliants' physical plot is uncomplicated. The story takes place in the prehistoric Greek past. The scene is set near the city of Argos. The orchestra, where the Chorus enters and dances while singing the odes, represents a shore. The raised stage behind the orchestra is a sanctuary crowded with images of gods—Zeus, Apollo, Poseidon, Hermes—and one altar common to them all. Enter the Danaids, the fifty virgin daughters of Danaos. Each carries a fresh-cut branch, the traditional symbol of suppliance. In Greek custom the suppliant petitioned from a shrine or sanctuary for asylum. At the moment of taking up the branch its bearer came under the jealous protection of the gods. Zeus, above all others, was thought to be the special guardian of those who sought asylum. In this role he was invoked as Zeus Suppliant. The epithet defines his protective function; there is no implication that the god himself was a suppliant. If asylum was granted to the petitioner, it was held to be a god-enforced, inviolable right.

The Suppliants immediately make it known that they are terrified fugitives from the land of Nile. They have fled marriage to their violently lustful cousins, the fifty sons of their father's brother Aigyptos (Egypt). At this very moment the would-be bridegrooms are swarming in swift-sailed pursuit. In a long choral ode (50–201 / 40–175) the Suppliants give thanks for safe arrival in Argos and express fear that their troubles are not yet ended. At the ode's conclusion their father enters and cautions them to take refuge in the sanctuary. Urging them to be calm, he warns that an explanation of their presence in Argos will soon be called for by the armed delegation now approaching. On its arrival the maidens ask the leader, Pelasgos king of Argos, to receive them as suppliants and they claim ancestral ties to his country. The petition presents Pelasgos with a choice of evils. If sanctuary is refused, the gods, offended by such sacrilege, will surely punish Argos. But if the Suppliants are sheltered, war with Egypt is a certainty, for the Egyptians do seem to have a valid legal claim upon the women. In either event the Argive people will suffer. The king's indecision and anguish are clear, but he is given direction by the Suppliants' threat to hang themselves from the images of the gods. And he agrees to put the case before the citizens, whose vote by Argive law must be final arbiter. He sends Danaos into the city to put branches on the temple altars and thus make the presence of suppliants known to the populace. After promising to speak to the people on their behalf, he, too, departs. The Danaids, now alone on the shore, sing and pray. As they deliver their most heartfelt praise of Zeus the Allfather, their own father re-enters with the glad news that the citizens' vote was affirmative. While the Danaids bless the Argive land and people in another ode (861–942 / 625–709), he climbs to the sanctuary, a vantage point from which he soon sights the Egyptian ships. Though he tries to reassure his daughters by saying that it takes time to moor a fleet, they are terrified. But, telling them that the gods protect them, Danaos leaves to muster help. The women's fears are not unjustified. Before help arrives, an Egyptian herald and a troop of armed men come ashore. The herald orders the Suppliants shipward. When words fail to move them, he uses force. But in the nick of time Pelasgos enters with soldiers. The herald makes war-talk but departs. Pelasgos asks the Suppliants to let him escort them to the city, but when they refuse to leave the sanctuary without their father, he, too, departs. Danaos soon returns with an honor guard of spearmen. And, to the singing of a recessional ode (1345–1422 / 1018–73), *exeunt omnes* to the city.

But that is merely the play's immediate action. There is a superplot that takes place in the remote past. Throughout the play, the Suppliants sing the story of the princess Io, their four-times-great grandmother, whose Argive birth reinforces their claim to asylum. Io, keeper of the keys to Hera's temple, attracted the attention of Zeus and was transformed by the ever-jealous goddess into a cow guarded by Argos, the thousand-eyed watchman. But Hera's precautions did not avail. Hermes slew Argos, and Zeus, lusting still, turned himself into an amorous bull. Hera again attempted to put an end to her consort's dalliance by sending a gadfly to torment Io. To escape its merciless stinging Io fled from the very shore on which the Suppliants stand. Maddened by pain, she swam the sea and galloped over Asia until, circling southward, she came to the land of Nile, where she fell exhausted in a meadow sacred to Zeus. There he again visited her and restored her to human form by breathing upon her and touching her. By his divine breath and touch alone she conceived and bore a son, Epaphos, whose name means touch or caress. The Suppliants see Io's sufferings as parallel to theirs, and they hope for a release as gentle as hers. At play's end it seems that this hope may be realized, for Argos has accepted and promised to defend them.

Plot and superplot are linked by more than apparently parallel action. There is an interweaving of rich thematic images. Over and again the Io-cow and the Zeus-bull are evoked in other contexts. The Suppliants see themselves as a driven herd and compare their plight to that of a lost heifer harried by wolves. They pray for the fertility of Argive herds and sing of pastures and refer to brideprices paid in cattle by the Egyptians. The touch of Zeus also rests on the play. His palm, his caress, his unbruising fist are hymned in continuing counterpoint to the seizure by rough hands that the Suppliants fear. His breath, too, blows change-fully throughout as breeze and wind and hurricane. And Hera's gadfly achieves hideous new life in the "manswarm," the "wingèd horde," of Egyptians.

Other recurrent images serve to give the play integrity. Its air is filled with the rush of wings: hawks, a nightingale, carrion crows, vultures. The Suppliants cry out in "birdvoices," pain nowhere shows "the selfsame feather," and the very gaze of Zeus becomes a bird, alighting on rooftops and staining them as it perches. The play's earth is endlessly fertile: flowers, fruit, grasses, grain. The verbs of procreation are those used specifically for planting and sowing. The Egyptians are sprouts on an old vine, Danaos compares his daughters to succulent summerfruit, and Zeus "plants the lifepulse in green nature." And Earth's dust is con-stantly refreshed by sweet water: Nile, Io's fathering river, Argos' rivers that curl redgold toward the sunset, and its sun-oiled streams.

But where is tragedy? Though interlocking themes and pervasive imagery give the play a coherence of its own, it is not truly self-supporting. The plot finds no ultimate resolution. Little is known about the two lost plays, but mythographers have recounted the Danaid legend often enough so that we have a few of the details that must have shaped subsequent action, though they may not have been shown directly on stage. In their light *Suppliants* appears to be the prelude to tragedy.

The Egyptians did come, conquer, and claim their brides. On the wedding night, at Danaos' behest, all but one of the bridegrooms were stabbed to death. (The surviving couple, Hypermestra and Lynkeus, began a line notable for Zeus-luring daughters: Danaë, mother of Perseus who was conceived in the god's golden rain, and Alkmēnē on whom he fathered Herakles by assuming her husband's shape. But neither of these beguiling ladies takes part in the Danaids' story.)

Careful opinion holds that a trial figured in the trilogy's development. Murder was, of course, a polluting offense against men and gods. But so were vow-breaking and filial disobedience on the part of the daughter who swore to kill but spared her husband. It was apparently she who was tried and found innocent. It seems, too, that Aphrodite intervened on her behalf. A magnificent seven-line fragment from the trilogy's last play is logically given to the goddess. It celebrates sexual love and its object, reproduction, by praising the divine marriage of Earth and Sky. That wedding, sacred and fruitful, provides the cosmic model for mankind. And it must not be questioned.

No one knows what fate, if any, Aeschylus visited upon the murdering daughters. Legend says that they did eventually marry and that after their deaths they were eternally condemned to the task of carrying water in sieved jars. These late events are not at all likely to have figured in the trilogy.

Amymone, the lost satyr-play that followed the trilogy's performance, seems to have concerned itself with a lighter episode in the Danaids' lives. Danaos sent his daughters, Amymone among them, to find water. The quest appeared to be futile, for Poseidon, angry at Argos, had at that time dried every known spring, river, and pond. As the Danaids searched, Amymone threw a dart at a deer and struck a satyr, who immediately assaulted her. As she attempted to fend off his shaggy advances, Poseidon appeared, routed the satyr, and promptly thereafter carried out the satyr's lustful intentions on his own behalf. In fee he revealed to Amymone an unfailing source of water, the spring at Lerna.

III

Though the Greeks saw *Suppliants* as tragic in the context of its trilogy and said as much when they awarded Aeschylus first prize, it is not enough to accept their judgment. We cannot see the play as they did. The music, dances, and masks are irretrievably lost, and the ambience of performance. Only the verbifact endures, and it is no longer perfect. If the play is ever again to be perceived as more than a curiosity, it must by itself move emotions here and now. If it is to find new dramatic vigor, the one surviving element, the broken text, must contain an intrinsic something that withstands time travel and culture shock: a psychological plot that links its antiquity to our present moment. I have reread *Suppliants* as presenting a particular account of a timeless human occasion, an occasion that recurs constantly and is not itself changed—however much human responses to it do vary and change—by shifts in landscape, religion, law, customs, language, and notions of what drama and poetry are.

Enter the Suppliants, not fifty but twelve. They are drenched to the knees because they have just waded ashore from a boat. They are black because Nile's sun has looked upon them, and they are comely—bodies as curved and tempting as fruit ready to be picked, faces reflecting the fierce independence of desert nomads, clothes glittering with barbarous splendor, breasts bare. They are virgins of an age to marry. How old is that? Their father addresses them as children and girls, but they speak of themselves, and the king addresses them, as women. And indeed they are women fullgrown, the youngest provocatively nubile, the eldest middle-aged, perhaps greying, but still full of female juices. They are ripe and overripe for husbands and children.

But they will NOT marry (12–13 / 8–9):

> Agree to marry Egypt's sons unthinkable!
> skin shudders the unholy thought

Later, in a chilling lament (1027–98 / 776–824), they cry that they would rather be taken by death than forced to wed. And why not marry, when marriage is expected of all women? The reason given is that Egypt's sons are violent and marriage would give them license for repeated sexual brutality. Again and again the Suppliants mention Egyptian *hybris*, a word that signifies an arrogance that blinds its possessor to the might of the gods and makes him aspire to more than human status. In fifth-century Athens *hybris* was also a technical legal term meaning "rape." In the context of *Suppliants* it has been translated as "lust." For a reason to be given later, I think it cannot be simply "rape" or "lust," though it bears those emanations when it is applied to the Egyptians. I have instead translated it with various compounds using the key syllable "self-"—self-vaunting, self-serving, self-blindness, self-glory, self-love.

The Suppliants' desperation is extreme. Rather than marry Egypt's sons, who are in fact brutal and motivated by selfish lust, they have chosen secret flight. And when they appeal to the king for protection, they make it plain that if their god-honored suppliance is refused, they will choose a god- and man-shocking form of suicide—hanging themselves from the images of the gods. It is as if, in another day, they had threatened so to use a crucifix or the tablets of the holy ark.

At first the refusal to marry and the threat sound like the polemics of a women's liberation movement, the Suppliants raising their branches like fists clenched for self-determination. But no, it is soon clear that they expect the course of their collective life to be determined by others—their father, the king, the gods. And they have used past events, the Io-history, as predictions of their future. So often have they called to mind Io's agony and deliverance that they have come to think of it as their own experience not yet fully lived out. What was, shall be. They feel, they *know* that they, too, deserve to be gently freed from their trials. In justification of their refusal to marry they often cite *dikē*, the basic principle of natural order and rightness, the laws of heaven. They *know* that divine law sanctions their behavior. In the play's moment, however, they are panicky refugees who cannot read how far into the future their trials will last.

I read their beliefs as false. The Suppliants have mistaken terrified hope for preordination. They do little to save themselves but pray and threaten and curse, sometimes hysterically, while they wait for touch and breath. Their very panic, however, suggests that they do sense something amiss. They are, after all, suppliants begging for sanctuary in the name of Zeus and requesting human help, force if necessary, against the pursuing Egyptians. And until help shall come from gods and men, they defend themselves with a shield of fantasy, a dream of deliverance absolutely promised, that blocks their recognition of plain facts: time is irreversible, no one goes home.

The Suppliants' psychological predicament may be read, here and now, as a primeval variation of the Beauty and the Beast story. In its classic resolution the virgin Beauty at last leaves her father's house and accepts the Beast for the goodness of spirit concealed within his grotesque body and thereby also accepts, according to modern interpreters, the forever-joined contradictions that exist in all life: evil–goodness, ugliness–grace, animal urge–human will. She thus attains true womanhood and finds her own humanity of spirit. But the Suppliants' story is unresolved. Though in body they are grown women, they steadfastly reject the Egyptian "Beasts" and continue to live, archetypal victims of a father fixation, in their father's house. The play, moreover, asks an important question about the identity of that father. Is he the physical, human father Danaos? Or is he Zeus the Father, who as Io's lover was male parent of the Suppliants' line? The play begins with an invocation to Zeus "Father Protector" and soon turns to the Suppliants' "father on earth, heart's guide and guide for our footsteps" (14–15 / 11–12). By play's last third the word "father" is used twice in an ambiguous vocative that can refer to either one (1081 / 811 and 1173 / 885). At play's end the two are inextricably confused, and there are strong suggestions that the Suppliants harbor an unrecognized incestuous desire. If their release from suffering is truly to parallel Io's, this desire is insanely reasonable.

But the play deals with matters larger than problems of the female psyche. Marriage is not the critical issue. Nor are the Suppliants motivated by anything as narrow as fear of Egyptian brutality or a personal aversion to cousin-marriage, which Greek law permitted and sometimes mandated in the statutes declaring that fatherless daughters were bound to marry their next-of-kin. A father could so pledge his daughters before his death. Nor were the Suppliants driven, as has been surmised, by an inborn pathological loathing of all men or an inability to come to terms with their own sexuality. The rejection of marriage and the women's stubborn, childish, father-abetted fantasy are the play's metaphors for a refusal to assume adulthood. That refusal is, I believe, the cornerstone of the play's psychological plot. Of course, it is not a play just about women. Its specifics point to the general occasion that links its world with ours. The occasion is coming of age. And coming of age certainly means more than learning to live with sexuality. It means making a contract with one's society, even if the contract is some-times sealed with a resounding NO. It means reaching voluntarily and hopefully toward the unknowable future and trying to shape it. It has meant (till very recent attempts to limit population on a large scale) a millennia-long commitment to ensure human survival through the birth of new generations. It still means putting away the child's way of thinking that confounds metaphor with literal meaning and sees the childself as the center of the universe. Two resolutions are possible for the Suppliants: death or love. In the play's own terms: an insanely murderous defense of childishness or growing up. And here, surely, is tragedy—deeprooted and impossible desire set against inexorable biological, social, and psycho-logical necessity.

And what of Io, both Beauty and the Beast in one person? She and Zeus himself are invisible actors in the psychodrama, and it is their impalpable presences that enlarge the play by giving it a past and infusing its mortal moment with eternity. But Io's history that so encompasses and perme-ates the play should be a dreadful warning to her granddaughters. Until mid-play she is described flatly as girl or cow or mother. She is a person or animal referred to, remote and fabulous. Then, the Suppliants sing her story from beginning to end (684–813 / 524–599), and in the singing Io-sung appears. It is as if she is actually present, a figure as real as the Suppliants themselves. Flystung, stampeded, she "hurls her body down Asia toward unreachable sunrise." Valleys fall behind her, mountains rise in her footsteps as her mad flight transforms a continent. She is an

> undreamed apparition
>   grasseater, flyblown
> patchflesh halfhuman
> There
>   and there
>   she is cow
> and here
>   still woman lowing and marvelous

The people who see her are appalled; their hearts skip beats, they cannot help staring. Her shape is woman's but she is horned and patches of hair disfigure her skin like angry new grafts and her hands are hoofs, she must lie on the ground to feed. Hers is no natural cowness but the sign of an inward horror. There is a monstrously egocentric child inhabiting her mind and heart; it breaks through, begins to consume her. And she cannot be transfigured till she—*she*, not a god—releases that childself and turns futureward, a woman whole, full of the breath of life and touched by faith, hope, and confidence.

Her story is that of the Suppliants resolved on a divine level, the gentle, momentary fusion of mortal flesh and immortal spirit. The Suppliants believe, however, that Io remained virginal throughout her love affair. Or rather, they try not to disbelieve; they firmly reject Pelasgos' suggestions that Io and Zeus were entangled in the usual manner of man and woman and that their son's conception was something less than virginal. But their most secret feelings about that ancestral coupling slip out when they refer to it in words overtly reserved for the Egyptians: "force" and "seizure." The Suppliants nevertheless fail consistently, tragically, to read the lesson in Io's metamorphoses: that to persist in childishness is to become less than human.

And what of the Egyptians, Io's four-times-great grandsons? They appear like dogs, like spiders and vipers in a black dream out of Egypt. The women have fled them not so much because virginity is imperiled, marriage repugnant, and Egypt's sons violently lustful, but because the sons are also Io's children, the darkside of her moon. Whatever true legal claims they have to the Suppliants, their animal-like desires surely defy the laws of nature and natural order. Nor can they control the forces of humanity and bestiality that war within them. They are threatened by the same end—to lose all human qualities, to become animals irretrievably—that awaits the Suppliants should they persist in their flight, which is a flight not merely from marriage beds but from the demanding realities of life. Again, the Suppliants seem to sense the potential for wrong in their attitude. They resist the Egyptians, and that resistance is a last-ditch survival tactic, a gut reaction, to protect their own humanity. But marry the Egyptians, marry them not, the women are ironically doomed by their own *hybris*. The word they hurl at the Egyptians turns on them. Self-vaunting self-glory, self-righteous self-interest are their own blinding characteristics. They are damned unless they, like Io, can perform an act of self-transfiguration.

What is the nature of these women? The usual view has been that they are sweet, amiable, plaintive, modest, brimming with filial piety; that they personify virtue as the Egyptians personify evil. Vaporous Victorian maidens? Hardly. They are passionate, they are fierce, they tremble with barely suppressed sexual appetites. Their language is the language of thwarted fertility; it teems with genital symbols—flowers, rivers. Two of their many odes contain elaborate curses, one directed against Pelasgos (535–64 / 418–37), the other against the Egyptians (1120–68 / 843–81). Two odes are laments (50–201 / 40–175 and 1027–98 / 776–825), though, as they admit in the former:

> ... rites for the dead
> in fair times when death is a stranger
> surge godward bearing a bloodcurse.

They are as amiable as streams in spate, as innocent as murder. It is no wonder that Pelasgos, the model of reason, cannot easily decide to welcome them, however much he first admires what he thinks is the dauntless courage that brought them to his shore. The confrontation between Suppliants and king unfolds like a trial (426–517 / 348–406); they are at once petitioners and prosecutors, and he, somehow defendant and unwilling judge. At play's beginning the Suppliants are already spinning down into madness and dehumanization, a fate that is slowly made clear in piling references to defilement, murder, and death. In the opening lines of the play they protest their innocence, "Leaving it [Egypt] we flew, not outlaws hounded publicly for murder's blood on our hands, but fugitives ...." The protestation is an oracle: there shall be blood and death.

Yet the Suppliants are to be pitied. Though they have not understood their plight, their hope for deliverance and their fear are heart-breakingly real. Their prayers are heartfelt. Transfiguration is indeed imperative, but circumstances have not yet presented an appropriate means of release. Marriage is destiny in the Suppliants' world; not to marry is a violation of *dikē*. The Suppliants are caught in a dilemma. And, menaced by crude and loathsome cousins, they are at the mercy of strangers. Their father, "heart's guide," does in every way prompt their ultimately murderous intransigence.

Danaos' role in *Suppliants* has puzzled many critics. His part, in contrast to that of Pelasgos, has seemed naïvely written, and his presence nearly superfluous except when he assumes duties usually assigned to the tragic chorus, which the Chorus here cannot perform, taking as it does an actor's part. As quasi-chorus Danaos advises and chides and reports the offstage action—the citizens' affirmative vote, the arrival of the Egyptian fleet—that further stage action. (It is suggestive, though probably not significant, that in this two-actor tragedy the actor who played Danaos also took the Egyptian herald's role.) Danaos has most often been seen as a kindly old soul motivated by nothing other than genuine paternal concern for his daughters' well-being. How can such a man be father to insanity? How indeed?

I see him enter not when he first speaks (**202** / 176) but when he is first mentioned (**14** / 11). Bent and ancient, he comes in silence, mounts the place of gods, and assumes a silhouetted attitude of prayer. In his shadow-stillness it is as if he is become a god, listening. Soon he hears his daughters tell the eerie story of a woman changed into a nightingale and kept from rest in her "green leafrivers." As she flies, hawk-pursued, she sings her home- and heartsickness, and (**76–79** / 64–67)

> ...the notes spill old tears with new
>   as she sings her son's doom:
> he was killed and she by her
> own hand's anger unmothered.

The Suppliants are most obviously comparing the nightingale's flight and grief-song with their own; in the next verse they say, "My human voice is also sorrow's friend." But what extraordinary, what monstrous prophecy! However unwittingly, the women have also compared themselves to a murderess, a filicide. After this play's end they shall at their father's command kill the Egyptians and kill as well a chance to bear children. They shall sever themselves from the life-continuum. And at the moment of singing the murderess they must feel in a deep, unacknowledged corner of their souls that their father is also killing their own capacity to act as godly human beings. At one point Danaos even seems to identify himself with Zeus; he speaks of his own gazing eye (**946** / 713) with the Greek word used elsewhere for deity's vigilant gaze (**476** / 380, **877–78** / 646–47, **1046** / 786). The play has a madman, and it is Danaos, author of his daughters' lives and their plight and their deepening insanity. He, more than the Egyptians, is villain. He, too, is Io's son.

His absolute power over his daughters is made clear from the play's beginning. And as the play unfolds, it is his counsel that repeatedly urges them to reject society's expectations and to suppress their quite natural sexual stirrings. Even after it seems that the women, accepted as refugees, will be saved from forced marriage to the Egyptians, he admonishes them, saying, in a final speech that borders on the salacious, that they are like succulent summerfruit and that their voluptuousness will inevitably entice men. "Do not shame me," he warns. "Guard a father's commandments; love your chastity more than your lives." He will not have them marry anyone. Why not?

The play does not offer reasons that will satisfy a modern audience. But myth does, and an ancient audience might well have known them, though such knowledge would not necessarily have enhanced fifth-century appreciation of the trilogy. The myth appears in many conflicting versions, but one detail common to them all is that Danaos quarreled with his brother Egypt. Some versions give an immediate sequel to the quarrel: Egypt suggested reconciliation and as proof of good faith offered his sons as husbands for Danaos' daughters; when Danaos refused the suit, Egypt vowed to kill him and his daughters. In that vow alone there is motive enough for the flight from Egypt. Danaos has cause to fear the Egyptians as much as the Suppliants do, for his own skin is at stake. Several versions also add that before Danaos left the land of Nile, an oracle had told him that his son-in-law would kill him. Thus, while there is only one threat to his daughters' lives, Danaos is twice-menaced, by his brother's known hand and the hand of a nameless son-in-law. To save himself he encourages his daughters' tragic dependence and drives them to a lunatic fear of marriage and sexuality. Later, the mass marriage accomplished, it is his command that thrusts the knives into Egyptian hearts.

Pelasgos' role counterpoints that of Danaos. The two have been seen as playing somewhat similar parts, that of the Protector and that of the Parent. But as Egyptian maleness and force are antithetical to the Suppliants' femininity and weakness, so Pelasgos and Danaos represent opposites. There is an obvious black and white difference in appearance; Danaos comments (**652** / 497–98): "Nile and Io's fathering river, each nurtures its own race." And their characters are as dissimilar as their skins. Pelasgos looks outward to law and reason for solutions to the problems presented by the Suppliants; Danaos consults inner experience. Pelasgos acts out of consistent concern for the public good; Danaos, out of self-interest. Granted that the Suppliants' world is a patriarchal one in which women were usually subject to men's wishes, still Pelasgos makes suggestions to them and solicits their understanding; Danaos dictates. Pelasgos stands on the side of peace and life; Danaos brings with him an unbreakable promise of war and death.

But at play's end not one drop of blood has been spilt. In the concluding ode (**1345–1422** / 1019–1173) ambiguous notes are sounded, portending grief to come. The Suppliants, leaving for their new home, laud the country and its gods in a recessional literally overflowing with sexual imagery:

> No more shall we sing hymns to quell Nile
>> spilling its siltflood into the sea
> Sing praise to rivers that rise here
>> and thrust through homefields

the sun-oiled streams
 that here shed their pleasurous waters
 to sweeten the dust of the mother Earth
and fulfill her with life upon life.

In the very next breath, however, madness cries to Artemis, goddess of chastity, "Help us withstand the womb's need for fullness that opens virgins to Aphrodite's act."

They are immediately rebuked. The next lyrics have been given by one scholar, at least, to the honor guard of spearmen accompanying Danaos; most critics believe, however, that they are to be assigned to a sub-chorus of Egyptian ladies-in-waiting who came ashore with the Suppliants and now, after a thousand lines of silence, burst into song. The words do seem most appropriately spoken by women. And I think that it is more dramatically effective, here and now, to put them in the mouths of Argive women, brought from the city by Danaos to attend his daughters. These servants are not able to accept the Suppliants' repudiation of woman's proper social role:

But Aphrodite is not slighted here
 nor do her rites lack eager celebrants...
And she is thanked, guile-dazzling
 goddess, for her solemn games.

And the Suppliants are warned that they may claim no special grace from heaven. They answer with a cry to Zeus that he deliver them as he delivered Io, though they are ready to admit that the final triumph they ask for may not be entirely favorable to them. But partial victory is better than none at all: "Better the half-light than utter dark." They have in their own minds behaved with guiltless obedience to heaven's laws; they are certain in their fantasy that they must be rewarded with heaven's benevolent attention.

To us who have not learned our myths in the cradle, the play falls on its back, not on its feet. We have been prepared for storms, but nothing happens. The actors depart, the play is over. The psychological tensions—forecast horrors, slowly piled thunderheads of coming violence—linger undissipated. Members of the antique audience would have known full well that darkness would almost totally eclipse the Suppliants. But, unacquainted with the story and hampered by the loss of the plays that swept the trilogy to its end, we are left unsatisfied with an empty stage.

From the second play, *Egyptians*, one word of Dionysiac ecstasy is left. From the third, *Danaids*, there survive two solidly attested fragments, a three-line excerpt referring to wedding customs and the earlier-mentioned benediction spoken in praise of marriage and fertility. Scholarly research has also assigned several one-line fragments to *Danaids*, and a few Aeschylean lines not attributed to specific plays seem as if they could have been fatherly maxims spoken by Danaos. I have combined all of these into a postlude that carries the Suppliants to their storm's end; it will be found in the section entitled "On the Translation."

IV

There are no hard facts of literary history to account for *Suppliants'* structural peculiarities, such as the preponderance of lyrics and the Chorus as protagonist. But if the text is read as an account of an occasion, coming of age, that has been immemorially ritualized, like the occasions of child-naming and marrying and dying, then the drama may play out in imagination like a rite of passage. Procession of ode and episode, the structure suggests the solemn public patterns of liturgy, patterns meant in themselves to evoke a sense of the sacred, patterns that seem to echo the lost rituals of a strictly choral type of pre-tragedy. Introit through recessional to the last lovely benediction sung by the goddess, the play's real drama is as invisible as transubstantiation. It should enact itself within players–audience–lone reader like a gale, like a god's breath, buffeting everyone with ritually worked changes of feeling, great leaps from hope to sorrow and terror to hope again.

It is not of course a rite. It never was. Rite deals with the desire for continuity in human life; tragedy with breaks in the relationships between men and men, men and their gods. But *Suppliants* can be seen as a piece of ritual theater that combines the patterned emotional transformations of rite with a kinetic visual experience, no matter that the experience may now be one solely for mind's eye. No oratorio or cantata this, with only the choir's lips moving. The lyrics are immensely pictorial; images—birds, cattle, the sea, ships, rivers, mountains, breezes, and tempests—flash swift and kaleidoscopic through the imagination. And the singers become their songs, they dance the nightingale and her flight, they *are* Io. They grow larger than their physical selves to become all girls on the threshold of maturity.

Suppliants' ritual aspect seems inherent. If so, it would help to account for the apparently archaic form into which Aeschylus cast a well-known myth. And the words I use to re-create it are words that I hope will speak to whatever is left of a modern sense of the ceremonial and the sacred and so make the play's antique strangeness somehow familiar and bring its timeless emotions home.

V

This translation is, admittedly, a sometimes radical reappropriation of *Suppliants'* one surviving element, the Greek text. Its aims are three and equal. The first is homage. For the sake of verbal access to the play Aeschylus' images and metaphors are translated with fidelity. Cattle graze, rivers stream, and Zeus holds the scales. I have strived for some reproduction of Aeschylus' remarkable compound words, verbal balances, and even syntactic distortions where they point up poetic and dramatic ambiguities. The plot, of course, unfolds just as it does in the Greek. The second aim is that of making the play emotionally accessible. Aeschylus' irreproducible meters must yield to the English and circadian rhythms that seem affective equivalents. Dead allusions are replaced by phrases meant to evoke felt responses here and now. When there is conflict between literal accuracy and what I believe is an accuracy of feeling, the latter prevails. Lexical readings, however, are given their due in the notes, which are keyed to the numbering of both the English and the Greek lines. The third aim is playability. *Suppliants* was composed to be danced and sung and spoken. It should still have a chance for oral publication, either in the speech of players or a silent voice in the mind's ear of a reader.

Readers will notice that the English version is many lines longer than the Greek. The disparity is more apparent than real. Much of it is accounted for by the fact that I have often translated one long Greek line as two, sometimes three, short English lines. And some of it stems from explanation; a concept expressed by a word or two of Greek may need fuller treatment to be understood by today's reader.

Throughout, the only rule has been, Trust the poet. If Aeschylus implies that Zeus' gaze is a bird, then the gaze is not *like* bird but *is* bird. And he knows that man, to be man, bleeds and dies but never is there blood on divine hands. I have tried most of all to preserve, in ways intelligible to a secular time, the ancient sense of awe, pity, and terror that pulses in the lines.

The translation is based on the texts of H. Weir Smyth, *Aeschylus*, volume I, Loeb Classical Library (Harvard University Press, 1922), and of H. Friis Johansen, *Aeschylus: The Suppliants*, volume I (København, 1970). Where the texts differ, I have freely followed the version that seems to me more effective. My choice and its reasons appear each time in the notes. There will be those who feel I have taken monstrous liberties in translating feelings rather than words, and to them, if they are Greekless, I commend the sober and faithful prose readings accompanying both texts *en face*. Or better still, the study of Greek.

Many other books have been helpful in bringing *Suppliants* to life in my mind. Three must be individually acknowledged: A. F. Garvie's *Aeschylus' "Supplices": Play and Trilogy* (Cambridge University Press, 1969); Robert Duff Murray's *The Motif of Io in Aeschylus' "Suppliants"* (Princeton University Press, 1958); and Margaret Alexiou's *The Ritual Dirge in Greek Tradition* (Cambridge University Press, 1974).

And people—most important are the people who have continually encouraged me, offered scholarly criticism, pulled the reins when my fancies flew headlong, and just plain listened. James Hynd, of the University of Texas, deserves great thanks for tape-recording *Suppliants* so that I could hear the Greek rhythms. William Arrowsmith gave needed polish, especially in matters theological, to my understanding of fifth-century thought. And there are two who have been extraordinary partisans from the beginning. Words enough to thank them do not exist. To Donald Carne-Ross and John Herington, therefore, this version is dedicated.

JANET LEMBKE

ON THE TRANSLATION

In honor of Aeschylus the translation stays as close to fifth-century concepts as it can without becoming just one more piece of word-for-word prose broken into lines that have the appearance but not the substance of poetry. Here, however, are some of the un-Greek, unstoppable ideas that rose in my mind during the three years that I lived deeply with *Suppliants*. All are personal views. None will enlighten the student who tries to understand the workings of Greek tragedy. Some might help a director re-create the play, though I cannot imagine, can only hope, that it will someday be given the physical translation of a performance.

Little is certain about the original staging and actors' masks. Ancient rumor reports that Aeschylus was a master of spectacle. The early classical stage on which *Suppliants* was probably performed is described briefly in section II of the Introduction. Through Danaos (**226** / 189) Aeschylus asked his audience to imagine that the raised stage was a rocky height. We do know that real statues of the gods and a real altar stood on that stage. And here knowledge ends, fancy begins.

THE ULTIMATE QUESTION

Suppliants is a play of many questions. The hardest to answer is, Can it be translated? Transformed and transfigured, made human again, without losing its mystery and poetry? How can anyone now hope to find the right, charged words when Aeschylus has already found them? If only everyone could read Greek! How, in a secular age, can anyone be brought to believe in the holiness that indwells words, rivers, sea, earth, sky, stones, pastures, cows? If only everyone *were* Greek!

COWS

The fact that I grew up with cows has made more trouble for me in coming to grips with *Suppliants* than any single problem in the play itself. All my life I've known cows—Guernseys, Jerseys, Holsteins, Herefords, Angus, Charolais. The word "cow" has always been denotative. It triggers memories of real moos and bawls, clanking stanchions, hoofs stomping straw-covered concrete, the swish of flywhisk tails, mucus-damp noses, calf-tongues rasping my fingers, shaggy patable winter coats. Dull silver tags clipped on golden ears. The fusty sweet warm snuffling dark of a cowbarn at night. Tests for Bang's disease and TB. I know that sturdy bovine bodies are slung from bony ridgepoles totally unsuited to bareback riding. I know that in an Ohio springtime raw milk has a special April flavor of onion grass. Barn cats like it; I don't. And I know that milk cows can be intractable about letting down milk to inexperienced fingers. Milking takes the dexterity of a pianist and the knotty strength of an Indian wrestler; my twelfth summer was a summer of aching forearms. Granted, some cows, especially the beef breeds, can be mighty mean, but I've always known Cow in general as a plodding, gentle ungulate whose miracle is that quadripartite stomach. Cow has never, ever, seemed frightening and tragic.

I read *Suppliants* clean to mid-play with old friends Boss and Caramel chewing their cuds and supplying prosaic mental pictures for Io. Why could she not have been transformed into a beautiful animal, a deer or a tawny lioness? It was no help to remember that in ancient Greece sheep and goats were the common domestic animals and only rich men, aristocrats and Homeric kings, maintained herds of cattle.

And then, in the Suppliants' account of her torment and deliverance, Io came alive. Half-cow, half-woman, she was not the lumbering barnyard animal I know but a magical creature who epitomized a true and crippling human condition, who was healed of her sickness. What was that condition? Back to play's beginning and a re-reading of myth's implications. Faith was placed in Aeschylus the poet rather than in the latter-day dicta of people who deal in prose. Lexicographers, especially, tell unintended lies; the alphabetically entombed verb is not the verb given life by rhythm and context. I relied instead on intuition and gave imagination its head. A risky act.

Twice I've seen calves die of exuberance. Both, released from the barn into the first springtime of their lives, leaped and ran, crazy with sun and new grass, and careered into the pasture gate and broke their necks.

THE GODS

I see, I feel:
A time of spirit that transcends finite body-time.

A place that is called Argos but can be any place of hot light and heart's darkness.

A beach and a central mound of earth where immense god-images are gathered: a sunburst, a trident, a winged phallos, an eagle with wings upstretched as if it had just fallen from heaven upon its prey. The names of the gods in this world are Sun and Ocean and Fool, and the greatest of them all is simply God. In front of their images is the low stone rectangle of their flame-crowned altar. Behind them, not concealed by them, is a fifth image that serves a dramatic purpose in imagination, though it is not mentioned in *Suppliants'* catalogue (**260–68** / 210–20): a round earth-shape with a figure curled motionless in its central hollow. All the images are capable of movement, all are alive.

THE SONS OF EGYPT

Over and again the Suppliants describe the Egyptians in animal terms. Io's grandsons are dogs, carrion crows, spiders, pit vipers, a wingèd horde, a black dream out of Egypt. Egypt, yes. Apis, Anubis, Set, and Thoth. The sons' torsos and limbs are human, but their heads are animal—bull, jackal, snake, lion, vulture, baboon, crocodile. They appear on imagination's stage like divine beasts or brutalized gods, apparitions from an adolescent's erotic daydreams.

A POSTLUDE

Suppliants' unbroken tensions oppress its readers. Is it possible to restore the play a little to its ancient serial context? Can I use here the plastic method I've used to recombine and translate archaic Latin lines that have lost their poems? The Latin lines arranged themselves by imagery and themes into groups that could be translated as complete poems. To break and end the storm, to release myself, I have taken the fragments mentioned in section III of the Introduction and imagined a postlude. Here, for the curious, are the fragment numbers given by H. Weir Smyth, *Aeschylus*, volume II, Loeb Classical Library (Harvard University Press, 1926): 197, 223, 206, 162, 163, 24 (wedding customs), 223, 208, and 25 (Aphrodite's benediction). Zagreus, the single word left from the second play, was suggested by Garvie, p. 163. It is an epithet of Dionysos, god of wine and manic ecstasy. Its use in the play is unknown, but it piques my fancy because it was associated with a bull-form of Dionysos and with flesh-eating rites.

The Suppliants, Danaos, and their attendants *exeunt* right. The stage is deserted for seconds, minutes. The light begins to darken toward a feeling of late afternoon, first streaks of sunset on the sky. The sons of Egypt in full battledress enter left, their animal heads cruel against the grey and rose. The sounds are those of military precision, armor clanking rhythmically, feet marching in measured cadence. And the Egyptians *exeunt* right. The stage is again empty of everyone but the gods. The sunset reddens. Offstage sounds of battle rise, peak, and give way to the lamentations of women.

SUPPLIANTS Io io ioioioioioooooooo
        You   YOU sowed my life, YOU would lay it waste.

DANAOS It pleases God to spend His might for the troubleworn.
        The sons of Egypt, true, weave clever snares.
        But there are subterfuges heaven sanctions.
        God shall not stand aside.
        There is a season, too, for lies.
        And God shall honor them.
        When sun's first clear light stanches rosy dawn,
        I will wake you, as custom bids,
        and the bridegrooms whose sleep you have
        enchanted with the grace deserved.
        And may this night bear heavy fruit.
        Courage.   God lends His might to the troubleworn.

Silence. The sky turns to a bloody night. A woman cries out inarticulately, and the gods surrounding the altar come alive, glittering, bending, whirling. The altar-fire swells and leaps. This is murder's hour.

SUPPLIANTS ZAGREUS
            GOD
                HUNTER
                      HELP US HELP US
                              HELP US

At their height the invocations suddenly cease. The altar-fire dwindles, the gods become still. The Suppliants, cloaked and veiled, enter right with Danaos.

DANAOS Children,
        circle the altar and its beckoning flame,
        and, yourselves encircled
        by the gods' escapeless, everlasting battleranks,
        for your unbedded innocence
        give thankful praise.

The Suppliants, followed by their father, climb to the sanctuary and stand before the gods. Danaos approaches his daughters, and in turn they tear off their veils, their faces are only half-human, horns sprout from their heads. Proudly they whip forth obedient bloody hands. He nods, his pleasure wordless and lunatic, until he sees that the last pair of hands is clean, the face whole. The one surviving bridegroom enters right, his animal mask in his hands, and his face is as beautiful as that of Osiris risen. And out of the one god-image that has not moved, the earth-shape, the goddess Love uncurls herself, stretches, and stands.

LOVE Desire   yes   Sky's holy quickfire longs
      to pierce the curvèd world
      Desire desire   grips Earth and reels her
      toward the coupling
      And Sky's rain   showered in their blissful bed
      impregnates Earth
      And she gives birth   the herds' grass and the grain
      for man's joy and continuing
      By that torrential wedding   life learns its seasons
      the sprout, the flower, the completed fruit
      And I am the divine accomplice
      Love

JANET LEMBKE

SUPPLIANTS

Translated by

JANET LEMBKE

CHARACTERS

SUPPLIANTS

DANAOS their father

PELASGOS king of Argos

SPOKESMAN a son of Egypt

CHORUS of Egyptians

CHORUS of Argive women
Argive soldiers and spearmen

Line numbers in the right-hand margin refer to the English translation only, and the Notes beginning at p. 267 are keyed to these lines. The bracketed line numbers in the running headlines refer to the Greek text. Lines bracketed in the translation are reconstructions, based on context, of Greek lines that are now corrupt or completely lost.

An Argive shore with a raised sanctuary where the gods offer asylum. Grouped around a common altar, images of Zeus, Apollo, Poseidon with trident, and Hermes.

Enter the SUPPLIANTS *from the left. Each carries the emblem of suppliance, a branch wreathed with white wool.*

SUPPLIANTS ZEUS MEN APHIKTOR Shining Father
                Protector of suppliants   shine freely
here   on this voyage of women   who set sail
where Nile twists through saltpolished
sand   Hallowed netherland whose sunbruised
boundaries graze desert   leaving it
we flew
          not outlaws hounded publicly
for murder's blood on our hands
         but fugitives   10
escaping self-built prisons for our own flesh
Agree to marry Egypt's sons   unthinkable!
skin shudders   the unholy thought

                DANAOS *enters left and climbs to the sanctuary.*

Our father on earth   heart's guide
and guide for our footsteps   gambling
all for the best among sorrows
                  decided
we fly before we were pinioned   over a trembling sea
to light on this earth cupped in the day's hand
and here   it must have been   our lives,   20
our voyage time out of mind began in
     droning of flies round a heifer
     warm palm of heaven
     blue breathing of Zeus   yes
we swear it!
     Land?   shall you welcome
     our coming?

With these mightiest swords we implore you   with
branches flowering white unspun wool

O home   30
O earth and sundazzled water
Highblazing gods and slowgrinding earthpowers
          vital in coffins
O Saviour Zeus
     guarding the flesh houses
of men who honor You   receive as Your suppliants
our fleet of innocence   and breathe
a soft air of mercy onshore

                              But the night-thick
manswarm   self-vaunting, spawned out of Egypt   40
before one foot pierces the shallows
before sailwings fold   God!
send them seaward   breathe rain, ice, and winter
caress them with lightning, thunder, hail
let them face gnashing waves
                              let them die
before they can man themselves   decency forbid!
in cousin-beds, in bodies seized and
     brutally entered

          Putting down their branches, the SUPPLIANTS *sing and*
                                        dance.

O be joyful now sing   50
     the Zeus-calf born over the sea
          to right an old wrong
          son of our flowerpastured first mother
          child of the heifer filled by Zeus' breath
          caress-child whose name,
               given at birth, proves the virginal
          truth of his fathering:
Epaphos, Caress-born
Sing joy sing homecoming!
     These green shores nourished   60

    our earliest mother
  while her body learned the first stings of suffering
Remember her pains   count and recount them,
proofs of our good faith
    proofs to astonish the land's children
  till they know truth
abides in our unfinished story

If a diviner of birdsong comes near
  a landsman who hears our heartfelt lamenting
he will think that he listens   70
    to her who was wife and now
sings out heart's darkness,
a hawk-shadowed nightingale

Barred from her nest in the green leafrivers
  she trills strange sweetness lamenting her exile
and the notes spill old tears with new
    as she sings her son's doom:
he was killed and she by her
own hand's anger unmothered

And singing Io's song   80
my human voice is also sorrow's friend
Mourning fingers rake smooth cheeks
    Nile's endless summer burnt
Tears corrode a heart unused to tears
I pick grief's flowers in the shadow of fear
    Are there friends here?   Or kin?
    For us who fled that land wide as air
    who will here lament and bury us?

But gods who gave me life
O hear me, stand vigil over heaven's laws   90
Grant innocence no wedding night
    that thrusts against fate
Self-serving lust!   Welcome it with hate
that saves me rightfully from wedded rape
    Even the battle-weary who run

find an altar, a sword-free no-man's land,
within their fearful love of heaven's powers

And Zeus!   grant that my hopes all come true
   But Zeus' desire is not easily traced
   for the paths of His mind   100
   maze through dusk and briers
   and my eyes cannot follow

It falls surefooted, not on its back,
   whatever command Zeus shakes from His head
   And it flares in the dark
   and carries black portents
   that men cannot read

And He hurls men down from hope's
heaven-tempting towers   their bodies
lie broken   But He needs no force   110
to complete His armor

   Out of that pure center where He sits throned
   unmoving He moves
   and His will has been done

Let Him look down and behold brute
self-seeking   how green the old
vine grows   new sprouts shooting forth
to entwine us in marriage
answering their untrainable hungers

   They run drunk and wild, goaded by lust   120
   And mad loins breed
   a madness in their minds

Disasters of pain
   I tell them in funeral cadences
keening, griefheavy, tearstormed
alalala
         lamentations
My voice is the wail of all funerals

I live I chant my own deathsong

    Lighten me   healing Hillpastures   130
    My cry holds Egypt's savagery but
    Mother-earth   you know my voice
      I try I try with mourner's hands
      to tear the fine-spun veil
      that shrouds my sight

But rites for the dead
  in fair times when death is a stranger
surge godward bearing a bloodcurse
ulululu
      pain unfathomed   140
Where will its waves wash me?   where break?

    Lighten me   healing Hillpastures
    My cry holds Egypt's savagery but
    Mother-earth   you know my voice
      I try I try with mourner's hands
      to tear the fine-spun veil
      that shrouds my sight

Broad oars, yes, and a house of planks
  bound with cord stitches to keep out the salt
brought me homeward unstormed on wind's steady breath   150
  Not do I complain

But my heart thinks of death
Father Allvisioning
  grant it lifegrace again

    If only the seeds
    of a godembraced mother
    might fly from men's beds
      away away away
    unmated, unraped away

See me!   stainless daughter of Zeus   160
  safekeeper of gates to your maiden shrine

I would guard my chastity as you guard yours
   but I am pursued

With your hunter's strength
as virgin for virgin
   save me from touching man

     If only the seeds
       of a godembraced mother
     might fly from men's beds
       away away away   170
     unmated, unraped away

If not, black flowers
forged by Nile's beating sun
shall seek
   that earthen hostelry
   where the Zeus rich in guests
   finds room for the lifeweary
and shall knock with suppliant branches
and enter noose-hung into death
     unless the gods on the skysummits hear us   180

     Zeus!   revenge against Io
     collects endless payment
     O I know Your queen's
     heavendaunting envy
       A day of hard wind
       blows a night of storm

And if I die
shall a just indictment not
trap Zeus:
     that He has disavowed   190
     the heifer's child, the son
     He fathered long ago
because He turns His countenance
away from supplicating prayers?
     But God in the highest   NOW hear our crying

Zeus!   revenge against Io
collects endless payment
O I know Your queen's
heavendaunting envy
    A day of hard wind   200
    blows a night of storm

DANAOS Children!   be cautious.
Caution disembarked you here, and trust
in the elder wisdom of your captain-father.
Standing now on firm ground,
looking futureward, I warn you.
Guard the words, carve them on memory,
for I see
      dust, voiceless messenger
of an army on the march.   210

But its wheels are not silent,
they squeal round the axles.
A mass of troops, yes,
shieldenclosed and spearbristling,
I see the shapes,
the horses, the curved chariots.

We are the likely cause:
this country's leaders
would confirm with eyes
what ears have learned from messengers.   220
But be it harmlessly or be it
sharpened by raw anger
that this march is risen toward us,
it better suits all frames of temper
that you sit, sheltered in your innocence,
upon this rock where gods are met.
Stronger than any fortress, an altar;
no mere man can breach its shield.

Quickly, quickly, rise, climb,
your whitecrowned emblems   230

that especially delight Zeus' pity
held solemn in the hands of luck—
those on your heart's side.

> *The* SUPPLIANTS *pick up their branches. Some move*
> *toward the sanctuary, some linger.*

In sorrowing, respectful, modest,
and most needful voices
you shall answer the strange host
as befits an uninvited guest.
Tell them plainly of your flight:
it was not murderstained.
And let birdvoices hold no brash notes.   240
No doubts must furrow
the smooth brow of your self-control,
no flirtation gleam in virtue's eyes,
and no forereaching, no backdragging
rule your words, for either breeds
a swift opposition in these men.

Remember, bend!
You are in want, strangers, fugitives,
and rash tongues do not suit
the part of weakness.   250

A SUPPLIANT Father, yes,
your caution speaks to mine.
Memory shall guard the treasure of your words.
But Zeus!   First Father, SEE US!

DANAOS May His eye hold you tenderly.
Don't loiter now. Borrow strength from purpose.

A SUPPLIANT From you, I want to stay near you.
O God, this weariness, have pity.
Shall I never be free?

> *The last* SUPPLIANT *reaches sanctuary.*

DANAOS *moves from image to image. As he identifies each
one, the* SUPPLIANTS *severally lay branches at the base.*

DANAOS Zeus does as He wishes. Praise Him.   260

A SUPPLIANT Praise takes wing, flies toward the sun.

DANAOS And Apollo, god who spent a year on earth.

A SUPPLIANT Who knows, then, about human troubles.

DANAOS Knowing them, he may defend you.

A SUPPLIANT Will other powers here fight for us?

DANAOS This trident is a god's weapon.

A SUPPLIANT Poseidon's waves were kind to us.

DANAOS And one more, Hermes, honored in Greek custom.

A SUPPLIANT Let him herald our freedom!

The SUPPLIANTS *sit at the feet of the images.*

DANAOS All heregathered are your lords.   270
Praise them with trembling.
Settle in their cleanness,
a pitying of doves who know hawkfear:
wingèd kin for hating,
blood cousins desecrating their own kind.
Bird that feeds on bird, how is it clean?
And one who preys upon a girl
against her will, and mine,
can he be cleansed?
                    Never!   280
Even after death there is no flight for him:
he shall be charged for an unnatural act,
and wrong shall be avenged.

Rumor says there is another Zeus
who sits in Hades and chars
final vengeance into all who have
worn out their earthly lives.

Remember:
guard your eyes, speak softly, bend!
Be sure of victory.   290

                    PELASGOS *enters right with his soldiers.*

PELASGOS Where
           have you come from?   A congregation
glittering, bizarre in alien robes and diadems,
and womanly, yet gaudy as no women
I have ever known or dreamed.
And how
           have you come here?   Without forewarning
or invitation.   Helped and guided
only by a reckless courage.   I am amazed.
But the branches   300
           that lie beside you in godshadow
seem lawhonored signs that you claim asylum.
At this one point perhaps your world meets mine.

Conjecture can solve every riddle.
What answers will your voices bring?

A SUPPLIANT My clothes, my branch:
your observations are not-false.
But whom do I answer?   Private citizen,
spokesman, priest or holy prophet?
Or the people's leader?   310

PELASGOS Reply to me, speak directly in good faith to me.
For I am Pelasgos,
           sprung from the seed of this Ancient Ground

that grew in Earth's womb.   I rule this realm.
And I
    for these good reasons stand first
among the land's many sons who harvest
    her deep sweetness.
Over plains, over valleys
    where rivers curl redgold   320
toward the sunset, I hold all power.
Beyond eyes' north horizon
    to mountains that build immense palisades
against the wild tribes,
    to foothills where oaktrees
rustle their oracles,
    until sea restrains me
with its bluesalt marches, I hold all power.
And the region around us
    has been called immemorially   330
Bull's Pasture in thankful memory of a healer.
Apis, God's Bull, was his name,
    and he sailed here,
a hero with healing visions, Apollo's own son.
And he cured our fields of mansavaging predators,
cleared our houses of the choking dragoncoils
that sick Earth, drenched,
    infected by the bloody stains
of ancient murders, had spawned in agony.
With such finecutting, freeing surgery   340
did he excise her pain that Argos still pays
his reproachless name a fee of prayer.
You have my credentials now.
Claim your lineage and corroborate it
quickly.
        My home has never cherished empty speech.

A SUPPLIANT My history is brief and plain. Argos
            cradled me.
                        I claim it proudly as birthright
            through a childblessed cow. All this is true!   350
            I offer proof: a few more words.

PELASGOS Strangers spin me incredible tales. How
can Argive soil and air be yours by birth?
Women seeded in the fields of Libya, surely you
resemble them rather than our native daughters.
And Nile might nurture such luxuriance.
And, Cypriot craftsmen do stamp male conceits
of female forms like yours on copper blanks.
And like you the nomads I hear of, sunburnished
women who saddle their humpbacked horses,   360
the camels, and ride Ethiopia's borders.
And, the husbandless, fleshfeasting Amazons—
if you bore weapons, certainly you would be they.

But tell me more. Perhaps I may then understand
how birth and heritage make Argos yours.

A SUPPLIANT A keeper of the keys to Hera's house,
the girl Io,
                    do people say she lived in Argos?

PELASGOS They say it and believe it.

A SUPPLIANT And say that Zeus Himself desired her?   370

PELASGOS No secret from Hera that deflowering.

A SUPPLIANT Outrageous! What did she do?

PELASGOS A cow, our goddess turned girl into cow.

A SUPPLIANT Did Zeus go near the horned cow?

PELASGOS They say He took bull's form and covered her.

A SUPPLIANT So they say. What did Zeus' bedmate do next?

PELASGOS She set a thousand eyes to guard the cow.

A SUPPLIANT An allseeing herdsman for one cow. Who?

PELASGOS Argos, son of Earth. Hermes killed him.

A SUPPLIANT Did she do something else to the unlucky cow? 380

PELASGOS She sent a cattlegoad, biting, bloodsucking—

A SUPPLIANT A fly, Nile's people say a blowfly.

PELASGOS —that drove her from land when she tried to outrun it—

A SUPPLIANT Yes, our stories interlock!

PELASGOS —but she found lower Nile and the city of sphinxes.

A SUPPLIANT Yes! God's hand caressed her and planted His seed.

PELASGOS Who is the cow's Zeus-calf?

A SUPPLIANT Epaphos, named for the true way Zeus took His prize.

[PELASGOS And his child?]

A SUPPLIANT Libya, great and fertile. 390

[PELASGOS And her bounty?]

[A SUPPLIANT Agenor was her firstborn.]

PELASGOS Had she another offshoot?

A SUPPLIANT Baal, father of two sons and one MY father.

PELASGOS Now tell me his respected name.

A SUPPLIANT Danaos, whose potent brother has fifty sons.

PELASGOS His name? Don't hold it back.

A SUPPLIANT EGYPT!

Now you know how ancient blood flows new in me.
I beg you, act. Raise me from this holy refuge.   400
TAKE ME HOME!

PELASGOS   You seem to inherit true communion with my country,
and out of the deepest past. But, familiar houses,
how had you courage to abandon them?
    What rush of fortune swept you here?

A SUPPLIANT   Pelasgos, lord of my people,
human sufferings change color in a flash; pain
never lets one glimpse the selfsame feather.
Who wished unexpected flight? foresaw that terror
would impel your kin by ancient marriages to cower here,   410
refugees, hating the thought of bridal beds?

PELASGOS   Explain more clearly why you stand suppliant before the gods.

A SUPPLIANT   Not to be enslaved by Egypt's brood!

PELASGOS   Because you hate them? Or have they violated laws?

A SUPPLIANT   What woman would marry a slavemaster?

PELASGOS   But marriage means clan-strength and man's increase.

A SUPPLIANT   If marriage fails, divorce is easy.

PELASGOS   How is a godfearing man supposed to help you?

A SUPPLIANT   Never give me to Egypt's sons, no matter what they claim.

PELASGOS   You ask me to bear the burden of a new war.   420

A SUPPLIANT   But heaven's law protects its human allies.

PELASGOS   Yes, *if* that law was always party to the case.

The SUPPLIANTS *rise and hold their branches over the images.*

A SUPPLIANT I crown your state's helmsmen. Respect them!

PELASGOS My skin crawls when I see my gods overshadowed.

A SUPPLIANT No man can bear the burden of Zeus Suppliant's wrath.

SUPPLIANTS Son of this Ancient Ground, let kindness
    hear me   Lord of my people, let heart's vision
    see me
        a suppliant, a refugee running here, there
    wolfharried   430
         a calf trapped on a mountain ledge
    trusting her life to the rockshield, bawling again
      again to the herdsman
    Fear   Weariness   Save me

PELASGOS I can see,
    beneath new-cut branches, shadowy
    newcomers thronging the presence of my gods.
    I wish it harmfree,
      this right that strange guests claim to our houses.
    Or shall it bring to pass,   440
      uninvited by my people, unforestallable,
    a bloodfeud, the visitant no people welcome?

SUPPLIANTS Bear witness, Suppliant Themis, daughter
    of Zeus Jury-Appointer: my flight harms no one.
    And you
        lord full ripe in wisdom, learn from the later-sown
    Human cries
        for heaven's help and man's are due respect
    and when the altar shields a suppliant, then
      you, a king, must show the gods   450
      fear   trembling   obedience

PELASGOS But you do not sit
    as claimants to the safety of *my* private hearth.
    It is the body politic, the people,
      that may be contaminated;

in concert *they* who must then cure their houses
    and their lives of bloodghosts.
And I, one man, can offer you no contract
until the citizens, all of them,
    publicly debate your case.   460

SUPPLIANTS You   the people!   You   the government!
A pharaoh chosen, unimpeachable   you
sustain the fire blazing on the country's altarhearth
    with single-voiced decrees, your own,
and single-handed from your sovereign bench   you
bring all debts to final reckoning
    Beware heaven's curse

PELASGOS Heaven's curse—
    may it fester only in my enemies. But you—
I cannot war on your behalf without incurring damages   470
nor yet, lightheartedly, dishonor your petition.
I am made weaponless.
    Fear beats in my body like a pulse:
to act, or not to act and let chance deliver
    its blind verdict.

SUPPLIANTS His gaze is vigilant   O lift your eyes
to Him Who guards all trial-torn humanity
Shall one who sits before her own kind pleading heaven's law
    find no relief mandated
in the laws of men?   Zeus Suppliant's anger   480
burns unquenchable though its victim
    lament to the end

PELASGOS If—hear me!—
    if power over you is vested in Egypt's sons
by the law you were born to, because they are
your nearest kin, who would contest it willingly?
It is compulsory—do you hear me?—
    that your defense spring from the law you fled:
that therein they have no jurisdiction,

        none whatever, over you.   490

SUPPLIANTS Never
       not ever
       may the power of a male fist crush me
       With help instead from sailorguiding stars
       I chart my own course   flight
       from a loathsome marriage

           As your ally now choose heaven's law
             Decide!
                Offer loving fear to the gods

PELASGOS There is no facile judgment for the case.   500
           Choose not me as judge.
       I have told you, tell you now, not without
           the polity's consent
       may I act on the question, not even though I rule,
           lest in time to come,
       if anything in any way untoward should happen,
           the householders convict me:
       Aliens. When you honored them, you damned your people.

SUPPLIANTS We share
       one blood and   510
       spring from one vigilant God Whose hands
       weighing human differences fairly dispense
       vengeance to the profane
       blessings to the reverent

           Heaven finds balance but you scruple
             Why?
                Earthly justice is yours to achieve

PELASGOS There is need—see it!—
           for deep and saving counsel,
       just as a diver descending the fathoms needs   520
       a clear eye undazed by the sea's winy rapture.
       Counsel, so that foremost your suit bring

no hurt to my people,
and counsel, for my own sake, that it be
    settled peacefully
and no force roughly seize its prize,
nor may we surrender you while you sit
    before the court of gods
lest Zeus Alldestroyer break holy,
heavy into our houses and we bring upon ourselves   530
    His ceaseless vengeance
that even after death lets no man go free.

Consider! Can you not see now
    the need for counsel that saves us all?

SUPPLIANTS Be counseled   and become
             it is your   allredeeming right
        our dutiful heavenwary
        advocate
                 The refugee   do not betray her
        farflung and cast upon this shore   the waif   540
             unholy lustfulness pursues

        Nor witness me   from the seat
             of a godhost   roughly prized
        reclaimed like a thing stolen
        O you in whom
                         rests ALL power   from sea to mountains
        Wake now to the self-adoration   of Egypt
             Beware an eversearching wrath

        Nor bear   to watch idly as one sanctuaried
             is forced from the godstones   550
                 though asylum is my heavensent right
        and dragged off
             a wild colt
                 my crownband
        the halter   my hair, fine rope   and strange
             hands pawing my flesh

        And know   to your children and their generations
             it shall be given

236

            whichever groundwork you now lay for them
        to pay Doom   560
            full tribute in

                                    death or
        rejoicing   Reflect   How just the power
            downstreaming from Zeus

PELASGOS Doubt not,
            I have reflected,
            and thought grounds here:

            harsh war
            in one cause or the other
            and I must fight: 570

            last nail driven home,
            the ship held in winches
            strains toward the sea:

            but there shall be no landfall free from pain.

            If treasures have been looted from a house,
            then may Wealthguarding Zeus [in jealous charity
                make good the loss,]
            and if a tongue shoot words that hurt,
            then may speech enchant speech back to wholesomeness
                [or twist the arrow in the wound.]   580

            But that there come no murder of blood kin

            I must
            offer sacrifices,
            victims must fall:

            the gods
            in their multitude demand
            a multitude as ruin's cure.

            Your animosity
            repels and pulls me in
            though I have wished   590

for ignorance,
not knowledge,
of a killing night:

and still I hope
against all reasonable hope
for peace, for light.

A SUPPLIANT Pity me. And listen to my final argument.

PELASGOS Argue on. I shall hear every word.

A SUPPLIANT I have a breastband and ribbons to fasten my dress.

PELASGOS Things common, no doubt, to women everywhere.   600

One SUPPLIANT *removes her breastband and collects two others. Handing the ends to another* SUPPLIANT, *she begins to make a braid.*

A SUPPLIANT Now out of them—look closely—an eloquent device.

PELASGOS Singing tongues, rhythmic hands. Put words to your music.

A SUPPLIANT If you can make us no firm promise—

PELASGOS Cat's-cradle. What purpose in your game?

A SUPPLIANT New strange offerings to give the godstones splendor.

PELASGOS A riddle for an answer. Speak plainly.

The finished braid is knotted into a noose.

A SUPPLIANT To hang myself, and now, AND FROM THESE VERY
                                            GODS!

PELASGOS Your words are whips that flay my heart.

A SUPPLIANT You understand! Now I have made your mind's eye wake.

PELASGOS Yes.   610

    And the truth is as hard to grapple as a river.
    Evils in surfeit crest sudden, sweeping me down
    to an unchartable sea of tears and death. The depths
    open, and nowhere a port safe from evils.

        If I do not discharge the debt
        owed you in heaven's name,
        your sworn befouling of both gods and men
        shall never be outshot.

    But if I stand, back to the wall, and battletest
    the issue with your cousins, Egypt's sons,   620
    shall not the cost be bitter: men drenching
    trampled earth with blood, and all in the name of women?

        Yet, that any of us live, I must
        revere the lethal holiness of Zeus,
        for He is Stay of suppliants,
        and mortal flesh owes Him its highest fear.

    (to DANAOS)
    And you,
        respected father of unmarried daughters,
    bundle their branches quickly in crooked arms,
        take them   630
    to other altars of my country's guardian powers,
    and lay them down,
        tokens for the eyes of all men
    that you have come in suppliance.
        Otherwise their tongues
    will send a spate of arguments against me,
    for people here enjoy disputing leadership.
    But,
        if the sight of branches stirs their pity,
    then shall they despise a male armada's selfishness,   640

then shall my countrymen grant you their welcome.
All men recognize some sympathy for helplessness.

DANAOS It is worth much to us, understanding
that a godmoved voice will plead a stranger's cause.
But, companions, guides with native knowledge of the land,
send them with me to the altars of the tutelary gods,
    those city-guarding crocodiles that slumber
    in the lifestream of your nation,
so that I find the temples easily, walk the streets
in safety: 650
        my dress, my face are not like yours.
Nile and Io's fathering river, each nurtures its own race.
Beware: overconfidence gives birth to fear,
and men have cut down friends they did not recognize.

PELASGOS (*to his soldiers*)   Men in the first rank, march with him.
The stranger our guest speaks persuasively.
Guide him to the city's altars, where gods abide,
and when you meet others, no need to be garrulous
about this voyager you steer to safety
    at the firesides of gods.   660

> DANAOS *takes some of the branches and exits right with a*
> *detachment of soldiers.*

A SUPPLIANT You instructed him and he has gone.
But I? What am I to do?

PELASGOS Come. Leave your branches there.

A SUPPLIANT Yes, I'll leave them as you ask.

> *The* SUPPLIANTS *place the remaining branches on the*
> *altar.*

PELASGOS Here, below the altar's rock, you may exercise.

A SUPPLIANT Unconsecrated public ground! How can it keep me safe?

PELASGOS We shall not give you to the wingèd horde.

A SUPPLIANT They are more poisonous than snakes!

PELASGOS I speak to you reasonably. Reply in kind.

A SUPPLIANT But they frighten me.   670

PELASGOS You have nothing to fear.

A SUPPLIANT Then encourage me by what you say and do.

PELASGOS Not long, not long shall you be left fatherless.
          And I—
                there are people to be called from fields and hills.
          I, too, must go
                to soften them toward accepting you with friendship
          and tell your father how to please their ears.
          Wait here. There are gods
                in the earth, on the heights, in this air.   680
          Hymn them. Pray that your desire be fulfilled.
          I shall do as much as one brief man can do.
          May persuasion guide me, and good fortune follow.

                  PELASGOS *waits until the* SUPPLIANTS *descend and exits*
                                      right with his soldiers.

SUPPLIANTS Lord over lords   of the everblest
           Most Blest   of prayer's answers
           Answer Perfected
                            Zeus God
                Whose wealth is the earth and the heavens
           let prayer now win You
           From Your own daughters   690
           ward off the manpride that stalks us
                Hate it with splendor
           Down seadeeps grave it
                                  Sea's blue night
           will heal over slashing black oars

Look now on women   look kindness
upon us   whose line reaches back
to the longfabled past
                              to her
    who began it, the woman You cherished   700
Renew within us
her glad deliverance
Court memory, how gently Your
    palm caressed Io our mother
Zeus Father
                    WE ARE YOUR DAUGHTERS
and hers who was forced from this home

As the SUPPLIANTS *sing Io's story, they dance it in spectacular*
pantomime. Through them Io becomes an overwhelming,
                    though unseen, presence on the stage.

Ancient days, ancient footprints
    I move now among them
My mother flowerbrowsing,   710
sleeplessly watched,
    here foraged on spring grasses and from here
flystung, stampeded,
mindbroken she runs

Many many the nations of men
            She has transgressed them
        Sea sunders land from land
    To the east, helpless, doomstormed
    she tears a dry wake through the windblasted water
till she marks solid ground,   720

hurls her body down Asia
    toward unreachable sunrise
Sheepgrazing solitudes,
straight through them she drives
    to the teeming squares and alleys of towns
And she tramples valleys,
mountains rise in her footsteps

Many many the faces of earth
          She has transformed them
          Forever swift rivers well   730
     in her track, her rush harrows stone,
     unburies the earthquake, the speed of her flight
scythes grain in the fields

And now she arrives
     body plundered by bites
     of the whinywinged drover
at the green oasis holy to Zeus
where all creatures may pasture
     on snowsuckled grasses
where quick showers strike   740
and air
          thickens
                    to rainsmoke
and here
          to Nile's incorruptible water
demented she comes   her anguish unearned
mindsick and bodysick   goaded
tormented   a shebeast
     infected and holy

And the people whose lives   750
     the rich land sustains,
     corpsegreen their horrorstruck faces
Hearts skip beats, eyes cannot stop staring:
undreamed apparition
     grasseater, flyblown
patchflesh halfhuman
There
          and there
                    she is cow
and here   760
          still woman lowing and marvelous
And now in extremity   who shall transfigure her
body and mind   wretched
farharried   flycursed
     and burdened with horns?

Who lives without end
   King of gods and men
Zeus ...
In the fist of unbruising power
In the radiant storm of His breath   770
she found rest
   tears fell
      washed away
         all grief and disfigurement
Zeus-filled she conceived
               IT IS NOT FALSE!
and bore Him a son immune to reproach
who lived a life
   crowned with years and gold
All lands under heaven rejoice with singing   780
Zeus Who plants the lifepulse in green nature
surely quickened this child and his children
Who else
   could arrest
      a goddess-born
         mortal infection?
Zeus alone, and we
          IT IS TRUE!
are daughters born to His hand's Caress

                     DANAOS *enters right.*

On earth a godhost gives   790
   order to nature
      Which god shall I cry to?
      Whose acts will answer me?
The Father
   Urge of my green life
   Whose own hand has sown me
Lord
   Ancient in wisdom Who crafted my people
   Allhelp
   Whose fair breath has sped me   800
Zeus

In high fiery places He sits
  suppliant to no throne
    nor derives His might
    from a more potent king
No other
  enforces His homage
  nor is He valley overshadowed by summits
But He
  acts in the instant of speech   810
  His word
  has completed whatever His will
conceives

O Father Lord Zeus no other but He conceives Father

The SUPPLIANTS *chant and rechant the last words until*
                    they are hysterical.

DANAOS Calm yourselves, children.
        And be joyful.
        The citizens play their part well.
        In the assembly all-enabling measures have been passed.

A SUPPLIANT Elder statesman!
        You bring the news most hoped for.   820
        Tell me, tell me,
        what decision has been made? Where
        did the hands of the majority
        show winning strength?

DANAOS The men of Argos voted not ambivalently
        but so that my old veins ran hot and young again.
        In full assembly every man raised his right hand—
        air bristled!—to confirm this resolution:

THAT WE BECOME SETTLERS IN OUR MOTHERLAND,
FREE, SECURE IN OUR PERSONS   830
AGAINST ALL SEIZURE AND HUMAN REPRISAL;
THAT NO MAN, EITHER NATIVEBORN OR ALIEN,
DRIVE US OUT INTO CAPTIVITY,

BUT, IF FORCE BE EXERCISED,

HE WHO DOES NOT AID US,

THOUGH IT IS HIS RIGHT AND DUTY TO BEAR ARMS,

SHALL LOSE ALL RIGHTS,

HIS EXILE MANDATED BY HIS PEERS.

And with what style did he prevail on our behalf,

Pelasgos lord of the Argive people,   840

speaking of Zeus Suppliant's wrath and its immensity;

warning that never in all time to come must people fodder it;

and saying that if we, doubly guests and kinsmen,

should cause a double mist of blood to shroud the people,

it would breed past human cure the fatted beast of ruin.

Hearing this, hands high,

not waiting for the usual reading,

the assembly voted:

LET IT BE LAW.

O they were easily persuaded,   850

listening to the twists of rhetoric.

But it was Zeus Who sealed the resolution.

He climbs to the sanctuary and stands looking left toward

the sea.

A SUPPLIANT Come sisters

come sing for the people of Argos

blessings of thanks in return for their blessings

And Zeus Guest and Stranger!

keep watch over strangers

that the prayers on our tongues come true

that now and tomorrow

no one reproaches them   860

HALFCHORUS Now   O gods

OF created of God   hear us now

SUPPLIANTS We overflow with prayers for our people

Never may they know the peace
that scorched earth brings
nor hear the famished glee
of carnal Ares
who harvests flesh
where men have sown their seed
For they pitied us   870
and cast a fair vote
and they respect the suppliants of Zeus
   this herd no one envies

HALFCHORUS Nor did they vote
supporting their own sex   and so
dishonor the fury of women

   For they considered Zeus
   Avenger's eye
   No battling that gaze, no house
   would have it light   880
   staining the thatch
   It perches heavy, hard

For they respect their kin
who supplicate Zeus
and their altars cleansed by reverence
   they shall delight heaven

HALFCHORUS O God!   though our mouths
lie in shadow   let our prayers
blaze far with friendblessing light

   Never may a plague   890
   of men drain this nation
   nor strife bloody Earth's breast
   with the bodies of her sons

Flower of youth   bud unstemmed
Ares Manmurderer
who heats Aphrodite's bed
must not mow down the finest blooms

HALFCHORUS   And altarhearths
                    where greybeards cluster   let your fires
                    glow in bright welcome to wisdom   900

                         Nation!   be governed well
                         by godfearing men who
                         fear Zeus Guest and Stranger most
                         By greymaned law He casts our lots

                         Earthguardians!   rise evernew
                         throughout all time to come
                         Artemis! Hekate!   guard
                         women brought to bed with child

HALFCHORUS   And no murderous
                    clanfeuds uprise   910
                    in this nation to divide it

                         Danceless tuneless
                         Tearbreeder Ares
                         howls and clatters in the men who
                              arm him

                         And Sickness   settle your joyless
                         swarm far from the people's heads
                         And Apollo of Wolves   show mercy's bite
                         to every tender child

HALFCHORUS   And Zeus!   grant perfect
                    ripening to Earth's   920
                    fruit in every season

                         And grazing cattle
                         breed countless calves
                         Earthpowers, skypowers nourish all who obey them

                         And altars   echo gladly poets'
                         godinvested hymns of thanks

And godbreathed prophecy   chant home to heaven
from tongues burnt clean by awe

HALFCHORUS Guard your mortal rights
     O citizens   Be unafraid   930
       Here is the state's core and its strength:
       your rule of foresight and concern for common good
     And to all strangers give fair hearing
       before grim Ares marches panoplied
     Concede inviolate our godsent rights

HALFCHORUS This is home earth for gods
     First, keep them blessed evermore
       And praise them as your fathers did:
       laurels highheld, oxen sacrificed, the rising smoke
     And honor parents in supreme   940
       obedience to the third commandment
     written in godgiven law

DANAOS Sane prayers. I second them, my filial daughters.

Now let no witless panic rout you as you hear
a father's news of unexpected and rising danger.
From this high holy refuge the eye gazes far.
I see the ship.
           She is well marked.
I make no mistake: the cut of her canvas,
hide safety lines strung along the gunwales,   950
and the bow that has eyes for scanning the searoad
yet far too blindly answers directives
from the helm astern. She freights us no love.

How clear they are—manshapes, the crew, black
arms, legs stark against snowy uniforms.
And following, a fleet—escorts, troopships,
all glinting clear.
           The flagship has a wide lead;
she stands inshore, canvas already struck.
That steady clack of oars will soon bring her in.   960

But you must stay here making no noise.
Use self-control in facing this predicament.
Nor slight the gods.
And I shall come back when I've summoned
advocates who speak with swords,
in the event that someone — herald, deputation —
approaches, rough hands intent
on seizing you like stolen chattels.

NOT ONE SHALL DARE TOUCH YOU.
No need to dread them, no need to run.   970
Far better, should help's march be delayed,
never to forget the altar's present shield.

Courage.
Relentless time appoints the day, the very hour,
that godscorning flesh shall bow to vengeance.

A SUPPLIANT   Father, I'm frightened   the ships   how swift
their wings   In time's midst, no time left

A SUPPLIANT   Fear winds a sheet round my body
          Truth stops my breath
Far-racing flight   what was the earthly use?   980
My flesh feels thick and numb, I'm dying   Father!

DANAOS   You are protected by the Argive vote.
They shall fight for you, I promise it, I *know*.

A SUPPLIANT   They are a shoal of sharks   fleshmad   Egypt's sons
their battlethirst unslakable   This too you KNOW

A SUPPLIANT   Hulls quest, shot spears, through the water
          Proweyes pierce the sea
The fin-sailed ships   too soon rage thrust them here
A legion, strong, stormblack   rides in their bellies

DANAOS   And it shall meet a legion, whose sword-arms   990
have been honed to muscle by hard work.

A SUPPLIANT To be alone!   Don't leave me, Father   please
A woman alone, a nothing   empty of war

A SUPPLIANT But THEY are
blood-impelled and born to treachery and
crammed with unclean hungers   carrion crows   to whom
altars mean nothing

DANAOS (*pointing to the trident*) But how useful to us, children,
if they make the gods hate them.

A SUPPLIANT No godspear   no sign glorious to the gods   1000
will cut their grasp on us   FATHERRRR

A SUPPLIANT For THEY are
blood-obsessed   wound fast in shameless heat
slavering and fleshcrazed   brazen dogs   that know
nothing of gods

DANAOS It's said that wolves are stronger than dogs,
that papyrus cannot seed the grainfields.

He descends from the sanctuary.

A SUPPLIANT Casual lusts, easy angers own them   They are
animals   empty of the laws that heaven gives men

A SUPPLIANT I must guard myself quickly!   1010

The SUPPLIANTS *cluster around* DANAOS, *who indicates
that they must again take sanctuary. They hesitate,
reluctant to let him go.*

DANAOS Not quick at all, the arrayal of a seaborne taskforce
nor its mooring. Sternropes must be hauled ashore
before they're made fast, and when the anchors bite in,
not even then are the ships' herdsmen satisfied,
especially if they've made a portshy coast
after the sun begins its stride toward night. And Night

251

likes mothering birthpains in the watchful helmsman.
I see no army successfully debouched
until the ships themselves feel snug at their moorings.   1020
And you, be cautious though fear beats at you.
Do not neglect your gods.
                          [I will return]
as soon as help is mustered. A call to arms—
no, the people won't reproach its clarion,
an old man lent youth by his quick-tongued wits.

He exits right. The SUPPLIANTS *linger on the level ground.*

HALFCHORUS io io ioioioioio
            O Earth
               O healing hills
                  Allholy law whence comes my strength   1030
            what shall I suffer?
               Where shall I flee in this country
            of pastures?   Is there a dark burrow?

               Let my blackness be smoke
               sister to God's clouds
                  All unseen
                  let me whirl up
                  secret as wingless dust
                              Let me be lost

HALFCHORUS io io ioioioioio   1040
            No flight
               no time to hide
                  Inhuman cruelty leaves no escape
            My heart beats darker
               dashes like a small trapped creature
            A father's eye snares me, fear haunts me

            Let my bondage to doom
            end in a slipnoose
               Before a man

     I wish unborn   1050
     can touch my flesh, O come
          husband me, Death

HALFCHORUS How shall I reach a throne in mid-air
     where the clouds' white night turns to snow?
   Or a sheer slick
     goatfoiling
     unpointed out
     lone-spirited
     vulture-reeling peak
   to jut in witness   1060
       above my valleyed corpse?

     Must I be forced against heart's dream
     into a murderous bed?

HALFCHORUS No! first dogs shall eat and birds make feast
     A godless grave, I do not care
   To die, to ease
     free from wail-
     exciting pain
     Cease, doomed breath
     Come come, Death, before   1070
   that other dying
       in the bridal room

     What saving channel must I cut
     to escape a marriage bed?

HALFCHORUS Toll, doomcry, on the sky's bluest shores
     Tell tell the gods
      I wail for my dying
   Make it true
     Release me
      Heal me of storms   1080
   Look peace on me, Father
         Whose lawgiving eye
   looks no light on brute force

    Send blessings to those
    who entreat You
    Earthcradler Allguiding Zeus

        Offstage, men's voices grunt and shout.

HALFCHORUS Egypt's get, how ugly their self-glory
    how hardpressing
        their misbegot maleness
    I have fled   1090
      They track me
        Found earth
    They bay and they clamor
                 with lawbreaking lust
    to take me by brute force

    Zeus! You hold the scales
    Who other than You
    can steady the deathbound?

        The SUPPLIANTS *run to the foot of the sanctuary*
                       and begin to climb.

A SUPPLIANT No   No   No   NO NO-O-O-O-O

A SUPPLIANT Rapists   seafoulers   shorecrawlers   1100

A SUPPLIANT Before you take me   die die die

SPOKESMAN (*offstage*) Down.   Come down, you.   Now.

A SUPPLIANT Cry cry   fill air with anguish
    I see looming shadows   acts of pain
    force impaling me

SUPPLIANTS   No   No   NONONONONO

A SUPPLIANT Climb   fly   HERE is our only strength

A SUPPLIANT Beasthearted lechery burdening the sea the shore

                The Egyptian SPOKESMAN *and an armed guard enter left.*

SUPPLIANTS Lord on earth   stand before us

SPOKESMAN Sssssssssssssssssssss——   1110

            So.   You.   Move move.   To the ship's
            boat.   On your feet.   HUP

            You won't, won't you?

            Hair torn, torn out, skin stung.
            Bloodrivers, you beg for murder.
            Chopnecks, toppleheads,
            move.   Move!
                            Then be damned, damn you,
                            there on your dunghill.

A SUPPLIANT I wish   1120
                weltering waves had
                    flooded the saltroad
                and you   with your slavemaster's self-love
                and you   in your brassbolted hulls
                        I wish you had foundered

[SUPPLIANTS Rather bleed   sweeten this hill with my death
            than go down to the ship]

[EGYPTIANS Bloody hill   reek of death
            Go down to the ship]

SPOKESMAN I order: stop this madmouth   1130
            crazy woman cursing.
            You and you, all of you,
            get up, march down to the landing craft.
            You—honorless, homeless,
            not worth my love or fear.

255

A SUPPLIANT I wish
             you never again see
                the springflooding water
             Only there   can you trade your cattle for brides
             Only there   can your lifebearing blood   1140
                arrive at full flower

[SUPPLIANTS My earth is here   my old and noble line
             my home my throne]

[EGYPTIANS My earth   my line
             your home is mine]

SPOKESMAN You, yes, you'll board the ship
          and fast, willing, unwilling,
          forced alive, forced till life runs out.
          [Shegoats are for covering and giving birth,
          and then for butchering.]   1150

A SUPPLIANT ah-aiaiai
             that you
                were hard-driven   helplessly lost
                   in the holy blue groves of Ocean
                wind-battered   cast aground
                your wanderings tombed
                   in a wilderness of spumy sand

SPOKESMAN Yowl and caterwaul and clamor at the gods.
          There's no outleaping Egypt's craft.
          Yelp and bleat.   Keep on.   1160
          Add bite to your dreary noise.

                                        He starts climbing.

A SUPPLIANT oh-ohohohoh
             how you
             lash upward   brooling bloodlust
                a crocodile bloated with sureness
             The Nile moves   vast in you
             May it wind away

from that morass where your self-blindness thrives.

The SPOKESMAN *reaches the sanctuary.*

SPOKESMAN Go down, I order it.   Board the boat.
Its eyes turn home.   1170
Fast as you can.   No more loitering.
Dragging has no love for ladycurls.

A SUPPLIANT Oh-oi   Father!   Godstones' rescue
cheats me   Saltward he presses
spiderish   one step, two
Dream!   Black   dream!

SUPPLIANT OTOTOTOI   MA GA   MAAA   GAAAA

A SUPPLIANT Mama   Earth   Mother me
His snarl
I'm scared   Keep him away   1180
O Pa   Earth-child   O God!

SPOKESMAN I fear none of your demonhost.
They didn't give me suck,
won't nurse me to my old age.

A SUPPLIANT Lustmad   deathmad   he winds closer
hissing   two-leggèd mansnake
pit viper   striking out
Fangs   hold   tight

He grasps her arm.

SUPPLIANTS OTOTOTOI   MA GA MA GA MA GAAAA

A SUPPLIANT MA GA   EARTH   MOTHER ME   1190
His clutch

I'm scared   Tear him away
O PA   GAS PAI   ZEU!

SPOKESMAN If none of you agrees to board ship,
             then ripping shows no pity for your skirts.

                              He does as he says.

A SUPPLIANT Generals   princes of my people
                 I am breaking

SPOKESMAN Be dragged by your pullaway hair.
             You are not quick enough to catch my words.

A SUPPLIANT Hope dies   High lord, I live on in pain   1200
                 beyond speaking

SPOKESMAN Many lords, sons of Egypt,
             soon you'll see them every one.
             Here's comfort:
             you won't squeal then that you lack rule.

                   PELASGOS *enters right with a company of soldiers.*
                   The SPOKESMAN *descends from the sanctuary.*

PELASGOS Who are you? What
              are you doing? What presumption
            leads you to defile a country rich in men?
            Do you think you come to a nation of women?
            Savage,   1210
               you insult Greeks far too carelessly.
            Your fancies mistake their target;
               not one flies straight.

SPOKESMAN Have I done anything unlawful?

PELASGOS Strangers should behave decently. You don't.

SPOKESMAN How not? I find lost property and take it.

PELASGOS Who protects your interests here?

SPOKESMAN Hermes the Searcher, a master protector.

PELASGOS Your tone is irreverent.

SPOKESMAN I left my reverence beside the Nile.   1220

PELASGOS You mean, these gods are nothing?

SPOKESMAN I'll take my women if no one spirits them away.

PELASGOS You'll howl for mercy if you touch them.

SPOKESMAN Strangers deserve a better welcome.

PELASGOS Not strangers who rob the gods.

SPOKESMAN Those words will anger Egypt's sons.

PELASGOS Don't threaten me.

SPOKESMAN But the more I know, the more clear my report;
my duty is to bear exact intelligence.
What shall I tell them? Who steals for himself   1230
this company of women, our own blood cousins?

Ares does not judge a case
by hearing windy words. He takes no silver
to blunt men's swords. Before the end comes:
many thudding bodies, many kicked-off lives.

PELASGOS What need to give you my name?
    In time you shall learn it,
you and your shipmates, and learn it well.
Yet, with their heartfelt, reasoning consent,
you still may take the women if—   1240
    if godfear comes alive in your inducements.

But my assembled people, voting as one,
have shown their will:
    This mission of women shall never
    be surrendered into forceful hands.

259

And a nail is so exactly driven
through that promise, it shall hold everfast.

None of this is published
    on deepcarved stone or bronze
nor sealed in the pages of official documents.   1250
Clear facts:
    you hear the truth voiced freely by a candid man.

Get yourself gone. You foul my sight.

SPOKESMAN I warn: you bind yourself to new bonecracking war.
Victory, power, glory! Let them come to real men.

PELASGOS Men, yes. My earth supports fullblooded men.
Here you'll find no breed that swills malt-wine.

The SPOKESMAN *and his company exeunt left.*

(*to the* SUPPLIANTS)
You are all in the care of friends.
Retrieve your brave hopes. Come
    to the city's safekeeping.   1260
Thick stones circle it, the towers
    grow from deepest roots.
Come with me now.

The SUPPLIANTS *do not respond.*

Do you wonder where you'll live?
Many houses offer ample public lodging,
and I myself am not housed in pinched quarters.
We are ready to welcome you as honored guests
in any of our lively households. But,
    if you prefer,
you may choose to live alone, sequestered quietly.   1270
Whichever best pleases you, enheartens you most,
pick that flower.
    We shield and defend you,

I and all my countrymen, whose vote has taken
full effect. Come.
                              Why wait? For higher authority?

A SUPPLIANT May goodness blossom to reward your goodness,
              most godly of men.
              But send, please send us
              our father, sureminded Danaos,   1280
              prophet and heart's guide.
              His plans grow from judgment far richer than ours.
              He knows where we should live
              and knows the city welcomes us
              and knows that people anywhere will cry
              blame on the foreign-tongued.

                  Let everyone be pleased
                  and no one angrily defame
                  our innocence.

                          PELASGOS *and his soldiers exeunt right.*

              Sisters, my friends and my sisters, be calm.   1290
              Our father allots each one her dowry:
              to serve a virgin future.

                      DANAOS *enters right with an escort of spearmen*
                              and a chorus of ARGIVE WOMEN.

DANAOS Children,
          we must thank the people of Argos with prayers
          and sacrificed animals and red wine outpoured
          as if we thanked the highest gods.
          These mortal men are saviors, weighed
          and found not wanting.

          My account of our trials moved them to support their kin
          and fired their bitterness against your cousins.   1300
          For me they marshalled this flourish of skilled spears
          that I might have the honor due my rank

and not be ambushed by spearkilling fate, and die,
for then my living ghost would place a burden on the land.

They have rescued you.
From the helm of virtue thank them,
praise them with chastity,
increase their honor by preserving yours.

Now write these words,
add them to the treasury   1310
of paternal maxims written earlier on your minds:
An unknown congregation is tested by time.
People everywhere are quick to wag
cruel tongues against an alien;
with ease they speak befouling slander.
You have my warning:
do not shame me.

There glows in you a season that makes men turn
    and hunger.
The succulence of summerfruit is never guarded
    well enough.
Animals paw it, batten on it; so do men. Why not?   1320
Some monsters soar and strike, others roam earth
    on two feet.
[When the fruit blushes ripe, Aphrodite bells a summons
and sets out feasts behind downtrampled gates.]
And when voluptuousness shapes unmated beauty,
every passing eye shoots arrows of enticement
as every passing man falls victim to base appetites.

Be circumspect.
We have already sailed
high seas and seas of trouble
to leave behind *that* suffering.   1330
Our disgrace would feed joy in my enemies.
New lives are near, and a twofold gift of houses,
in virgin cloisters or among the people.
The way of life we choose shall cost us

nothing but sustained decorum.
Easy terms!

But one last warning:
guard a father's commandments;
love your chastity more than your lives.

SUPPLIANTS I pray the high gods look fortune upon me.   1340
And summer's fruit?
                        Be trustful, Father.
Unless godplans have sent new storms onspinning,
my heart shall not be turned from its first-followed path.

They take their branches from the altar and descend from
                                        the sanctuary.

Go forth in brightness exalting
    home's highest lords
the blest gods
        who guard the lifestream of the nation
        who hallow the landloving rivers
        till their agelong white rush enters the sea   1350

Believe!   all you who attend us
    receive
our choired promise
        Fame shall embrace this city and people
        No more shall we sing hymns to quell Nile
    spilling its siltflood into the sea

Sing praise to rivers that rise here
    and thrust through homefields
the sun-oiled streams
        that here shed their pleasurous waters   1360
        to sweeten the dust of the mother Earth
        and fulfill her with life upon life

But see us!   unbroken Artemis
    be fierce
for our voyage

        Help us withstand the womb's urge to fullness
          that opens virgins to Aphrodite's act
        Out of that prize wells the river of death

ARGIVE WOMEN But Aphrodite is not scanted here
          nor do her rites lack eager celebrants.   1370
        She wields such lightning that she,
        with heaven's queen, stands next to Zeus.
        And she is thanked, guile-dazzling
          goddess, for her solemn games.
        And in her motherlight soft daughters walk,
          Passion and one who brooks no denial,
          spellchanting Persuasion.
        To Union then is given the share of love
          that touches and whispers
        and follows the well-traveled paths.   1380

        But you are fugitives. And fear for you
          sends chills of warning through the summerheat.
        Somewhere a storm gathers dark breath:
          cruelty and suffering and bloodblack war.
        What good the fair winds of your passage
          that also sped heelnipping hounds?
        Fate spins each beginning to its only end.
          The Godmind's mystery is impassable;
          no man may overreach it.
        And now, as it has ever been and shall be,   1390
          marriage is destiny,
        and a woman's consummate crown.

A SUPPLIANT Zeus!   O cover me conceal me
        Marry Egypt's brood?
                    I cannot

A WOMAN But marrying would best serve peace.

A SUPPLIANT You chant spells to the spelldeaf.

A WOMAN YOU know nothing of the future.

A SUPPLIANT How can I futuregaze Zeus' mind?
           His eye holds the abyss   1400
                         It blinds me

A WOMAN Be temperate when you cry to Him!

A SUPPLIANT What will that teaching profit me?

A WOMAN To claim no special grace from heaven.

SUPPLIANTS Zeus!   Lord on high!   deprive me
           of marriage   man-built prison
           that stabs and kills
                         It was Your breath
           that transfigured Io   It was
           Your hand   1410
                         healing, triumphant
                                    that held her
           down as You planted Your sweet force

           Glory and power   stream them
           on women   Better the half-light
           than utter dark
                         That I accept
           for heaven's law follows   the lawful
           My hands
                         see! no wrong stains them   1420
                                         O save me
           God, end and beginning of help

                    The SUPPLIANTS *hold their branches high.*
                    ALL *exeunt slowly, ceremoniously right.*

NOTES

1 / 1 *ZEUS MEN APHIKTOR* The Suppliants' initial cry to Zeus is transliterated from the Greek. It means, roughly, *Zeus of Suppliants* or *Zeus Suppliant-Protector*.

1–2 / 1 *Shining Father / Protector of suppliants; Our father on earth* The first phrase is an expanded gloss on the transliterated Greek; the word for *father* does not appear in the text. The literal reading of the second phrase (l. **14 / 11**) is *Danaos father*. The Greek, however, contains a pair of particles—*men / de*, on the one hand / on the other—that contrasts the names of Zeus and Danaos. Because fatherhood is an important issue in the play, it seems fair to emphasize the contrast in translation.

3 / 2 *voyage of women* I have used *voyage* as a collective noun to translate the Greek word *stolos*, company or band or troop. The Suppliants have, after all, just completed a sea journey.

6 / 5 *boundaries graze desert* The Greek reads *Syria*, not *desert*. But in my pursuit of the evocative word I have decided to use a word suggesting the harshness the Suppliants fled rather than to retain a concrete geographical reference that does not again appear in the play.

11–13 / 8–10 *escaping self-built prisons for our own flesh . . . the unholy thought* The lines, not at all clear in Greek, have been the subject of much scholarly conjecture. Do the Suppliants loathe only the idea of marrying the Egyptians? Or do they hate all men, all thoughts of marriage? I suspect that an intrinsic poetic ambiguity is in part responsible for these questions. The Suppliants do reject marriage to the Egyptians, and they express this rejection in terms that conjure the Io-history. There is, I think, a comparison of their own plight with that of Io: marriage would imprison them much as Io was held under Argos' neversleeping guard. The crucial, implicit difference is that Io's captivity was divinely devised, divinely ended, while marriage would be a captivity the Suppliants would take upon themselves without hope of heavenly intervention. Aigyptos is called Egypt throughout the translation.

14 / 11 *Our father on earth* No one knows today at what point Danaos originally made his entrance. It has been placed at play's beginning or immediately prior to his first speech. I see him enter, however, when his name is first mentioned.

28–29 / 21–22 *With these mightiest swords...branches flowering white unspun wool* The latent ferocity of the Suppliants glints briefly here in the comparison of their suppliant emblems to weapons that can kill. And in tragedy death dealt by a sharp blade was a typically feminine form of murder. The Greek is more pointed; it uses a word that means *dagger*, not *sword*.

30 / 23 *O home* The Greek says *O polis*. *Polis* is a loaded word that is all too often flatly translated as *city*. But the ancient *polis* was more, much more, than a collection of stones and timbers. The word rather describes a social organization, a way of life, and by extension can be read as referring to the *place* in which social life was lived. According to context, I have translated *polis* in many ways: home, people, nation, state, and, yes, as city when the material aspect of *polis* seems uppermost.

34 / 26 *Saviour Zeus* Zeus, all-knowing and all-experiencing, has many aspects and many epithets. In *Suppliants* he also appears as Zeus Aphiktor (1 / 1), Father Allvisioning (152 / 139), First Father (254 / 206), Zeus Suppliant (425 / 347, 480 / 385, 841 / 616), Zeus Jury-Appointer (444 / 360), Zeus Alldestroyer (529 / 403), Wealthguarding Zeus (576 / 445), Zeus Guest and Stranger (856 / 627 and 903 / 671), Zeus Avenger (878 / 647), and Earthcradler (1086 / 816).

40 / 30 *self-vaunting* Here Aeschylus writes *hybris*.

47 / 37 *decency forbid!* The Greek calls upon Themis, the moral basis of law and justice.

50–201 / 40–175 *O be joyful now sing...blows a night of storm* The Suppliants' first and longest ode begins in joy but soon turns eerily, prophetically, into lamentation. Laments are far from unusual in Greek tragedy. It is suggestive to remember that tragedies were performed at festivals that took place in the spring and that spring is a time of both grief and joy. Christianity's Holy Week provides a familiar analogue in its mourning for Christ crucified and its celebration of His resurrection. The Suppliants, however, move from happiness to sorrow.

For those who are interested in such matters, it may be helpful to explain a little about choral odes and the ways in which I try to recreate the odes of *Suppliants*. In classical Greek practice such odes were tightly patterned in paired stanzas—a strophe that is followed by an antistrophe repeating the metrical structure. The terms "strophe" and "antistrophe" are now both used with the sense of "stanza," but they mean "turn" and "counterturn" and presumably referred to the dance movements of the Chorus. In choral lyrics strophe and antistrophe may be accompanied by an epode, an "after-ode." The three epodes of *Suppliants* are found near the end of the first long lamentation, and they can easily be distinguished because they act as a reiterated refrain. In all the odes sung by the Suppliants, words and ideas that occur in the strophe often recur significantly in the antistrophe; sometimes they occupy similar, if not identical, positions in the lines. Lines 766 / 574 and 778–79 / 582 provide an example: Zeus "who lives without end" and his son Epaphos "who lived a life crowned with years and gold." Such correspondences are readily translated. The Greek meters, however, cannot be reproduced in English because the sound properties of the languages are intrinsically different. But to convey some idea of the discipline that informs the Greek, I have translated each strophe and its antistrophe into twin stanzas linked by close syllabic and rhythmic similarities.

58 / 47 *Epaphos, Caress-born* The proper name Epaphos signifies *touch* or *caress*.

71–79 / 60–67 *to her who was wife . . . own hand's anger unmothered* The Suppliants here combine two ancient nightingale stories. In the text they speak of the wife of Tereus, Aēdōn, whose name is the Greek word for nightingale. In the *Odyssey* (19.518ff.) Homer briefly mentions a nightingale, *aēdōn*, once wife of Zethus, who killed her son Itylos and ever after on spring nights sang in lamentation. Tereus, king of Thrace, figures in a bloodier myth told by Apollodorus (3.14.8) and Achilles Tatius (5.3, 5). Pandion, king of Athens, had two daughters, Procne and Philomela, and to reward Tereus for helping him in battle, he gave Procne in marriage to the Thracian. She bore him one son, Itys. But she was lonely in barbaric Thrace and sent Tereus to Athens to bring her sister for a visit. On the journey north Tereus raped Philomela and cut out her tongue to keep her from telling Procne of the assault. Philomela, however, wove a tapestry that pictured the event. And Procne sought revenge. She killed Itys, boiled him, and served him as dinner to her faithless husband. The sisters fled, but Tereus, soon realizing what he had eaten, seized an axe and hunted them down. When they saw his murderous rage, they prayed that the gods turn them into birds. Prayer was answered. Philomela became a songless swallow, and Procne a nightingale whose trill, *ity ity*, repeats the name of her dead son. And Tereus, changed to a hawk, hunts them still.

80 / 69 *And singing Io's song* The literal reading is *lamentation in Ionian measures* or *in the Ionian mode*, a direct reference to musical practice. But the adjective *Ionian* certainly evokes Io. And the Greek word *nomos* that I have translated as *song* is close in sound to a word signifying *pasture*. Aristophanes makes a pun on the correspondence in *The Birds*, l. 1287.

88 / 76 *who will here lament and bury us?* This entire line interprets a single Greek word, *kēdemōn*. Translators of this play have let it off too lightly as *kinsman* or *protector*, which is its classical sense. But I look back to Homer, who uses the word only for someone who is charged with the care and ritual burial of the dead. In the context of *Suppliants* it seems most appropriate to see it as signifying "a person with enough family feeling to see that mourning and burial are properly performed." (Thank you, Margaret Alexiou, for your concurring letter.)

90 / 78 *heaven's laws* Here and elsewhere the words translate references to the concept of *dikē*.

98–107 / 86–95 *And Zeus! grant that my hopes all come true . . . that men cannot read* Editors vary in their arrangements of these lines. I have followed Johansen's order.

126 / 114 *alalala* Greek tragedy has a large store of grieving cries, and the Suppliants wail many of them. Some I have simply transliterated: *aiai, ototoi*. Others have been adapted to the needs of the English: *ululuu* for the Greek *iō iō*; *away away away* for the Greek *eé*. Exactly such inarticulate expressions of grief may be heard today on the tongues of Greek village women.

130 / 117 *Hillpastures* The Greek words are *Apian bounin*; the literal reading is *Apian land-of-hills*, an apparently straightforward description. But the words reverberate. The adjective *Apian*, as applied to Argos' hills, summons the healer Apis who came to Argos and cured the polluted earth (331 /

260 and **342** / 269). And *bounin*, a rare word, calls to mind the Greek word for cow, *bous*.

131 / 118 *My cry holds Egypt's savagery* I have given this line a double meaning that may not exist in the Greek. *Egypt's savagery* can refer both to the Suppliants' foreign-flavored Greek and to the savage murderousness that sleeps within them.

132 / 118 *Mother-earth* Again there are two references, one to the primal Gaia, the goddess Earth, and the other to the home earth of the Suppliants' maternal ancestor Io.

134–35 / 121–22 *the fine-spun veil / that shrouds my sight* The passage in Greek refers to nothing other than the physical action the Suppliants perform to accompany their words. In a traditional gesture of mourning they rip their veils of "fine Sidonian linen," as the Greek has it. I have gone beyond these bounds to suggest the Suppliants' blindness to their plight.

136–38 / 123–24 *But rites for the dead...bearing a bloodcurse* The storm-shadow darkens. The suppliants know their premature sorrow is an act of ill omen, but uncontrollably they persist in lamentation. The same superstition figures in the *Iliad* (6.500) and at least five other tragedies, Aeschylus' *Persians*, Sophocles' *Elektra* and *Antigone*, Euripides' *Alcestis* and *Hecuba*. Here the picture is especially chilling, for the Suppliants mourn themselves.

160 / 145 *stainless daughter of Zeus* Artemis is the goddess invoked. The text does not name her, nor is it now clear about what, exactly, she is doing. The Greek seems to see her as holding a shrine wall securely or keeping her face safely. I have chosen the former image for its sexual suggestiveness in relation to the Suppliants' predicament.

180 / 161 *gods on the skysummits* Olympos is the summit mentioned in the text.

208–9 / 180 *for I see / dust* Danaos describes what he actually sees and at the same time seems to prophesy the advent of the Egyptian army that will, after this play ends, vanquish Argos.

254 / 206 *Zeus! First Father* The Greek says *Zeus Progenitor*. I wish to suggest both his divine fatherhood and his actual fathering of the Suppliants' line.

258–61 / 210–13 *O God, this weariness...Praise takes wing, flies toward the sun* Though the meaning of this passage seems clear in the Greek, the arrangement of the lines is uncertain, and one line spoken by the Suppliants is known to be missing. I have followed the Loeb order. The missing line is ignored, for conjecture would here add nothing to the general tone of troubled invocation.

262 / 214 *And Apollo, god who spent a year on earth* Myth says that Apollo's son, the physician Asklepios, once used his healing powers to bring a man back from the dead. This misapplication of godgiven skill enraged Zeus, who hurled his lethal thunderbolt through doctor and patient. In retaliation for his son's death Apollo killed the thunderbolt-makers, the Cyclopes. For this act Zeus condemned Apollo to ever-lasting punishment in Hades, but Leto, Apollo's mother, interceded and the sentence was commuted to a year of shepherding the earthly flocks of King Admetos.

273 / 223 *pitying of doves* The Greek says a *swarm of doves*, using the same word that denotes the Egyptian *manswarm* (*swarm of males* in literal translation) and brings to mind Io's tormenting fly. But I could not resist here employing an old and genuine collective term—as genuine as covey of quail and murder of crows—that both describes the Suppliants as a group and says something about their state of mind.

286 / 231 *final vengeance* The Greek refers to *dikē*, which both benefits and punishes.

291 / 234 PELASGOS By a curious inversion that may have held no significance whatever for the poet or the original Greek audience, Aeschylus chose to name the Greek king "Pelasgos." Some versions of the myth give the king's name as Gelanor. Pelasgos, in *Suppliants* the archetypal Greek, was, in Greek legend, the eponymous ruler of a pre-Greek people, the Pelasgi, who inhabited the mainland during that time now called the Neolithic and whose non-Greek language and ways persisted in isolated pockets well into classical times. Aeschylus presents Danaos, on the other hand, as a black foreigner. Danaos was, to be sure, of Greek descent, but his line was four generations removed from Argos. Yet, it is the alien Danaos whose name is given, in Homer and elsewhere, to the Danaans. And Danaans is simply a generic term for Greeks.

294–95 / 236–37 *and womanly, yet gaudy as no women / I have ever known or dreamed* Pelasgos says literally, "Not Argolid your women's dress, nor from any place in Hellas." He implies that the Suppliants' appearance is beyond his experience and imagining, and so have I translated.

313 / 250 *Ancient Ground Palaikhthon* is the ancestral name given by Pelasgos. Uncapitalized it is a compound word that means nothing other than *ancient-ground, ancient-land*. Pelasgos is not, however, saying merely that he was born on Argive soil. Rather, he claims descent from a divine son of the goddess Earth.

315–17 / 252–53 *and I / for these good reasons stand first / among the land's many sons* The Greek yields, "And for me, their king, the tribe of the Pelasgi... is appropriately named." Pelasgos is telling the Suppliants indirectly that he is not an absolute king but a leader, *primus inter pares*. The Suppliants, unfamiliar with Argive government, do not catch his meaning.

319–28 / 254–59 *Over plains, over valleys... until sea restrains me / with its bluesalt marches* Aeschylus' geography is more specific than mine. According to Johansen's edition, the Greek says, "And over all the region through which pure Strymon flows—there toward the setting sun, I rule. And I am bounded by the Paionians' land that lies beyond Pindos, near the Perrhaibians and the mountains of Dodona. And the boundary of the moist sea cuts me short." Pelasgos claims territory far north of the Argolid peninsula. Strymon is a river in Thrace. Pindos is a mountain range in northwestern Greece. Dodona, renowned seat of a pre-Greek oracle, lies in Epirus. Because the names of tribes and places are non-evocative in English and would only, at best, send a few diligent readers to a map, I have tried less concretely to suggest the immensity of Pelasgos' claims.

329–42 / 260–70 *And the region around us... his reproachless name a fee of prayer* Argos and Egypt are in many ways linked in *Suppliants*, and these lines show a most subtle connection. The Greek says: "The region where we now stand was long ago called Apian in gratitude to a mortal man, a healer. For, coming from neighboring Naupaktos [a port on the northern shore of the Gulf of Corinth], Apis, healer-and-prophet, son of Apollo, cleansed this land of wild, man-destroying beasts, to which injured Earth, besmeared by the pollutions of ancient blood-deeds, had given birth.... For cutting out and loosening these pains irreproachable Apis is remembered in the Argive land and given recompense in prayer." Naupaktos notwithstanding, Apis is the bullheaded Egyptian god, son of Isis, who is portrayed with horns or a crescent moon on her head. The close physical correspondence between this pair and Io-Epaphos is obvious. Aeschylus surely recognized it and also the near identity of Apis' and Epaphos' names. The connection is clear in the reference here to "irreproachable Apis" and later to Epaphos "son immune to reproach" (777 / 581). Danaos seems to try to put himself into this picture when he tells his daughters that he is going to the city of Argos to muster help: "A call to arms—no, the people won't reproach its clarion" (1024–25 / 774–75).

352–62 / 277 *Strangers spin me tales...fleshfeasting Amazons* Aeschylus' geography here leaves Greece and sweeps through the eastern Mediterranean to "Ethiopia's borders," which in classical times meant India, and rests finally on the shores of the Black Sea, homeground of the Amazons. The imagery invests the Suppliants with lush sexuality, and they are made to seem potentially dangerous.

366–98 / 291–323 *A keeper of the keys to Hera's house...EGYPT!* This passage bristles with problems. First, it is corrupt; lines and phrases have been lost. Then, editors do not agree about who says what, who asks, who answers. There is disagreement, too, about which lines are questions. I have followed the Loeb version throughout, partly because I think that dramatic irony is well served by having the Suppliants interrogate Pelasgos rather than the other way round. That they immediately take the offensive and make Pelasgos defend himself does show a desperate cunning in their characters. They are as fierce as they look. I have also accepted the Loeb conjectures about the missing lines; such are bracketed in the translation.

Textual difficulties do not obscure what I believe is a third geography. Pelasgos has described his realm; he has speculated about the Suppliants' homeland. Here Io's line is described as producing gods and nations. The Epaphos-Apis correspondence has been mentioned. Belos can be undisguised as Baal, the golden calf, another bull god. Libya and Egypt are the eponymous founders of the lands that bear their names; Agenor can be equated with Canaan. It is almost as if the earth without Io would have been an earth without North Africa, Palestine, and the pyramids.

366 / 291 *Hera's house* Her temple. Hera, patron goddess of Argos, presided over the sanctity of marriage. A love affair between her priestess and her consort was sure to arouse queenly wrath.

385 / 311 *lower Nile and the city of sphinxes* The Greek says *Canopus and Memphis*. Again I replace ancient names with words that are meant to be evocative for the reader here and now.

390 / 317 *Libya, great and fertile* The line is not clear. It seems to say *Libya who harvests the greatest* word missing *on earth*. Though Libya now appears

in imagination as an arid land where the greatest harvest is subterranean oil, it was anciently much admired for its fertile soil. Herodotus speaks of its three yearly harvests, each successively farther inland and at higher altitudes (*Histories* 4.199). I chose to emphasize fertility in the translation because of the play's general obsession with the subject and because of the vegetable image in the near line, "Had she another offshoot?" The Greek word *blastēmos*, scion or sprout or offshoot, is an urgent green word.

414–25 / 336–47 *Or have they violated laws . . . the burden of Zeus Suppliant's wrath* Again, the text is not easy to interpret, and two lines are missing. I have not tried to re-imagine them. Despite corruption, the dialogue seems packed with implications. Pelasgos tries to understand the Suppliants' motive for seeking asylum. Hatred, to his good Greek logic, is too intangible a reason for behaving in a fashion that defies social expectations. Women in his world marry; love and hatred do not figure in the arrangements. He seeks a reason that he can accept: perhaps the Egyptians have performed a criminal act that would cause the Suppliants to reject and denounce them. The Suppliants, however, appeal to Pelasgos' emotions, not his reason, and they avoid giving a direct answer. Though they cite heaven's law and suggest that it overrides any manmade law, the conclusion to be drawn is that the Egyptians do indeed have valid legal claim to the women. Pelasgos' earlier hunch that these Suppliants endanger Argos receives confirmation. From his point of view their response is lunatic. But his reverence for the gods outweighs his fear that the women bring sure calamity in their train.

423 / 345 *your state's helmsmen* The idea of the state as a ship is frequently expressed in Greek literature. And what more natural for a seafaring people?

426–517 / 348–407 *Son of this Ancient Ground . . . Earthly justice is yours to achieve* The exchange between the Suppliants and Pelasgos is truly an adversary proceeding. The Greek resounds with legal terminology. The stage becomes a court of law. And it is not only the Suppliants and Pelasgos who are at odds, but two kinds of law: the unwritten code of heaven and the rules legislated by men. Try as he will, Pelasgos cannot explain to these alien, and increasingly alienating, women how firmly he is bound to respect his country's laws and its form of government. Some scholars have felt that Aeschylus, letting his pen run away with him, overstressed Argive democracy or that he was making a point we cannot now grasp. To me, however, the confrontation seems not to be imbalanced or obscure. The conflict here becomes polarized. Rationality is set against irrationality, moderation against excess. The Suppliants, whose foreign-ness is brought into high relief, are shown retreating from reality into fantasy.

443 / 360 *Themis* The Suppliants cry out to the personification of the moral basis of manmade laws and customs. The invocation holds a horrible irony.

444 / 360 *Zeus Jury-Appointer* The epithet could be translated as *Apportioner* or *Lot-Caster*. Juries were chosen by casting lots, and I have emphasized this aspect of the epithet.

453 / 365–66 *my private hearth* The hearth was the heart, warm and sacred, of an ancient household.

461 / 370 *You the people!* The Greek says *You indeed the polis*. See note above (l. 30 / 23) on the word *polis*.

462 / 371 *pharaoh* The Greek word is *prytanis*, which generally signifies *ruler* or *lord* and can also denote a tribal leader or a magistrate. Pharaoh, however, seems a title that would slip easily from the tongues of Egyptian refugees.

476 / 381 *His gaze* A fatherly eye—Greek *skopos*, literally *look-out*—rests on the play. To have and to be *skopos*, to possess such an all-seeing outlook, is a gift usually reserved for deity. See notes below, ll. 877–79 / 646–48, 946 / 713, 1046 / 786.

483–90 / 387–91 *If—hear me! . . . none whatever, over you* Pelasgos again indicates his suspicion that the Suppliants may be breakers of man's law. The issue of their defense, however, is moot; in this play it does not come to the test. It is perhaps easiest, here and now, to read the passage as one more attempt on Pelasgos' part to make the women see reason. Their response is again emotional.

511–12 / 403 *God Whose hands / weighing* The image of Zeus weighing or balancing scales is used directly once again in the play (1096 / 822–23). And Aeschylus worked two oblique changes on the picture, both in reference to the men of Argos who vote "not ambivalently" (825 / 605) and are "saviors, weighed / and found not wanting" (1297–98 / 982).

521 / 409 *eye undazed by the sea's winy rapture* The Greek speaks of an "eye not over-intoxicated." The phrase has often been understood as signifying an eye not confused in its perceptions; most translators omit any suggestion of

the effects of alcohol. The Greek words, however, are not metaphoric. And the Greeks, as a sea people, surely knew about nitrogen narcosis, that rapture of the deep, which can make the fathoms-down diver feel as drunk as a toper. Pelasgos' language here and elsewhere is salted with sea imagery.

535–64 / 418–37 *Be counseled and become...downstreaming from Zeus* These four stanzas are nothing other than a good old-fashioned curse, calling heaven's wrath upon Pelasgos and his descendants, should he thwart the Suppliants.

550 / 429 *godstones* The Greek word, *bretas*, signifies a wooden image. But because the modern mind will probably imagine the gods in terms of museum marbles, I substitute stone for wood.

571–73 / 440–41 *last nail driven home...strains toward the sea* Aeschylus' metaphor has undergone (I refuse to say suffered) a seachange. In the original it is a highly compressed nineteen syllables, a line and a half, and it is not translatable without resort to paraphrase. The gist is, "And as a ship's hull, the nails driven in, is held fast in shipyard winches, so am I held fast." In my version, nails, ship, and winches remain, but I inject the idea of a launching, of future events now set into unrecallable motion. Either way, Pelasgos means that he is gripped by the absolute necessity of making a decision he can never change.

576–77 / 444 [*in jealous charity / make good the loss*] This is my guess. The line is grievously damaged. It seems to say something about cheating and refilling with plenteous cargo.

580 / 448 [*or twist the arrow in the wound*] Again, a guess. The line is either corrupt or interpolated. As it stands, it seems to mention grief of spirit and agitation.

588–89 / 452 *Your animosity / repels and pulls me in* The single verb that I have translated as *repels and pulls me in* is a verb with many shades of meaning that all involve either *go* or *come*. The line literally says, "Truly, deeply, I much shrink-from / am-brought-into these quarrels."

593–96 / 453–54 *a killing night...for peace, for light* No, Aeschylus' poetry does not rhyme. And the Greek says, "I wish to be ignorant of evils rather than wise in them, but may matters go well, though my opinion is that they won't." But such a bald translation has no force as poetry in English.

646–48 / 493–94 *of the tutelary gods / those city-guarding crocodiles that slumber / in the life-stream of your nation* These lines translate three words, *tōn polissoukhōn theōn*, which usually appear in English as *of the city-protecting gods*. *Polissoukhos* (nominative form of the adjective) is, however, a rare compound that I think must be loaded with connotations. *Polis*, of course, is the word signifying people-nation-state-society. And if one reads through the alphabetized list of *polis* compounds in the lexicon, sure enough, there is the definition, *city-protecting*, for the double-barreled word. But, when one looks up *soukhos* alone, the definition given is *crocodile*. In the mind of Danaos the Egyptian, why should Argos' gods *not* seem to be crocodiles, as hidden and holy and dangerous as Nile's sacred beasts?

652 / 497 *Io's fathering river* Inakhos, the Argive king who fathered Io and a river and a river deity therefore, is the name given in the text.

660 / 503 *the firesides of gods* The Greek says *hearths* and refers to the fires that burn on the altars of the gods' temple-houses.

661–66 / 504–9 *You instructed him...How can it keep me safe?* And why does Pelasgos instruct the Suppliants to leave the safety of the shrine? Aeschylus as playwright had a purely technical reason for moving the women from the sanctuary height to level ground or, in stage terms, from the raised stage to the orchestra. After Pelasgos makes his exit, the Suppliants sing and dance. The raised stage was not the conventional place for choral dancing. In the Greek, Pelasgos merely tells the Suppliants to descend to level ground and, though they are reluctant to abandon their refuge, he reassures them and they descend. In the translation I have added an explanation to Pelasgos' instruction so that a lone reader, not necessarily concerned with such ancient details, can imagine that the Suppliants might welcome a chance to stretch their legs after huddling in the sanctuary.

684–813 / 524–99 *Lord over lords...has completed whatever His will / conceives* At play's mid-point, in this magnificent central ode, the Suppliants act out their deepest wishes when they sing and dance the prayer-framed story of Io's torment and transfiguration. As a poet I feel that strange things are happening. In the evocation of Io, time collapses as her ancient past enters and fills the play's present moment. And in the simultaneous existence of past and present, the finite stage reaches into the universe and the mortal Suppliants glow briefly with divinity.

714 / 542 *mindbroken she runs* Yes, Aeschylus does use the present tense. It has been thought of as an historical present and is often, therefore, translated as a past. In the lines that follow I have made free with the tenses originally used because after Io here moves into the present, I prefer to keep her there as if she were actually on the stage.

721–33 / 547–55 *hurls her body down Asia . . . scythes grain in the fields* A fourth geography (see also ll. 319–27 / 254–59, 329–42 / 260–70, 366–98 / 291–323), and I have taken great liberties with it in order to make evocative English poetry. For the Greekless here is a literal translation of the lines: "And she hurls herself through Asian lands, straight through sheepgrazing Phrygia. And she passes the town of Teuthras the Mysian, and Lydian valleys; and through the mountains of the Cilicians, of the Pamphylians, too, she rushes on to everflowing rivers and deep-rich soil and Aphrodite's grain-fertile fields."

737 / 558 *at the green oasis holy to Zeus* Io arrives in Egypt. The Greek says not *oasis* but *sacred grove* or *precinct*. I choose a word that refugees from Egypt might use.

740–43 / 559–60 *where quick showers strike . . . to rainsmoke* The Greek has Typhō striking or attacking "the snowsuckled pasture." Typhō is, in one view, the personification of a whirlwind. In Greek imaginations he was the monstrous child of Earth and Tartarus. After he had variously attacked the Olympian gods, they fled to Egypt to avoid his assaults. Zeus at last managed to catch him and bury him beneath Mount Aetna, where his smoky breath still erupts. His name, in fact, signifies smoke and smouldering. He has also been equated with the Egyptian deity Set, who killed Osiris, the husband of Isis. And Isis, as has been mentioned, was the crescent-horned mother of Apis. Some mythologists see her as a nature goddess and the murderer Set, therefore, as destruction or decay in nature. I dodge all these complications and settle for *rainsmoke* and *quick showers.* Typhō's attacks appear only as a series of curt English k-sounds.

750–51 / 565 *And the people whose lives / the rich land sustains* The Greek moves here into the past tense and merely says *the people who at that time lived in the land.* I retain the present because I feel that Io is still onstage.

768 / 575 *Zeus . . .* This one word is all that is left of a seven-syllable line.

771 / 578 *she found rest* Past tense in English, past tense in Greek: I think that this is the moment at which the Suppliants release Io and let her return to her own elder time.

789 / 590 *Danaos enters right.* Most editors and translators see Danaos entering immediately after the Suppliants have finished singing their ode. I think that an entrance at this point is more dramatically effective in modern terms.

794–95 / 592 *The Father / Urge of my green life* Yes, the Greek says patēr, father. The Suppliants' confusion about their father's identity begins to show.

829 / 609 SETTLERS IN OUR MOTHERLAND The word *settlers* indicates that Danaos and his daughters have not been granted citizenship, which carried with it voting rights for men and certain rights of property and inheritance. They are all, nevertheless, granted freedom of the *polis* and full protection. As for *motherland*, the Greek merely says *land*. I add the qualifier to evoke Io.

843–44 / 618–19 *doubly guests and kinsmen...double mist of blood* Because the Suppliants are both guests and distant kinsmen of the Argive people, any evil they might cause would have a twofold effect. The lines recall the healing work of Apis, who once cured Argos of a hideous pollution, and they also foreshadow events to come. The Suppliants will indeed stain Argive soil with blood.

861–942 / 630–709 *Now O gods / created of God...written in godgiven law* I have imagined this ode sung in antiphonal choruses, one of high bright voices, the other of dark-timbred voices. The strophes seem to divide themselves into two somewhat alternating groups. Some blessings are couched in positive terms: "Nation! be governed well." Others catalogue horrors that the Suppliants hope will *not* decimate the Argive people: "Never may they know the peace / that scorched earth brings." The storm gathers force. War and sickness and murder are the housegifts that the Suppliants bring to their Argive hosts.

877–79 / 646–48 *Zeus / Avenger's eye / No battling that gaze* Here again is skopos (see note, l. 476 / 381), the divine ability to see everything, everywhere. In these lines the god's eye, his steady gaze, becomes a bird.

890–91 / 659–60 *Never may a plague / of men drain this nation* The Greek is as ambiguous as the English. Plague may be understood as epidemic sickness or as an attack force of soldiers, *of men*. Both can drain the nation, the *polis*, of her men.

895 / 665–66 *Ares Manmurderer* Ares, too, bears epithets. Soon hereafter he is called Tear-breeder (l. 913 / 682).

907 / 676 *Artemis! Hekate!* Artemis, as a goddess with special interest in women's affairs, not only kept an eye on chastity and unmarried girls, but also protected women in childbirth. The goddess Hekate, at Zeus' behest, guarded the well-being of children. By invoking her, the Suppliants bless not only women in labor but also the infants that are struggling to be born. In light of the Suppliants' determination not to marry, the blessing is ironic.

917 / 686 *Apollo of Wolves* The Greek calls him *Lykeios*, an epithet that is closely related to the word for wolf, *lykos*. Apollo was thought to be both a protector of wolves that might threaten a man's enemies and a killer of wolves that attacked herds. Surely the Suppliants here call to him as one who keeps cattle safe.

936–42 / 704–9 *This is home earth for gods . . . written in godgiven law* The Greek uses only the adjective *triton*, third, as I have used it. The two preceding rules are not enumerated. They are, however, plainly there in the passage. (Thank you, John Herington.)

946 / 713 *From this high holy refuge the eye gazes far* That gazing eye is *skopē* here, a *place of look-out*. The word is perilously similar to *skopos* (see note, l. 476 / 381). Danaos does not use a pronoun to qualify the gaze but it is patently his. Nevertheless, he manages to claim a god's talent for himself. Does he confuse himself with Zeus?

947–53 / 713–18 *I see the ship. / She is well marked . . . from the helm astern* What a vivid picture Danaos creates! And here one catches sight of the notion that an inanimate thing, a ship, is somehow alive. The eyes painted on the bows possess a mysterious but very real ability to see.

969–70 / 729 NOT ONE SHALL DARE TOUCH YOU! / *No need to dread them, no need to run* The literal translation of the Greek is tedious: "But nothing shall come of these things; do not flee-in-fear from them." But, O but, the Greek is full of hard, short d-sounds and t-sounds. I try to reproduce them.

984 / 741 *They are a shoal of sharks* Aeschylus does not mention *sharks* but describes Egypt's offspring as *margon*, an adjective with multiple meanings—lustful, mad, gluttonous. I have used the shark image for two reasons. First, it pictures concretely the mindless greed implied by *margon*; the Egyptians' seaborne pursuit of the Suppliants is activated by an impulse akin to the one that triggers a feeding frenzy. Then, it complements the animal images

that do appear in the text soon hereafter when the Suppliants compare the Egyptians to other carnivores, *dogs* and *carrion crows*.

986 / 743 *Hulls quest, shot spears* The Greek says *sturdy-timbered ships*, ships that are well built. For the sake of a vivid picture in English I have made much of the fact that the Greek words for *timber* and *spear* are similar in appearance and sound, if not in etymology. I see sleek ships slicing the water with unstoppable force.

1006-7 / 760-61 *It's said that wolves... / that papyrus cannot seed the grainfields* These expressions are clearly proverbial. The literal reading of the second is, "Papyrus' fruit does not prevail over grain." I think that my version points up the play's emphasis on fertility without sacrificing the proverb's sense.

1016-17 / 769-70 *And Night / likes mothering birthpains in the skillful helmsman* This odd expression—odd, at any rate, to us—is quite literally translated. Don't disbelieve it. The thought is that the primordial goddess Night, obscuring human vision, takes divinely malicious pleasure in spawning anxiety and fear in all men, and most especially in one who must perform his task in darkness. One might paraphrase the lines this way: The skillful helmsman, charged with securing a ship at night in a strange harbor, has his stomach tied in knots.

1020 / 772 *until the ships themselves feel snug at their moorings* Again, an indication that ships are alive and sentient. It is the *ships*, not the helmsmen, who must feel secure.

1027-98 / 776-824 *io io ioioioioio / O Earth... can steady the deathbound?* This ode, like the first one that the Suppliants sing, is a lament. Thoughts of death and marriage are intertwined and sung in grieving voices. It may be of interest to note that ritual lamentation, a Greek practice with a traceable literary history spanning two and a half millennia, is not necessarily confined to the occasion of death. Emigration, exile, and marriage have also given rise to dirges. In the case of marriage there seem to be several initiating impulses. One is simply the structural similarity of Greek wedding and funeral rites. Another is symbolic similarity; the girl leaves her father's house and her childhood as truly and forever as the dead leave earth and life. In the Suppliants' song the two occasions fuse. They sing their own bridal dirge, and Death is the husband they would embrace.

1046 / 786 *A father's eye snares me* Once again, *skopos* (see note, l. 476 / 381). The Suppliants seem to say two things in one: "What my father Danaos has seen now closes in on me like a snare" and, as if a brief recognition of their wrongheadedness bursts forth, "Zeus the Father's eye holds me in a snare from which I cannot escape."

1056 / 794 *goatfoiling* The Greek says *goatless*, and the adjective describes a rockface that is too precipitous to be climbed even by agile wild goats.

1063 / 799 *murderous bed* Greek and English both carry twin readings: that the Suppliants feel that marriage will kill them and that they will kill if they are forced to marry.

1064–65 / 800–801 *No! first dogs shall eat . . . a godless grave* In Greek the Suppliants say that they do not refuse to be dogs' prey and a feast for native birds. I add an interpretation that I think would have been implicitly grasped by the ancient audience. To escape marriage the Suppliants would go to the shocking extremity of forfeiting the funeral rites that the living and the dead were owed as a religious duty. And such unhallowed burial could bring pollution in its train. But the Suppliants in their desperation care for no one but themselves.

1073 / 806–7 *What saving channel must I cut* Again both Greek and English hold twin readings: statement and prophecy. The Suppliants refer here to their recent flight across the sea and they also foreshadow murder-to-come, the stabbing—"cutting"—of the bridegrooms.

1081 / 811 *Look peace on me, Father* The word *Father*, vocative in Greek, is ambiguous and can refer to Zeus or Danaos.

1087 / 817 *Egypt's get, how ugly their self-glory Genos gar Aigypteion*, the Greek stutters hard g-sounds. Self-glory is, of course, *hybris*.

1099–1205 / 825–910 *No No No NO NO-O-O-O . . . You won't squeal then that you lack rule* The text throughout has been severely damaged. Phrases have been compacted into single nonsense words; lines and passages are garbled or lost. Line order is sometimes uncertain. Nor are editors always sure about who speaks, Suppliants or Egyptian Spokesman or, in Johansen's guess, a chorus of Egyptians. The confrontation is nevertheless the most active, the most powerful scene in the play. And a translator falls back on intuition to bring into English the vigor that still resides in the corrupted Greek.

1109 / 835 *Lord on earth* The Suppliants cry out to the absent Pelasgos. The Greek word is *gaïanax*, which signifies *earthlord* or *lord-of-the-land*.

1110 / 836 SPOKESMAN The Spokesman is a herald delegated to herd the Suppliants to the ship and to bring back intelligence. I imagine him, however, as one of the sons of Egypt and have so treated him in the translation.

1110 / 836 Sssssssssssssssssssss——Hurry hurry (*sousthe sousthe*) says the Greek. I like those hissing s's.

1111–17 / 836–42 *So. You. Move move…Chopnecks, toppleheads, / move* Here and in his other speeches the Spokesman seems to use a broken Greek. It is the kind of speech that a foreigner unfamiliar with a language might employ.

1114 / 839 *skin stung* Io's gadfly is evoked.

1119 / 842 *on your dunghill* The Greek says *epamida* or *ep' amada*; the significance is utterly lost. The usual translation, based on contextual guesswork, is *to the ship*. But the Greek word is divisible into the preposition *epi* and the noun *amis*. The lexicon defines the latter as *chamber pot* and cites its seeming occurrence here as a false reading, that is—the result of a copyist's mistake or misinterpretation. How, then, can I possibly arrive at dunghill? I hope to suggest many things: the chamber pot's contents, the height on which the Suppliants take sanctuary, the dung of cattle, and the Egyptian Spokesman's utter lack of respect for Greek gods. There is, irrelevantly, an ancient proverb involving *amis*: "Don't throw grain into a chamber pot." Nor cast pearls before swine.

1120–68 / 843–81 *I wish / weltering waves had…from that morass where your self-blindness thrives* The Suppliants now curse the Egyptians. In this passage both of the English compounds using *self-* are translations of *hybris*. The bracketed lines are re-imaginations of jumbled, run-on words that do, for all their unintelligibility, suggest such ideas as blood and sweetness and nobility and goats.

1138 / 855 *the springflooding water* Nile, of course.

1139 / 855 *Only there can you trade your cattle for brides* The Greek line says *alphesiboion hydōr*, which is usually read as *cattle-nourishing* or *cattle-producing water*. That is, water that greens pastures which in turn produce fat cattle. But again I look back to Homer, who applies the adjective *cattle-*

producing to the noun for an unmarried girl. It signifies that the girl will fetch a good brideprice. I could not resist using the adjective to recall Io and her transfiguration, the divine union in which she traded her cow-form for womanhood. And I hear the Suppliants obliquely telling the Egyptians that they, the women, are not cattle who will become brides.

1140–41 / 856–57 *Only there can your lifebearing blood / arrive at full flower* The metaphor expresses the not-uncommon archaic notion that whatever encourages growth in the natural world also mysteriously promotes human growth and maturity. As water is needed for vegetable fertility, so is it needed for human "flowering."

1144–45 / 859–60 [*My earth my line / your home is mine*] The Egyptians remind the Suppliants that they, too, are Io's descendants. Their claim to Argos is equally strong.

1156 / 869–70 *your wanderings tombed* The Greek mentions, instead, *Sarpedon's sandy promontory-bank-tumulus.* In any case a headland on the coast of Asia Minor is indicated, for there Sarpedon, one of the sons born in Crete to Zeus and Europa, died and was buried.

1159 / 873 *Egypt's craft* I introduce a double reading—*boat / cunning*—that does not exist in the Greek, which simply says *boat.*

1165 / 878 *a crocodile* Not *soukhos* (see note, ll. **645–47 / 493–94**) but *khampsa* is the word translated. Herodotus says the latter is the Egyptian word for crocodile (*Histories* 2.69). The usual Greek word for the beast has a familiar ring, *krokodeilos.* Aeschylus seems to use the unusual word to emphasize, once again, the Suppliants' foreignness.

1173 / 885 *Father!* Zeus or Danaos? Either and both.

1177 / 889–92 and 1193 / 899–902 *OTOTOTOI MA GA* and *O PA GAS PAI ZEU* The Greek has been transliterated. In their terror the Suppliants revert to an infant babble and cry out in elemental Indo-European monosyllables that I think need no translation. MA and PA: eternally mother and father. GA: Earth. *GAS PAI:* Earth's child. *ZEU:* vocative of Zeus. And *OTOTOTOI:* the chatter of terror.

1179 / 890 and 1191 / 900 *His snarl* and *His clutch* In both places the Greek word indicates the sound—a howl or a cry—that the Spokesman makes. I work a small change to suggest evil manifestations of breath and touch.

1194–1205 / 903–10 *If none of you agrees to board ship . . . you won't squeal then that you lack rule* The order of these lines is most uncertain. I have followed Johansen's arrangement.

1200 / 908 *High lord* Pelasgos.

1257 / 953 *malt-wine* The Egyptians were beer drinkers.

1258 / 954 *You are all in the care of friends* The Greek says, "But all of you with your friendly female companions in attendance." Here is the text's first suggestion that the Suppliants are accompanied by maidservants, who may have occupied the stage from play's beginning. I do not reject this possibility outright. But these ladies have not survived translation because I think that it is too much to ask of a contemporary reader that he accept such a minor chorus, whose lines (**1369–1404** / 1034–61, if they did utter these lines at all) can be given with more here and now dramatic logic to others (see note below, l. **1369** / 1039).

1264–70 / 957–61 *Do you wonder where you'll live . . . sequestered quietly* The question of the Suppliants' lodgings, mentioned here and in lines **1332–33** / 1009–11, has provoked debate. There are those who think the matter peculiarly overemphasized; there are others who believe that the Suppliants' choice had significance in the trilogy's lost plays. In Greek feeling the place in which a crime occurred had bearing on the crime's gravity. And where did the Suppliants commit murder? In a sacred spot, in the king's house, in private lodgings? No one knows. I have tried to translate around these problems so that a reader will not be puzzled but rather hear Pelasgos trying both to talk the Suppliants down from sanctuary and to find his own explanation for their lack of response. In the lines that follow immediately the father-dominated Suppliants do give him an explanation that he can accept: they are waiting for Danaos in a commendably filial fashion.

1291–92 / 977–79 *Our father allots . . . to serve a virgin future* The Greek, which is made somewhat difficult here by the loss of several preceding lines, seems to say, "Take your places, dear maidservants, in the way that Danaos assigned you as a dowry of service to each of us." Dismissing the problematic servants, I have again taken great liberties and reworked the lines to voice the Suppliants' unrealistic expectations.

1292 / 980 DANAOS *enters right with . . . a chorus of* ARGIVE WOMEN Though I have sent away the maidservants, a chorus of women is called for later (**1369–1404** /

1034–61). Danaos' entrance seems an appropriate moment to bring them onstage.

1295 / 981 *red wine outpoured* The Greek says *poured libations*. I hope to suggest not only libations but the red blood that the Danaids shall spill.

1299–1339 / *983–1013 My account of our trials...love your chastity more than your lives* Perhaps I have overplayed Danaos' homily to his daughters. But the Greek, which is usually translated as the good and gentle advice of a devoted father, seems to me to strip Danaos of all pretense. He is revealed as an egotistical old man full of despair at dwindling virility. If his lusty days are over, then his daughters' days of lovemaking shall not begin. Brackets indicate my reconstruction of two lines that are almost unintelligible in the text; the only words that come through clearly are *Kypris proclaims*. Kypris, the Cyprian, is one of Aphrodite's epithets.

1345–68 / 1018–33 *Go forth in brightness exalting... Out of that prize wells the river of death* O the phallic rivers! And O the Suppliants' absolute rejection of their fertilizing flow! In the Greek, as in the translation, the movement from praise to rejection is abrupt and takes place in midstrophe. Madness has pulled its snare tight.

1349 / 1020 *who hallow the landloving rivers* The Greek mentions the gods who "around-dwell the ancient stream of Erasinos." I drop the now-unresonant name and make use of its similarity to the word *eros*.

1368 / 1033 *the river of death* The Greek says, "Would that this prize come to the ones I hate." One may also translate the last phrase as "to the stygian ones." And another river is brought by name into the Suppliants' ode. The river Styx—the river Hate, that is—was the black stream across which the dead were ferried into Hades.

1369 / 1034 ARGIVE WOMEN These are the women that I would have Danaos bring onstage to replace the maidservants whose thousand-line silence does not make much sense. And the lines seem to imply local knowledge that foreign maidservants simply would not have had. Johansen has assigned the verses to Danaos' honor guard of spearmen. I cannot accept his suggestion because the words are, in my opinion, women's words and they would not sit easily on a spearman's tongue.

1372 / 1035 *heaven's queen* Hera.

1378 / 1041 *Union* The goddess is the Greek Harmonia, daughter of Aphrodite and Ares. She presided over all things joined, from ship's planking to strings-and-instrument and people coupled in love.

1405–22 / 1062–73 *Zeus! Lord on high! . . . God, end and beginning of help* I have taken such liberties with strophe and antistrophe that it is only fair to give the Greekless reader a prose approximation of them. Hyphenated words indicate some of the readings possible in the Greek:

"Zeus lord, may he avert-withhold-rob me of destructive marriage to an evil man, for Zeus is the very one who with goodwill loosed Io from her miseries with his healing-triumphal hand that possessed-held her down and planted his kind force.

"And may he extend power-rule-mastery to women. I will be content with whatever is the better thing than evil, even the two-thirds share. And in accord with my prayer, may heaven's justice follow the just, with my deliverance granted by the means-devices that come from a god."

PROMETHEUS BOUND

Translated by

JAMES SCULLY

and

C. JOHN HERINGTON

INTRODUCTION

I   THE MYTH

The *Prometheus Bound*, unlike any other extant Greek tragedy, carries us back almost to the beginnings of this universe. It is set in a period when the Olympian Gods were new, and when even the elemental powers of Sea, Earth, and Sky had not yet withdrawn into inert physical matter, but were tangible personalities—loving, begetting, and warring. The great cosmogonic myth to which these monstrous characters belong is older than Greek civilization, and far more widespread. Many elements of it can now be traced in ancient Near Eastern mythology, and some as far afield as ancient Gaul and India.[1] That international dream of our beginnings is in some ways infinitely remote, especially to the imagination of the modern, scientifically educated, reader. Yet its outlines are still worth the effort to grasp, as one approaches the *Prometheus Bound*. For the supreme miracle of the play is perhaps this: out of a far-off creation-story Aeschylus has conjured a political and religious figure whose influence has expanded rather than decreased with the centuries. Today his Prometheus has transported the memories of the myth far beyond its ancient territory—even across the boundaries that have been set up by the ideologies of the twentieth century. Several translations have been published in postrevolutionary Russia, and in 1961 a Chinese translation (with the *Agamemnon*) appeared in the People's Republic of China.

The creation myth must have been known to Aeschylus in many versions that no longer exist, but luckily we still have the version that

---

1.   There is a survey of this question in M. L. West's *Hesiod: Theogony* (Oxford, 1966), which is the standard commented edition of Hesiod's poem. For English translations of this and the other works of Hesiod to be discussed in this section, the reader is referred to *Hesiod, the Homeric Hymns and Homerica*, ed. H. G. Evelyn-White (London and Cambridge, Mass., 1936).

was probably the most familiar to him and to his intended audience in the middle years of the fifth century B.C. It is embodied in the poems of Hesiod (flourished about 700 B.C.): mostly in his *Theogony*, but also, to some extent, in his *Works and Days*. The *Theogony* teaches how our universe, once it had been formed out of primeval Chaos, fell successively under three régimes, representing three generations of the same divine family. Schematically, and with innumerable figures left out, the family tree given by Hesiod looks like this (the royal consorts in each generation being shown in capital letters):

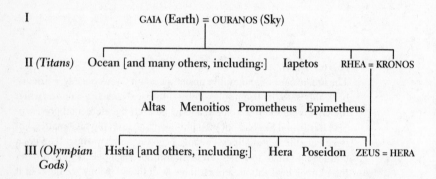

The fates of the three divine governments were varied. Ouranos was castrated by his youngest child Kronos, and dethroned. But Kronos' children were rebellious in their turn. The time came when they revolted under the leadership of the youngest of them, Zeus. They overcame Kronos in a cosmic war and cast him into the lowest pit of Tartaros, along with most of the other Titans. Since that stupendous upheaval, according to Hesiod, Zeus has reigned in Heaven, secure in his possession of thunder and lightning (*Theogony* 71–72), and attended by his ministers Rivalry, Victory, Power, and Violence (*Theogony* 383–403). Yet two of the older deities managed to survive these heavenly revolutions unharmed: Earth and Ocean. (Ancient myth, for all its strangeness, usually holds fast in its own way to the observable realities. The solid land and heaving waters, as well as the bright, passive sky, couldn't be abolished; they could at best be distanced.) Earth, the aged grandmother of the divine dynasty, lives on throughout Hesiod's story, influencing events by a unique power of her own: *she knows!* She has an awareness of destiny, of the way things really are, that is denied even to the highest male Gods, Ouranos, Kronos, and Zeus himself. Ocean is less important to Hesiod's narrative. He stands somewhat aloof from the politics of the universe, attending conscientiously to his profession, which is to encircle the known world with his massive stream.

Compared to any of these magnificent beings, Hesiod's Prometheus holds a rather insignificant status. He is not at all involved in the great revolution of the Olympians against the Titans. He appears merely as a son of the Titan Iapetos, and he and his three brothers (Atlas, Menoitios, and Epimetheus) are allowed only one, dubious distinction: all of them sinned against Zeus and failed to get away with it. It is true that Hesiod shows a marked interest in Prometheus' misdeeds and punishment (*Theogony* 507–616, and again in *Works and Days* 42–105), but the moral of the story, as he tells it, is, bluntly, *that you can't trick Zeus* (*Theogony* 613, *Works and Days* 105). Prometheus' most notable sin, the theft of fire for mankind, was punished by chaining, and by an eagle that was sent to gnaw his liver; only long afterwards, according to a passage of the *Theogony* whose genuineness has sometimes been doubted (526–534), did Herakles slay the eagle, "not without the will of Zeus who is Lord on high." Oddly enough, Hesiod's wording does not make it clear whether or not Herakles also released Prometheus. The sin for which Prometheus thus paid so heavily did not even benefit mankind. The gift of fire, which is the only gift that Hesiod mentions, led simply to what (in the eyes of that deplorably antifeminist poet) was unqualified disaster: the first woman, Pandora!

So far as we now know, Prometheus was felt by the Greeks generally—and even, to some extent, by Hesiod himself—as semi-comic: an impudent wag who tempted Providence in unusually ingenious ways and was properly put down for it. It is a remarkable fact that almost all the ancient Greek literary accounts of Prometheus that survive, whether complete or in fragments, are either overt comedies or at least written in a humorous manner. There was a lost comedy by Aeschylus' Sicilian contemporary, Epicharmus, entitled *Prometheus or Pyrrha*, and Aristophanes' extant *Birds* contains an uproarious Prometheus episode toward its end. As late as the second century A.D. the Greek satirist Lucian still extracted some tame, civilized fun from Prometheus in his dialogues *Prometheus or the Kaukasos* and *You Are a Verbal Prometheus*. Even the great myth of Protagoras about the creation of mankind (as reported in Plato's *Protagoras* 320c–322d), profoundly serious as its implications are, does not treat Prometheus himself with any great respect and treats his brother Epimetheus with outright levity. Strangely enough, Aeschylus himself seems originally to have shared the general attitude toward Prometheus. His earliest extant play, the *Persians* of 472 B.C., formed part of a trilogy of tragedies, which was followed, according to the custom at the Dionysiac competitions, by a light-hearted satyr-play. The title of the satyr-play in that production was *Prometheus*, almost certainly with the subtitle *Pyrkaeus* ("the Fire-Lighter"). Not so long ago, a song probably sung by the satyr-chorus in this play came to light on a papyrus. Fragmentary though it is, it allows glimpses of a wild dance, in which the Satyrs caper round "the unwearying glare" of the fire newly given by Prometheus, and praise him for his boon to mankind; they also hope that they'll be joined by a Nymph or two, to complete the pleasure of the occasion.[2] Prometheus was still on Aeschylus' mind—and *still* in a satyric context—in 467 B.C., when he produced his tetralogy on the Theban story (including the extant *Seven against Thebes*). One of the very few fragments of the satyr-play of that production, the *Sphinx*, mentions Prometheus and his garland—a garland that is "the best of chains."[3] That mysterious garland chain, as will be seen, recurs later in Aeschylus' work, but then in the altered context of a *tragedy*. For it seems that very near the end of the poet's life Prometheus began to take on an utterly different shape in his imagination, and to assume, for the first time, the Titanic and tragic stature that is now so familiar to the reader of Goethe, Shelley, or Karl Marx.

II   THE PROMETHEUS BOUND

Aeschylus first competed at the Dionysiac festival in or about 500 B.C. During his long career as a playwright he composed, probably, almost ninety tragedies and satyr-plays. Of all that output, only seven tragedies survive complete, dating from the last sixteen years of his life. The *Persians* was produced, as has been mentioned above, in 472 B.C., and the *Seven against Thebes* in 467. In some subsequent year (there are some grounds for putting it at 463 B.C., but they are not absolutely conclusive), Aeschylus produced the tetralogy whose one surviving play is *Suppliants*. In the spring of 458 he produced the *Oresteia* tetralogy, of which we have all the tragic plays (*Agamemnon, Choephoroi, Eumenides*), but not the accompanying satyr-play (*Proteus*). Shortly afterward he left Athens for a voyage to Sicily, from which, as it turned out, he never came back; he died in the Sicilian city of Gela in 456–55 B.C., at the age (probably) of sixty-nine. Unfortunately there exists no direct evidence about the dating of the *Prometheus Bound*. To arrive at a date one's main resource is to compare the play's style, technique, and themes with those of the remaining, dated plays, but the students who have attempted to apply this method have come to very diverse results.

2.   The fragments of this song are translated by H. Lloyd-Jones in his appendix to H. W. Smyth, *Aeschylus* (London and Cambridge, Mass., 1957), II, p. 566.
3.   The fragment is translated in Smyth, *Aeschylus* (see preceding note) II, p. 460.

Almost all have agreed that the *Prometheus Bound* cannot be as early as the *Persians*. A minority has even held that it cannot be by Aeschylus at all, but must have been composed at some time after his death. The majority, perhaps, in recent years, has concluded that it must be later than the *Oresteia*, and therefore must date from his last visit to Sicily. The question is not an easy one, and a complete consensus on the answer is hardly to be expected unless some fresh evidence turns up. On the evidence we have, however, the present writer is of the opinion that the last-mentioned conclusion is by far the most likely: the *Prometheus Bound* should belong to the final two years of Aeschylus' life. Most of his reasons are of a technical nature,[4] but one, perhaps, is worth a brief mention here. In the *Suppliants*-tetralogy, and even more in the *Oresteia*, we become aware of two related tendencies in Aeschylus' imagination: a growing preoccupation with the nature of Zeus, and an insistence on the idea of a split between the divine powers of the universe. Neither of these tendencies is visible in the two earliest plays, the *Persians* and the *Seven against Thebes*; on the other hand, they are brought to a crashing climax in the *Prometheus Bound*, where the human action has become almost insignificant, the split between the divine powers is apparent at the very opening of the play, and the nature of Zeus is questioned as fiercely as it ever was in any ancient pagan work. If this view of the matter is right, then Aeschylus discovered, very late in his life, that the lowly Prometheus who had been on his imagination for at least fourteen years might now be made to serve him in his last and most radical effort to convey his vision of the human and divine state. We shall next try to follow the process of transformation that resulted, so far as the evidence allows.

In general, the picture of the Universe and of its early history that Aeschylus presupposes in the *Prometheus Bound* is very similar to the picture presented by Hesiod. The significant differences relate to the achievements and genealogy of Prometheus. Aeschylus lays so much emphasis on these differences, especially in the earlier part of the play, that one may well believe that they were strange even to his intended audience; in other words, that at these points he is introducing entirely new material. Thus the first and second episodes (284–576 / 193–396, and 620–764 / 436–525) consist largely of straight exposition of the immensely important role that Prometheus has played in divine history and in the civilization of mankind respectively. Such static expository passages, noble poems though they may be in their own right, are rare in

---

4. They are presented, with references to differing views on the question, in C. John Herington, *The Author of the Prometheus Bound* (Austin and London, 1970).

Attic drama. Can it be mere coincidence that Hesiod had been completely silent about Prometheus in his roles of cosmic kingmaker and inventor of all human arts? The suspicion grows that in these two episodes Aeschylus is freely inventing—and consequently that the reader here, no less than the original audience, is actually privileged to be in at the *creation* of that towering Prometheus who has so influenced the modern imagination. Another difference from the Hesiodic tradition, and perhaps the most crucial one of all, is genealogical: Aeschylus makes Prometheus not the grandson of Earth, but her son. The point is emphasized (again, as if it were quite strange to the audience) in lines 311–13 / 209–10. There, and also in lines 35–36 / 18 and 1334 / 873–74, Earth is identified, most unusually and no doubt significantly, with the goddess Themis, "Right." In this way Prometheus becomes a member of the older divine generation, the Titans, and uncle to Zeus instead of an obscure cousin. Of his brothers, Aeschylus retains only the spectacular and magnificently suffering figure of Atlas, probably because he felt that the comic, dim-witted Epimetheus and the vague sinner Menoitios were below the dignity of his new Prometheus. A further, and momentous, result of Prometheus' new genealogical position is that in becoming Earth's son he is brought into direct contact with her prophetic powers. He is thus able to share knowledge that is concealed even from Zeus— above all the secret that Zeus, unless warned in time, will some day lie with a girl whose son is fated to be greater than its father. This secret is in fact Prometheus' only weapon in the struggle against Zeus. He naturally will not be heard to name the girl in the course of the *Prometheus Bound*, but from other evidence we gather that she was the sea-goddess Thetis; and that in the end the Gods judiciously married her off to a mortal, Peleus...(The issue of that marriage was Achilles, mightier indeed than his father or any other hero of his time). But in Aeschylus' *Prometheus Bound* all that is in the unborn future. The secret of Thetis' strange destiny is known only to Earth, and to her son Prometheus. Hence, in fact, comes the tension that is built up in the course of the drama. Zeus, who has recently conquered in the war against the Titans, now possesses all the physical power available in the Universe; while Prometheus possesses the knowledge that can, in time, render that power useless and topple Zeus from his throne.

The way is now clear for a consideration of the general structure of the play that Aeschylus proceeded to create. Apart from its tempestuous prologue and finale, there is little physical action. For most of its course the central character, inevitably quite motionless, conducts a series of conversations with a procession of visitors—the Chorus, Ocean, Io, and Hermes—and of these visitors only the Chorus stays for more than a single episode. But before the crude conclusion is drawn (as it often has been) that *nothing happens* between the prologue and the finale, we ought to recall that we are in the presence not of Shakespeare or Webster or Euripides, but of Aeschylus. This is a playwright who, admittedly, rarely does anything twice in the same way; standing as he does so close to that miraculous point in Western history at which *poetry* was transfigured into *drama*, he is freer and less easy to fit into any pattern than most of his successors. But in one respect his method—or is it rather his vision of the way life works?—is consistent. He habitually treats a given physical event as merely the visible manifestation of a vast complex of ideas and moral forces, which sometimes (especially in his later surviving plays) extend to the very boundaries of the Universe. In his best-known play, for instance, the *Agamemnon*, there is far less physical action than in the *Prometheus Bound* itself. Even the single physical event that matters there, the murder of the great king, takes place offstage and is in a sense thrown out of focus by being seen in detail, by Kassandra, some minutes before it happens. The bulk of the *Agamemnon* explores not that event in itself, but its causes and its significance. Seen from this point of view, the apparently *staccato* episodes of the *Prometheus Bound* present a steady and harmonious progression of ideas. By the end, Prometheus and Zeus and the entire situation within the Universe have been transformed: nothing remains in the same state as it was in the noisy and violent prologue, where the silent fire-thief was being passively clamped to the rock for a seemingly limitless and unchangeable punishment. We have already seen how the two episodes following that prologue transform the fire-thief into a cosmic figure. After them, the next great movement of the play is comprised in lines 765–1392 / 526–907. Up to now, Prometheus' knowledge of the Marriage-Secret has been mentioned only with mysterious obscurity (249–62 / 168–75, 277–83 / 186–92, 743–64 / 511–25); this movement will bring it as far into the open as Prometheus dares, will reveal its central importance, and will also lead directly on to the final catastrophe. The long Io-episode is here framed by two choral odes (765–821 / 526–60 and 1363–92 / 887–907), which are linked thematically, and also musically—the distinctive variety of meter used in the Greek of both odes is particularly striking because it occurs nowhere else in Aeschylus' extant work. The odes both reflect on the irresistible power of the Olympian Gods, on the defenselessness of all lesser beings in the face of it, and on *sexual union*, which will be the dominating theme of this entire movement. The first ode, however, ends with the solemn, ritual union of Prometheus with his equal Hesione, in marriage, whereas the second dwells on the stark terror of an unequal, violent mating between God and inferior. The long

Io-episode that lies between the odes is a specific, and horrible, instance of such divine cruelty. As a result of Zeus' lust, and of the jealousy of Hera, this young mortal girl has been warped in body and mind, and driven from her home to journey in torment. Here the imaginative boundaries of the play suddenly burst outward from the desolate rock on the Kaukasos range. The accounts of Io's past and future wanderings conduct the hearer in a vast clockwise sweep from her father's palace in Argos, through Prometheus' place of suffering, onward to the monster-peopled far East, then south to the territory of the Ethiopians, and finally down the Nile, from its fabled source to the Delta. This supreme example of the oppression of humanity by God, expressed in sexual terms, spurs Prometheus to reveal at last the details of the threat that he holds over Zeus. In a dialogue placed at the center of the Io-scene (1138–51 / 757–70), he discloses the secret almost in its entirety, short of giving the name of the girl whom Zeus will choose for his fatal liaison.

The climax of this theme, however, is reserved until immediately after the Io-movement. In a thunderous speech (1393–1425 / 908–27), Prometheus furiously shouts his secret at the sky, in a direct challenge to Zeus. The scene is now set for a second confrontation between Prometheus and the powers of Olympos, of infinitely wider implications than that which took place in the prologue. It is now a war between brute force and unbending knowledge, between the reigning monarch of the Universe and the patron of suffering mankind. The challenge brings Hermes plummeting from heaven, to threaten Prometheus ultimately with Zeus' only available resource—more violence. The Titan still refuses to name the girl, and the play ends in a cosmic storm amid which he sinks into the rock.

The *Prometheus Bound* as a whole thus seems to present a coherent development, even though it is a development of *ideas* rather than of *actions*. In detail there still remain many problematic passages, and we have not yet touched on the most interesting problem of all: the religious and political significance of the story. These questions will be approached in the following section.

III   THE PLAY AND ITS SEQUEL

The long history of the interpretation of the *Prometheus Bound* is almost the history of a mirror. Romantics, liberals, and socialists, gazing into these disturbing depths, have found there an Aeschylean justification of romanticism, liberalism, and socialism, respectively. Authoritarians on the contrary, from the medieval Byzantines onward, have emphasized with approval the crushing punishment ultimately accorded to the rebel against the Supreme Authority. In a word: *Tell me what you are, and I will tell you what you think of the* Prometheus Bound.... The present writer has no reason to believe that he has been specially exempted from this law. The following interpretation is therefore put forward with humility. It is meant not as a definitive pronouncement, but as an indication of some factors that may help the reader to make up his own mind.

We may at least begin with a statement on which, probably, all critics can agree, whatever their ideologies: in the dramatic present of the *Prometheus Bound*, Zeus' government of the Universe is represented as a despotism of the most brutal kind. The supreme God is made to look the very pattern of an ancient Greek tyrant (in the most unfavorable sense of that word), and there can be no doubt that this is deliberate. He is given all the stock attributes of the tyrant that are found in Greek historians and political thinkers from Herodotus to Aristotle: he rules without laws (**223** / 150, **278** / 186–87), he seduces his female subjects (Io is one example), he plans indiscriminate murder of his people (**345** / 232), he is so suspicious that he does not even trust his friends (**334–36** / 224–25).[5] But the *Prometheus Bound* goes far beyond citing the traditional Greek attributes. Here we reach one of the more uncanny aspects of the play: especially in the prologue and the final scene with Hermes, it presents a study of tyranny *in action*, and its effects on victims and agents alike, which has no parallel at all in ancient literature, and foreshadows the methods of twentieth-century totalitarianism. The following summary of a recent investigation into contemporary brainwashing techniques is worth a few moments' pause: "Isolation, deprivation of sleep, intimidation, endlessly repeated accusations of lying, maintenance of very painful postures, abrupt change of attitude by the interrogator, from vilification to friendly understanding and compassion, and then back again to severity...these are basic features.... [The prisoner] might have leg chains and manacles applied."[6] Almost every feature of the twentieth-century prison camp can in fact be paralleled in the *Prometheus Bound*, without pressing the evidence. We see here a political offender whose will must be broken by the régime at all costs, by isolation from all fellow beings, by torture, by chaining, and even by

---

5. These points are established, with full references to the Greek historians and philosophers, by George Thomson, notably in his edition of the *Prometheus Bound* (Cambridge, 1932), pp. 6ff. Of particular interest is the sketch of a tyrant in Herodotus, *Histories* 3.80, which was written only a decade or two after the presumed date of our play.

6. *Times Literary Supplement*, August 14, 1969, p. 893: from a review of S. M. Meyers and A. D. Biderman (eds.), *Mass Behavior in Battle and Captivity* (Chicago, 1969).

psychological means (Power's final effort to pervert Prometheus' very name, 130–31 / 85–86, is noteworthy); the too-familiar callous police-agents, Power and his female colleague Violence,[7] who in a modern production might appropriately be clothed in neat black uniforms and jackboots; the gentle, nonpolitical technician, Hephaistos, pressed in to misuse his skill for the régime's infamous purposes; and finally the high-ranking Party official, Hermes, who does not dirty his own hands with violence but proceeds like an expert brainwasher, alternating between threats and confidential appeals to reason. These parallels between the ancient play and the modern prison seem to confirm the fact that in the *Prometheus Bound* Zeus' régime is being represented as an odious tyranny—not only by the criteria of the ancient Greek city-state, but also by the standards of all democratic societies in all ages.

This factor in the dramatic situation thus seems certain, and it is tempting, with some earlier readers, to come to rest in that sublime and appalling concept: *God is a Tyrant*, bent on suppressing mankind's benefactor and on preventing the awakening of humanity! But unfortunately, it really is not so simple as that. There are two further factors that seem equally certain and must equally be taken into account by anybody who wishes honestly to decipher the message of Aeschylus. These factors may be summarized thus:

1. The contradictions in Prometheus as they appear in the extant *Prometheus Bound:*
2. The evidence about the now-lost sequels to the extant play—above all, the fragments of the *Prometheus Unbound*.

The contradictions in Prometheus may first be illustrated from his great opening utterance (134–89 / 88–127), which happens to be metrically unparalleled in all Greek drama in that it modulates from speech, to chant, back to speech, to full song, and back to chant, combining, in fact, all the three levels of delivery that were at the disposal of a Greek playwright (these will be further discussed in section IV). Or perhaps "happens" is not the correct word. It may be argued that Aeschylus is deliberately emphasizing at the outset, by musical means, the unparalleled nature of his protagonist. The utterance opens (134–42 / 88–92) with Prometheus' calm, majestic appeal to the elements, which is delivered in unaccompanied speech. Then, very abruptly, Prometheus slips into a chant (143–51 / 93–100) in which he laments his horrible and

---

7. The Greek gender of her name indicates almost beyond doubt that Violence is a *female* police-agent.

apparently limitless suffering; but equally abruptly (**152** / 101) reverts to speech, now asserting that he can foresee every detail of the future, and must endure it. Yet he has already begun again to lament his fate when he is interrupted by the as yet unidentifiable sound and fragrance of the approaching Chorus, which spur him (**173** / 115) to a burst of full song. At line **181** / 121 he reverts to chant, at first proudly defying the Gods, but then again collapsing into sheer panic: *"I'm afraid whatever comes!"* This strange pattern repeats itself in his ensuing lyric dialogue with the Chorus, although it is now no longer accentuated by abrupt changes in the Greek meters. Here his utterances are desperate lamentations, until line **249** / 168, where he threateningly mentions the mysterious plan by which Zeus' throne will be endangered. The dialogue closes (**277–83** / 186–92) with an even more extraordinary shift of attitude—the vision of a future in which he and Zeus will love one another as friends.

Even on the evidence so far mentioned, Prometheus appears to be deliberately represented as an unstable compound of mortal sufferer and immortal prophet—much as Io, in this same play, is an unstable compound of human and heifer (her heifer-element being expressed most brilliantly, though not solely, in her opening and closing songs). At one moment Prometheus is totally absorbed, as any of us human beings would be, in the emotions and the agonies of the present, while at another he has the limitless and timeless vision of a God. This being so, his moments of inspired prophecy deserve careful inspection by anyone who would understand Aeschylus' total conception of the Prometheus story. They transport us, as they transport Prometheus himself, far away from the hideous dramatic present into a very different future. Most important of all from this point of view is surely Prometheus' culminating prophecy in the Io-scene (**1276–1336** / 844–74), which is pointedly prefaced by a convincing proof of his mediumistic powers (**1240–75** / 823–43), and concluded by the solemn statement that it is derived from Earth-Themis. In the far future that is opened up by this passage, Zeus does *not* ultimately lie with Io but merely restores her to herself and caresses her "with a hand you no longer feat," miraculously begetting a child, Epaphos; from that child descends in turn a long and noble line, culminating in the greatest of all heroes, Herakles; and Herakles frees Prometheus.

Yet in Prometheus' very next speech (**1393–1425** / 908–27, following the exit-song of Io and the choral ode), the gentle Zeus, the sane Io, and his own release by Io's descendant have all vanished from his thoughts as if they had never been. Several more such apparent inconsistencies occur in the play; compare the content of lines **143–51** / 93–100 with that of **385–88** / 257–58, **743–64** / 511–25, **1135–37** / 755–56, **1152–55** / 771–74. But Prometheus is inconsistent with himself in other respects also.

Although he is a bitter adversary of tyranny and oppression in the dramatic present, he admits to responsibility for the staffwork that resulted in the defeat and imprisonment of Kronos and his fellow-Titans (326–29 / 219–21), to having "helped [Zeus] set up his tyranny" (454–55 / 305), and to having organized the power structure of the victorious régime (625–27 / 439–40). The second of these admissions may have sounded particularly sinister to an Athenian audience, for in the Greek Prometheus uses the same words that are used in the ancient Athenian law directed against anyone who set up, or *helped to set up, a tyranny* in their city.[8] Equally strange are Prometheus' contradictory attitudes to truth-telling, in the Io scene. At one moment he is promising Io the full, undisguised truth (896–99 / 609–11, 909 / 617, 1230–32 / 816–17), at others he is denying it to her (913 / 621, 1157 / 776) or masking it in oracular obscurity (1155–56 / 774–75). Finally, it has recently been shown, with an overwhelming number of examples, that almost all the odious characteristics attributed to Zeus in this play (mostly by Prometheus)—stubbornness, anger, rashness, harshness—are also attributed to Prometheus himself by other characters, including sympathizers like the Chorus.[9]

In view of these phenomena, we probably have to recognize that the *Prometheus Bound*, like the *Agamemnon*, is very far from being a simplistic opposition between blameless virtue and incurable wickedness. Rather we are at a nightmare stage of this universe, in which the true nature of any character, at any level, is hopelessly elusive. Is Io a mad heifer or the mother of heroes? Is Prometheus a human sufferer or a divine seer, a champion of humanity or a discontented member of the divine totalitarian party? Is Zeus the pitiless dictator of the universe, or its beneficent father? From the bottom to the top of the chain of being the ambiguities persist, and there is no point where the mind can rest in moral or political certainty, with one possible, mysterious exception: the wisdom and foreknowledge of Earth. Perhaps the most tormenting ambiguity of all, for those who have been conditioned to read the *Prometheus Bound* as committed partisans either of Prometheus or of Zeus, will be this: *there is a strain of Zeus in Prometheus himself.*

Could there, conversely, have been a strain of Prometheus in Zeus? And could it be that at some time when the universe had grown older, and the echoes of the terrible convulsions at its beginning had died away, the good qualities in *each* character, by mutual attraction, might bring the two together? This is a strange, perhaps to some even an

8. The law is cited by Aristotle, *Polity of the Athenians*, 16.10.
9. This important point was demonstrated by A. J. Podlecki in an article, "Reciprocity in the *Prometheus Bound*," in *Greek, Roman, and Byzantine Studies*, vol. 10 (1969), pp. 287–92.

unwelcome, outcome. Yet it actually seems to be foreshadowed in one of Prometheus' earlier prophetic moments (280–83 / 189–92); and once, in the most deliberate of his prophecies, near the end of the Io scene (1283–89 / 848–49), we glimpse a Zeus who shows a Promethean gentleness toward a human being. But the testimony of the *Prometheus Bound* can carry us no farther than that. The moment has arrived when we must look at some other, too often neglected, evidence: the lost play or plays that Aeschylus composed as an immediate sequel to the *Prometheus Bound*. For if one thing is absolutely certain, it is that he never meant the extant play to be a self-contained dramatic unity—that when Prometheus vanishes into the rock at its end we are not witnessing the coda of Aeschylus' symphony, but only the close of a movement. The composition and order of the sequence of Prometheus-plays that Aeschylus originally composed has been very much debated, but the majority of modern students of the subject would probably agree on the following statement.[10] The *Prometheus Bound* was undoubtedly followed immediately by a play entitled *Prometheus Unbound*, of which quite a number of fragments survive. There is some very slight evidence to indicate that the *Unbound* in turn may have been followed by a third play, the *Prometheus Pyrphoros* ("Fire-Carrier") of which there are only three, not very informative, fragments. This sequence presumably constituted a tragic trilogy to be performed together on one occasion, just like the *Oresteia* (and indeed like the majority of Aeschylus' known productions). It will therefore not have been so much three dramas as a single superdrama falling into three movements, with the action and the ideas developing continuously from the first movement to the last. By all analogies the trilogy should have been concluded by a satyr-play, which would be an independent, semi-comic unit; but if a satyr-play was ever composed for this production, we have no way of identifying it. The tragic trilogy thus reconstructed is often referred to as a whole by modern writers as the *Prometheia*, and this is a convenient, time-saving title—provided one bears in mind that there is no ancient authority for it.

All the fragments of the *Prometheia* that seem to be of the least significance for the understanding of Aeschylus' original design are translated and discussed in the Appendix to the present edition. To our knowledge this is the only such collection of the evidence—including nearly all the ancient *allusions* to these lost plays, as well as the verbatim quotations from them—available in English translation. The fragments include some wonderful moments of imaginative poetry, but as a whole they are definitely not easy reading. At this point, therefore,

10. A discussion of the technical evidence available is given in *The Author of the Prometheus Bound* (above, note 4), Appendix A.

we shall merely survey the general conclusions that seem to emerge from them, referring the reader to the Appendix for details.

Above all, the fragments confirm the hypothesis that Prometheus' moments of solemn prophecy in the *Prometheus Bound* are to be accepted as describing what actually happened later in the trilogy. Prometheus was released in the end, and by Herakles, the descendant of Io. The episode of the Garland (Appendix, fragments 15 through 17), so far as it can now be made out, suggests even that Prometheus' vision (*Bound*, 282–83 / 191–92) of a spontaneous, mutual friendship between himself and Zeus was fulfilled. The general drift of the trilogy now becomes clear, also; it is a universal progress from confusion and torment, at all levels of the universe, toward peace and joy. Phrases of the type "release from sorrows," "freedom from agony," "end of toils" recur like a *leitmotiv* in the extant *Prometheus Bound*; we count twenty-one instances of them in the Greek text, which is only 1,093 lines long.[11] Such verbal recurrences on such a scale are unique in Greek tragedy, and we can only account for them as being subliminal preparations of the audience for vast changes that were to take place later in the trilogy. In fact, Prometheus' prophecies in the *Bound* and *Unbound* (to Herakles), as well as the action of the *Unbound* in itself, show that such changes actually occurred. All the major characters—Prometheus himself, Io, and Herakles—seem to have moved on from torment to release. *And Zeus?* Here we know all too little; but there is some evidence to show that, at least, totally new facets of him moved into the spectator's vision as time progressed. We have already seen how, in the far future, he would cease to lust after Io, or to cause her fear. Further, in fragments 11 and 12 of the *Unbound* Prometheus actually envisages Zeus as *pitying*, an emotion that is utterly alien to Zeus in the *Bound* (1500 / 980), being there attributed to Prometheus alone (e.g., 514 / 351). It thus seems likely that to the thesis of the *Prometheus Bound*, "Zeus is a Tyrant!" the *Unbound* responded with the antithesis, "Zeus is a Savior!" and that in the light of this response a synthesis became possible: the reconciliation of the almighty power of Zeus with the civilizing intelligence of Prometheus. Many people may find such a development difficult to imagine, in view of the hideous portrait of Zeus that is painted in the *Prometheus Bound*: could the God's reputation ever be salvaged after that? But in fact there is a close parallel to the process in another extant work by Aeschylus, composed near the end of his life. In the first third of

11. In translating, it did not seem possible to give the same literal rendering to each of these phrases each time it occurred, without producing an effect of artificiality. But the *idea* has almost always been kept; examples will be found at l. 151 "end this pain," ll. 396–97 "break free of your agony," ll. 470–71 "find a way free of these agonies," l. 483 "try to have you freed from these agonies."

the *Eumenides* (part of the *Oresteia*, of 458 B.C.), the Furies are represented as the filthiest of Hell's monsters, hated by the bright Olympian
Gods and irreconcilably opposed to their claims. In the middle third this
aspect fades out, and we begin to understand them as earth-powers
capable of blessing the soil as well as of blasting it. In the finale of the
Eumenides their beneficent aspect is entirely uppermost, and they are
persuaded to join forces with the once-hated Olympians in prospering
Athens. Yet if only the first third of the *Eumenides* had survived no
student, however adventurous, would have dared to predict that outcome. In the *Eumenides*, as in the whole *Oresteia*, Aeschylus admits no
absolutes into this universe until the very end. He is willing to postulate
that not merely humanity, but even the Gods, even the supreme God
himself, are ambiguous, many-sided phenomena, good and evil; and
that only time will painfully uncover the good in any of them, making
possible a harmonious world. The appalling realism of the first half of
this postulate, and the soaring optimism of the second, are neither of
them easy to grasp in this age of gray ideologies. Yet it may, possibly, be
one clue to the *Prometheia*.

Even if this parallel holds good, however, we still have to confess
defeat on most fronts. The story told in the entire trilogy as Aeschylus
conceived it, its mechanisms, and the motivations of its participants,
remain beyond us. The negligence of ancient scribes (or was it just the
quiet, aimless work of mice or moths in some Byzantine library?) has
deprived us of two-thirds of the poet's design; and in so doing has carried
away much of the evidence for the interpretation even of the extant one-
third, the *Prometheus Bound*. It is difficult to make up one's mind
whether, in the long run, this loss has harmed or profited the imagination of mankind. We may well have been denied one of the most
magnificent political and religious dramas ever composed in the Western world, and yet, and yet ... the solitary play that survives has generated
new poems and new theories in cultures and languages that
Aeschylus never knew. Perhaps the greatest reward of a reading of the
Prometheus Bound in any century since the fall of Rome has been
that the reader has been forced by it to construct for *himself* some
response to the play's fearsome thesis on humanity, God, and government. So, where the ancient poem now abandons him, only one-third
of the way through its course, an eternally modern poem begins:
his own.

IV   STAGING AND STAGE DIRECTIONS

In the matter of staging, as in almost every other, the *Prometheus Bound*
presents special problems. There is no reliable information about the

way it was first performed—nor indeed about when or where the performance took place. If we are right in dating the play to the very end of Aeschylus' life, during his residence in Sicily, then the poet did not live to see it staged in his own city. On the other hand, the parodies in Aristophanes (especially at the end of the *Birds*, of 414 B.C.) leave little doubt that by this comedian's time the *Prometheus* had been performed before Athenian audiences. We know, in fact, that Aeschylus' son Euphorion later produced a number of his father's unpublished tragedies (presumably found among his papers after his death in Gela) and won four victories with them in the Dionysiac competitions. The *Prometheus* and its trilogy could well have been among these. As a setting, then, for the first production, it is reasonable to envisage the Theater of Dionysos at Athens. There will be a *skēnē* or background building with two projecting side wings, an actor area in the long narrow rectangular space extending between those wings, and a round dancing floor for the Chorus in front of the actor area. For specific information about the staging of the *Prometheus*, our first recourse must be—as usual—to the Greek text itself. From this one can deduce with almost complete precision (a) the points where characters enter and exit and (b) the manner in which each part of the play was delivered. Item (b) may require some explanation. There were three types of delivery in the Athenian theater, each traditionally associated with its own meter or meters. Since the meter is, of course, still preserved in the Greek verses, we can in almost all cases state how any given section was uttered. The Greek tragedian had at his disposal (1) *unaccompanied speech*, associated with the six-foot iambic line, which is the almost universal dialogue-meter in Greek drama; (2) a delivery known in Greek as *parakatalogē*, which was accompanied instrumentally, and was something midway between speech and melodic song, like our modern recitative; it was mostly associated with the rapid-moving anapestic meter. In our stage directions this kind of delivery is referred to as *chant*. In the *Prometheus* its use nearly always indicates rising emotions, quickening tempo; a good example is in the finale (1593–1670 / 1040–93), where it marks the coming of the great storm. Lastly, there is (3) fully melodic *song*, instrumentally accompanied, and associated with an almost endless variety of lyric rhythms. There can be great fascination in following Aeschylus' handling of these three types of delivery for dramatic purposes. Here, long after every ancient lyre has been broken and nearly every written note lost, there is still some possibility of appreciating him in his aspect of operatic musician, and a virtuoso at that. There are even passages, above all the opening speech of Prometheus, which was analyzed above, where an understanding of the variations in delivery seems almost essential to an understanding of Aeschylus' meaning.

A few further indications about the staging can be extracted from the Greek text. The mask of Power seems to have been hideously ugly (120 / 78). The mask of Io was crowned, grotesquely, with heifer horns (1002–3 / 674). Ocean somehow appeared mounted on a monster that was winged, and yet had four legs (433 / 286–87, 572–74 / 394–95). Beyond this, all is uncertain. In the ancient Greek commentary on Aeschylus' seven plays preserved in our oldest surviving manuscript (the venerable "Medicean manuscript" in the Laurentian Library, Florence), there are a few notes referring to the staging of the *Prometheus Bound*. They run as follows:

> On line 190 / 128 (*opening words of the Chorus*): "They utter these words while being swung in the air by means of a *mēchanē* [crane]; for it would be absurd that they should converse from below with Prometheus, who is high up. But while he is talking to Ocean [i.e., in the scene that begins at 431 / 284], they come down to the ground."
> On line 431 / 284 (*opening words of Ocean*): "The arrival of Ocean provides the Chorus with a suitable opportunity to get down from the *mēchanē*.... Ocean is riding on a four-legged griffin."
> On line 577 / 397: "The Chorus, having come down to the ground, sings the *stasimon* [ode]."

The authorship and date of these notes are unknown; at most we can say that they can hardly have been compiled less than two centuries after Aeschylus' death, and that they may be several centuries later still. One is at liberty, if one will, to assume that they may preserve genuine information about the original production of the *Prometheus*, or at least of *some* production in classical times, and quite a number of students have done so. In that case Prometheus will somehow be elevated high above the stage, and the entire Chorus (numbering twelve or fifteen) will be swung in on a crane and will hover around him until Ocean enters, when they will descend to stage-level and disembark. But we confess that our imaginations boggle at the implied spectacle, and we prefer to believe that the flight and descent of the Chorus were represented simply by mime (see, further, our note on 190–283 / 128–92). On the other hand, the ancient commentator's assertion that Ocean and his monster were brought in on a crane seems acceptable. Indeed, it is hard to imagine any other way of doing it; and there are many parallels in fifth-century drama (even as early as the lost *Psychostasia* of Aeschylus himself) for the introduction of a winged character, or a character on a winged mount, by such mechanical means.

The reader now has before him such meager ancient evidence as exists concerning the staging of the *Prometheus*. The stage directions that we have inserted in the present edition are mostly inferences from the text itself; one or two depend on the ancient notes that have just been described; here and there we have added our own brief hints as to staging or delivery. But the reader is urged to bear in mind that none of these directions derives from Aeschylus himself, and to exercise his own judgment accordingly.

The question of physical staging is, of course, one thing, while the fantastic scene conjured in the imagination by Aeschylus' verse is quite another. The latter could never be reproduced in its fullness on any stage, whether ancient or modern (*film*, unfortunately, has never yet been properly exploited as a medium for Aeschylean drama). The imagined setting lies where, for Aeschylus, the world ends — the Kaukasos range, probably thought of as extending between the further end of the Black Sea and the encircling Ocean.[12] Across some chasm high in those desolate mountains, Prometheus is fettered. Far below he can glimpse the endless glitter of the waves (**137 / 90**); and somewhere down there, within earshot of the tremendous clang of Hephaistos' sledge, are the sea caverns where Ocean and his daughters dwell (**193–97 / 130–33, 444–47 / 299–301**). Thus the setting remains until the great storm at the end, which, again, must always have been realized for audiences primarily by the magic of Aeschylus' verse. The ancient theater had its primitive thunder-machines, and the modern producer might make effective use of drums here; but neither will carry one far, in comparison with the words. In this final upheaval of the elements Prometheus will be swallowed by the mountain chasm, as Hermes has threatened (**1551–55 / 1016–19**). What becomes of the Chorus is not clearly indicated in Aeschylus' text, but we prefer to imagine that they disappear — also swallowed up by the collapsing rocks — somewhat before Prometheus' last terrible appeal to the elements. "*Everyone else having left*, Prometheus speaks his words to the bright sky [*aithēr*], just as he did in the beginning," was the guess of one of the greatest of medieval Byzantine scholars, Demetrios Triklinios, in his commentary on lines **1661–63 / 1091–92**. It is only a guess (Demetrios probably had no more reliable information than we do on such points) but it makes sense. Prometheus' last words, like his first, will thus be spoken in utter loneliness — except for the eternal, mysterious presence of the elements.

C. John Herington

---

12. The Caspian Sea was not generally known to be an inland sea until the time of Alexander the Great, more than a century after Aeschylus' death.

ON THE TRANSLATION

Any language is a unique complex of cultural associations, so we have tried to translate not only the words but also the realities they are charged with. That is, this translation starts from commonplace assumptions and intentions. Nonetheless it has turned out to be more idiomatic, yet also more literal, than other versions of the play. We have been somewhat literal in our handling of metaphor. Wherever possible, Aeschylus' "metaphors"—which are not metaphors, strictly speaking, but the images generated by his unabstracted apprehension of the world—have been kept more or less intact. For instance, line 646 / 450 is usually rendered as "houses made of bricks," whereas here it is "brick-knitted houses" ("brick-woven" would be the literal translation, but "woven" is so overused as a metaphor that it seems inert, no longer image-able). We have held to this and other images not merely because they are there, though that might be reason enough, but because they are startlingly right and precise. In its context, the image of "brick-knitted houses" does more than note the cultural advance signaled by the move from caves into houses. It evokes a profound technical breakthrough: the discovery that bricks might be made and built with . . . if, instead of being heaped or stacked atop one another, they were overlapped or staggered. Aeschylus' phrase, which also suggests the texture of brick, is a fresh realization of something that almost anyone else would have taken for granted. The realization is condensed, fleeting, but it is there and ought to be preserved. It has something to tell us.

To keep faith with the spirit of the Greek text, we have at times had to reach through its "letter" so as to draw submerged metaphors nearer the surface. Io characterizes Argos as being "unmixed in his rage." Those are her actual words. Here, however, those words are translated as "his rage the rage / of raw wine" (1010–11 / 678), for the simple reason that a word-for-word translation would have given little clue as to their significance, their cultural ambience. In fact the original phrase conceals a wine metaphor. The Greeks believed that the drinking of unmixed wine, wine undiluted by water, drove men crazy. Argos' rage, then, was unadulterated and therefore mad, barbarous.

This translation also tries to be idiomatic: partly to convey the familiarity of concepts that really are familiar, but which seem remote when couched in translatese; and partly to simplify. Aeschylus' text suffers no serious distortion if "we come in winged rivalry of speed" or "in swift rivalry of wings" is rendered as "we raced ourselves here" (192 / 129–30), especially as the "wings" in the Greek are probably no more than a stage direction, a notation on the costume of the Chorus. Mostly, however, idiomatic speech has been used to take graphic but alien images and, without rubbing off *all* their strangeness, make them accessible. At one point, one point only, we have dovetailed a literal and an idiomatic translation of a single line. The Greek: "Who, then, is the helm-swinger of Necessity?" And the English translation: "But who swings the helm? / who brings Necessity about?" (751–52 / 515). By observing the second part of that line, which contains a nautical metaphor that has been worn down into idiomatic usage, one may have some sense of the transformations that have occurred between the original text and its translation. We have, then, tried to render the play idiomatically without, in the process, domesticating it. Aeschylus' audacity and "otherness" should come through untamed. He is not, and should not seem to be, our contemporary. Immediately present, yes. But as himself, not quite as one of us.

As we note in the introduction, verse distinctions among speech, chant, and song are essential dramatic properties of the play. Naturally we have tried to maintain those distinctions, although it should be noted that possibly the least Aeschylean aspect of this translation is in the speech rhythms. These rhythms, as the narrative manners of Prometheus himself, start from one basic assumption: that their function is not merely to convey certain information, but to communicate *the experience of* that information. Which is what Prometheus does with kennings. For example, his "seawandering / linen wingd / chariots for sailors" (677–79 / 467–68) forces us to reimagine ships, to encounter them as a marvelous, primitive invention before it has evolved its own proper name. So, too, the delayed timing of Prometheus' descriptions: "And their three sisters live nearby: / repulsive with hair / not hair, they're wingd / snake wool! it's / GORGONS!" (1196–1200 / 798–99). Once a thing is "named," its mystery and spring and terror are muted, locked up. But here as elsewhere, Prometheus witholds the domesticating name until the last possible moment. Truly to know what "Gorgons" are, one has to sweat out the disorienting, by turns dawning and erupting, realization of them. In this translation we have attempted through our rhythms to keep touch with this nervous, muscular, sensuous process. At some level it seems to bear not only on the rhetorical devices of Prometheus, but on the sensibility of Aeschylus as well.

This is one play that seems to have been written with the head, hands, and heart: bunched, impacted, in the solar plexus. Ideally it would not be read or seen, but undergone. Of course the translation does not pretend to approach the standards suggested here; it attempts, simply, to acknowledge them.

JAMES SCULLY

PROMETHEUS BOUND

Translated by

JAMES SCULLY

and

C. JOHN HERINGTON

CHARACTERS

POWER male, an agent of Zeus

VIOLENCE female, an agent of Zeus

HEPHAISTOS blacksmith, fire worker, god of craftsmanship

PROMETHEUS

CHORUS the daughters of Ocean

OCEAN old god of the world's waters

IO the heifer girl

HERMES the messenger god

Line numbers in the right-hand margin of the text refer to the English translation only, and the Notes beginning at p. 371 are keyed to these lines. The bracketed line numbers in the running headlines refer to the Greek text.

PROMETHEUS *is dragged by* POWER *and* VIOLENCE; HEPHAISTOS, *lugging chains and blacksmith tools, trails after them.*

POWER   And so we've come to the end of the world.
To Scythia: this howling waste
                            no one passes through.
Hephaistos, now it's up to you.
What the Father wants done
    you've got to do.
On these overhanging cliffs
    with your own shatter-proof irons
you're commanded:
Clamp this troublemaking bastard to the rock.   10

After all, Hephaistos, it was *your* glowing flower
    FIRE
  —the power behind all
        works of hands—
he stole it, he gave it away
to *human beings.*
That's his crime, and the Gods demand
    he pay for it.
He must submit
    to the tyranny of Zeus   20
and like it, too.
He'll learn.

He's got to give up
feeling for humanity.

HEPHAISTOS   Power and Violence . . . you've already carried out
      your orders from Zeus.
you're free to go now.
But me, I haven't the heart to chain this god
    this brother!

to this stormbeaten ravine.   30
        And yet I must.
        It's heavy business
to shrug off the Father's word . . .

Prometheus, I know you for what you are:
the headlong, steep thinking son
            of Themis: your levelheaded mother.
Yet against my will, as against yours
I'll spike you to this
            inhuman cliff.
Nobody's here, no human voice   40
will come through to you.
When the bloom on your cheek is burnt
        black by the sun
you'll be glad when night with her veils of starcloud
covers up the glare,
And again glad when at dawn, the sun
        scatters the hoarfrost off.
But always you'll be crushed by the load
        of each, every moment.
The one who will set you free   50
hasn't even been born.

This is what you get
for loving humankind.

You, a god, outraged the Gods.
Weren't you afraid?
You gave mere people
what people should not have
        Prometheus!
Now you must stand watch
over this brute rock   60
and never bend your knee,
you won't sleep, won't move,
no you'll
        sigh and howl

and won't be heard. No

Zeus is not
    about to mellow.
Every ruler who's new
is hard.

POWER   MOVE damn it! What good's your pity?   70
       Why don't you hate the god
          the Gods hate?
       Didn't he betray you? He gave humans a power
       meant for you!

HEPHAISTOS   We're family, we're friends: there's power in that, too.

POWER   Sure. But how can you refuse the Father's
          orders!
       Don't *they* scare you even more?

HEPHAISTOS   (*groaning*)
       You *are* pitiless...shameless too. You always were.

POWER   No use whining about it. He's had it.   80
       Don't work yourself up
          over a lost cause.

HEPHAISTOS   It's this work, these masterful hands of mine—
       that's what I hate!

POWER   What for? Fact is, the craft you work at
       wasn't to blame for this.

HEPHAISTOS   Still, I wish it had fallen to someone else.

POWER   Every job's a pain, except
          for the God at the top.
       Only Zeus is free.   90

HEPHAISTOS (*gesturing toward* PROMETHEUS)
           Obviously. What can I say.

POWER   THEN GET A MOVE ON! Throw the chains on him—
        before Zeus sees you loafing on the job.

HEPHAISTOS Look here, the iron's at hand. You aren't blind.

POWER   Clamp his wrists, real hard. Now the sledge: with all
        your might, quick, spike him to the rock!

HEPHAISTOS OK, OK, I'm doing my job. I'm doing it right.

POWER   Strike! Strike! Harder. Squeeze. He's too shrewd:
        where there's no way out, still, he'll find one.

HEPHAISTOS Well, here's one arm he'll never work free.   100

POWER   Then spike the other, hard. He's got to learn:
        'intellectual' that he is, next to Zeus he's stupid.

HEPHAISTOS No one can say I didn't do
                        justice to this job!
           Except Prometheus.

POWER   Now the arrogant jawbone, of *wedge*: batter
        it hard, you, crunch through his chest!

HEPHAISTOS (*cries out: striking, recoiling*)
           PROMETHEUS! it's *your* agony I cry for!

POWER   You shying off again? Moaning over enemies of Zeus?
        Watch out, or you'll be moaning for yourself.   110

HEPHAISTOS You see something no one should see.

POWER   I see this bastard getting what he deserves.
        Now! Slap those iron bands around his ribs.

HEPHAISTOS I do what I have to do. Don't push it.

POWER I'll push you alright! the way a hunter sics his dogs.
Now get under. Shackle those legs.

HEPHAISTOS (*having gotten under, getting hastily back up*)
There, the job's done. I've made short painless work of it.

POWER Now, hard as you can, hammer the shackles INto him!
Watch it now. The Boss checks everything out.

HEPHAISTOS I can't tell which is worse: your looks or your loud mouth. 120

POWER So *be* a bleeding heart! Me, I'm thick-skinned,
but don't blame me for that. I am what I am.

HEPHAISTOS Let's get out of here. He's ironbound, hand and foot.

(HEPHAISTOS *hobbles off.*)

POWER (*finally addressing* PROMETHEUS)
You cocky bastard: *now* steal
powers from the Gods.
And for what?
Things that live and die!
Tell me sir, can humanity drain off
a single drop of your agony?   130
The Gods called you "Resourceful,"
that's a rich one.
You'll need resources, to squirm out of this
first-rate ironwork.

(POWER *strides away. After a moment* VIOLENCE *follows
him, silent as ever.*)

PROMETHEUS (*alone: speaking, invoking*)
Light, light, you
bright sky, winds on the wing, you rivers
springing up, and you
the waves the immense laughter easing the sea—

       now
Earth, mother of us all
      and you, Sun, watching over all: 140
        see
what a god can suffer at the hands of the Gods!

(*chanting*)
      These are the tortures
      I must struggle with: through ten thousand years
      of flesh raked away.

      This new Dictator
      of the Fortunate . . . *He* had these chains made
      to put me to shame!

      This agony I
      feel, I feel it coming too! At what point   150
      will He end this pain?

(*speaking*)
Wait, what am I saying?
I know how it all turns out:
      no unforeseen
heartbreaks for me.
        I see,
I do what I'm bound to do, and take the consequence
      as best I can.
I know: no one
wrestles Necessity down.   160

Yet it's hard to speak, and just as hard
not to speak, of what has happened . . .

For the power, the glory I gave to human beings
      I'm bound in irons.
I tracked down fire, where it springs from.
And stole it. I hid
      the spark in a fennel stalk, and brought it
to human beings. Now it shines

forth: a teacher
showing all mankind the way to all the arts there are.   170
That's my crime. That's why
I'm hammered in chains under the open sky.

(A *distant throbbing arises, approaches*: PROMETHEUS
                                        bursts into song.)
But what's that sound, that perfume? I can't see
                what flies at me!
                Is it a God
        or is it human, or a mingling of the two,
                who comes to this rock
                at the edge of the world?

(*breaking off*)
To make a show of me? Or what?
Then look! At a god savaged by irons   180

(*chanting*)
        an enemy of Zeus

        hated by all those Gods
        who strut through His vestibule,

        hated because I love
        mankind more than I should.

        Still it comes! But what?

        Light air whispers
        fluttering with wings!

        I'm afraid whatever comes!

        (DAUGHTERS OF OCEAN, *a chorus of barefoot girls*
        with the wings of sea birds, flock breathlessly in.)

CHORUS (*dancing, singing*)

> Don't be afraid: we came   190
>   because we love you.
> We raced ourselves here.
>
> Old Father Ocean
>   groaned, but let us go.
> High winds lofted us here.
>
> The pounding irons rang
>   right through our cave.
> We were beside ourselves!
>
> We forgot to be shy: look
>   we come barefoot.   200
> Our wings hurried us here.

PROMETHEUS (*chanting*)

> Ah, children of Tethys
> mother of so many others!
> You're your father's daughters
> too, I see—
> old Ocean
> who never sleeps, but streams
> coiling around the world!
>
> ...Look! Look at me.
> Chained in the rockpeaks   210
> of this ravine,
> I'll stand a watch
> no one envies me.

CHORUS (*dancing, singing*)

> Prometheus, I see
>   but through a mist of fear.
> Tears darken my eyes.
>
> I see, I see your body
>   withering on this rock,
> racked by unspeakable irons.

New masters sail Olympus.   220
   Look now, how Zeus lords it!
His rules are new, they're raw.

He rules beyond the law.
   Giant Things that used to be
He wipes out completely.

PROMETHEUS (*chanting*)
                    He should have buried me
                    under this earth, and under
                    Hades, cave of the dead,
                    down bottomless Tartaros.
                    With breakproof chains, with torture   230

                    still, that would be better.
                    No God there, no no one
                    could make a fool of me.
                    But here, while I hang
                    the winds toy with me

                    I writhe, my enemies smile.

CHORUS (*dancing, singing*)
                    What brute hearted God
                       would smile at this?
                    Who wouldn't howl feeling with you   240
                       at this outrage?
                    None but Zeus. His spite, His will
                       won't bend: but crush
                    the children of Father Sky.
                       Zeus won't let up
                    till Zeus has had enough

                    unless, against all odds, He's over-
                    thrown by ambush! Done with!

PROMETHEUS (*chanting*)
                    My day will come: though this

Commander of the Fortunate
tortures me, chains me up,   250
yet still my day will come.
He'll need me, to tell Him how
a new conspiracy
(I see it even now)
strips Him of His scepter
and all His privileges.

He'll never mystify me,
not with honey tongued charms
singing, to draw me out.
Never, I'll never cringe   260
to tell these things, despite
His lead heavy threats.

Not till He breaks these chains.

Not till He pays me all
He owes for this outrage.

CHORUS (*dancing, singing*)
                          You're brave, you won't
                                give in to pain.
                    And yet, your speech is much too free.
                          Fear quick fear
                          pierces our fluttering hearts: 270
                    whatever must become of you
                          on this sea of pain,
                          and when will you
                    arrive, safe on the shore?

              Your words can't touch, your words won't move
                    the brute heart of Kronos' Son.

PROMETHEUS (*chanting*)
                    He's savage, I know. He keeps
                    justice in His fist.
                    But with this hammer blow

He'll soften, He'll calm down   280
His blind stubborn rage.

He'll come to me, as a friend,
I'll love my friend again.

(*The music ends:* PROMETHEUS *and the* CHORUS *speak*
without accompaniment.)

CHORUS O tell us, tell us everything!
Having arrested you,
on what charge does Zeus
torture, humiliate you?
Tell us the whole story, please
... but only
if it doesn't hurt to tell.   290

PROMETHEUS It's painful to speak, it's painful
not to.
Every way, there's misery.

As soon as the Gods broke into factions
civil war was breaking out.
Some wanted to unseat
old Kronos.
Imagine! they wanted Zeus to rule.
Others though were deadset against it,
against Zeus   300
lording it over them.
Bringing good advice then, I went to the Titans
—the sons of Father Sky
and Mother Earth—
and went for nothing.
They brushed off
my sophisticated stratagems.
By sheer willpower and brute force
they dreamed
they would win with ease.   310

My mother Themis, who is also called Earth
    (she's one, only one, always the same form
       though she has many names)
she had sung time and again
the way the future goes:
how the war is won
    not by brute force
but by cunning, as fate would have it.
Yet even while I spelled this out for them
they wouldn't so much as look at me.   320
What could I do?
As things stood then, it seemed best
    to take my mother, and together
      we went as volunteers
                into the open arms of Zeus.
Thanks to the strategy I devised
the black hole of Tartaros holds and hides
    archaic Kronos
and all his allies too.
This Tyrant of the Gods   330
    so profited from my help
He paid me back in full,
with evil.
      Because all tyranny
is infected with this disease:
it never trusts its friends.

But you asked why He tortures me.
Listen. I'll make it clear ...

The war's no sooner over
    than there He is, on His father's throne,   340
dealing out priyileges to the different Gods.
And so, He makes a hierarchy of powers.
But for the suffering race of humankind
    He cared nothing,
He planned to wipe out the whole species
and breed another, a new one.

And no one dared stand up against this thing
    but me!
I alone had the courage.
I saved humanity from going down   350
    smashed to bits
into the cave of death.
      For this
I'm wrencht by torture:
    painful to suffer,
      pitiable to see.
I began by pitying people (things that die!)
    more than myself, but for myself
I wasn't thought fit to be pitied.
Instead, I'm brought to order   360
    without mercy—
a sight to bring
disgrace on the name of Zeus.

CHORUS What iron heart what breast hacked out of rock
would not howl
    feeling with you
      Prometheus!
I would not have wished to see this
yet now I do see, I'm   370
heartstruck.

PROMETHEUS Yes, this is a pitiful sight . . . to my friends.

CHORUS You didn't, perhaps, go beyond what you've told us?

PROMETHEUS Humans used to foresee their own deaths. I ended that.

CHORUS What cure did you find for such a disease?

PROMETHEUS Blind hopes. I sent blind hopes to settle their hearts.

CHORUS What a wonderful gift you helped mankind with!

PROMETHEUS What's more, I gave them fire.

CHORUS   Flare-eyed fire!?
                Now! In the hands of these
                          things that live and die!?   380

PROMETHEUS Yes, and from it they'll learn many skills.

CHORUS So these are the charges on which Zeus

PROMETHEUS   TORTURES ME
                and in no way eases these agonies!

CHORUS But isn't there a fixed point at which
                your agony must end?

PROMETHEUS None. It will end
                only when HE sees fit.

CHORUS When He sees fit! What hope is that?
                Don't you see,   390
                      you went wrong!
                But then, it gives me no pleasure to tell you
                      how you went wrong,
                besides it's painful for you to hear.
                So, enough of that.
                You must find a way to break
                free of your agony.

PROMETHEUS It's easy enough for the bystander,
                who's not bogged down in sorrow,
                to advise and warn   400
                the one who suffers.

                Myself, I knew all this
                and knew it all along.
                Still,
                      I *meant* to be wrong.
                I knew what I was doing.
                Helping humankind
                      I helped myself to misery

And yet I never dreamed it would be like this,
    this wasting away against the air hung cliffs   410
    the desolate mountain top
       the loneliness
So don't now, don't
    cry over *this*, the sorrow that is.
But come down to earth.
Hear what's to come, hear the story to its end.

Obey me, obey!
Bear with me
    now it's *my* turn for misery.
Sorrow wanders about the world   420
touching on each of us, and each in turn.

CHORUS (*wheeling deeper into the ravine, nearer* PROMETHEUS:
                                   chanting in gusts)
              Prometheus
        we come and gladly,
          glad you called to us.
      Out of the pure clean air
          O air currents
            the birds ride
       I come, coming to set my light
          foot on this harsh rock,
     I'll hear out your sorrows to the end.   430

    (*Suddenly a birdhorse billows down with an over-*
      whelming rider on its back: this is OCEAN.)

OCEAN (*chanting*)
      At this point my long journey ends, Prometheus,
      because here you are. Didn't use the reins, either,
      I just steered this wingéd monster by sheer willpower.
      But you may rest assured, my *heart* goes out to you—
      it couldn't do otherwise, seeing that we're kin,
      and even if we weren't, it would: for there's no one,
      no one I respect more than you. You can believe that.

I haven't it in me to go around mouthing
highsounding hollow words. Look I'll prove it: tell me
what I can do for you ... and then you'll never say   440
you have a steadier friend than your friend Ocean!

PROMETHEUS   What's this! Have you too come
                    to witness my pain?
            How did you dare abandon
                    the great stream that bears your name
                        and the rock arches of the sea caves
                            the sea itself has made—
            to come to this, this
            motherland of iron!
            And why? To see what's happened to me?   450
                    To howl feeling with me?
            Well here's a show for you: look at this
                    friend of Zeus!
            I helped Him
                    set up His tyranny,
            now I'm wrencht with torture
            ordered by Him.

    OCEAN   I do see, Prometheus. And what I wish to give you
                    (smart as you are)
            is the best advice of all: 460
                            Know thyself.
            Also, rehabilitate yourself.
            The Gods have a new Tyrant,
                    follow the new line!
            If you throw such sharp words around
            why even Zeus, even though He's seated way up there,
                    may hear!
            Then agonies that crowd you now
            will seem like child's play.
            You're suffering: calm down, find a way   470
                    free of these agonies.
            This may sound old-fashioned, but
            The braggart gets more than he bargained for.

You don't keep your profile
        low enough, you don't
    give in to torture: you insist
        on more of the same!
Let *me* be your teacher, and you won't
        stick your neck out,
not when there's a hard Chief-of-State   480
in power, accountable to no one.

I'll go now, and try to have you
        freed from these agonies.
Meanwhile keep quiet, don't run off at the mouth.
Clever as you are, you should know by now
To a loose tongue, punishment comes.

PROMETHEUS (*ironically*)
        How I envy you:
having been such a great help in my struggle
        you're beyond blame!
Now too, leave me alone, forget it.   490
You won't ever change His mind, it's set.
You look out for your*self*, you're headed for trouble.

OCEAN   You give advice better than you take it,
    look at you!
        I'm going now, don't try to haul me back.
I'm confident, absolutely confident
Zeus will grant what I ask:
to free you from these agonies.

PROMETHEUS   One thing I admire in you, and always will:
    you're not at a loss for good intentions.   500
    But don't bother,
            it's useless to bother on my account
            ... that is, if you really intend to.
    No, keep quiet, stay out of this.
    I've my misfortune, but that's no reason for me to wish
            as many as possible should suffer too,

not when I'm already
    torn by the anguish
of Atlas, my brother:
            who stands where evening is,   510
    pressing his shoulder to the unbearable
        pillar that holds
the sky from the earth!

Pity cut me to the quick, too, when I saw
    that child of Earth,
the hotblooded monster of the Cilician caves,
        Typhon
    with his hundred flickering heads
as he, too, was overpowered by violence.
He stood up against all the Gods: 520
    terror
    hissed through his horrible jaws, his eyes
glared, a lightningd
  DEATH'S HEAD!
As though he'd explode the tyranny of Zeus
by violence!
But then on *him*
    Zeus drove the sleepless thunderbolt,
    plunged the fire spurting shaft
down, it slammed   530
the loud bragging pride out of Typhon—
    struck through, scorcht
      his heart out, it
thundered his strength away.
Now that helpless sprawl of a body lies
    near the sea narrows,
clenched by the massive roots of Etna,
    while at the summit
Hephaistos sits, pounding the glowing mass of iron.
    One day in time to come   540
fire rivers will gush up: white hot fangs will gouge
the smooth, fruitful fields of Sicily!
That will be Typhon
    fuming:

though Zeus' lightning bolt has burnt him out, still
    he'll boil up, he'll jet
fountains of rage and fire.

But you've been around, you don't need me
to teach you this.
Save yourself any way you can.   550
I have, now, my own misfortune: which I'll bail to the dregs
    until the wrathful mind
        of Zeus . . . lets up.

OCEAN   Don't you know, Prometheus:
a sick mind may be cured by words.

PROMETHEUS Yes, if the time's right. But when that mind is still
infected with rage, you can't force the swelling down.

OCEAN All right then, teach me this: what's the harm
if daring is mixed with good intentions?

PROMETHEUS Useless makework! simplistic innocence!   560

OCEAN Then let me suffer such disease.
When one is wise, it's wisest to seem foolish.

PROMETHEUS As will be seen: that's my condition, not yours.

OCEAN Your drift is obvious: you want to send me home.

PROMETHEUS Yes. If you feel sorry for me, you'll get yourself hated

OCEAN by Him? the One newly seated on the Throne of Power!

PROMETHEUS Yes. Watch out, or His heart may turn angry on you.

OCEAN I learn that, Prometheus, just by looking at you.

PROMETHEUS LEAVE! GET GOING! NOW YOU'VE GOT THE
                POINT, KEEP IT IN MIND!

OCEAN Before the words are out of your mouth   570
     I'm going!
  My four-legged bird
   strokes the smooth
  skyways with his wings.
  For sure: he'll be glad to bed down
  at home, in his own stall.

    (OCEAN *and his monster swing upward, and away*.)

CHORUS (*dancing and singing an ode*)
     Prometheus, your savage fate
      has made me cry.
     My cheeks are wet
    with tears welling from my delicate eyes   580
     as river water, or the falling dew.
    It's horrible: Zeus dictates with laws
      He made Himself,
    He bares the spearpoint of His pride, over
     the Gods that used to be.

    The whole earth now howls with grief:
      everything mourns
     the bold, emblazoned
    glowing ancient glory that used to be
  and be yours and your family's, before this grief.   590
     And those peoples who have set
      their roots in the plains
     near Asia's holy ground,
     they feel your howling pain

     as do the girls of Colchis
     who never tremble in battle;
     and, too, the Scythian horde
     camped by Lake Maiotis
     where earth comes to an end

     and, too, the flower of   600
     Arabia: the wild

warriors who guard the steep
acropolis by Kaukasos,
a thunderhead bristling with spears.

The only other Titan I have seen
so trapped, so infinitely abused
was Atlas
god Atlas:
his awful strength
he mourns with his back.   610

The waves break
the surf moans,
the depths sound and sound,
the black
bottomless deep
hollows back,
and the pure springs of rivers and brooks
all for you

sorrow

PROMETHEUS I say nothing, but don't think that means I'm   620
arrogant or stubborn.
I see myself abused, bullied, and . .
     Brooding
eats my heart away.
After all, who apportioned the privileges
    among these latter-day Gods?
      Who but I?
But I won't go into that,
you've heard it all before.
    Instead, hear   630
what wretched lives people used to lead,
how babyish they were—until
I gave them intelligence,
    I made them
masters of their own thought.

I tell this
    not against humankind, but only to show
how loving my gifts were . . .

Men and women looking
    saw nothing,   640
they listened
    and did not hear,
but like shapes in a dream dragging out their long lives
        bewildered
they made hodgepodge of everything, they knew nothing
                  of making

        brick-knitted
    houses the sun warms,
nor how to work in wood.
They swarmed like bitty ants
    in dugouts   650
in sunless caves.
They hadn't any sure signs of winter, nor spring
    flowering,
nor late summer when the crops come in.
All their work was work without thought,
until I taught them to see
what had been hard to see:
            where and when the stars
            rise and set.

What's more, for them I invented   660
    NUMBER: wisdom
above all other.
    And the painstaking, putting together of
LETTERS: to be their memory
of everything, to be their Muses'
    mother, their
      handmaid!
And I was the first to put brute beasts
under the yoke, fit them out
    with pack saddles, so they could take   670

the heaviest burdens off the backs of human beings.
Horses I broke and harnessed
        to the chariot shaft
so that they loved their reins, they showed off
the pride and wealth of their owners.
I, I alone invented
        the seawandering
            linen wingd
chariots for sailors.

All these devices, I invented for human beings.   680
Yet now in my own misery, I can't devise
        one single trick
to free myself from this agony.

CHORUS You've been tortured, humiliated, so that your mind
                        wanders
driven to distraction.
Like a bad doctor fallen sick
        you grope, desperate
for what you can't find:
the drugs that will make you well.   690

PROMETHEUS But hear the rest, you'll be more amazed:
what arts, what
        resources I worked out!
And the greatest was this . . .
If someone fell sick
        there was nothing for it: nothing to eat, drink
nor rub into the skin.
Without drugs
people wasted away,
until I showed them how to mix   700
        soothing herbs
to ward off every sort of disease.

I marked out the many ways men might
        see into the future.

I was the first to realize what dreams are bound
to wake up: real.
And snatches of speech
    caught in passing, and chance meetings along the road,
these too have secret meanings.
I showed them this.   710
        And clearly analyzed the flight
  of birds with crookt claws—
    what ones
      bring luck, and which
    are sinister—
and the way each species lives,
what hates it has, what loves,
what others it settles with.
I looked into
    the silky entrails, I showed them   720
what color gall bladder meant the Gods were pleased,
and the liver's
    lovely marbled lobe.
And thigh bones wrapped in fat, and long backbones
    I burned,
I showed humans the pathway into an art
hard to figure.
I gave the fire
    eyes, so that its signs
      shone through   730
where before they were filmed over.

So much for these. As for the benefits to humankind
hid under the earth (the copper the iron
      the silver the gold)
who but I could claim he discovered them?
No one, except a babbling idiot.

In a word: listen!
All human culture comes from Prometheus.

CHORUS Don't go out of your way to help humankind, yet
    neglect your own misery!   740

I'm hopeful, now, that once you're freed from these chains
you'll be powerful as Zeus.

PROMETHEUS Fate, that concludes everything, is not
                    fated to make that happen—
              not yet, not this way.
              Ten thousand
                    sorrows must wrench me. *That's* the way
                          I escape my chains.
              Art is far feebler
              than Necessity.   750

CHORUS But who swings the helm?
                          who brings Necessity about?

PROMETHEUS The three bodies of Fate, and the unforgetting Furies.

CHORUS Is Zeus really less powerful than *these*?

PROMETHEUS Well...He can't escape His fate.

CHORUS But what *is* His fate, except to rule forever?

PROMETHEUS Don't be so insistent. You're not to learn that. Not yet.

CHORUS This secret must be awesome, you keep it so close...

PROMETHEUS Talk about something else!
              It's not the time to speak out, not yet.   760
              Whatever happens
              the secret has to be kept,
                    it's all I have
              to escape this shame, this torture, these chains.

CHORUS (*dancing and singing an ode*)
                          May Zeus never turn
                          His world
                          wide
                    power against my mind

may I never
hesitate   770
to approach the Gods
with holy feasts
of blood drenched bulls
where Father Ocean, our father, streams and streams

may I never
say a sinful word

may this be ever
engraved in my mind
not melt
as words on wax   780

Nothing is sweeter
than life
lived
as long as this may be

always to hope
and feast, keep
the heart while it throbs
alive, lit up
with happiness
O but my blood runs cold, I'm cold, seeing you   790

raked over with
ten thousand tortures

you won't cower for Zeus,
you've a mind of your own
and you
honor humans

too much! Prometheus!

Tell us, what's the use of doing good

when there's no good in it
for you?   800

These things that live and die—
what help are they?
You must have seen
how blind and weak, like prisoners of a dream,
the human beings
are.
Can the plans of things that live and die
ever overstep
the orchestrated universe of Zeus?

This is what we've learned, Prometheus,   810
seeing your murderous
fate . . .

My heart flutters, I ache
to sing for you,
but not the song
I sang blessing your bridal bath and bed,
that bed you shared:
when
with gifts you courted Hesione
our dear sister,   820
persuading her, who gladly went home with you

(*Suddenly* IO *bursts in: a beautiful young girl horned like
a heifer.*)

IO (*chanting*)
Where is this?
Who lives here?
What *is* this
stormbeaten thing
yoked by rock?

Speak to me!
What did you do
to deserve this?
Where on earth   830
have I strayed to?

(*A sudden lowing shriek: it wells up through her, a voice
beyond her own, breaking out into wild unstructured
song.*)

again
it's the horsefly
it bites
my poor body!

No ... it's the ghost of Argos
born out of earth
EARTH MAKE IT GO AWAY!
Herdsman I see
scaring me   840
with all his eyes!
He stalks by, the eyes give me
sly looks.
But he's dead! why can't the earth
hold him under?
From the dead dark he comes
to hound me
drive me
so that I starve
by the sands of the seashore   850

(*still singing, but in her own voice now, and less wildly*)

And always I hear the awful drone
the drowsy hum of reed-pipes bound in wax.
(*moaning, lowing*)   No
it's so far, where am I going?
Son of Kronos

you've yoked me to this misery,
what did I do wrong?
why this horsefly?
why this horror
driving a wretched thing out of her mind!   860

BURN ME WITH FIRE

BURY ME IN EARTH

LET ME BE SWALLOWED BY BEASTS OF THE SEA

I pray you, Master! I'm put through
my paces
enough now!
I don't know how
to get away from this misery.

Hear her now? Hear the girl
who's horned like a cow!   870

PROMETHEUS (*speaking quietly, as though to himself*)
Of course I hear. It's the child of Inachos
driven by the horsefly.
Zeus was hot for her,
Now she's hated by Hera
whose violence puts her through
these neverending paces.

IO (*singing*)
How do you know my father's name?
Who are you? Speak to the unhappy girl:
you, who
grieve as I do, how could you say   880
what my name is,
how could you know what winged disease from the Gods
stings me on? I'm near
eaten away!

(*bellows*)
                    Tortured sick, hungry, I kicked up, came here

            STORMING STAMPEDED TERRORSTRUCK

            IT WAS HERA WHO BROKE ME

            HER SPITE BROKE MY SPIRIT

                    Who of all the unfortunate
                            suffers   890
                        as I do?
                    In plain words now
                    tell me: how much more must I endure?

                    Where's the cure? If you know
                    tell the wandering girl!

PROMETHEUS (*speaking*) All you want to know, I'll tell you,
            not weaving it into riddles
            but straight out: the right way
            to speak to a friend.
            You see the one who gave mankind   900
            fire:
                    Prometheus.

        IO (*speaking*) PROMETHEUS, patron of the whole human race!
                    Unhappy thing
            you suffer, what have you done?

PROMETHEUS A moment ago, I

                            . . . have ended the song of my suffering.

        IO Well, then, won't you grant me this other favor?

PROMETHEUS Name it. Ask me whatever you wish.

        IO Say who wedged you into this ravine.   910

PROMETHEUS Zeus, with His will. Hephaistos, with his hands.

  IO But the crimes you're paying for, what were they?

PROMETHEUS No more! It's enough that I've told you this much.

  IO   Tell more! At what point
        does my wandering end, how long must I suffer?

PROMETHEUS You're better off not knowing that.

  IO What fate must I suffer? Don't hide it from me.

PROMETHEUS It's not that I grudge you this gift.

  IO Then why hold back? Why not tell it straight out?

PROMETHEUS Not out of meanness.   920
              It's just... I'm afraid
        I'll crush you with it.

  IO Don't be kinder to me than I myself would like.

PROMETHEUS All right, listen! If you insist, I have to give it to you...

  CHORUS Wait, not yet!
        Let us
              have our share of pleasure.
        Let's ask her
              her disease,
        let's hear from her own lips   930
        what fate wastes her.
        After that, she can learn from you
        the ordeals to come.

PROMETHEUS It's up to you, Io, to do them this favor,
        especially since they're your father's sisters.

345

Then too it's worth troubling yourself
to weep over your fate . . . when there are others
who will weep with you.

10 I don't see how I can refuse you.
I'll tell you   940
all you want to know.
Although, even as I speak
        I'm ashamed, recalling
the storm the God let loose
        —my lovely body
                ruined—
and the One who drove it winging down
on me, wretched thing.

Always at night, haunting softspoken dreams
would wander into my bedroom   950
(where no man had ever entered)
whispering whispering
                "Happy, happy girl
you could marry the greatest One of all,
why wait so long
        untouched?
Desire's spear has made Zeus
burn for you. He wants to come
        together with you   960
making love.
Don't, dear child, turn skittish
        against the bed of Zeus. Go out
into the deep grasses of Lerna, where your father's
        cattle and sheep
                browse. Go,
so the eye of Zeus will no longer
be heavy-lidded with longing."

        Such dreams obsessed me
night after night. I was miserable.
Until, finally, I brought myself to tell my father   970
these dark-roaming dreams.

He sent many messengers off
                              to Delphi, and towards Dodona,
            to find out
        what he must do, what say
to please the Gods—
and they came back reporting
the shifty words of oracles,
        doubletalk
no one could make out.   980
At last, word came to father;
it was clear, and it was an order:
            "Drive her out of home and country,
            let her wander
                untouchable, footloose
            to the far ends of the earth.
            If not, Zeus will fire His thunderbolt
                down,
            your whole people
            will be exterminated."   990
Those were Apollo's oracular words.
Father gave in.
Against his own will
        as against mine
he drove, locked me out.
The bridle of Zeus
forced him to it.
            Suddenly   1000
my body, my mind
        warped,
my head
        horned—
            look at me!
Under the sharp bites of the horsefly
I kicked up, making
a mad dash for the sweet water
        at Kerchneia, and the spring
            called Lerna...
Suddenly Argos the earthborn herdsman

was following me: his rage the rage   1010
    of raw wine, staring with thick packt eyes
he crowded my every step.
      Until an unforeseen abrupt fate
cut him   from life!

Yet *still* the horsefly
goads me,
   the God's switch
lashes me land to land . . .

You've heard what was done.
Now tell me, if you can,   1020
the sorrows to come.
Don't for pity's sake
   try to warm me with lies.
To me, lies are the shamefullest disease.

CHORUS (*bursting into song*)
                   NO
                   NO
         make it go away!

(*individually*)
         I never dreamed I'd hear
           so horrible a story,

         such barbaric words   1030
       such pain,   such filth
    it's not to be seen, not endured!

         My heart's
        goaded stabbed
          iced

      It's FATE! your FATE!

         Io
       I shudder at

PROMETHEUS Too soon you cry out! all brimming with fear!
            Wait: till you've heard what's to come.   1040

CHORUS Go ahead, tell her. When you're sick it helps
        to know beforehand: what pain waits for you.

PROMETHEUS Your first appeal was not—for me—hard to grant.
            You wanted to hear this child
                recite with her own lips
            her own agony.
            Now hear the rest, what
                misery she's in for—
            this young girl, hated by Hera.

            You too, Io, daughter of Inachos,   1050
                take my words to heart.
            Then you will know
            at what point your journey ends.

            To begin: from here you must turn
            towards where the sun comes up.
            And walk on, across unplowed meadows,
                till you come to the roving Scythians
            who live in air, within reed huts
            on wagons with sturdy wheels.
            They're armed with long range bows   1060
            so don't get near them.
            Keep by the sea, let your feet
                trail through the surf
                    where the waves moan
            And so, pass through that country.

            To your left there'll be
            the Chalybes: those ones
                work iron.
            Watch out for them, they're savages,
            strangers can't approach.   1070

                        Next

you'll come to the Arrogangos, a river
that lives up to its name.
Don't cross though. It won't be crossed
    till you come to Kaukasos itself
            the highest of mountains: from whose very brow
the river in all its fury
gushes out.
Those peaks
    stand off among the stars, and those   1080
you must cross.

Head south then
till you find the man-hating
    army of Amazons.
One day they'll settle by the Thermodon, in Themiskyra,
where Salmydessos
    that haggard rockmouth of the sea, that
stepmother of ships, welcomes
sailors to death.
On *your* way, though, they'll help you   1090
and help you gladly:
        you'll come to the Crimea,
    the isthmus
by the narrow gates of the lake.
But leave this behind: for with a strong heart
    you must cross that channel.
Channel of Maiotis now, but ever after
men and women will speak of your crossing:
they'll call it Bosporos,
    Place Where The Heifer Girl Crossed,   1100
in honor of you.

    But now you
have left Europe, you move on
    into Asia . . .

(*to the* CHORUS)
NOW do you see? This Dictator of the Gods

is violent in every way
    to everyone!
With this girl, this human,
    this God
wanted to make love.   1110
After *her*
      He drove this curse, this wandering.

Io, the suitor for your marriage
    has been a savage.
As for all you've just heard, believe me: it isn't even
the prelude to your song.

(IO *cries out*)
    Howling and snorting again?
How will you take it, then, when you hear
the terrors to come?

CHORUS To come? You've *more* pain to tell of?   1120

PROMETHEUS A wintry sea of   sorrow.

IO Then what good's life? Why haven't I
thrown myself off this harsh rock,
smashed myself against the earth
    and so
        freed myself from *all* suffering!

Better to die once and for all
than drag out my days in misery.

PROMETHEUS   Then you'd be hard put
to bear this agony of mine.   1130
My fate is
    I cannot die.
Death would be
freedom from sorrow, but now ...

There's no end
        point to my misery, none
until Zeus falls from power.

IO Can Zeus ever, ever fall from power?

PROMETHEUS I suspect . . . you'd be glad to see that come about.

IO Of course I would, why not, isn't Zeus my oppressor?   1140

PROMETHEUS Then take it from me: these things *are*. They're so.

IO Who'll rob Him of His scepter, His power?

PROMETHEUS He'll do it Himself, through His own mindless schemes.

IO But how? Tell me, if there's no harm in telling.

PROMETHEUS He'll marry, and someday that marriage will trouble Him.

IO With a human being? a God? Tell me, if you may.

PROMETHEUS What difference does it make? Anyway, it's not to be told.

IO Who drives Him from His throne—His wife?

PROMETHEUS His wife. She'll bear a child greater than its Father.

IO And there's no way He can get around this?   1150

PROMETHEUS None . . . except, if I were freed from these chains.

IO But who's to free you against the will of Zeus?

PROMETHEUS As fate has it: one of your descendants.

IO What! You'll be freed from evils . . . by a child of *mine*?

PROMETHEUS Yes: the tenth, tenth then third, of the line following from
you.

IO You sound like an oracle: I can no longer follow you!

PROMETHEUS Don't, then, try to find out how far your sufferings go.

IO Please! Don't reach out a helping hand
then take it back again!

PROMETHEUS I've two stories—I'll give you one of them.   1160

IO What are they? Tell me, let *me* choose between them.

PROMETHEUS Then choose. Shall I tell you in plain words
what more you'll suffer, or who will set me free?

CHORUS Give her the benefit of one, please, and give
us the other.
You can't grudge us our fair share of the story.
Tell Io
how far she still has to go.
Tell us
who will set you free,   1170
that's what *we're* dying to hear . . .

PROMETHEUS Since you're so anxious, I won't refuse to tell you
all you want to know.
First, Io, I'll tell you
your wandering, whipt about like a top.
Inscribe this in your mind's
tablet, where memories are kept.

Having crossed the stream between Europe and Asia
—towards that dawnworld where the sun
walks, flare-eyed—   1180
you'll move on
over swells of an unsurging sea.

These
    are dunes, it's desert!
You'll reach the Gorgonian flatlands, in Kisthene,
where the daughters of Phorkys live:
    three girlish hags
        shaped like swans.
Between the three, they've got
just one eye   1190
    and one tooth.
The sun doesn't ever
    beam on them,
nor will the night
    moon.
And their three sisters live nearby:
    repulsive with hair
not hair, they're wingd
    snake wool! it's
                GORGONS!   1200
No human being will ever look on these and breathe
one breath more.

So much for the guardians of that land.

    Next comes
a horrible sight: Zeus's
    hunting pack, but sharp beakt, they don't bark
but lunge! They're GRIFFINS.
Avoid them, them and the one-eyed army
mounted on horseback, they're
    ARIMASPS   1210
by the River Wealth
rippling with gold . . .
    Stay away!

You'll come, then, to a land at the world's end
where tribes of black people live,
where the Fountains of the Sun
    gush

and the River Aithiops flows.
Follow that river's bank, till you come upon
sheer waterfall plunging   1220
          down from the Bybline Hills,
     hills bubbling
the sweet blessed waters of the Nile.
And he, that river, will lead you to
a three-cornered land:
          the Nile delta.
Io, here is your destiny.
Here, you with your sons
found your far-off, longstanding colony.

     ...If anything's obscure   1230
ask me again, and again
till it comes clear.
I've more spare time than I could wish for.

CHORUS If you've left anything out, or if there's
               more to her disastrous wandering,
          why then tell her.
          Otherwise, grant what we asked.
          You remember what that was.

PROMETHEUS She's heard the endpoint of her journey.
          She should know, too, that what she's heard   1240
               is true.
          I'll prove it.
          I'll tell her what agonies she went through
          to get *this* far.

          (*to* IO)
          ...There's such a crowd of words
          I'll skip most of them, and push through
          to the endpoint of your wanderings.

          After you had moved on
               to the Molossian meadows,

then to the sheer ridges
    ranged around Dodona   1250
(where Thesprotian Zeus
        is enthroned as oracle)
     you came upon
something incredible, wonderful: oak trees
    that spoke to you.
Without riddles, in luminous words
they saluted you:
(*his voice changing*)
               You, who are to be the glorious
                    wife of Zeus   1260
Remember, Io? Doesn't this
nuzzle your memory . . .
    But then
the horsefly bit you,
     again
you bucked up, plunging along the coastal road
to the great Gulf of Rhea—
                  where suddenly
    you were stormed back in a blind rush.
Yet now and for all time, believe me,   1270
that inlet of the sea will be called
    Ionian,
all humankind will recall your passage there.

This then is proof: my mind *sees*
    more than may be seen.

(*to the* CHORUS)
Now—picking up the trail where I left off
    in my earlier story—I'll tell
you, and her as well,
what lies ahead.

Where Egypt ends, where silt   1280
    bars the mouth of the Nile
there's a city called Kanobos.

There I see
        Zeus...
He's bringing you back to your senses,
        stroking you
with a hand you no longer fear.
He merely
        touches you. Yet that's enough
to father your black child   1290
Epaphos (or Touchborn)
        who'll harvest
                as much of the land
as is watered by the broad flooding Nile.

The fifth generation following from him, a family of fifty
        girls will hurry against their will
back to Argos.
They want to escape
marrying their cousins.
But those men with their hearts worked up,   1300
        closing in on them
                as falcons on doves, will come hunting
a marriage that should not be pursued.
Yet the God will grudge them
the girls' bodies.
The Pelasgian earth
takes them in

when, daring
        during the nightwatch,
woman's war   1310
will make man a corpse.
She cuts
        his life out: tempers
her double-whetted blade, glowing red
in her lover's throat.
I wish my enemies could have
        such love made to them!
Yet one of the girls... desire

has her, spellbound.
He lies beside her, yet she cannot　　　　　　　1320
　　kill.
In her, the murderous edge
goes blunt.
Her choice is
　　she'd rather be called coward
than guilty of blood.
In Argos, your homeland,
that girl, your descendant,
will bear a line of kings.

That's another story, a long one, but I'll say this much:　　1330
that from her seed
　　a brave man will grow, a famous archer
who'll free me from these agonies.
This was prophesied by the Titan Themis, my mother
　　born in archaic time.
She explained it to me.
It would take too long to say
how it will come about,
　　and besides
it's of no use for you to know.　　　　　　　1340

10 (*bellowing horribly: thrown back into the present, again*
　　　　　becoming heifer, she breaks away chanting)
　　　　spasm! again
　　　　what manias
　　　　beat my brain
　　　　hot I'm hot
　　　　where's the fire?
　　　　here's horsefly
　　　　His Arrowhead
　　　　not fire forged
　　　　but sticks: heart
　　　　struck with fear　　　　　　　1350
　　　　kicks at my ribs
　　　　eye balls whirl

spirally wheeld
by madness, madness
stormblasted I'm
blown off course
my tongue my tiller
it's unhinged, flappy
words words thrash
dashed O at doom   1360
mud churning up
breaking in waves

(10 *charges off.*)

CHORUS Wise, yes, that man was wise

(*dancing and singing an ode*)
who first weighed this in mind,
then shaped it
on his lips:
"Marry your own kind, within your own class,
there is no better way."
As for people puffed up with money
or the arrogance of birth,   1370
no worker should want to marry the likes of those."

Great Fates: never, never
may you see
me coming
to be the mistress in the bed of Zeus,
nor would I be the bride
of any God come out of heaven,
I dread it: seeing Io's
manshunning maidenhood driven wild by Hera.

(*individually*)
For me,   1380
when equals marry
there's no terror.

What I'm afraid of is the Stronger Ones,
                what if their love
            should stare me down?
        There's no getting away.

    That would be a war that's not a war,
        where struggling more is more
                giving in.

    I don't know what would become of me,   1390
        I don't see how I could avoid
                Zeus' design.

PROMETHEUS   As for Zeus, His heart's
                stubborn.
            But take my word for it, He'll be humbled yet.
            He's getting ready to marry
            ah, what a marriage . . . it will throw Him
                out of His throne and His tyranny,
            He'll end up nowhere.
                    His father, Kronos, as he fell from his ancient throne 1400
                cursed Him.
            Zeus, then, will have consummated that curse.
            None of the Gods can show Him the way
                out of these troubles.
            Except me. I know these things
            and how they will happen.

            So. Let Him sit there, dreaming He's safe
                making sky high thunder, rattling
            a fistful of fire spurting rockets.
            Nothing will save Him from the sharp   1410
            plunge into shame,
                excruciating ruin.
            Even now, He Himself is working out the wrestler
            who'll take Him on.
            What an unbeatable
                wonder it is, this giant who'll discover

fire hotter than lighting, explosion
outroaring thunder!
As for Poseidon's three-pointed pitchfork
    that makes the sea heave and the earth quake,   1420
he'll knock it flying...
Stumbling up against this terror, Zeus will learn
what a difference there is: between
   being a power
and being a slave.

CHORUS This curse on Zeus—it's only your own wishfulness!

PROMETHEUS It *is* what I wish. But also, in fact, it's bound to happen.

CHORUS You mean, we can expect someone to lord it over Zeus?

PROMETHEUS Yes. And His neck will bend under worse pains than these.

CHORUS Aren't you afraid, throwing such talk about?   1430

PROMETHEUS Afraid? Why? I'm not fated to die.

CHORUS He could make you suffer worse than this.

PROMETHEUS So let Him! I know what to expect, I'm ready for it.

CHORUS Those who are wise
                bow down to the Inevitable.

PROMETHEUS Honor! adore! go crawling before
whatever ruler rules
   today.
Me, I couldn't care less for your Zeus.
Let Him act willful, let Him lord it   1440
   this little while,
He won't lord it over the Gods for long.

                  (*out of the blue*: HERMES *appears*)
Look now, here's Zeus' errand boy,

special assistant to the new
   Dictator. No doubt
he's come to hand out some news.

HERMES You there!
      Yes,
you . . . are, I presume, the bitter, too bitter, intellectual
who committed crimes against the Gods,   1450
who gave their glory away
to things that live and die,
the one who stole
              our fire!

Well. The Father demands to know
   what's this marriage you're shouting about,
the one you infer
will depose Him.
A detailed explanation, please, and no doubletalk.
Don't make me come back a second time.   1460
In cases like this, as you're well aware, Zeus is not
inclined to go easy.

PROMETHEUS You've got an insolent
         pompous mouth,
you sound just like the Gods'
     puppet god.
You're all so young, newly in power, you dream
    you live in a tower
       too high up for sorrow.
Haven't I seen two tyrants   1470
thrown from that height?
And won't I witness the third, this latest
   God of the hour,
as He too falls?
It will be sudden, and most shameful.

Well? Do I seem afraid? Do I cringe
before the new Gods?
      Far from it. Not one bit.

Now scurry on back the way you came.
Whatever you ask, you'll get nothing out of me.   1480

HERMES Once before, by just such stubbornness as this
you came to moor yourself in these miseries.

PROMETHEUS Get this much straight: if I could trade
all my misery for your servility
I wouldn't.

HERMES Really. I suppose it's better to serve this rock
than be, say, Father Zeus' trusted
minister? His messenger god!

PROMETHEUS When you're insolent, that's the insult you're reduced to.

HERMES You seem to glory in your present situation.   1490

PROMETHEUS Glory in it? I wish my enemies such glory!
                                        Including you.

HERMES Me? You blame me too for this disaster?

PROMETHEUS To put it simply: I hate all the Gods
who, when I helped them, wronged me.

HERMES You're insane, you're sick, and what you say is sick.

PROMETHEUS Agreed . . . if it's sick to hate one's enemies.

HERMES If you were doing well, you'd be insufferable.

PROMETHEUS (*involuntarily, screaming his pain*) **AIE!**

HERMES "Aie . . . ?" That's one word Zeus doesn't understand.   1500

PROMETHEUS (*regaining composure*)
Time, as it grows old, teaches all things.

HERMES   Really? But you still haven't learned to be sensible.

PROMETHEUS   No, or I wouldn't be talking to a puppet.

HERMES   Then you won't, it seems, give the Father
the information He demands.

PROMETHEUS   Sure! Since I owe Him a great favor, on demand
I'd be more than pleased to pay Him back...

HERMES   You're teasing me, treating me like a child!

PROMETHEUS   But aren't you childish, I mean
sillier than any child, expecting *me* to tell *you*   1510
anything?
Zeus doesn't have one torture, not one ingenious device
to pry this out of me—
not till He eases
these shameful chains.
Let Him rocket His lightning
the bolts trailing smoke!
With white wings of snowflakes,
with earth shattering
thunder,   1520
let Him heave together everything there is
in one confusion!
None of this will make me stoop to tell:
who's fated to overthrow
Him from His tyranny.

HERMES   Think now: will any of this benefit your case?

PROMETHEUS   I thought this out, and came to my conclusions, long ago.

HERMES   Come round, you fool! Consider what
pain you're put through: come to your senses at last!

PROMETHEUS   Why waste your breath? You might as well   1530
preach at the waves.

Don't think I'm so terrified by the will of Zeus
I'll turn womanish, turn
      my fluttering palms up, and beg the One I hate
to free me from these chains.
I'm a long ways from that.

HERMES All I say, apparently, I say for nothing.
I've begged you, and still
you haven't softened or mellowed:
but like a newly harnessed colt   1540
      you grind at the bit,
you buck, you fight the reins.
But really, this tactic you put such raving faith in
      is ineffectual.
When you're wrongheaded, it gets you less than nowhere
to be stubborn.

My *words* won't persuade you? Then think
what a storm, what a towering wave of ruin
      rushes down on you!
Your can't escape it.   1550
First, the Father will flash
      lightning and thunder down, and pound
this jagged ravine into an avalanche
to bury your body in it.
Arms of stone will hug and hold you.
And so, you'll travel through the vast tracts
    of time. And at last
come back up into sunlight.
        Then
Zeus' feathered hound, the blood red golden EAGLE   1560
will tear your flesh
      into flapping rags.
It won't be invited, but it will come:
all day
      feasting, its beak
         stabbing your liver black.
Blood black.

At no point can you expect
an end to that anguish.
　　　Until perhaps   1570
a God comes, willing to suffer
your pain for you,
willing to sink
　　down into lightless Hades and the dead dark
　　　　hollows of Tartaros.

Well, there you have it. Now make up your mind.
I haven't concocted a fiction, no bluff,
　　it's all too true.
Besides, Zeus cannot tell a lie,
He doesn't know how to.   1580
Whatever He says, it happens.
Now, Prometheus, give this careful consideration,
reflect on your situation.
Don't think it's better
to be stubborn, than to be sensible.

CHORUS   To us, it seems
Hermes has a point:
that you should give up your stubbornness, follow the trail
　　of good sound advice.   1590
Listen to him.
It's shameful for one so wise to be so wrong.

(*music: from here on, all is chanted*)

PROMETHEUS   Before he said one word
                  I knew what he would say!
                  Yet when an enemy's
                  hurt by an enemy

                              why, there's no shame in that!

                  Let forkt lightning coil
                  down on my head

Let sky shudder thunder
with wind spasms   1600

Let hurricane shake
earth from its roots

Let waves surge and moan
as savages

      overwhelming the tracks
      high stars leave

Let Him hurl my body
utterly down

      the black pit
      of Tartaros, down   1610

      the stiff whirlpool
      Necessity...

Come what may: He won't
put *me* to death.

HERMES   These are the words, these are the dreams
of lunatics.
What part of this peculiar prayer
is *not* insane?

(*to the* CHORUS)   You, girls, who cry over his pains,
get out of here —   1620
before Zeus' lowing thunderclap
stuns you senseless.

CHORUS   Say something else, give us advice
we'll listen to!
We can't put up with this
aside, these words you've dragged up in passing.

How could you order me to be
a coward, how?
I'll suffer by his side
whatever comes, because I've learned to hate   1630

treachery: to me, the filthiest disease.

HERMES Remember what I proclaim to you: when
doom hunts you down
don't blame your luck, don't say Zeus hurled you down
to unforeseen pain.

Not so. For you'll have brought this on yourselves.
There'll be no surprise
either, no tricks: for you'll be tangled up
within the boundless

net of disaster, and through your own madness.   1640

(HERMES *vanishes; the storm breaks out.*)

PROMETHEUS No more words.
Now it's things.

Earth staggers to!
Rolling thunder
hollowing up
bangs at rock.
Lightning coils
gutter and flash!

Whirld winds suck
up clouds of dust,   1650
winds of the world
all dance around,
winds war winds!
Burning blue air
swirls up with
the heavy sea!

(*The* CHORUS *is gone.*)

Out in the open
it's Zeus, it's Zeus
come down on me,
howling terror!   1660

MAJESTY OF MY MOTHER!
and of
SKY SKy Sky sky

wheeling your light
over us all,
watching all of
us, in common

see how I suffer,
how unjust this is

(*Blinding flash: blackout: howling darkness swallows rocks, all; until only the voice
of* PROMETHEUS, *going back into the Greek it has come out of, rages still among the
elements.*)

ESORAIS M' HOS EKDIKA PASKHO!

NOTES

1–189 / 1–127 [The Prologue:] This falls into two movements. In the first, Prometheus is dragged in and chained, to the accompaniment of a dialogue between the coarse, sadistic Power and the pitying Hephaistos—both of them very clearly characterized by their language. Hephaistos leaves the scene after line 123 / 81, and Power does so after line 133 / 87, followed by the ever-silent policewoman, Violence. In the second movement (134–89 / 88–127) Prometheus, now entirely alone, speaks for the first time. For the unique metrical character of his speech, and its shifting attitudes to the future, see Introduction, page 301.

35–36 / 18 *the headlong... mother* In the Greek this is a single line, containing two massive compound adjectives; literally, "Of straightplanning Themis O steepthinking son!" An important contrast between the character of Themis (=Earth) and that of Prometheus is clearly implied by this, the first direct address to Prometheus in the play. How the contrast was worked out later in the trilogy we can no longer tell, but it is noteworthy that Earth appeared onstage in the play in which Prometheus was released, the *Unbound* (see fragment 3).

130 / 85–86 *The God called you "Resourceful"* There is a Greek word *promētheia* meaning "forethought," and the Greek noun-ending *-eus* often denotes an agent. To a Greek ear, therefore, the name "Prometheus" sounded like "fore-thinker" or "resourceful one." Here Power cruelly denies that even Prometheus' name has any meaning left in it.

173 / 115 *that perfume?* The "odor of sanctity," an idea familiar enough to Christians, was also attributed by the pagans to supernatural beings. Compare, for example, Euripides' *Hippolytos*, line 1391.

176 / 116 *a mingling of the two* That is, something midway between god and man; to a Greek this will mean a demigod or hero.

190–283 / 128–92 [The entrance-song of the Chorus, and Prometheus' chanted responses.] Just how the Chorus makes its entrance is an unsolved problem. The ancient commentary discussed in the Introduction assumes that the entire group is swung in on a crane, and remains aloft until just before the appearance of Ocean (**431 / 284**), when it descends and disembarks. The wording of Aeschylus' text at line **192 / 129–30**, literally "with swift rivalries of wings," and lines **425–27 / 279–80**, literally "leaving my swift-rushing seat, and the bright sky, the holy path of birds" presents further complications. Some modern commentators have deduced from this that the Chorus was not merely swung in, but swung in seated in a large winged chariot—or even in a flock of little winged chariots, one to each girl, and hotly competing with each other! We, however, prefer to suppose that the Chorus danced in on foot in the usual way, with much use of mime, and that the "swift-rushing seat" of line **425 / 279** is a metaphorical expression for their *imagined* station, hitherto, in the clear windy skies. Such a metaphor would not be at all too violent for Aeschylus.

248–65 / 168–77 *My day will come...outrage* This is Prometheus' first allusion to the Marriage-Secret (discussed in the Introduction, pp. 296–97), but it is as yet expressed in very obscure language.

277–83 / 186–92 *He's savage...my friend again* Here only in the trilogy, so far as it has survived, Prometheus foresees a total reconciliation between himself and Zeus. See Introduction, pp. 302–4.

284–576 / 193–396 [The First Episode:] like the Prologue, this episode is in two movements. In the first, Prometheus describes his part in the Titan War and its aftermath, and stresses that he has given not only *fire* to mankind, but also *hope*. In the second (**431 / 284ff.**), Ocean arrives and offers to mediate with Zeus but in vain.

431–576 / 284–396 [Ocean's intervention:] See Appendix, for the possibility that this scene belongs to a sequence of element-scenes originally extending through the trilogy; and the Introduction, p. 307, for a discussion of the manner in which Ocean's entry was staged. The tone in which this scene should be acted has been a matter for much debate. On our reading of it, the opening and close are almost comic. Ocean begins with elaborate professions of friendship, and with much proverbial wisdom, declaring that nothing will prevent him from going straight to Zeus and arranging for Prometheus' release. He ends by departing for his own home, on the not too convincing pretext that his monstrous steed is panting to return to the stable. His switch in attitude seems to be brought about, above all, by Prometheus' terrifying speech describing the physical power of Zeus, manifested in the punishments of Atlas and Typhon. That speech is one of the most majestic descriptive passages in all Aeschylus, and no doubt should be delivered with an appropriate seriousness; during the rest of the scene, however, we envisage Prometheus as impatient and slightly sarcastic, Ocean as well-meaning but pompous and timid.

514 / 351 *Pity cut me* . . . For the following passage, see Glossary, ETNA and TYPHŌN. Prometheus stresses the folly of Typhon in trying to oppose Zeus' violence by yet more violence (notice the deliberate repetition in 519 / 353 and 526 / 357). *Knowledge* is the only possible weapon against the physically omnipotent God, as the rest of this play will indicate.

577–619 / 397–435 [Choral Ode:] This simply constructed but powerful song moves from the mourning for Prometheus of the Chorus itself, through the lamentations of Asia and the tribes who dwell about the Kaukasos, to . . . the howling of the water in the seas and rivers. Only one stanza, lines 605–10 / 425–30 ("The only other Titan . . . with his back"), interrupts its smooth progress, and that stanza is also the one passage of any length in the whole *Prometheus Bound* where the Greek text given by the manuscripts is seriously corrupted. We have translated what we take to be the general drift of the partly unintelligible Greek at this point: it is a lament for the sufferings of Atlas (cf. 507–13 / 347–50) as he bears up against the weight of heaven. But this sudden switch from Prometheus to Atlas as an object of sympathy violently interrupts the sequence of thought. The problem has not yet been solved to anyone's satisfaction, but in general there seem to be two possible approaches to it: (1) the passage simply does not belong to the original ode, but has been wrongly inserted in it—for example, a quotation from some lost drama, written in the margin as a parallel, was mistaken for part of the actual text by an early scribe; or (2) the corrupt Greek must be rather drastically emended. It is in fact possible by such means to produce a text meaning "I have seen only one other Titan so trapped in pain before now, . . . and *he too* laments you," which would at least restore some coherence to the thought.

595 / 415 *girls of Colchis* These are Amazons (see Glossary and also 1083–89 / 722–27).

614 / 433 *the black bottomless deep hollows back* Again, the Greek seems to have been corrupted here, but this time not so seriously. As given in the manuscripts, it reads "and the black abyss *of earth of Hades* hollows back." Following a hint by Wilamowitz, one of the greatest editors of Aeschylus, we have cut out the two expressions here italicized, assuming that both of them are separate (and unintelligent) attempts by early annotators to explain the word "abyss." In fact, the context suggests strongly that the "abyss" is that of the waters.

620–764 / 436–525 [The Second Episode:] In two great speeches Prometheus describes how he brought the arts of civilization to mankind. The episode closes with a mysterious dialogue between him and the Chorus, in lines 739–64 / 507–25; see the note on those lines.

670 / 463 *pack saddles* We have here followed the Dutch scholar Pauw, who emended the Greek word given in the manuscripts, *sōmasin* ("bodies"), to *sagmasin* ("pack saddles").

703–31 / 484–99 *I marked out . . . filmed over* Prometheus here explains how he introduced the art of prophecy, enumerating many of its major ancient techniques: dream-interpretation; the interpretation of words overheard from passers-by; the interpretation of encounters in the street; augury, or the art of foretelling the future from the behavior of birds (711–18 / 488–92); extispicy, or prophecy through the examination of the entrails of sacrificial victims (719–23 / 493–95); and finally empyromancy, or the discovery of omens in the flames of the sacrificial fires, as certain parts of the sacrifice were burned. To a modern reader, the idea of *prophecy* as one of the civilized arts will seem strange, but two points are worth his consideration. First, the majority of ancient thinkers, lacking our data, supposed that the future of human affairs might be predicted by attention to the right phenomena, just as the future of the weather and of the starry sky could be (and still is) predicted. In that light, this discourse on prophecy makes good sense in the context. It is an important illustration of Prometheus' general theme, that he brought human beings from total inability to understand or control their environment, to full knowledge. Second, not all the techniques mentioned are obsolete even by modern scientific standards: Freud and others have taught us that at least the first two phenomena in Prometheus' list may actually provide some data for the understanding of a man's personality—and so of his destiny.

739–65 / 507–25 *Don't go out of your way . . . this torture, these chains* In this solemn passage Prometheus touches once more on the Marriage-Secret, and also approaches—as nearly as he ever does in the extant parts of the *Prometheia*—the question of who actually steers the destiny of the universe. Both topics are treated with a deliberate obscurity at this point. Later in the play, confronted with the appalling presence of Io, Prometheus will reveal far more of the Marriage-Secret. If the second question was ever answered in full, this must have occurred in some now-lost passage of the trilogy, perhaps at its very end. Our only clues to Aeschylus' thinking, and uncertain ones at that, may be sought in the last play of the *Oresteia*, the *Eumenides*. In that play Zeus is faced by rivals in the government of the universe—again the Furies (and also their ancient sisters, the Fates). Only in the finale do the two parties reach an understanding, and so make possible a stable universe.

766–1392 / 507–25 [The Third Episode, and the Choral Odes on either side of it:] This long and crucial movement of the play, and its probable significance, are discussed in the Introduction, pp. 297–98.

809 / 551 *orchestrated universe* The Greek word here, *harmonia*, is ambiguous—no doubt deliberately so—and we have tried to capture the ambiguity. *Harmonia* essentially means "a fitting-together" and would be applicable to all sorts of processes, e.g., carpentry, government, and music. In its musical sense, which is common, it can mean "tuning," "musical scale," or just "music."

813–21 / 555–60 In recalling the marriage of Prometheus with Hesione (also a daughter of Ocean), the Chorus introduces a major theme of this movement: sexual union. Here, however, the union is between equals, is brought about by *persuasion* (819–21 / 559–60), and is accompanied by the traditional customs of an ancient Greek marriage—the bride-gifts, the ritual bathing and bedding, the hymenaeal song. In all this it contrasts with the unions represented in the Io-scene and in the final choral ode.

896–1340 / 609–876 The spoken part of this episode is primarily concerned with the story of Io (see Glossary). This heroine, like Prometheus himself, seems to have preoccupied Aeschylus as she preoccupied no other Greek tragedian. In the *Suppliants* (between 466 and 459 B.C., perhaps 463) she does not actually appear, but the Chorus of Daughters of Danaos, who are her descendants, constantly appeals to her story. For them it is the supreme example of deliverance by Zeus at the end of long torments and wanderings. There is some reason to think that her story may have had the same significance in the context of the *Prometheia* as a whole; in the *Prometheus Bound*, of course, the main emphasis is laid on her sufferings at the hands of the Gods, but even here there is a prophecy of her final deliverance by an altered Zeus (see the Introduction, p. 304).

The story is told almost, but not quite, in chronological order. Aeschylus begins at the beginning, with the tale of how Zeus fell in love with Io, and how she was metamorphosed into a heifer, narrated by Io herself (949–1018 / 645–82). Next Prometheus prophesies her wanderings from the place where he is bound to the border of Europe and Asia (1054–1104 / 707–35); and follows this by a prophecy of her journey through Asia and Africa until she reaches the Nile Delta (1178–1229 / 790–815). In his final great speech of this scene he looks out into the furthest future, from Io's healing at the Delta, through the return to Argos of her descendants, the daughters of Danaos, to his own release by her remote descendant, Herakles (1280–1333 / 846–73). But this culminating prophecy is prefaced (1248–73 / 829–41) by a brief account of her wanderings between Greece and the Kaukasos; thus the last gap in her story is filled in.

The geography of Io's wanderings, like the geography of the *Odyssey*, is baffling, once we pass beyond the area that was familiar to the Greeks and their navigators. Aeschylus seems not to have known, or—more likely—not to have cared particularly, just where lay the natural and supernatural terrors which Io was to pass through, before she reached peace in Egypt. What mattered to his poem were the terrors themselves which confronted the lonely girl at this troubled stage of the universe. All we can tell for certain is Aeschylus has her wander in a clockwise direction from the peak in the Kaukasos, through part of what is now European Russia, into the far East and South, and finally up the Nile to one of its mouths at Kanobos (Canopus).

935 / 636 *your father's sisters* Io's father is Inachos, a river-god of Argos. Rivers in general were thought of as sons of Ocean and Tethys (Hesiod, *Theogony* 337), and Aeschylus here implies the same parentage for Inachos (cf. the later mythographer Apollodorus, *Bibliotheca* 2.1.1, where it is explicitly stated). Thus Inachos is a full brother of the Daughters of Ocean and Tethys who form the Chorus.

985 / 666 *untouchable, footloose* The Greek adjective here used by the Oracle is *aphetos* (literally, "let-go"), which is a highly technical religious term, properly applied to animals consecrated to a God and allowed to wander freely in his sacred precinct. Its relevance to Io is manifold. She is shortly

to be turned into a quasi-animal, to be dedicated (in a sense) to Zeus, and to be sent roving across the world—His sacred precinct?

1072 / 717 *Arrogangos* The Greek name here is *Hybristes*, but no such river name is found on any map, ancient or modern. There is a strong presumption that Aeschylus actually invented the name, just as he seems to have invented the Gorgonian Flatlands of Kisthene (1185 / 793), the River Wealth (1211 / 806), and the Bybline Hills (1221 / 811). If so, his intention here will have been to echo the names of actual rivers of the distant East (e.g., Araxes, Hydaspes), and at the same time to convey a terrible suggestion of violence—for *hybristes* is also a regular Greek word, meaning "violent," "insolent," or "lecherous." Our imaginary name tries to render these implications.

1085–86 / 725–26 *Thermodon . . . Salmydessos* For these place names see the Glossary. As names, they are magnificently sonorous (one remembers similar geographical roll calls, with similar effects, in Miltonic poetry), but the topography is disconcerting: Themiskyra is not close to the river Thermodon, and Salmydessos is on the opposite side of the Black Sea to either of them! Aeschylus, however, is thought to be indicating merely the general area in which, on his understanding, the Amazons would later settle. In Prometheus' present narrative they are located somewhere north of the Crimea.

1117–71 / 743–85 *Howling . . . dying to hear* Midway among the great solo speeches of the Io-scene stands this brisk dialogue between Prometheus, Io, and the Chorus. In it, for the first time in the play, Prometheus reveals two crucial prophecies in some detail, instead of alluding to them by vague and mysterious hints. Zeus, unless warned, will marry a woman whose child is fated to be greater than its father, and so will lose his throne; and Prometheus himself will be released by a descendant of Io's in the thirteenth generation. (As the Greek spectator probably knew, or guessed, that descendant would be Herakles himself. Herakles is never named in this play, even in the more specific prophecy at lines 1331–33 / 871–73. In the following play, however, the *Prometheus Unbound*, he appeared onstage and fulfilled the prophecy.)

1182 / 791 *unsurging sea* The Greek text is very uncertain at this point. The manuscripts give various readings, none of them perfectly intelligible; we have here followed the suggestion of the French scholar Girard in reading *ponton peros' aphloisbon* at line 791 of the Greek. The resultant conception of the desert sands as a "surgeless sea" would be characteristic of

Aeschylus, who loved such riddling expressions (there are examples in his descriptions of the Gorgons and Griffins, just below).

1211 / 806 *the River Wealth* a river in the far East, apparently invented by Aeschylus. The Greek name *Ploutôn* suggests the fabled wealth of the east but also suggests death via one of the most common names of its lord, Pluto.

1239–1340 / 823–76 *She's heard . . . no use for you to know* In this, his last speech during the Io-scene, Prometheus' prophetic powers are shown at their most intense. His knowledge seems to crowd in on him (cf. **1245 / 827**), and there is an immediacy and exactness of vision that is lacking elsewhere in his prophecies. The *truth* of this narrative of the far future is emphatically guaranteed in two ways. First, Prometheus employs a device that is also used by the prophetess Kassandra at Aeschylus' *Agamemnon* 1194–97, and is commonly employed by fortune-tellers to this day: to show his knowledge of the future, he recounts some events from his hearer's past (**1248–73 / 829–41**). Second, he refers to his wise mother Earth-Themis (**1334–36 / 873–74**) as his authority for the prophecy.

1295–1329 / 853–69 *The fifth generation . . . a line of kings* This story was treated, like that of Io herself (see note on **896–1340 / 609–876**) in Aeschylus' *Suppliants*, and in the trilogy to which that play belonged; again—like so much in the Io-episode—it involves an attempt at love-making against the will of the beloved, a long journey in terror, and some kind of redemption at the end. It is further relevant to Io in that the girls concerned, her descendants, traveled back from the Nile Delta to her ancient home, Argos (thus completing a vast predestined cycle); and in that one of those girls was in turn the ancestress of the greatest of all heroes, Herakles.

Aeschylus here assumes a great deal of knowledge in his audience—knowledge that not every modern reader will share. In brief, the myth runs: the fifth generation of Io's descendants consisted of two brothers, Aigyptos and Danaos. The former begot fifty sons, the latter fifty daughters (usually known as the Danaids). The male cousins tried to marry the female cousins against their will, whereupon the girls, led by their father Danaos, escaped from Egypt to Argos. The males pursued them thither, and in the end a marriage was arranged between the fifty couples. On the wedding night, however, the indignant brides took revenge on their pursuers by stabbing them to death—all except one, Hypermnestra, who had come to love her partner Lynkeus. From this couple descended the royal line, which culminated in Herakles.

1341–62 / 877–86 *spasm!...breaking in waves* Io ends her scene as she began it: a maddened heifer, just—but only just—able to express her sensations in human language. Our translation attempts to bring out the great speed of this final chant, and the rapid succession of not quite coherent images. The imagery in lines **1358–62 / 885–86** is particularly uncertain; a literal prose translation of the Greek would run: "and muddied words thrash aimlessly against waves of grim doom."

1363–92 / 887–907 [The last Choral Ode:] This short, low-keyed song, its detached deliberation contrasting with the violence of Io's chant just before, sums up the dominant themes of the entire Io-episode: equality and inequality in the union between the sexes, and the overwhelming terror of a God's love for an inferior. Both themes will recur in the scene that follows, but in a different context—Zeus' coming love for a woman whose name cannot yet be spoken (it is, in fact, Thetis) and the disastrous consequences.

1383–86 / 902–4 *What I'm afraid of...no getting away* The Greek text is slightly corrupt, and several reconstructions in detail are possible. We believe, however, that there is little doubt about the general drift, as rendered here.

1393–1670 / 908–1093 [The Exodos, or final scene:] The last scene balances the Prologue in many ways. Both contrast with the central scenes of the play in the extraordinary rapidity and violence of their respective actions. In both, Prometheus is confronted by servants of Zeus, sent to execute the God's will. Both, in the Greek, show notable correspondences in phraseology and imagery. Yet all these parallels, in their various ways, only serve to accentuate the immense difference in the situation of the universe that has been brought about during the play. At the beginning, a lonely sinner was being chained in an apparently endless punishment, in the presence of the serene elements. At the end, a Titanic Prometheus confronts Zeus with the threat of dethronement, and all the universe is in turmoil.

1416–21 / 922–25 *this giant...knock it flying* This account of the unknown child who would be born if Zeus should marry Thetis is paralleled in Pindar's version of the legend (*Isthmian Odes*, VIII.34–5), where the child

> "shall wield another weapon, stronger
> than the lightning-bolt,
> and than the unconquerable trident."

Yet at least one modern commentator (E. Beaujon, *Le Dieu des Suppliants* [Neuchâtel, 1960], p. 177) has had the fancy that the tremendous explosive force foreseen in Aeschylus' more vivid description is none other than the nuclear bomb . . . in which case the Child who will dethrone Zeus is, presumably, Man. This is a fancy only, but it seems worth a mention—there are, after all, uncanny insights elsewhere in the *Prometheus*.

1435 / 936 *the Inevitable* There is no precise English equivalent to the Greek word used here: *Adrasteia*, which is somewhere between the proper name of a rather impersonal goddess, and an abstract noun. We have chosen to render the latter facet of the word. The Goddess Adrasteia, who appears rarely in Greek literature, was identified with Nemesis, that divine power who remorselessly chastises human pride.

1443 / 941 *Look now* There is no clue, in the text or ancient commentary, to the manner of Hermes' entrance. J.S. suggests: *Feathery footsteps echoing as in a long corridor: Hermes appears.*

1470–71 / 956–57 *Haven't I seen . . . from that height?* Prometheus refers to the dethronements of Ouranos (Sky) and of Kronos.

1570–75 / 1027–29 *Until perhaps / a God comes . . . Tartaros* Following hints in the Greek commentaries (see on fragments 1–3), we take this to be spoken in savage irony; Hermes implies "any God who tries to help you may expect the same punishment." Many modern commentators, however, see here an allusion to an obscure Greek myth, in which the Centaur Cheiron, in the agony of a mortal wound, offers to go down to Hades in Prometheus' place (Apollodorus, *The Library*, tr. J. G. Frazer [London and New York, 1921], vol. I, pp. 193 and 229–31, is the only ancient source). But this interpretation involves great difficulties, especially in the reconstruction of the *Prometheia* as a whole, and we prefer the simpler solution. There is a careful discussion of the Cheiron myth, and its problems, by D. S. Robertson, "Prometheus and Chiron," in the *Journal of Hellenic Studies*, vol. LXXI (1951), pp. 150–55.

1640 / 1079 *your own madness* There is no indication in the text as to when Hermes exits, but this is the most likely point. J.S. suggests:
Hermes takes off so rapidly he seems to vanish
        at once
utter disruption makes everything utterly clear, everyone knows who
                stands where.

1656 / 1088 *the heavy sea* Again, the text does not show when—or how—the Chorus exits. For the reason given in the Introduction, p. 308, we have tentatively placed its disappearance here.

1670 / 1093 *ESORAIS M' HOS EKDIKA PASKHO* Literally, "you see me, how unjust things I suffer."

APPENDIX:
THE FRAGMENTARY
PROMETHEUS PLAYS

These "fragments" (the term as used here embraces any ancient evidence referring to the lost plays) have been preserved, practically, by blind chance. They are cited in the ancient sources for almost any odd purpose, *except* that of satisfying the literary critic's curiosity about the plot mechanics or motivations of the lost plays. Galen, for instance the great physician, has preserved fragment 8 of the *Unbound* merely as an illustration of an obsolete Greek word; and the geographer Strabo quotes fragments 5, 10, and 11 in connection with antiquarian and geographical problems of his own. Even so, the outlines of the *Prometheus Unbound*, at least, emerge with a fair certainty. The play began with the entrance of a Chorus of Titans, arriving to visit Prometheus and chanting about the vast territories they had crossed to do so. (Already, then, it is to be inferred, the political atmosphere of the universe has lightened somewhat since the last play: Zeus must have relented from the dire punishment he imposed on the Titans in *Prometheus Bound*, 326–29 / 219–21.) Prometheus, now restored to the light from his rock-prison, but suffering the torments of the eagle (all as Hermes had threatened, in *Prometheus Bound*, 1551–67 / 1016–25), gave the Chorus an account of his new sufferings. The long fragment 6, which describes these, may well be the most horrific passage in ancient drama; Prometheus seems very close to collapse. At an unknown interval after that, Herakles entered, and Prometheus delivered a speech, or series of speeches, in which he foretold Herakles' further wanderings. These would take him counterclockwise around half the world, first northwards through the freezing Russian winds, then westwards past the mouth of the Rhône, and finally (according to Strabo, in fragment 11) to the Garden of the Hesperides — which most ancient writers imagined as somewhere on, or near, the

North African coast. This scene was thus a counterpart to the Io-scene in the *Prometheus Bound* and completed a magnificent poetic survey of the entire world, as Aeschylus envisaged it. Herakles, like Io, will probably end his strenuous wanderings somewhere on the African continent. Either before or after this great prophecy (there is no evidence to indicate which), Herakles shot the eagle with his bow, and then, as fragment 14 shows, he released Prometheus, confirming the latter's prophecy to Io long ago. Yet fragment 14 also seems to show that the release was carried out before Prometheus and Zeus had been reconciled (compare, perhaps, *Prometheus Bound*, 1152 / 771, where Io is made to ask, "who's to free you *against the will of Zeus?*").

What happened next? The only remaining solid literary evidence is the brief fragment 15, which shows that mankind was at last reintroduced into the trilogy, as forever wearing the garland—a symbol of festivity— "as a recompense for [Prometheus'] chains." If this mysterious statement may be interpreted in the light of the two related (but not certainly Aeschylean) statements in "fragments" 16 and 17, we must conclude that Prometheus and Zeus eventually came to terms, but that Prometheus agreed to save Zeus' face by continuing to wear a chain of sorts—in the form of a garland! Recently some evidence of a quite different kind has been published, which seems to support this conclusion. It is an Apulian red-figure vase-painting, assigned to the third quarter of the fourth century B.C. (A. D. Trendall and T. B. L. Webster, *Illustrations of Greek Drama* [London, 1971], p. 61; here will be found a photograph, further references, and a discussion to which the present account is much indebted). At the upper center of the picture is Prometheus, a grandiose bearded figure, still fettered to his rocky chasm. At the left of him stands Herakles, with his club and bow: the Eagle is toppling, mortally wounded, into the lower register of the picture, which contains some female figures that seem to symbolize Hades. To the right of Prometheus stands a stately female figure, who might be Earth: and to the right again sits Apollo, the God to whom Herakles prays in fragment 13 of the *Unbound*. Most interesting of all, in view of our fragment 15, is the figure on the extreme left of the picture; here the goddess Athena sits quietly, as if waiting. She has her regular attributes of helmet, shield, and spear, but also holds up prominently, in her left hand, a very unusual attribute indeed: *it is a leafy garland*. There can be no reasonable doubt that this vase-painting bears some relation to the later scenes of the *Prometheus Unbound*. Unfortunately the ancient vase painters very rarely reproduce a given scene from drama with literal precision, but tend to paint generalized views of the mythological situation concerned, often adding or subtracting characters at will. The painting, therefore, cannot be taken as proving that all the figures shown were characters in Aeschylus' *Prometheus Unbound*. But at least it seems to confirm the indications of fragments 15, 16, and 17, that Prometheus was given a garland in exchange for his chains, and it may even add a highly significant detail—that none other than *Athena*, the favorite daughter of Zeus and the goddess of Athens, finally conferred this garland on Prometheus. Athena's specially close relationships both with Zeus and Athens, it will be noted, are celebrated in a great song of joy near the end of Aeschylus' *Oresteia: Eumenides*, 916–1020 (above all in the stanza 996–1002).

At this point the evidence for the story told in the *Prometheia* finally gives out. It is useless to conjecture about the narrative of the final play, the *Prometheus Pyrphoros*; all that can be said with reasonable certainty is that its dramatic time was set *later* than the release of Prometheus (*Pyrphoros*, fragment 1). Yet there remains one further aspect of the trilogy to be considered, and that is the progress of the Elements through it. Prometheus' first utterance in the *Prometheus Bound* (**134–39** / 88–90) is apparently a solemn appeal to the four elements—the deep bright sky (the Greek word is *aithēr*, often used for the element fire), the winds, the waters, and Earth. In the course of the action he is visited by the Daughters of Ocean, who form the Chorus, and even by Ocean himself (**431–576** / 284–396); this first play is thus, in a sense, dominated by the watery element. Ocean's offer to intervene with Zeus, however, comes to nothing, for Prometheus' fearsome descriptions of the violence of Zeus eventually drive him and his monstrous steed back to the safety of home. The critics have never been able to make much sense of the Ocean episode in the context of the *Prometheus Bound* alone, and it is at least worth raising the question whether that episode may have been part of a chain of element-scenes, proceeding through the trilogy and only understandable in that greater context, if only we had it in its entirety. Certainly the final cry of Prometheus in the *Prometheus Bound* is an appeal to Earth and Sky alone—as if Ocean no longer counted? And in fact, one of the stage characters of the *Prometheus Unbound* was Earth herself (*Unbound*, fragment 3; compare, perhaps, the standing woman on the Apulian vase-painting mentioned above), while the Chorus consisted no longer of Ocean's Daughters but of Titans—who are the children of Earth and Sky (cf. the *Bound*, **302–4** / 204–5). At this point, as so often in the exploration of the *Prometheia*, we are simply deserted by the concrete evidence. But the pattern established so far is striking enough; it suggests that there may have been a kind of elemental sub-plot to the trilogy, a groundbass accompanying the melody of the Prometheus-Zeus story. One may speculate that the progression from

Ocean in the first play through Earth in the second might imply the intervention of Sky (or *aithēr*, fire), in the final play. At least, that play's probable title, *Prometheus Pyrphoros* ("Prometheus Fire-Carrier"), contains that element in itself. But that is, admittedly, a speculation and no more.

We may now present our translations of the ancient evidence on which the above account is based. The fragment numbers are our own, but for the convenience of any reader who may wish to refer to the original Greek and Latin texts we have added in square brackets the numbers used in an edition of the fragmentary plays of Aeschylus: H. J. Mette, *Die Fragmente der Tragödien des Aischylos*, Berlin, 1959 (here abbreviated to "M"). *Verbatim* quotations from Aeschylus are translated in verse and printed in italics.

"PROMETHEUS UNBOUND" FRAGMENTS

1–3: *General information about the play*

These three fragments are preserved in the Medicean manuscript of Aeschylus, in the Laurentian Library, Florence. It contains, besides the text of Aeschylus' seven surviving plays, a Greek commentary that was compiled in the classical period, evidently by somebody who was acquainted with much now-lost Greek literature—including the *Prometheus Unbound* and *Prometheus Pyrphoros*.

1. [M fr. 320] Medicean Commentary on *Prometheus Bound* (lines 743–45 / 511–12). "That is: It is not yet my destiny to be released. For in the following play he is released, as Aeschylus indicates here."

2. [not in M] Medicean Commentary on *Prometheus Bound* line 759 / 521 ("Talk about something else"): "He reserves his words for the following play."

3. [M fr. 325] The dramatis personae of the *Prometheus Bound*, as given in the Medicean manuscript and several others, includes:
   "EARTH;
   HERAKLES."

Fragments 1 and 2 indicate that the *Unbound* immediately followed the extant play, and that in it Prometheus was released and probably mentioned the Marriage-Secret. Fragment 3 presents a strange problem.

Neither Earth nor Herakles, of course, appears in the *Prometheus Bound*; but Herakles is known to have been introduced in the *Unbound* (see below, fragments 11, 12, and 14). It is therefore conjectured that Earth, also, appeared in the *Unbound*. Some early ancestor of our existing manuscripts may have contained both the *Bound* and the *Unbound* together, with a consolidated list of characters at the beginning; hence the accidental survival of these two names from the now-lost play.

Fragments 4 through 7: The entry-chant of the Chorus of Titans, and Prometheus' speech to them

4. [M fr. 322] A Greek writer of the second century A.D., Arrian, writes in his *Navigation of the Black Sea* (ch. 19): "And yet Aeschylus in the *Prometheus Unbound* makes the River Phasis the borderline between Europe and Asia: in him the Titans say to Prometheus:

> We come to see
> these your sorrows, Prometheus,
> and this agony of your chains . . .

Then they tell how much country they have traversed:

> . . . where the Phasis, the great
> twofold boundary of Europe and Asia . . ."

Here Arrian's quotation ends, but a little more information is given by the sixth-century A.D. historian Procopius, who mentions that Aeschylus placed this passage "right at the beginning of his tragedy" (*History of the Gothic Wars* 4.6.15).

5. [M fr. 323] The Greek geographer Strabo, who lived from about 64 B.C. to 21 A.D., says that the following passage occurred in the *Prometheus Unbound* (*Geography* 1.2.27):

> "And the Red Sea's holy
> flood with crimson bed,
> and the Aithiopians' Lake
> tendering food to all
> —a coppery glitter
> there, by Ocean's side—
> where Sun, that sees all,

under the stroking of
the warm river revives
his tired horses, and
his own deathless body."

The quotation from Aeschylus in 5 is in the same meter (anapestic) as that given in 4, and it may reasonably be assumed to come from the same entry-chant. The Titans, or some of them, will be describing how they have come from the uttermost south to visit the suffering Prometheus.

6. [M fr. 324] Cicero, the Roman statesman and philosophical writer (106–43 B.C.), quotes the following iambic verses as having been spoken by Aeschylus' Prometheus "when bound to the Kaukasos" (*Tusculan Disputations* 2.23–25, from a philosophical discussion on the endurance of pain). Cicero gives the lines in his own Latin verse-translation, but other examples of his translations suggest that he will have rendered the original Greek fairly faithfully.

"Titans

     blood brothers

          children of Sky

look at me! moored, chained
fast to the choppy rock —
   the way, towards nightfall, sailors in the howling narrows
      panickt
         secure their ship.
   In this way
Zeus, Son of Kronos, had me moored in iron.
Through Hephaistos' hands, His will became
   fact.
With cruel, painstaking craft, he slogged
   wedge on wedge
into me: splitting, sticking.
Thanks to that, I stand watch
mourning, at this castle of the Furies.
And always on the third day, for me, the light of day
is black,
when Zeus' horrible pet glides in at me —
      the EAGLE
that digs in with crookt claws

gouging out
          her feast, until her crop's
bloated, rich with liver.
                    Then
screaming
          wheeling skyward . . . her tail feathers
drag through blood,
my blood.
And once again, my rag of a liver
                    swells up like new, and again
the bloodthirsty banqueter comes back for more.
In this way
          I feast my prison warden:
who in turn, by deathless outrage,
tortures my live
          body—
look! Zeus' chains
clench me, I can't
          protect my chest from that
filthy thing.
Only, myself
          gutted, take what
agony comes, grope for an end to pain
and burn, like sex, for death.

But by the will of Zeus
I'm exiled far away from death.
Century has swarmed on shuddering
                    century
around this old anguish, this
wedge through my body

whose drops of blood
          melted in the flaming sun
over Kaukasos, rain
endlessly on rock."

Fragment 6, though its position in the play is not stated by Cicero, may well come from Prometheus' answer to the entry-chant of the Titans.

7. [M fr. 336a] Plutarch, the Greek essayist and biographer (*fl. ca.* 100 A.D.), discussing mankind's dominance over the other animals in his essay *On Fortune*, writes: "According to Aeschylus, Prometheus— that is, Reason—is responsible, for he

> *gave horse and donkey and the breed of bulls*
> *to be as slaves to us and bear our burdens."*

Fragment 7, to judge by its strong resemblance to lines 668–75 / 462–66 of the *Bound*, may also have belonged to a speech made by Prometheus to the Titan-Chorus further describing his benefits to man. This, how- ever, is not certain, since Plutarch does not expressly attribute his quotation to the *Unbound*.

Fragments 8 through 12: Prometheus foretells the wanderings of Herakles in the north and west

8. [M fr. 327] Galen, the famous Greek physician who lived from *ca.* 129 to 199 A.D., writes in his *Commentary on Hippocrates' Epidemics,* 6.1.29, that he found the following iambic lines in Aeschylus' *Prometheus Bound* [sic: this is either a slip for "*Unbound,*" or Galen is using "*Prometheus Bound*" as a generic title for the whole trilogy]:

> *"Follow straight along this pathway.*
> *You'll come, first, to the high winds*
> > *of Boreas.*
> *Take care:*
> > *for fear*
> *the hurricane with its wintry blasts*
> *will howl down*
> *whirling you into the sky."*

9. [M fr. 329] Stephanos of Byzantium, a Greek geographical writer who is thought to have lived in the fifth century A.D., quotes the following iambic lines on the Scythian tribe *Gabioi,* from "Aeschylus in the *Prometheus Unbound*":

> *You'll arrive, then, at a just*
> *community, more just than any other*
> *and friendlier.*
> > *These are the Gabioi.*

> Here, no plow, nor any hoe
> hacks at the land
> but the plains plant themselves,
> the harvest is endless."

10. [M fr. 328] Strabo (on whom see fragment 5) writes as follows in his *Geography* 7.3.7.: "Aeschylus concurs with Homer [*Iliad* 13.4–6] in saying about the Scythians,

> But Scythians, well-governed,
> who feast
> on maresmilk cheese ..."

11. [M fr. 326a] Strabo (on whom see fragment 5) discusses in the fourth book of his *Geography* the scientific problem presented by a pebble-strewn plain that lies in southern France between the Rhône estuary and Marseilles. He mentions (4.1.7) a mythical explanation of the phenomenon in the following words. "In (Aeschylus) Prometheus, advising Herakles about that journey of his from the Kaukasos to the Hesperides, says:

> You'll come upon
> the Ligyes, a horde
> that doesn't know what fear is.
> Fierce a fighter as you are, you won't fault
> their fighting.
> As fate has it: you'll run out of weapons,
> you can't grab even
> one stone off the ground
> because the plain is soft, it's
> dust.
> But Zeus will see you
> bewildered there
> and pity you, and cast a stormcloud
> to shadow the earth
> in a flurry of rounded rocks.
> You'll heave them, and with ease
> batter the Ligyan horde back."

12. [M fr. 326c] Hyginus was a Latin mythological writer who drew heavily on Greek sources, especially tragedy; his date is uncertain, but he may well have lived in the second century A.D. In his *Astronomy in the Poets*, 2.6, he discusses the myth underlying the constellation called *Engonasin* (Hercules in modern star-maps), in the following words:

> "But Aeschylus in the play entitled *Prometheus Unbound* says that Herakles is not fighting with the Dragon, but with the Ligyes. His story is that at the time when Herakles led away Geryon's cattle he journeyed through the Ligyan territory. In trying to remove the cattle from him they came to blows, and he pierced a number of them with his arrows. But then his missiles gave out, and after receiving many wounds he sank to his knees, overpowered by the barbarian numbers and by the failure of his ammunition. Zeus, however, took pity on his son, and caused a great quantity of rocks to appear around him. With these Herakles defended himself and routed the enemy. Hence Zeus set the likeness of him, fighting, among the stars."

Fragments 11 and 12 clearly refer to the same passage of Aeschylus, and fragment 12 proves that that passage occurred in the *Unbound*. It is extremely likely that 8 and 9 also belong to Prometheus' prophecies of Herakles' wanderings. Fragment 10 is attributed only conjecturally, on the ground that it, too, refers to the great Russian land mass and its inhabitants.

Fragments 13 and 14: Herakles rescues Prometheus

13. [M fr. 332] Plutarch (on whom see fragment 7) discusses in his dialogue *Amatorius*, 757E, how various Gods are invoked for various purposes. In the course of the discussion he remarks: "But Herakles invokes a different god when he is going to raise his bow against the bird, as Aeschylus says—

> *Let Hunter-Apollo level straight this shaft!"*

14. The same Plutarch begins his *Life of Pompey the Great* by commenting on the contrast between Pompey's popularity and the extraordinary hatred felt for his father, Pompeius Strabo. The opening words of the *Life* run: "From the first the Roman people seems to have felt towards Pompey as Prometheus in Aeschylus feels towards Herakles when, after being rescued by him, he says—

> This dearest child of
> the Father I hate!"

Although Plutarch does not name the play from which he is quoting in fragment 13, the only known mythological situation which the quotation would fit, among the lost works of Aeschylus, is the shooting of the eagle in the *Unbound*. The Apulian vase discussed above (pp. 384–85) perhaps lends further support to the attribution. Fragment 14 must certainly refer to the *Unbound*; its implication that Prometheus continued to hate Zeus even after the rescue is noteworthy.

Fragments 15 through 17: The Garland of Prometheus

15. [M fr. 334] Athenaeus, an enormously learned Graeco-Egyptian scholar, compiled his *Deipnosophistae* in about 200 A.D. In Book 15, p. 674 D of that work, during a discussion of the custom of wearing garlands, he writes: "Aeschylus in the *Prometheus Unbound* expressly says that it is in honor of Prometheus that we put the garland about our heads, as a recompense for his chains."

16. [also M fr. 334] Another passage from the same discussion by Athenaeus (Book 15, p. 672 F); here he is quoting a story from an earlier historian, Menodotos, concerning a strange penalty laid upon some ancient inhabitants of the isle of Samos: "Apollo through his oracle told them to pay that penalty which in times gone by Zeus laid upon Prometheus for his theft of fire. For after Zeus released him from those most cruel chains, Prometheus consented to pay a voluntary but painless requital; and this is what the Leader of the Gods ordained that he should have. Whence it was that the garland was revealed to Prometheus, and not long afterwards it was inherited by mankind also, whom he had benefited by the gift of fire."

17. [not in M] Hyginus (on whom see fragment 12), *Astronomy in the Poets* 2.15, writes as follows: "Several people have said that he (Prometheus) wore a garland in order that he could say that he had been the victor, since he had sinned without being punished for it; and for that reason mankind began the custom of wearing garlands in moments of their greatest joy, and in victories."

Fragment 15 alone attributes the story of the garland expressly to Aeschylus. We have tentatively included 16 and 17 because they seem to throw a little further light on the brief statement given in **15**, and because it is possible that the solution that they indicate could have originated, in outline, with Aeschylus. The vase-painting discussed above also suggests that a garland was somehow associated with Prometheus' release in the *Unbound*.

THE FRAGMENTS OF THE "PROMETHEUS PYRPHOROS" ("FIRE-CARRIER")

1. [M fr. 341] The Medicean Commentary (for which see the note on fragments **1–3** of the *Unbound*) has the following note on *Prometheus Bound* line **144** / 94–95 ("ten thousand years"): <That is,> many years; for in the *Pyrphoros* (Aeschylus) says that (Prometheus) has been bound for thrice ten thousand years."

2. [M fr. 351] Aulus Gellius, a Roman literary scholar of the second century A.D., quotes the following line from "Aeschylus in the *Prometheus Pyrphoros*" in his *Noctes Atticae*, 13.19.4: "*Quiet, where need is; and talking to the point.*"

3. [M fr. 340] In the Medicean manuscript of Aeschylus (for which see the note on fragments **1–3** of the *Unbound*) and two other manuscripts, there is included an extensive catalogue of the plays of Aeschylus, which must go back to classical times. Among the titles there given occurs:

"PROMETHEUS PYRPHOROS."

Those three fragments are the only classical evidence we now have about the *Pyrphoros*. Fragment **1** seems to show that the action took place later than that of the *Bound*; **3** simply confirms that the play was once in existence; **2** (as a devoted student of Aeschylus, George Thomson, once remarked) offers excellent advice to would-be reconstructors of its plot.

GLOSSARY

Note: In the case of *Persians*, two groups of names have been omitted from this Glossary. First are the very numerous geographical names that occur—most of them on one occasion only—in the Messenger's narrative of the Persian retreat, and in the choral ode on the conquests of Darius; they are explained in the Notes on those passages. Second is the even more numerous group of names of Persian warriors in the three "roll-calls" (see the note on **1542–1625** for *Persians*). Relatively few of these names occur more than once in the play; some of them are thought actually to have been invented by Aeschylus; and even where a name can be shown to be genuinely Persian, and to occur in Herodotus' lists of the Persians involved in the expedition, identifications are not often certain. In short, it seems likely that even Aeschylus and his audience would in most cases have known little more about them than we do. There thus seemed to be no point in loading the Notes or Glossary with repeated entries of the type, "*Egdadatas*: name of a Persian known only from *Persians* **1618** / 997." What little definite information is known about the Persian names—and it is information of more importance to Indo-European philologists and professional historians than to readers who are interested in Aeschylean poetic drama—is conveniently assembled in Appendix V to Broadhead's edition of this play.

With regard to *Prometheus Bound* and the Fragments of the Prometheus plays, it should be noted that Aeschylus shows a strong tendency to free invention of mythological data and geographical names. In compiling this Glossary, we have therefore relied primarily on the information given in Aeschylus' own text. Where that has failed, we have had recourse primarily to Hesiod (whose works Aeschylus knew) and to Herodotus (who wrote not very long after Aeschylus' death) in order to fill in the mythological and geographical details, respectively.

In such cases, of course, one cannot always guarantee that the resulting picture was the picture envisaged by Aeschylus, but it is the best that can be given in the circumstances.

ADRASTOS: King of Argos and commander in chief of the Argive army; the only Argive leader not killed in the attack on Thebes.

AGENOR: Third-generation descendant of Io; son of Libya; brother of Baal. When he was king of Canaan, his daughter Europa was seduced by Zeus, who disguised himself as a bull; his son Kadmos founded Thebes.

AIGYPTOS: See EGYPT.

AITHIOPIANS: A generic Greek name for the peoples who inhabited the unknown southern parts of the earth. Aeschylus seems to have thought that they extended even as far as India (see note on *Suppliants*, 352).

AITHIOPS: A river, imagined by Aeschylus to be in the farthest South.

AJAX: Greatest Greek warrior at Troy after Achilles, venerated as a sacred hero on his home island of Salamis. After the Trojan War, his younger brother, Teucer, colonized the other Salamis, in Cyprus.

AKTOR: Son of Oinops; Theban captain at the Northern gate.

AMAZONS: A matrilineal tribe of female warriors said to dwell on the southern shore of the Black Sea; Greeks regarded them as a historical people (e.g., Herodotus, *Histories* IV.110–17). They were renowned for their fierce use of the axe and the bow, and for their contempt of males, with whom they would associate only for child-bearing purposes.

AMPHIARAOS: Son of Oikles; priest of Apollo, Argive captain at the Homoloian gate.

AMPHION: A Theban hero, who caused the walls of Thebes to rise by playing on his lyre. His grave was near the Northern gate.

ANTIGONE: Daughter of Oedipus and Jocasta.

APHRODITE: Goddess of sexual love, who rose from the sea-foam near Cyprus.

APIS: A healer and a hero to the Argive people, who honored his memory in prayers because he had cured their land of a grievous pollution.

APOLLO: An Olympian God, son of Zeus and Leto; god of light reason and order; patron of athletic skill and the arts, including music and mathematics. In the *Prometheus* he is mentioned only in his capacity as the oracular God of the shrine at Delphi.

ARABIA: Usually thought of by the Greeks as lying in the area now called Saudi Arabia. Aeschylus, appears to place some Arabians in the neighborhood of the Kaukasos (*q.v.*) as well.

ARES: God of war and the personification of strife; father by Aphrodite of Harmonia (*q.v.*).

ARGOS: (1) A city located in the northeast peninsula of the Peloponnese and a state claiming territory far into northwestern Greece; the home of Io; (2) The watchman, covered with eyes all over his body, whom Hera ordered to guard Io after the latter had been turned into a heifer, but was soon after slain by Hermes. In the *Prometheus*, he is called a child of Earth.

ARIMASPS: A fabulous race of one-eyed men, placed by Aeschylus somewhere in the far East. Herodotus, *Histories* III.116, and IV.13, reports a story (which he himself refuses to believe) that the Arimasps' occupation consisted in stealing gold from its monstrous guardians, the Griffins (*q.v.*).

ARROGANGOS: Punning translation of Aeschylus' fictitious river-name, "Hybristes." See note on *Persians* 1072.

ARTAPHRENES: A Persian noble, described in *Persians* **1279** / 776 as having been a leader in the conspiracy to assassinate the usurper Mardos in 521 B.C. He is probably identical with the individual whom Herodotus names Intaphrenes in his story of that conspiracy (*Histories* III.70, 78). See also MARDOS. (A different Artaphrenes is named among the Persian warriors at *Persians* **29** / 21.)

ARTEMIS: Goddess of untamed creatures and virgin wilderness, archery and the hunt, the moon and all matters pertaining to women; twin sister of Apollo.

ATĒ: Personification of folly; a kind of blindness or insanity that makes men act in defiance of moral law.

ATLAS: A brother of Prometheus. In Hesiod (*Theogony* 517–19, 745–46), Atlas is punished by being made to bear the sky on his shoulders, somewhere in the far West. In *Prometheus Bound* his punishment is not clearly explained, but it seems to consist of propping up a presumably unstable pillar that separates the earth from the sky.

ATOSSA: Queen Mother of the Persian realm. A daughter of Cyrus the Great, she was married three times: first to her brother Cambyses, then to the usurper Mardos, and finally to Darius. Herodotus, *Histories* III.134 and VII.3, emphasizes her influence over Darius, especially in persuading him to designate their son Xerxes as his successor to the empire. See further the note on *Persians* **194**.

BAAL: Third-generation descendant of Io; son of Libya; brother of Agenor; father of Danaos and Egypt.

BACTRIA: One of the easternmost provinces of the Persian empire, in the region between the River Oxus and the range of the Hindu Kush. Bactrian infantry and cavalry contingents served in Xerxes' expedition (Herodotus, *Histories* VII. 64, 86).

BOREAS: God of the North Wind.

BOSPOROS: "Cow-ford," named for Io's crossing from Europe to Asia. In *Persians* (1179 / 723, 1215 / 746), it refers to the Hellespont (Dardanelles). In most other Greek writers it denotes the "Thracian Bosporos," the strait that joins the Sea of Marmara to the Black Sea.

BYBLINE HILLS: A fabled range in the far South, first heard of in Aeschylus and perhaps invented by him on the basis of the word *byblos* (= the Egyptian papyrus). Here he locates the springs of the Nile.

CHALYBES: A tribe somewhere in the East, to whom the Greeks attributed the first working of iron. Some historical reality no doubt underlies the vague legends; Xenophon, in his great march through Asia Minor, actually fought with a tribe of this name. But the Greek poets generally are uncertain about the whereabouts of the Chalybes. In Aeschylus' account they seem to dwell somewhere north of the place where Prometheus is bound.

CILICIA: A territory on the southeast coast of Asia Minor, where the monster Typhōn (*q.v.*) dwelled; CILICIANS, inhabitants of the region that lies along the southern coast of Asia Minor.

COLCHIS: A city at the eastern end of the Black Sea.

CRIMEA: (Greek Isthmos Kimmerikos, whence the modern name is derived.)

CURSES: The personified prayers for justice of those whose rights have been violated. They are implemented by the Fury.

CYRUS: Called The Great, in effect the founder of the Persian empire (cf. the Introduction to *Persians*, p. 5). Cyrus ruled from 559 to 529 B.C., and was succeeded by his son Cambyses, who—perhaps because his character and reputation were so disastrous, at least as the Greeks perceived them—is not expressly named in Darius' account of the Persian Kings, but is merely alluded to as "Cyrus' son" in *Persians* 1275 / 773. Cambyses' reign (described in Herodotus, *Histories* III.1–65) lasted from 529 to 522 B.C.

DANAOS: Fourth-generation descendant of Io; brother of Egypt; father of the fifty Suppliants.

DARIUS: Ascended the Persian throne in 521 B.C., after the assassination of the usurper Mardos (q.v.), and ruled until he died in 486 B.C. Taking Atossa as his chief wife, he was by her the father of Xerxes. All the historical sources indicate that he was a wise and, on the whole, magnanimous ruler, although his reign was less serene, and less unbrokenly successful in war, than the *Persians* would have us believe (cf. note on *Persians* 1398–1469).

DELPHI: A town in central Greece, famous for its sanctuary and oracle of Apollo.

DIKĒ: Personification of the natural order and the divine justice that governs that order.

DIRKE: One of the springs of Thebes.

DODONA: An ancient sanctuary of Zeus, in the far northwest of Greece. The shrine was famous above all for its oracles, supposedly delivered by speaking oak trees. The shrine lay in a valley of the Molossian hills, east of the region named Thesprotia.

EARTH (Greek *Gaia* or *Gē*): Wife of Sky; the couple, according to Hesiod, were the first divine pair to rule the Universe. In *Prometheus Bound*, Earth is represented as the mother of Prometheus, and is also identified with the goddess Themis ("Right"). In *Suppliants*, EARTH is the ur-grandmother of Pelasgos.

EGYPT: Fourth-generation descendant of Io; brother of Danaos and uncle to the Suppliants; father of fifty sons.

EGYPTIANS: The fifty sons of Egypt and fifth-generation descendants of Io; nephews to Danaos; first cousins of the Suppliants.

EKBATANA: Modern Hamadan, was the capital city of the Medes (see MEDE). Built with great splendor by the Median king Deiokes (Herodotus, *Histories* I.98), it continued to be an important center, and one of the royal residences, under the Persian Empire.

ENYO: Goddess of war-like frenzy.

EPAPHOS: Son of Io, miraculously conceived by the touch of Zeus (the name signifies caress) in the Nile Delta. He became ruler of Egypt and ancestor of a line of kings. Many Greek writers identified him with the Egyptian bull-god Apis.

ETEOKLES: Son of Oedipus; Theban captain at the seventh gate.

ETEOKLOS: Argive captain at the gate of Neïs.

ETNA: The volcanic mountain in northeast Sicily; its spectacular eruption in (probably) 479/78 B.C. In *Prometheus Bound*, Typhōn (*q.v.*) is imagined as buried below the mountain and responsible for its fires.

FATES (Greek *Moirai*): The three goddesses who are in charge of destiny. In Hesiod they are the daughters of Night, and their names are Klōthō, Lachesis, and Atropos.

FURIES (Greek *Erinyes*): A group of ancient goddesses of indeterminate number, primarily concerned with the punishment of blood-guilt and the enforcement of oaths. A single FURY (*Erinys*) is generally the personification of the wrath that pursues the violators of *Dikē*, and thus often the personification of a familial curse.

GABIOI: A Scythian tribe, already renowned for justice in Homer (*Iliad* XIII.6, where they are called *Abioi*).

GORGONIAN FLATLANDS: A geographical name apparently coined by Aeschylus from the name "Gorgons" (*q.v.*). He places them in the far East.

GORGONS: Three monstrous snake-haired sisters, the most famous of whom is Medusa. Aeschylus places their home in the far East. Usually thought of as daughters of Phorkys (*q.v.*) and Kētō, and sisters of the Graiai.

GRIFFINS: "Are beasts which are like lions, but have the wings and beak of an eagle" (Pausanias, *Description of Greece* I.24.6). Herodotus heard legends that these monsters dwell in the far North or Northeast, guarding great quantities of gold, which the Arimasps (*q.v.*) are forever trying to steal from them (Herodotus

III.116, IV. 13). Aeschylus seems to place them in the far East or South.

HADES: A God, brother of Zeus and ruler of the world of the dead below the earth. In English usage—which we have followed—the name is often used to mean that world itself.

HARMONIA: Daughter of Ares and Aphrodite; wife of Kadmos.

HEKATE: Goddess associated with crossroads and magic, especially commissioned by Zeus to protect children.

HELLĒ: Child, along with her brother Phrixos, of a king of Boeotia, Athamas, and of his first wife Nephelē. When Athamas remarried, Nephelē tried to save the children from the plots of their wicked stepmother by mounting them on a ram with a golden fleece, which bore them away from Greece through the sky. Hellē fell from the ram into the straits now called the Dardanelles, which thus became known as "Sea of Hellē," *Hellespontos*.

HEPHAISTOS: An Olympian God, borne by Hera without intercourse with Zeus. He is always represented as lame, but he is the great craftsman of the Gods, famed above all for his metal work.

HERA: Daughter of Kronos and Rhea, wife of Zeus, and jealous guardian, therefore, of all conjugal bonds; queen of the Olympian Gods and patron goddess of Argos.

HERAKLES: Son of Zeus and Alkmēnē, through whom he was descended, in the thirteenth generation, from Io. He was the greatest of all Greek heroes; among his many labors was the freeing of Prometheus.

HERMES: An Olympian God, son of Zeus and Maia. The chief among his many functions is that of herald and messenger of the gods.

HESIONE: A daughter of Ocean, and wife of Prometheus.

HESPERIDES: These nymphs (their name means "girls of the West," or "girls of the Evening") kept eternal watch over a garden in which grew golden apples. Hesiod places them in the far West, in the neighborhood of Atlas.

HIPPOMEDON: Argive captain at the gate of Athena.

HYPERBIOS: Son of Oinops; Theban captain at the gate of Athena.

INACHOS: Son of Ocean, and father of Io; he gave his name to the River Inachos, near Argos (1).

IO: Daughter of Inachos. Her story, as envisaged by Aeschylus, is given in full in the *Prometheus* and (with some differences in detail and emphasis) in the *Suppliants*. In brief: Zeus fell in love with her; she was turned into a heifer, and Hera set the many-eyed Argos (2) to watch over her; Argos was slain by Hermes; whereupon Hera sent the horsefly to torment Io and drive her over the earth. In the course of her wanderings she came to Prometheus, who, in the play of that title, prophesies her future fate. Her eventual union with Zeus began the Suppliants' line.

IONIAN SEA: This name is usually given to the stretch of sea between the west coast of Greece, the "foot" of the Italian peninsula, and Sicily; but some Greek writers, including (apparently) Aeschylus, extend it to the entire Adriatic.

ISMENE: Daughter of Oedipus.

ISMENOS: One of the streams of Thebes.

KADMOS: The legendary founder of Thebes, son of Agenor, king of Tyre. With his wife, Harmonia, he is the progenitor of the royal house of Thebes.

KANOBOS: Better known as Canōpus, a city on the Egyptian coast some fifteen miles east of what was later Alexandria.

KAPANEUS: Argive captain at the gate of Elektra.

KAUKASOS: Better known as the Caucuses, the mountain range east of the Black Sea, which was the scene of Prometheus' punishment. Greek writers, even long after Aeschylus, believed this range to be of vast extent. Aeschylus seems to imagine Prometheus as being chained on one of the lower peaks of the range, some distance from the great peak which he calls "Kaukasos itself," and which Io must cross in her later wanderings.

KERCHNEIA: A small town some fifteen miles southwest of Argos (1) and in its territory, with a spring of fresh water.

KISSA: A "Kissian land" is known to Herodotus (*Histories* III.91, etc.) as a district in the neighborhood of the Persian capital, Susa. Aeschylus evidently believes in the existence of a walled city, Kissa, comparable with Ekbatana and Susa in importance.

KISTHĒNĒ: A far Eastern place name, first found in Aeschylus and perhaps invented by him.

KRONOS: Youngest son of Earth and Sky, husband of Rhea, and king of the Titans. He has been conquered by Zeus, dethroned, and imprisoned in Tartaros (*q.v.*).

LAIOS: Father of Oedipus.

LASTHENES: Theban captain at the Homoloian gate.

LERNA: A coastal region of the territory of Argos (1), famed for its spring water.

LIBYA: Granddaughter of Io and Zeus; queen of the land that bears her name; by Poseidon she became the mother of Agenor and Baal.

LIGYES: Better known by their Roman name of "Ligurians," a people who inhabited the territory that is now the southeast corner of France and the northwest corner of Italy.

LYDIANS: Inhabitants of Lydia, the territory inland of the Ionian Greek colonies that occupied the central shoreline of western Asia Minor. A rich and powerful kingdom in the seventh and early sixth centuries B.C., it had been conquered by Cyrus; thereafter, according to Herodotus, *Histories* I.155–56, the Lydians had succumbed to the delights of the easy life, a belief alluded to in *Persians* 54–55 / 41–42. Its capital was Sardis (*q.v.*).

MAENAD: Frenzied woman worshiper of Dionysos, god of wine and ecstatic possession.

MAIOTIS: Lake, the inlet of the Black Sea east of the Crimea; now the Sea of Azov.

MARATHON: On the northeast coast of Attica, was the scene of the defeat of a great expedition dispatched by Darius against the Athenians in 490 B.C. (Herodotus, *Histories* VI.94–120.)

MARDOS: The usurper of the Persian throng whose rule intervened between those of Cambyses and Darius (*q.v.*) in 522–21 B.C. ("Mardos" is evidently Aeschylus' spelling of the name which appears as "Smerdis" in Herodotus.) In a dramatic passage of the *Histories* (III.61–79), Herodotus tells how this Smerdis, one of the priestly caste called the Magi, impersonated Cambyses' dead brother (who happened to bear the same name), and ruled until he was assassinated by a group of seven Persian grandees, including Darius and Intaphrenes (? = Aeschylus' Artaphrenes, *q.v.*). By an extraordinary maneuver (III.84–87), Darius then secured the kingdom for himself.

MEDE: (1) Media, an ancient kingdom to the northwest of Persia, was always joined to it in close political association; thus, after the foundation of the empire, the names "Medes" and "Persians" come to be bracketed together and "Mede" may be used to refer to either nation or both. (2) In Darius' list of earlier kings, the first is simply described as *Mēdos*, "Mede" (*Persians* 1265 / 765). The king concerned is generally thought to be the man known as Kyaxares, who ruled Media in the years around 600 B.C. His son (mentioned, but not named, in *Persians* 1266–67 / 766–67) was Astyages, whom the Persian Cyrus defeated, thus bringing the two kingdoms together under Persian sovereignty. For this story, see Herodotus, *Histories* I.95–130.

MEGAREUS: Theban captain at the gate of Neïs; son of Kreon, descended from one of the heroes that sprang from the dragon's teeth sown by Kadmos.

MELANIPPOS: Theban captain at the gate of Proitos; descended from one of the heroes who sprang from the dragon's teeth sown by Kadmos.

MOLOSSIAN (Meadows): See DODONA.

MYSIA: A territory in Asia Minor immediately north of Lydia; see further the note on *Persians* 1688.

OCEAN (Greek Okeanos): Son of Earth and Sky according to Hesiod; both a god of the Titan-generation, and a river—the greatest of all rivers, encircling the world. Ocean is husband of Tēthys, and father of the girls who compose the Chorus in the *Prometheus* (see next entry).

OCEAN, DAUGHTERS OF: In Hesiod, Ocean marries Tēthys and begets many water-nymphs; after naming a large number of them, the poet adds, "but there are many others, also; for there are three thousand slender-ankled daughters of Ocean, scattered far, taking care everywhere alike of the land and the depths of water, children glorious among goddesses." Of some of these, the Chorus of the *Prometheus* is composed.

OEDIPUS: Son of Laios; son and husband of Jocasta; father of Eteokles, Polyneices, Antigone, and Ismene.

PARTHENOPAIOS: An Arcadian, son of Atalanta; Argive captain at the Northern gate.

PELASGIA: An ancient name for Greece, and especially for the region around Argos (1), derived from the name of a legendary ruler, Pelasgos.

PELASGOS: King of the Argive people; descendant of the goddess Earth.

PHASIS: A river running into the eastern end of the Black Sea.

PHOBOS: Personified divinity of fear or battle terror.

PHOENICIANS: These dwellers on the shoreline of central Palestine, with their age-old maritime expertise, naturally provided Xerxes with his largest naval contingent (Herodotus, *Histories* VII.89, etc.). From one of their famous seaports, Tyre, they might also be referred to as "Tyrians" (*Persians* 1558).

PHOIBOS: Epithet of Apollo.

PHORKYS, DAUGHTERS OF: Three monstrous and aged sisters, who possessed only one eye and one tooth between them—which they used by turns. They are better known as the "Graiai." According to Hesiod their mother was Kētō, so that they were full sisters of the Gorgons (*q.v.*).

POLYNEICES: Son of Oedipus; Argive captain at the seventh gate.

POLYPHONTES: Theban captain at the gate of Elektra.

POSEIDON: An Olympian, son of Kronos and Rhea; god of the sea and its storms, of earthquakes, and of horses; his symbol is a three-pronged spear, the trident.

PROMETHEUS: A god of the Titan generation. In *Prometheus Bound*, he is said to be the son of Earth (*q.v.*), but his father is not named. His wife, Hesione, is one of the daughters of Ocean.

RHEA: Wife of Kronos (*q.v.*). The *Gulf of Rhea* is Aeschylus' name for the upper Adriatic.

SALAMIS: (1) The famous island off the west coast of Attica. Aeschylus also refers to it as the "isle of Ajax" (see AJAX), and as "Kychreian" (see note on *Persians* 922); (2) A city in Cyprus (see AJAX).

SALMYDESSOS: A city on the southwest coast of the Black Sea, about sixty miles west of the Bosporus (*q.v.*).

SARDIS: The ancient capital of the Lydians (*q.v.*). Renowned for its wealth and power under its native kings, Sardis continued to be an important city after Cyrus' conquest, when it became the seat of the Persian satraps (governors) of the region.

SCYTHIA: A vast tract of country, its outer limits undefined, but roughly co-extensive with European Russia. For an elaborate account of the land and its many tribes (generically called Scythians) as the fifth-century Greeks knew them, see Herodotus, *Histories* IV. 1–82.

SILENIAI: The stretch of the coast on the island of Salamis (*q.v.*) that faces the location of the naval battle.

SKY (Greek *Ouranos*): Consort of Earth, and also (according to Hesiod) her parthenogenetic son. The two together were the first divine sovereigns of the universe.

SPARTOI: "Sown men," the ancestors of the Thebans. They sprang from the soil where Kadmos (*q.v.*) sowed the dragon's teeth.

SPHINX: Threefold demon with the head of a beautiful woman, the body of a lion, and the wings of a bird; she killed those who could not answer her riddle.

SUPPLIANTS: The fifty unmarried daughters of Danaos and fifth-generation descendants of Io; first cousins of the Egyptians (*q.v.*).

SUSA: The city in northwestern part of ancient Persia where the action of *Persians* is set. It was the greatest of Persia's royal cities; Darius' palace there is said to have excelled, even that at Persepolis (Strabo, *Geography*, XV.729).

TARTAROS: The lowest and darkest depth in the universe, below Hades itself. Here Zeus imprisoned the defeated Titans and Kronos, hurling them (according to Hesiod) "as far below the earth as sky is above earth—that is the distance from earth to the dark mists of Tartaros."

TEIRESIAS: Blind Theban gifted with prophecy.

TĒTHYS: Wife of Ocean (*q.v.*).

THEMIS: The personification of the moral basis of human customs and laws; her name means "Right." She is identified with Earth (*q.v.*) in the *Prometheus Bound*, but elsewhere in Greek literature—even in Aeschylus' *Eumenides*—she is a daughter of Earth and Sky, and thus a sister of Kronos.

THEMISKYRA: A town on the south coast of the Black Sea.

THERMŌDŌN: A river running into the Black Sea on its southern coast.

THESPRŌTIA: See DODONA.

TITANS: The name for the race of ancient deities who were born of Sky, and rebelled against him under the leadership of their youngest brother, Kronos. They in turn were deprived of their power by the following generation, the Olympian Gods, led by Zeus.

TYDEUS: Argive captain at the gate of Proitos.

TYPHŌN (or Typhoeus):   The youngest child of Earth, begotten on her by Tartaros. A monster with a hundred snake heads, fiery eyes, and a tremendous voice, he rose up against Zeus after the latter's defeat of the Titans and was destroyed by the thunderbolts in a tremendous duel (see Hesiod, *Theogony* 820–80). *Prometheus Bound* adds that Typhōn's body was buried under Mount Etna.

TYRIAN: See PHOENICIANS.

XERXES: Son of Darius and Atossa; he inherited the Persian throne from his father in 486 B.C. As Aeschylus was aware (see note on *Persians* 1626), the disastrous outcome of his expedition to Greece in 480–79 B.C. in no way meant the end of his reign. He continued in office until 465 B.C., when he was assassinated by the captain of his bodyguard and was succeeded by his son Artaxerxes.

ZEUS: Ruler of the Olympian Gods, youngest son of Kronos and Rhea, husband of Hera. At the dramatic date of the *Prometheus Bound*, Zeus has only recently defeated the older divine generation of Titans and established his new régime. In *Suppliants*, he is great-grandfather of the daughters of Danaos four times over.

FOR FURTHER READING

AESCHYLUS

C. John Herington. *Aeschylus*. New Haven: Yale University Press, 1986. A brief, engaging, and beautifully written introduction.

Michael Lloyd, ed. *Aeschylus*. Oxford: Oxford University Press, 2007. A collection of influential critical essays, including papers on all the dramas in this volume.

Thomas G. Rosenmeyer. *The Art of Aeschylus*. Berkeley: University of California Press, 1982. A topical survey of the major aspects of Aeschylus' artistry.

Alan H. Sommerstein. *Aeschylean Tragedy*. Bari: Levante Editori, 1996. A substantial and informed introduction.

R. P. Winnington-Ingram. *Studies in Aeschylus*. Cambridge: Cambridge University Press, 1983. A valuable collection of his essays.

PERSIANS

David Rosenbloom. *Aeschylus: Persians*. London: Duckworth, 2006. A thoughtful introduction to the play and its cultural context, with rich bibliography.

Thomas Harrison. *The Emptiness of Asia: Aeschylus' "Persians" and the History of the Fifth Century*. London: Duckworth, 2000. A comprehensive reading employing both literary and historical approaches, with detailed assessment of earlier scholarship.

PROMETHEUS BOUND

Mark Griffith. *The Authenticity of "Prometheus Bound."* Cambridge: Cambridge University Press, 1976. The essential presentation of the case against Aeschylean authorship; well argued and very influential.

Stephen White. "Io's World: Intimations of Theodicy in *Prometheus Bound*," *Journal of Hellenic Studies* 121 (2001): 107–40. An original reading of the play's ideas of human progress and their implications.

SEVEN AGAINST THEBES

W. G. Thalmann. *Dramatic Art in Aeschylus's "Seven against Thebes."* New Haven: Yale University Press, 1978. Carefully argued and comprehensive.

Froma I. Zeitlin. *Under the Sign of the Shield: Semiotics and Aeschylus' "Seven against Thebes."* Rome: Edizioni dell' Ateneo, 1982. Brilliant and stimulating study using modern semiotic theory to illuminate a close reading, especially of the central "shield scene."

SUPPLIANTS

A. F. Garvie. *Aeschylus' "Supplices": Play and Trilogy.* 2nd edition. Exeter: Bristol Phoenix Press, 2006. Updated reprinting of an essential study, first published in 1969.

Froma I. Zeitlin. "The Politics of Eros in the Danaid Trilogy of Aeschylus." In Ralph Hexter and Daniel Selden, eds., *Innovations of Antiquity*. New York: Routledge, 1992. 203–52. A bold and demanding study that illustrates Aeschylus' complicated "choreography of male and female categories."